# Advance Praise for SEARCHING FOR THE SELF

"I am thrilled to see *Searching for the Self.* All the volumes in the *Library of Wisdom and Compassion* are a highly cherished treasure—they are profound yet easily accessible. *Searching for the Self* will help to open your wisdom eye to investigate emptiness. With that understanding, you can fly in freedom without grasping to illusory objects."—GESHE LHAKDOR, director, Library of Tibetan Works and Archives, Dharamsala, India

"It is refreshing to come across such a clear and in-depth study of the Middle Way teaching of no-self and emptiness as found in the Mahāyāna and Theravāda traditions. This remarkable book opens the door to a wide and profound understanding of those teachings and to the path leading to their realization."—AJAHN SUNDARA, author of *Walking the World, Seeds of Dhamma*, and *Pacupanna: The Present Moment*

"This seventh volume in the *Library of Wisdom and Compassion* is undoubtedly the masterpiece of H. H. the Dalai Lama and Thubten Chodron. *Searching for the Self* deals not only with the heart of the Buddhist view on emptiness, which distinguishes it from the great monotheistic religions, it also discusses the approaches of Pāli and Chinese Buddhism on the ultimate nature. A brave, impressive, and convincing presentation toward a theory of "Buddhist ecumenism," it enables Buddhists worldwide to speak in one voice about important issues that concern all of us today. At the same time, it gives non-Buddhists fresh insight into the world of Buddhist thought and practice."—DR. CAROLA ROLOFF (Bhikṣuṇī Jampa Tsedroen), Professor for Buddhism and Dialogue at the Academy of World Religions of the University of Hamburg

"With this book the authors have opened the door to a vast treasure of Buddhist ideas. Based on instruction given by the Dalai Lama to audiences around the world, it speaks directly to issues of the human condition. A valuable compendium of Buddhist philosophy that addresses both simple, grounded, spiritual practice, and the need to comprehend higher profound truths."—IAN COGHLAN (Jampa Ignyen), Monash University

THE LIBRARY OF WISDOM AND COMPASSION

*The Library of Wisdom and Compassion* is a special multivolume series in which His Holiness the Dalai Lama shares the Buddha's teachings on the complete path to full awakening that he himself has practiced his entire life. The topics are arranged especially for people not born in Buddhist cultures and are peppered with the Dalai Lama's unique outlook. Assisted by his long-term disciple, the American nun Thubten Chodron, the Dalai Lama sets the context for practicing the Buddha's teachings in modern times and then unveils the path of wisdom and compassion that leads to a meaningful life, a sense of personal fulfillment, and full awakening. This series is an important bridge from introductory to profound topics for those seeking an in-depth explanation from a contemporary perspective.

*Volumes:*

1. *Approaching the Buddhist Path*
2. *The Foundation of Buddhist Practice*
3. *Saṃsāra, Nirvāṇa, and Buddha Nature*
4. *Following in the Buddha's Footsteps*
5. *In Praise of Great Compassion*
6. *Courageous Compassion*
7. *Searching for the Self*

More volumes to come!

THE LIBRARY OF WISDOM AND COMPASSION • VOLUME 7

# Searching for the Self


Bhikṣu Tenzin Gyatso,
the Fourteenth Dalai Lama

*and*

Bhikṣuṇī Thubten Chodron


Wisdom

Wisdom Publications
199 Elm Street
Somerville, MA 02144 USA
wisdomexperience.org



*Library of Congress Cataloging-in-Publication Data*
Names: Bstan-'dzin-rgya-mtsho, Dalai Lama XIV, 1935– author. |
Thubten Chodron, 1950– author.
Title: Searching for the self / Bhikṣu Tenzin Gyatso and Bhikṣuṇī Thubten Chodron.
Description: First. | Somerville: Wisdom Publications, 2022. | Series: The library of wisdom and compassion; 7 | Includes bibliographical references and index.
Identifiers: LCCN 2021030593 (print) | LCCN 2021030594 (ebook) |
ISBN 9781614297956 (hardcover) | ISBN 9781614298205 (ebook)
Subjects: LCSH: Sunyata. | Buddhism—Doctrines.
Classification: LCC BQ4275 .B78 2022 (print) | LCC BQ4275 (ebook) |
DDC 294.3/42—dc23
LC record available at https://lccn.loc.gov/2021030593
LC ebook record available at https://lccn.loc.gov/2021030594

ISBN 978-1-61429-795-6 ebook ISBN 978-1-61429-820-5

26 25 24 23 22
5 4 3 2 1

Photo credits: cover, courtesy of His Holiness the Dalai Lama; pp. vi, xii, 196, Ānandajoti Bhikkhu / PhotoDharma.net; p. 4, Tibetan Nuns Project | TNP.org; p. 160, Leila Mills; pp. 228, 374, Olivier Adam; p. 320, Gen Heywood Photography
Cover and interior design by Gopa & Ted 2.
Interior typeset by PerfecType, Nashville, TN.

Printed on acid-free paper that meets the guidelines for permanence and durability of the Production Guidelines for Book Longevity of the Council on Library Resources.

Printed in the United States of America.

*Publisher's Acknowledgment*

The publisher gratefully acknowledges the generous help of the Hershey Foundation in sponsoring the production of this book.

# Contents

# Preface

MANY OF THE PRACTICES we do on the path to awakening are to prepare us to study, contemplate, meditate on, and realize the nature of reality, for this is the realization that has the power to cut our defilements from their root. So in the *Library of Wisdom and Compassion*, we now arrive at this topic. Although His Holiness has sprinkled his discussion of emptiness—the absence of inherent existence—throughout previous volumes, in this and the next two volumes he delves deeply into this topic, presenting it from a variety of approaches. This first of the three volumes on emptiness, *Searching for the Self*, focuses on identifying our erroneous views and directing us to the actual mode of existence of all persons and phenomena. Doing this will challenge some of our deepest-held beliefs—some false ways of viewing ourselves and the world that are so habitual that we don't even notice them. Get ready to be challenged and intrigued!

## *How This Book Originated*

The *Library of Wisdom and Compassion* has been many years in the making. As relayed in the prefaces of previous volumes, the idea for such a series began in the early 1990s when I requested His Holiness the Dalai Lama to write a short text that Tibetan lamas could use when teaching the Buddhadharma to Westerners and other non-Tibetans. His Holiness responded that we should write something longer first, gave me a transcript of one of his teachings, and sent me off to work.

In interviews with him over the ensuing years, the focus and scope of the series became clearer. The following is some of His Holiness' advice:

Our main aim is to help practitioners of the Pāli and Sanskrit traditions have a better understanding of each other's teachings and practice; a better understanding between the two traditions will bring closer contact, which will not only benefit individual practitioners but also enable the Buddhadharma to exist longer. In addition, it will enable Buddhist leaders from all traditions to speak in one voice about important issues in the world, such as climate change.

Except for minor differences, the Vinaya practice in all traditions is basically the same; the Vinaya and prātimokṣa are emphasized in both the Fundamental Vehicle and the Mahāyāna. The thirty-seven harmonies with awakening are also held in common. After reading this book, Theravāda practitioners will have clearer understanding that Mahāyāna practitioners also engage in these practices and Mahāyāna practitioners will know that Theravāda practitioners meditate on immeasurable love and compassion.

The Pāli tradition is the foundation of the Buddhadharma. Although there may be some people who think Vinaya is old-fashioned, that is a wrong view. The Buddha established the Vinaya, so deprecating the Vinaya and the value of monastic life is similar to dismissing the Buddha's wisdom and denigrating the path to awakening. It would be good to have more explanation in this series about the Theravāda tradition, especially its Vinaya practice—how ordination is given, the three monastic practices (*poṣadha, varṣā, pravāraṇā*)—and its practice of samādhi, insight, and the thirty-seven harmonies with awakening.[1] I know that some practitioners in Theravāda countries are very accomplished and some monks are considered arhats.

When I meet monks from Sri Lanka, Thailand, Burma, and so forth, we discuss Vinaya, the thirty-seven harmonies, the four truths, and so forth—Buddhist teachings that all of us share. When I meet Japanese tantric practitioners, we discuss tantra. But when Japanese tantric practitioners and Sri Lankan Buddhist monks meet, aside from the practice of refuge in the Three Jewels, they can discuss only a few common practices. That is sad. I would like us Buddhists to understand one another better.

> I also try to create closer understanding between Buddhists, Hindus, Christians, Muslims, and Jews. Theistic religions' emphasis on faith in God, the creator, helps people to live better. When they think that they are created in God's image, that God is like a protective father, and that everything is in God's hands, it helps them develop single-pointed faith. Such faith reduces self-centeredness and supports them in abandoning harm and extending forgiveness, kindness, and generosity to others. Based on pinpointing self-centeredness, anger, greed, fear, jealousy, and so forth as destructive emotions, we can understand and respect practitioners of theistic religions.
>
> In the Tibetan community, some people stress their identification with a particular Tibetan tradition, "I'm Nyingma, you are Gelug; I am Sakya, you are Kagyu." Doing this in a discriminatory way is silly. By seeing our commonalities, I hope we Tibetans will overcome old divisions and that these misconceptions will not spread to Western, Chinese, and other practitioners of Tibetan Buddhism.

With this in mind, we'll explore the Buddha's teachings on the nature of reality. Although there are many educational systems in the world, each with its own methodology, here we follow the Nālandā tradition of India. In some educational systems today, teachers explain topics to students who are expected to remember all the information. They then take tests on the material to see if they have memorized it properly. Students are not necessarily taught how to think about the material or to question the ethical value of exploring a certain field of knowledge.

In the Nālandā tradition, our motivation for education is to increase our ability to contribute to the well-being of others and to progress on the path to full awakening. Here a teacher's role is to put forth varying ideas and help students to investigate them one by one, stating their qualms and debating the issues. Teachers don't give students all the answers, but present different viewpoints and questions that the students discuss and debate among themselves. This functions to increase students' discriminating wisdom and their ability to think clearly. They learn what is true by refuting wrong ideas and establishing correct reasons.

The first book His Holiness and I did, *Buddhism: One Teacher, Many Traditions*, as well as the previous six volumes of the *Library of Wisdom and Compassion*, establish many of the common points shared among the prominent Buddhist traditions (there are many Buddhist traditions and ways of practice—too many for us to include in this series). Now we will turn to the cultivation of a special kind of wisdom: the wisdom that realizes selflessness and emptiness. This wisdom has the power to free us from saṃsāra forever.

In learning about selflessness and emptiness, you will encounter new words, definitions, and ideas. You may wonder: If reality is empty of all false ways of existence, why do we need so many complicated words and concepts to explain it? Shouldn't reality be simple to understand and easy to realize?

Once seen directly, emptiness probably seems obvious and easy to understand, but for the minds of us ordinary beings that are obscured by wrong views and disturbing emotions, discerning reality is not at all simple. If emptiness were easy to realize, we would have done so long ago and would have already become buddhas by now. But this is not the case. If emptiness were obvious, we would already have the correct view and would know how to meditate on emptiness correctly. This too is not the case. People have a variety of views, and even within one person there exist many contradictory ideas and perceptions. Look at ourselves, for example: Do all our perceptions and conceptions about reality form one logical, consistent philosophy, or do they sometimes contradict each other, leaving us confused?

The Indian and the Tibetan texts dealing with emptiness contain many debates that employ reasoning and critical analysis. This may cause us to wonder: Why is so much time and energy spent refuting others' wrong views? Shouldn't we be meditating instead? Reasoning and debate are tools that expose our own misconceptions. Although the texts ostensibly appear to refute others' distorted views, we may hold some of those very misconceptions and wrong views ourselves. Logic and reasoning are not employed for the egotistic goal of being the victor in a debate. Rather, they are employed to disprove the distorted views we cling to so strongly and ignite the light of wisdom in our minds.

Meditation on emptiness isn't the simple activity of closing our eyes, emptying all thoughts from our mind, and waiting for reality to magically appear to our consciousness. In minds that are crowded with wrong views and distracted by attachment to only the happiness of this life, there is no room for reality. We must clear away the wrong conceptions by means of reasoning and analysis so that we can see the ultimate nature that already exists in ourselves and in all phenomena around us.

For these reasons, we must continually cultivate enthusiasm and interest to understand emptiness deeply as well as to comprehend the words and concepts that lead to such understanding. Then we must meditate one-pointedly on emptiness to gain insight into emptiness, and then familiarize ourselves with that realization of reality to eradicate all afflictions and defilements in our mental continuum. I encourage you to be enthusiastic to study, reflect, and meditate on this topic for a long time.

## *Overview of the Book*

This volume begins with an introduction by His Holiness in which he places our study of reality within the framework of a compassionate motivation to benefit sentient beings. Since the value of whatever we undertake depends on our motivation, cultivating a motivation to contribute to the welfare of all beings places our study of emptiness in a beneficial context.

Chapter 1 explains why realizing emptiness is important and describes the qualities to develop to understand it correctly. Chapter 2 speaks of the Buddhist sages whose teachings are the most reliable for us to follow. It culminates with a praise His Holiness wrote that introduces us to the seventeen great scholar-adepts of the Nālandā tradition followed in Tibetan Buddhism. Then in chapters 3, 4, and 5 we explore assertions of both Buddhist and non-Buddhist philosophical tenet systems. This topic is vast, so only the important positions regarding the topics of the present volume—selflessness and emptiness—are spoken of here. Although initially this material may seem replete with new terms and ideas, as you progress in your study and practice to develop insight into emptiness, you will see the value of learning these because they point out some of our own incorrect ideas and direct us to views that are more reasonable.

Chapter 6 provides some of the epistemological material that helps us to understand both cognizing subjects and cognized objects, and chapter 7 fleshes out some of the mental states involved in both our ignorant and accurate cognitions. Chapter 8 discusses inherent existence and other fantasized ways of existence that comprise the objects of negation—what we seek to disprove when meditating on emptiness—and chapter 9 establishes the Middle Way view that has abandoned the extremes of absolutism and nihilism. The view of absolutism superimposes false ways of existence, whereas the nihilistic view negates what does in fact exist. Chapter 10 looks more closely at the extreme of absolutism, as this is the view that we ordinary sentient beings usually cling to.

Chapter 11 speaks of the two extremes as presented in the Pāli tradition and the three characteristics of impermanence, duḥkha, and not-self that counter the absolutist views. Chapter 12 goes into some of the many arguments presented in the Pāli tradition that help to overcome clinging to a false notion of the I. Although the arguments to support selflessness in the Sanskrit tradition are expounded in the upcoming volume 8 of the *Library of Wisdom and Compassion*, readers who are already familiar with these will see the similarities with arguments found in the Pāli sūtras.

The coda is designed for people who have studied the tenet systems in the Tibetan tradition as well as for followers of the Pāli tradition who want to learn more about their own Abhidharma system. Many Tibetans believe that modern-day Theravāda corresponds to the Vaibhāṣika and/or Sautrāntika systems as these systems are explained in the Tibetan tradition. However, this is not the case; although the Pāli tradition shares many commonalities with these two systems, there are some important differences. In addition, this coda orients the reader to some of the foundational, canonical ideas informing the Tibetan treatises on the nature of reality, selflessness, and emptiness. Being aware of the development of the Abhidharma provides background for the refutations in Nāgārjuna's *Treatise on the Middle Way*.

When His Holiness said he wanted me to include the perspective of the Pāli tradition in the *Library of Wisdom and Compassion*, his office gave me a letter requesting Theravāda monks to give me teachings and allow me to stay in their temple. Thus I spent two weeks studying and practicing with Ajahn Anan at Wat Marp Jan in Thailand. This was followed by studying Bhikkhu Bodhi's lengthy series of teachings on the Majjhima Nikāya and meeting with him to ask questions. This led to reading about the Pāli Abhidharma, participating in a vipassana retreat, and discussing the Dharma with Western monks and nuns whom I met at our annual Western Buddhist Monastic Gatherings. Having taught the Dharma in Singapore for almost two years, I also got to know some monks from that tradition, participated in panel discussions with them, and was invited to speak at their temples. This study and engagement with the Pāli tradition has helped my own Dharma practice considerably.

## *Please Note*

Although this series is coauthored, the vast majority of the material is His Holiness's teachings. I researched and wrote the parts about the Pāli tradition, wrote some other passages, and composed the reflections. For ease of reading, most honorifics have been omitted, but that does not diminish the great respect we have for the excellent sages, practitioners, and learned adepts. Foreign terms are given in italics parenthetically at their first usage. Unless otherwise noted with "P." or "T.," indicating Pāli or Tibetan, respectively, italicized terms are Sanskrit, or the term is the same in Sanskrit and Pāli. When two italicized terms are listed, the first is Sanskrit, the second Pāli. For consistency, Sanskrit spelling is used for Sanskrit and Pāli terms in common usage (nirvāṇa, Dharma, arhat, and so forth), except in citations from Pāli scriptures. Tibetan terms can be found in the glossary. The term *śrāvaka* encompasses solitary realizers, unless there is reason to specifically differentiate them. To maintain the flow of a passage, it is not always possible to gloss all new terms on their first usage, so a glossary is provided at the end of the book. "Sūtra" often refers to Sūtrayāna and "Tantra" to Tantrayāna—the Sūtra Vehicle and Tantra Vehicle, respectively. When these two words are not capitalized, they refer to two types of scriptures: sūtras and tantras. "Mahāyāna" or "Universal Vehicle" here refers principally to the bodhisattva path as explained in the Sanskrit tradition. In general, the meaning of all philosophical terms accords with the presentation of the Prāsaṅgika Madhyamaka tenet system. Unless otherwise noted, the personal pronoun "I" refers to His Holiness.

## *Appreciation*

My deepest respect goes to Śākyamuni Buddha and all the buddhas, bodhisattvas, and arhats who embody the Dharma and with compassion teach us confused beings who seek happiness but are ignorant of the means to create the causes for it. I also bow to all the realized lineage masters of all

Buddhist traditions through whose kindness the Buddhadharma still exists in our world.

This series consists of many volumes. For their aid in this seventh volume, I want to express my gratitude to His Holiness's translators—Geshe Lhakdor, Geshe Dorji Damdul, and Mr. Tenzin Tsepak. I am grateful to Geshe Dorji Damdul, Geshe Dadul Namgyal, and Bhikṣuṇī Sangye Khadro for checking the manuscript, and to Samdhong Rinpoche, Geshe Yeshe Lhundup, and Geshe Dhamchoe Gyaltsen for clarifying important points. Geshe Thupten Jinpa's help was always welcome, and Dr. Yakupitiyage Karunadasa and Stephen Wainwright kindly checked the coda. I also thank Bhikkhu Bodhi for his clear teachings on the Pāli tradition and for generously answering my many questions. He also kindly looked over the sections of the book on the Pāli tradition before publication. The staff at the Private Office of His Holiness kindly facilitated the interviews, Sravasti Abbey supported me while I worked on this volume, and Mary Petrusewicz skillfully edited this book. I thank everyone at Wisdom Publications who has contributed and continues to contribute to the successful production of this series. All errors are my own.

Bhikṣuṇī Thubten Chodron
Sravasti Abbey

# Abbreviations

ADK *Treasury of Knowledge* (*Abhidharmakośa*) by Vasubandhu. In *Abhidharmakośa of Ācārya Vasubandhu: English Translation from the French by Dr. Leo M. Pruden*. Edited by Lokananda C. Bhikkhu (Delhi: Buddhist World Press, 2018).

ADKB *Treasury of Knowledge Autocommentary* (*Abhidharmakośabhāṣya*) by Vasubandhu. In *Abhidharmakośa-Bhāṣya of Vasubandhu: The Treasury of the Abhidharma and Its Commentary*. 4 vols. Translated into French by Louis de La Vallée Poussin. Annotated English translation by Gelong Lodrö Sangpo (Delhi: Motilal Banarsidass, 2012).

ADS *Abhidharmasamuccaya: The Compendium of the Higher Teaching (Philosophy)* by Asaṅga. Translated into French by Walpola Rahula. English translation by Sara Boin-Webb (Fremont, CA: Jain Publishing, 2015).

AN Aṅguttara Nikāya. Translated by Bhikkhu Bodhi in *The Numerical Discourses of the Buddha* (Boston: Wisdom Publications, 2012).

BCA *Bodhicaryāvatāra* by Śāntideva. Translated by Stephen Batchelor in *A Guide to the Bodhisattva's Way of Life* (Dharamsala: Library of Tibetan Works and Archives, 2007).

BV *Commentary on Bodhicitta* (*Bodhicittavivaraṇa*) by Nāgārjuna. Translated by Geshe Thupten Jinpa.

CŚ *The Four Hundred* (*Catuḥśataka*) by Āryadeva. Translated by

Ruth Sonam in *Āryadeva's Four Hundred Stanzas on the Middle Way* (Ithaca, NY: Snow Lion Publications, 2008).

CTB *Compassion in Tibetan Buddhism* by Tsong-ka-pa. Translated and edited by Jeffrey Hopkins (Ithaca, NY: Snow Lion Publications, 1980).

DAE *Dependent-Arising and Emptiness: A Tibetan Buddhist Interpretation of Madhyamika Philosophy*, by Elizabeth Napper (Boston: Wisdom Publications, 1989).

DN Dīgha Nikāya. Translated by Maurice Walshe in *The Long Discourses of the Buddha* (Boston: Wisdom Publications, 1995).

EES Tsong-kha-pa Lo-sang-drak-pa's *Extensive Explanation of (Candrakīrti's) "Supplement to (Nāgārjuna's) 'Treatise on the Middle'": Illumination of the Thought.* Translated by Jeffrey Hopkins and Anne C. Klein. Unpublished manuscript.

EMW *Emptiness in the Middle Way School of Buddhism: Mutual Reinforcement of Understanding Dependent-Arising and Emptiness: Dynamic Responses to Tsong-kha-pa's "The Essence of Eloquence: IV,"* by Jeffrey Hopkins. Edited by Kevin Vose (Dyke, VA: UMA Institute for Tibetan Studies, 2019).

FEW *Tsong-kha-pa's Final Exposition of Wisdom.* Translated by Jeffrey Hopkins (Ithaca, NY: Snow Lion Publications, 2008).

HSY *How to See Yourself as You Really Are*, by His Holiness the Dalai Lama. Translated by Jeffrey Hopkins (New York: Atria Books, 2006).

Iti *Itivuttaka.* In *The Udāna and the Itivuttaka.* Translated by John D. Ireland (Kandy: Buddhist Publication Society, 2007).

LC *The Great Treatise on the Stages of the Path: Lam Rim Chen Mo*, by Tsong-kha-pa, 3 vols. Translated by the Lamrim Chenmo Translation Committee. Joshua Cutler, editor in chief. Guy Newland, editor (Ithaca, NY: Snow Lion Publications, 2000–2004).

LS *Praise to the World Transcendent (Lokatistava)* by Nāgārjuna.

Translated by Thupten Jinpa, 2007. http://www.tibetanclassics.org/html-assets/WorldTranscendentHym.pdf.

MMA *Supplement to "Treatise on the Middle Way"* (*Madhyamakāvatāra*) by Candrakīrti.

MMK *Treatise on the Middle Way* (*Mūlamadhyamakakārikā*) by Nāgārjuna. From *Ocean of Reasoning by rJe Tsong Khapa*. Translated by Geshe Ngawang Samten and Jay L. Garfield (New York: Oxford University Press, 2006).

MN Majjhima Nikāya. Translated by Bhikkhu Ñāṇamoli and Bhikkhu Bodhi in *The Middle-Length Discourses of the Buddha* (Boston: Wisdom Publications, 1995).

MP *Maps of the Profound: Jam-yang-shay-ba's Great Exposition of Buddhist and Non-Buddhist Views on the Nature of Reality*, by Jeffrey Hopkins (Ithaca, NY: Snow Lion Publications, 2003).

NT *The Nature of Things: Emptiness and Essence in the Geluk World*, by William Magee (Ithaca, NY: Snow Lion Publications, 1999).

OR *Ocean of Reasoning by rJe Tsong Khapa*. Translated by Geshe Ngawang Samten and Jay L. Garfield (New York: Oxford University Press, 2006).

P. Pāli.

PV *Commentary on the Compendium of Reliable Cognition* (*Pramāṇavārttika*) by Dharmakīrti.

RA *Precious Garland* (*Ratnāvalī*) by Nāgārjuna. Translated by John Dunne and Sara McClintock in *The Precious Garland: An Epistle to a King* (Boston: Wisdom Publications, 1997).

SN Saṃyutta Nikāya. Translated by Bhikkhu Bodhi in *The Connected Discourses of the Buddha* (Boston: Wisdom Publications, 2000).

Sn *Suttanipāta*. Translated by Bhikkhu Bodhi in *The Suttanipāta* (Somerville, MA: Wisdom Publications, 2017).

SRR *Self, Reality, and Reason in Tibetan Philosophy: Tsongkhapa's Quest for the Middle Way*, by Thupten Jinpa (New York: RoutledgeCurzon, 2002).

ŚS *Seventy Stanzas* (*Śūnyatāsaptati*) by Nāgārjuna. *Nāgārjuna's Seventy Stanzas*, by David Ross Komito (Ithaca, NY: Snow Lion, 1987).

T. Tibetan.

Vism *Visuddhimagga* by Buddhaghosa. Translated by Bhikkhu Ñāṇamoli in *The Path of Purification* (Kandy: Buddhist Publication Society, 1991).

VV *Refutation of Objections* (*Vigrahavyāvartanī*) by Nāgārjuna. In *The Dispeller of Disputes: Nāgārjuna's* Vigrahavyāvartanī. Translation and commentary by Jan Westerhoff (New York: Oxford University Press, 2010).

YDB *The Yogic Deeds of Bodhisattvas*, by Geshe Sonam Rinchen. Translated by Ruth Sonam (Ithaca, NY: Snow Lion Publications, 1994).

YS *Sixty Stanzas of Reasoning* (*Yuktiṣaṣṭikākārikā*) by Nāgārjuna. Translated by Geshe Thupten Jinpa. https://www.tibetanclassics.org/html-assets/SixtyStanzas.pdf.

# Introduction

WHENEVER I SPEAK with people, I think of myself as a member of their family. Although we may be meeting for the first time, in my eyes you are already a friend. When we share together, I don't think of myself as a Buddhist, a Tibetan, or as the Dalai Lama. I think of us as one human being speaking with another.

When we interact, I hope that you will think of yourself as a human being rather than as an American, Asian, European, African, or member of any particular country, ethnic group, gender, political party, age group, or religion. These conventional identities and loyalties are secondary, and sometimes they interfere with our connecting with and understanding one another. If you and I find common ground as human beings, we can communicate well; my being a monk, Buddhist, Tibetan, or man are peripheral in comparison to my nature as a human being.

Being human is our fundamental commonality; it is the foundation we will always share. Each of us is born as a human being, a fact that doesn't change until we die. Everything else—whether you are educated or uneducated, young or old, rich or poor, black, white, yellow, or red—is secondary.

In truth, you and I already know each other profoundly as human beings who share the same basic goals. All of us seek happiness and do not want suffering. Everyone, no matter where we live, is engaged in various projects because we are motivated by the desire to be happy. This is natural, and there is nothing wrong with it. However, we must keep in mind that too much involvement in the superficial aspects of life will not solve our bigger problems of discontentment and suffering. And too much self-centeredness will not make us fulfilled. Love, compassion, and concern for others are the real sources of happiness. When we cultivate these in abundance, we will not be disturbed by even the most uncomfortable circumstances. If we nurse resentment, jealousy, and hatred, however, happiness will elude us even if we live in the lap of luxury. So if we really want to be happy, we must widen the sphere of our love. This is both religious thinking and basic common sense.

Look at it this way: We are born helpless. We own nothing and cannot take care of ourselves. Without the kindness of our parents or another caregiver, we could not survive, much less prosper. Because the minds of small children are very delicate, their need for kindness is particularly obvious, but adults need kindness too. If someone greets me with a smile and expresses a genuinely friendly attitude, I appreciate it very much. Although I might not know that person or even understand their language, my heart instantly feels relaxed. On the other hand, if kindness is lacking, even if I'm with someone from my own culture whom I have known for many years, I feel an icy chill between us. Kindness and love—a real sense of sisterhood and brotherhood—are very precious. They make community possible and therefore are an essential part of any society.

On the last day of a visit to Los Angeles, the geshe and his students who organized the teachings, my staff, and security were walking to the hotel elevator on the way to the airport. I saw the maid who had taken care of my room and went over to thank her. To everyone's surprise, she reached up and gave me a quick kiss on the cheek. Everyone around was not sure how to respond; I think they were a little uncomfortable, thinking the kiss on my cheek was inappropriate, so they just kept silent. But after we got into the elevator, I told them that was a sweet kiss—the maid was just expressing natural human affection—and they relaxed.

As small children, we depend on the kindness of others. In old age, we again depend on the kindness of others. Between childhood and old age we falsely believe that we are independent beings who are in control, but this is not so. Human society exists because it is impossible to live in complete isolation. Especially with the present structure of society, a global economy, specializations in particular fields of study, and the pervasiveness of technology and industry, we are more dependent on one another than at any other time in human history. Interdependent by nature, we must live together. Since this is unavoidable, we must have concern for one another. The aim of society must be the compassionate betterment of everyone from one lifetime to the next; this endeavor must include all living beings on this planet, not just human beings.

As you gain more appreciation for both the kindness intentionally bestowed on you by others and the unintended kindnesses reflected in the goods and services you depend on daily, you will automatically want to repay that kindness—or pay it forward—by contributing to a healthier society so others will benefit. By benefitting others, you will improve your own lot too. Without appreciation of kindness, society breaks down.

When people in need are ignored, abandoned, or exploited for political or economic reasons, it reveals what is lacking in us human beings: although we are intelligent and powerful enough to destroy the planet, we lack genuine kindness and love for one another. There is an Indian saying: "When an arrow has struck you, there is no time to ask who shot it or the type of arrow it was." Similarly, when we encounter human suffering, we must respond with compassion rather than question the political, national, religious, or racial identities of those we help. Instead of asking whether their country is a friend or foe, we must think, "These are human beings; they are suffering and their right to happiness is equal to our own."

Consider, too, the animals who are being raised for slaughter, a number so great that the environment itself is harmed. These sad facts are the result of insufficient loving care. If humanity's sense of compassion for others increased, not only would people in the world be happier but so would the countless animals whose lives we directly affect.

A better society is not something that can be legislated. Our common well-being depends on each of us as individuals cultivating peace, tolerance, forgiveness, love, and compassion in our own hearts and minds. Even if others don't do this, we must. It is our personal contribution to world peace, and we must not back out with the limp excuse that others must be kind first, then we will return the kindness. Rather, we must go forward with optimism and determination and do what we know in our hearts is right.

With this awareness and an altruistic intention to benefit all beings, we will explore the nature of reality together. In doing so, we will examine a number of Buddhist and non-Buddhist assertions. This will prompt a lot of debate, where we compare and contrast different ideas and try to defend our own positions. The motivation for this is for all parties to develop their wisdom by closely investigating various philosophical assertions. Any dissecting of others' views is not done out of hostility, the wish to take others down, or the intention to criticize people who hold views that differ from ours. Rather, through discussion and debate all of us will benefit.

Bhikṣu Tenzin Gyatso, the Fourteenth Dalai Lama

Thekchen Choling

# 1 The Importance of Realizing the Ultimate Nature, Emptiness

THE PREVIOUS VOLUMES of the *Library of Wisdom and Compassion* predominantly explored the method aspect of the path—the topics leading us to aspire to be free from saṃsāra and to generate bodhicitta and joyfully work for the liberation of all sentient beings. The ultimate nature of phenomena was explicitly spoken of from time to time because it underlies all these topics. The emptiness of inherent existence is the space in which all phenomena exist.

Now we will turn to make the ultimate nature—the emptiness of inherent existence—the chief object of our exploration. Emptiness is the ultimate mode of existence, and the wisdom realizing it directly is the only medicine that can cure saṃsāra and its duḥkha once and for all. This wisdom, coupled with bodhicitta, removes both afflictive and cognitive obscurations, enabling us to become fully awakened buddhas who are of great benefit to all beings.

## *Why Realizing Emptiness Is Important*

All of us share the wish to be happy and to overcome duḥkha. Upon close examination, it is evident that the situation in saṃsāra is utterly unsatisfactory. Its faults—especially birth, aging, sickness, and death, which we undergo without choice—continuously plague us in one rebirth after another. All the seeming pleasures of saṃsāra are transient and leave us dissatisfied. Chasing after them ensnares us in a cycle of excitement followed by disillusionment and depression. When we become fully aware of our predicament in saṃsāra and the danger of it continuing, strong aspiration for liberation and full awakening arises.

Ceasing saṃsāra entails eradicating its causes—afflictions and polluted karma—which are rooted in the ignorance grasping persons and phenomena as inherently existent. To identify this ignorance and the false object it grasps necessitates observing our mind closely, seeing how we easily assent to and grasp as true the false appearance of everything existing under its own power, independent of all other factors. Correctly identifying this self-grasping ignorance that is the root of saṃsāra is extremely important, for without this we will not be able to eliminate it.

Having correctly identified self-grasping and its erroneous object, we must ascertain that such inherently existent persons and phenomena do not exist at all. Doing this involves refuting inherent existence, which is called the "object of negation" (*pratiṣedhya* or *niṣedhya*,[2] T. *dgag bya*), because we need to prove to ourselves that it does not and cannot exist. Through contemplating correct reasonings that refute inherent existence, a correct assumption regarding the emptiness of inherent existence will arise. There are many levels of correct assumption that are gained over time until a correct inference knowing emptiness is gained. This conceptual realization of emptiness is then combined with a mind of serenity to attain the union of serenity and insight on emptiness. Through familiarization with emptiness by meditating with the union of serenity and insight over time, the conceptual appearance of emptiness gradually fades away and profound wisdom increases until it directly perceives emptiness, the ultimate nature of reality.

Again, by meditating over time with the wisdom directly perceiving emptiness, the levels of afflictions and their seeds are gradually cleansed from the mindstream. Continued meditation gradually removes the cognitive obscurations—the latencies of ignorance and the factor of the appearance of inherent existence—from the mind. When this wisdom is complemented by faith, collection of merit, and bodhicitta, full awakening is on the horizon.

Thus if we seek true peace and if we take the Buddha's teachings to heart, there is no other choice than to cultivate the wisdom realizing emptiness. Āryadeva's *The Four Hundred* (CŚ 135cd–136ab, 288) tells us:

> All afflictions are overcome
> through overcoming ignorance.

When dependent arising is seen,
ignorance does not arise.

It is the only doorway to peace;
it destroys wrong views;
it [captures] the attention of all buddhas—
this is called selflessness.

All existents—be they impermanent or permanent—exist depending on other factors. Being dependent, they lack an independent, inherent essence that makes them what they are. These dependent arisings' lack of inherent existence is their fundamental or final mode of existence. It is the object realized by all buddhas of the past, present, and future; it is the object of the meditative equipoise of all śrāvakas, solitary realizers, and bodhisattvas. Through it, nirvāṇa and full awakening are attained. The *King of Concentration Sūtra* (*Samādhirāja Sūtra*) says (MP 71):

If phenomena are individually analyzed as selfless
and what has been analyzed is meditated on,
that is the cause for attaining the fruit, nirvāṇa.
Through any other cause one does not go to peace.

It is crucial to seek the correct antidote to ignorance. Although a variety of religious practices and philosophies benefit people, not all of them explain the correct view of the nature of reality. I have been to more than one Kumba Mela, a Hindu pilgrimage and festival held every twelve years at the confluence of the holy rivers Ganges, Yamuna, and the mythical Sarasvatī. It is one of the largest religious gatherings on the planet, attended by, among others, Hindu yogis who live in the Himalayas and meditate on the practice of inner heat (*caṇḍālī*). From the Buddhist perspective, although these yogis have great faith in their gurus and have renounced the pleasures of this life, they are not able to cut the root of self-grasping. Similarly, some of my Christian friends weep when they speak of their love of God, but they too aren't able to stop rebirth in saṃsāra.

Although we Buddhists learn and apply the antidotes to specific afflictions—such as meditating on impermanence to counteract attachment and on love to subdue anger—these antidotes alone cannot eradicate self-grasping ignorance. In *Clear Words* (*Prasannapadā*), Candrakīrti explains (FEW 37–38):

> Among the extensive teachings in nine divisions—discourses and so forth—rightly proclaimed by the Buddha,
> based on the two truths and corresponding to the forms of behavior of worldly beings,
> those spoken for the sake of removing attachment do not remove hatred,
> and those spoken for the sake of removing hatred do not remove desire.
>
> Moreover, those spoken for the sake of removing arrogance and so forth do not overcome other defilements.
> Therefore, they are not very pervasive, and those teachings are not of great import.
> But those spoken for the sake of removing confusion overcome all afflictions,
> for the Conqueror said all afflictions thoroughly depend on confusion.

Attachment, anger, arrogance, jealousy, and so forth are problematic in our lives and applying the specific antidotes to them—contemplating impermanence, cultivating love, rejoicing in others' good fortune, and so forth—subdues them temporarily. However, their seeds still remain in our mindstream, ready to rise up in an instant as full-blown afflictions. To cut these off so they can never reemerge, eradicating them from the root is imperative. The only antidote capable of eradicating self-grasping ignorance (also called "confusion") is the wisdom realizing the subtle selflessness of persons and phenomena. By realizing emptiness, we cease to assent to or grasp ignorance's false appearances. At that time, there is nothing that can act as a basis for us to give rise to afflictions such as attachment and anger.

## *What Is Emptiness?*

Emptiness is equivalent to suchness (*tattva*).[3] Candrakīrti describes it as the complete refutation of self-existence with respect to all internal phenomena (those conjoined with sentient beings' minds) and external phenomena (those not so conjoined).

Among Buddhists and non-Buddhists there are many different assertions regarding selflessness and suchness (emptiness). Those that are incorrect fall into two extremes: the extreme of nonexistence, deprecation, or nihilism where too much has been negated, and the extreme of absolutism, permanence, eternalism, or superimposition where not enough has been negated. In his commentary to the *Treatise on the Middle Way*, Buddhapālita says that in the first turning of the Dharma wheel, the Buddha presented selflessness as an antidote to counter distorted ways of viewing our aggregates as a self. However, the selflessness presented there is not the final understanding of selflessness, because not enough has been negated. Although the Yogācārins go a step further and reject the reality of the external material world, they still maintain the reality of the internal subjective consciousness. This, too, is a form of exaggerated views where not enough has been negated. Meanwhile Svātantrika Mādhyamikas, in their commentaries on Nāgārjuna's works, insist that phenomena possess some objectified basis on the conventional level. They, too, have fallen to the extreme of superimposition or absolutism. Materialists, on the other hand, say that the self and the world arise randomly without any causes, and people who misunderstand the Prāsaṅgika view say that according to that view nothing at all exists because ultimate analysis negates all existents. These people, who resemble scientific reductionists, also fall to the extreme of deprecation. The Middle Way view as presented by the Prāsaṅgikas avoids both these extremes by realizing the suchness that is the emptiness of inherent existence and still being able to establish conventional, dependent existence.

The view of superimposition exaggerates what exists by saying that dependent arisings exist inherently. This view is faulty because if things existed inherently, they would be independent of all other factors, such as causes and conditions, parts, and so forth. In this case, the person would be permanent because it would exist without depending on causes and conditions.

Such an independent, permanent self would continue unchanged eternally after death.

The view of deprecation denies the existence of what does exist. This involves thinking that if phenomena do not exist inherently, they do not exist at all. Those who hold this view say that if the inherent existence of impermanent, dependently arising things were negated, then these things could not perform the function of creating effects. In that case, when the person dies, he or she would become totally nonexistent, there being no continuity of the person and thus no rebirth.

Both extreme views are based on the premise that if phenomena existed, they must exist inherently, and if they don't exist inherently, then they don't exist at all. Those adhering to the view of absolutism say that since phenomena exist, they must exist inherently. Otherwise they would be totally nonexistent, and that is not acceptable. Those holding the view of deprecation assert that since phenomena don't exist inherently, they don't exist at all. People who fall to either of these extremes are unable to establish dependently arising phenomena. In his *Commentary on [Āryadeva's] Four Hundred*, Candrakīrti says (EMW 179):

> Therefore, here (1) this [deprecation] is an erroneous view of nonexistence due to deprecating—as nonexistent—dependently arisen causes within the thoroughly afflicted (saṃsāra), and [phenomena] within liberation or the very pure, which are compounded [by causes and conditions] and are like illusions, and (2) a view of thingness (inherent existence) also is erroneous because an inherently existent nature does not exist. Hence, in this way those who propound that things have an inherent nature incur the fault that dependent arisings do not exist and incur the faults of the views of permanence and of annihilation.

The correct view is the view of the Middle Way that proclaims the dependent arising of all phenomena and their emptiness of inherent existence are complementary. This book will delve into emptiness and explain how emptiness and dependent arising come to the same point. It will also enable us to gain a correct understanding of emptiness and develop the tools to realize it in our meditation.

## *Emptiness, Its Nature, Its Purpose, and Its Meaning*

The nature of emptiness is the mere negation of grasping inherent existence; the purpose of teaching emptiness is to eliminate that grasping that lies at the root of all afflictions and duḥkha; the meaning of emptiness is that all phenomena lack inherent existence and exist dependently.

The nature of emptiness is the absence of an objectified basis for grasping—anything in relation to which we could say "This is the self" or "This is such-and-such phenomenon." In his *Commentary on Bodhicitta* (*Bodhicittavivaraṇa*), Nāgārjuna says (BV 51–52):

> The abiding of a mind that has no object
> is defined as the characteristic of space;
> [so] they accept that meditation on emptiness
> is [in fact] a meditation on space.
>
> With the lion's roar of emptiness
> all [false] pronouncements are frightened;
> wherever such speakers reside,
> there emptiness lies in wait.

"A mind that has no object" is a mind that does not grasp any phenomenon to have an objectified or inherently existent basis. As long as we believe there is an objectified basis—something that by its own nature *is* that object—grasping its inherent existence will arise. That this happens is confirmed by the fact that we so quickly react to people, objects, and events with attraction and rejection, based on believing they have their own inherent nature; they exist as self-enclosed, independent things just as they appear to. In *Sixty Stanzas of Reasoning* (*Yuktiṣaṣṭikākārikā*), Nāgārjuna asks (YS 44):

> Those who assert the conditioned things
> as being established in terms of ultimate reality,
> why wouldn't the faults of permanence and so on
> not arise within their minds?

If the impermanent things that surround us in daily life existed independent of all other factors, they would be unable to change. Someone who asserts inherent existence should therefore believe conditioned phenomena are permanent, a view that our experience refutes, since we and everything around us is in constant flux.

To avoid these errors, it is crucial to analyze if the basis of objectification we believe exists is actually findable. When we search for an essence of things—a person, paycheck, or rainstorm—instead of finding an objectified basis, we find their emptiness of inherent existence. If we then search for the essence of that emptiness, we find in turn its emptiness. Seeking an essence, we find only essencelessness. This lack of an objectified basis applies when we search for the essence of persons, phenomena, and their emptiness.

At the end of our search for an objectified essence, all that remains is emptiness—the absence of inherent existence—which is like space. Space is defined only in negative terms; it is the absence of obstruction. Aside from this, nothing can be pointed to as being space. Similarly, when we search for the essence of any object with ultimate analysis, only emptiness—the absence of inherent existence—is found. In this way, the teachings on emptiness dismantle any basis for grasping, and the meditative equipoise on emptiness is called "space-like meditation."

Essentialists—philosophers who assert that the person and aggregates truly exist—do not refute enough and leave an objectified basis for grasping inherent existence. Although some of them, such as the Yogācārins, negate an external world, by affirming the true existence of consciousness they too maintain a basis for grasping. Svātantrikas leave room for grasping because they accept inherent existence on the conventional level. Prāsaṅgikas—those who negate inherent existence both ultimately and conventionally—dismantle any basis of grasping.

In the *Treatise on the Middle Way* (*Mūlamadhyamakakārikā*), Nāgārjuna states that whatever is dependent arising is empty, and that holding phenomena as being dependently designated is the Middle Way view. In other words, he equates the meaning of emptiness with the meaning of dependent arising. Understanding this prevents falling to the two extremes. Such a view is like a lion's roar that decimates all wrong views.

In the opening verses of chapter 24 of *Treatise on the Middle Way*, someone who misunderstands the meaning of emptiness thinks that Nāgārjuna's refutation of inherent existence undermines both the Buddhadharma and mundane conventions. Not accepting the meaning of the Perfection of Wisdom sūtras, he accuses Nāgārjuna of being a nihilist (MMK 24.1–6):

> If all these were empty [of inherent existence],
> there would be no arising and no disintegration,
> and it would [absurdly] follow for you
> that the four truths of the āryas would not exist.
>
> Since the four truths would not exist,
> knowing thoroughly, abandoning,
> meditating on, and actualizing [them]
> would not be logically feasible.
>
> Since those would not exist,
> the four fruits also would not exist.
> When the fruits do not exist,
> abiders in the fruit would not exist;
> approachers also would not exist.
>
> If those eight persons did not exist,
> the spiritual community would not exist.
> Because the four truths would not exist,
> the doctrine of the excellent also would not exist.
>
> If the doctrine and spiritual community did not exist,
> how would the buddhas exist?
> If emptiness is construed in this way,
> the existence of the Three Jewels is undermined.
>
> The existence of effects,
> what is not the doctrine, the doctrine itself,
> and all conventions of the world—
> all these are undermined.

The objector says that if everything is empty of inherent existence, nothing could arise and cease, and thus true duḥkha and true origins would not arise and could not cease. If that were the case, then true paths could not be cultivated and true cessations could not be actualized. In short, the four truths of āryas would not exist. If the four truths didn't exist, thoroughly knowing true duḥkha, abandoning true origins, meditating on true paths, and actualizing true cessations would not be possible. If these weren't possible, the four fruits of stream-enterer, once-returner, nonreturner, and arhat would not be feasible, nor would the four approachers to these states and the four abiders in them. In that case, the Saṅgha Jewel and the Dharma Jewel would not exist, and if these did not exist neither would the Buddha Jewel. Cause and effect, the Dharma teachings, and all societal conventions would be negated. In short, the objector claims that emptiness is equivalent to total nonexistence and would undermine both the ultimate truth (true cessations and nirvāṇa) as well as all mundane conventions (true duḥkha, origins, path, and everything else in the world).

Nāgārjuna replies that this person has misunderstood the nature of emptiness, its purpose, and its meaning, and as a result his mind is proliferating with many pernicious misconceptions. Nāgārjuna then explains that the nature of emptiness is peaceful (quiescent) and not fabricated by the mental elaborations of inherent existence; it is the absence of all dualistic appearances. The purpose of realizing emptiness is to eliminate afflictions, polluted karma, and cognitive obscurations, and the meaning of emptiness is dependent arising.

Nāgārjuna then directly confronts the objector's points, saying that his understanding is completely backward, and the situation is the opposite of what he believes: the fact that all phenomena are empty of inherent existence allows all the functions and relationships of saṃsāra and nirvāṇa to exist. If phenomena existed independent of all other factors, they couldn't interact with other factors and thus couldn't arise, change, function, or cease (MMK 24.14):

> For whom emptiness is feasible,
> all is feasible.
> For whom emptiness is not feasible,
> all is not feasible.

Since phenomena are empty by nature, all the faults the objector accuses the Mādhyamikas of having actually accrue to him. Nāgārjuna confronts the objector with the undesirable consequence of his wrong views (MMK 24.20):

> If all these were not empty [of inherent existence],
> there would be no arising and no disintegration,
> and it would [absurdly] follow for you
> that the four truths of the āryas would not exist.

Because phenomena lack inherent existence, they exist dependently. True duḥkha arises dependent on its causes, true origins. These can be overcome by realizing true paths, which bring true cessations. True paths and true cessations are the Dharma Jewel, and the Saṅgha Jewel, which includes the eight approachers and abiders to stream-entry, and so on, and the ārya bodhisattvas, has actualized them. Since the Saṅgha Jewel is feasible, the Buddha Jewel is also possible. All mundane and supramundane realizations and attainments are feasible, as are cause and effect and all worldly conventions.

In this way, Nāgārjuna clarifies that the meaning of the Perfection of Wisdom sūtras' statements about emptiness are definitive and can be understood just as they are expressed. In addition, the above argument clears away all doubt regarding the existence of the Three Jewels and the four truths: because phenomena are empty and arise dependent on other factors, all phenomena in saṃsāra and nirvāṇa are feasible.

## REFLECTION

1. Why is realizing emptiness important?
2. What is the purpose of realizing emptiness?
3. What are the disadvantages and inaccuracies of the view of superimposition and the view of deprecation?
4. Review Nāgārjuna's argument that because all phenomena are empty of

inherent existence and exist dependently, the four truths as well as the Three Jewels and the path to full awakening exist.

---

## *Suitable Vessels to Receive Teachings on Emptiness*

For teachings on emptiness to benefit us, we must be proper vessels. Scriptures contain warnings about the danger of teaching emptiness to those who are not suitable vessels, and doing so transgresses a root bodhisattva percept. The chief danger is that an untrained person will misunderstand the teachings, mistake the emptiness of inherent existence for total nonexistence, and fall to the extreme of nihilism (deprecation), thinking that nothing exists or that actions do not bring results. It is especially deleterious if people disbelieve the law of karma and its effects and cease to care about the ethical dimension of their actions. Behaving recklessly, they create destructive karma, winning for themselves only an unfortunate rebirth.

Alternatively, by misunderstanding the teachings on emptiness, someone may think that emptiness is nonsensical, thus hardening their belief that all phenomena inherently exist. Abandoning suchness, they close the door to liberation by falling to the extreme of absolutism (superimposition). Such wrong views perpetuate duḥkha in saṃsāra for a long time to come. The Sakya scholar-adept Drakpa Gyaltsen (1147–1216) summarizes the disadvantages of incorrectly understanding emptiness in "Parting from the Four Clingings" (26):

> There is no liberation for those who grasp at existence;
> there is no higher rebirth for those who grasp at nonexistence;
> those who grasp at both are ignorant;
> so place your mind freely in the nondual sphere.

Those who grasp inherent existence cannot realize emptiness; until they relinquish that view, they cannot attain liberation. Those who grasp nonexistence negate the law of karma and its effects and ignore the ethical dimension of their actions. As a result, fortunate rebirth eludes them. Those who hold both the view of absolutism and nihilism are confused and cannot progress on the path. The view of emptiness is the remedy of all these wrong views.

Āryadeva mentions the qualities of suitable disciples: they are open-minded and willing to hear new ideas, intelligent and able to discern the validity or error in those teachings, and earnest, having a sincere spiritual motivation. Some arrogant people erroneously think that they have understood the subtle meaning of emptiness. Teaching their wrong view to others, they not only harm themselves but also lead others astray.

Candrakīrti speaks of external signs that a teacher may look for to determine if a student is ripe to hear teachings on emptiness (MMA 6.4–5):

> Upon hearing about emptiness even while an ordinary being,
> whoever gives rise repeatedly to great inner joy,
> tears flowing from utter joy moisten the eyes,
> and the hairs of the body stand on end,
>
> they have the seed of the mind of complete buddhahood.
> They are vessels for the teaching of suchness.
> The ultimate truth is to be revealed to them.
> In him, qualities that follow after that will arise.

People familiar with the doctrine of emptiness from past lives and those who have wisdom arisen from hearing and wisdom arisen from reflecting on emptiness may have these physical reactions when they hear teachings on emptiness in this life. However, weeping or one's bodily hair standing on end during teachings do not necessarily indicate that a person is a completely suitable vessel for learning about emptiness, because these physical signs could occur for a variety of reasons. On the other hand, the absence of these signs does not mean that those people are not suitable vessels to hear teachings on emptiness. People who have heard teachings on the stages of the path, have conviction in the infallibility of karma and its effects, and do not stray from their teacher's instructions should learn and study emptiness and will receive great benefit from doing so.

Maitreya's *Ornament of Clear Realizations* says that suitable vessels for teachings on emptiness are students who have made offerings to the Three Jewels, created roots of virtue, and are under the guidance of a qualified and virtuous spiritual mentor. A great collection of merit is needed before learning about emptiness to ensure that the student will adequately think about the teachings, reach correct understandings, and thus benefit from the teachings. Students of the Buddhadharma must be willing to exert effort to examine the teachings on emptiness with unbiased wisdom and to persevere until they gain the correct view.

To make your mind receptive to emptiness, engage in practices to accumulate merit and purify negativities and develop a firm foundation in the Buddhist worldview and the four truths. In addition, cultivate humility and be willing to familiarize yourself with the foundational teachings, such as those on impermanence, duḥkha, and karma and its effects, without impetuously jumping ahead to more advanced teachings. By studying and practicing the foundational topics, your confidence in the Dharma and in yourself as a Dharma practitioner will increase.

Try to learn and reflect as your spiritual mentor and the lineage masters instruct so that you are not the confused students Āryadeva speaks about: people who, not understanding the teachings, fault the Buddha for not explaining them well, think emptiness means that nothing whatsoever exists, or favor views that make them feel emotionally comfortable although those views are not supported by reasoning. I heard a story about a Buddhist monk who converted to Christianity. When a friend asked him why, he responded, "Buddhism explains things that are impossible for me to do, such as realize emptiness. But in Christianity, I just have to have faith and God will provide for everything. I can do that."

Do not take the teachings about emptiness for granted. Following his awakening, the Buddha reportedly reflected:

> Profound and peaceful, free from elaboration, uncompounded
>     clear light—
> I have found a nectar-like Dharma.
> Yet if I were to teach it, no one would understand,
> so I shall remain silent here in the forest.

"Profound and peaceful" refers to the true cessation that is the focus of the first turning of the wheel of Dharma. "Free from elaboration" alludes to the content of the second turning of the wheel, and "uncompounded clear light" indicates the third turning of the wheel.[4] These teachings are precious, and fearing that no one would understand them, the Buddha almost didn't teach. Receiving these teachings is a dependent arising, and making ourselves receptive students prior to receiving the teachings and enthusiastically investigating the teachings afterward create the cause for our spiritual mentors to instruct us on emptiness.

If we follow an intelligent approach to the Buddha's teachings, diligently study them, and gain a correct understanding, the Buddhadharma will endure. But if we rely only on faith and worship the Three Jewels without valuing their realization of emptiness, how long will the Dharma exist in our world? If we can explain the Buddha's philosophical views on the basis of reason and science, people today will pay attention. Thus it is important to study the sūtras and the treatises, commentaries, and autocommentaries of the great Indian scholar-adepts. The classical Indian commentaries unlock the meaning of the terse root verses and enable us to discern the assertions of other tenet systems from those of our own.

When people who are suitable vessels hear teachings about emptiness, good qualities will arise in them. Candrakīrti says (MMA 6.6–7a):

> After adopting an ethical code, they will always abide in ethical conduct.
> They will practice generosity, cultivate compassion, meditate on fortitude,
> and fully dedicate the virtue of these toward awakening
> for the sake of liberating migrators.
> They will respect the exalted bodhisattvas.

Suitable disciples understand that emptiness and dependent arising are complementary, not contradictory. This increases and stabilizes their faith in karma and its effects, which is essential to avoid the extreme of nihilism. Convinced that realizing emptiness is the key to awakening, they are keen to learn, reflect, and meditate on emptiness from one life to the next without interruption. To ensure they have future lives with all the conducive conditions to do this, they create the causes for fortunate births by cherishing ethical conduct and purify any previously created causes so they cannot ripen. To prevent poverty from interfering with their ability to receive teachings and practice in future lives, they create the causes to receive life's necessities by practicing generosity.

Aware that realization of emptiness conjoined with compassion will bring full awakening, bodhisattvas cultivate compassion and bodhicitta to ensure that they will continually follow the Mahāyāna and attain buddhahood. To prevent anger from creating destructive karma, destroying virtue, and propelling them to an unfortunate rebirth, they practice fortitude. Practicing fortitude also brings a pleasant appearance, so they can meet more people, especially āryas who will instruct them. Knowing that familiarizing themselves with emptiness is the way to overpower afflictions and defilements, they learn, think, and meditate on emptiness as much as possible and cultivate serenity focused on emptiness. To direct the merit from the above practices to full awakening, they dedicate it to attain buddhahood. Their respect for bodhisattvas increases exponentially because they understand that only buddhas and bodhisattvas can teach emptiness using a myriad of reasonings. To repay the kindness of the buddhas, they engage in the four ways of gathering disciples that give them the opportunity to instruct others on emptiness.

In short, suitable vessels do not erroneously think that the method aspect of the path, which includes compassion, bodhicitta, the collection of merit, ethical conduct, generosity, fortitude, and so on, is only to be practiced by those who have not understood emptiness. They know that although these practices are empty of inherent existence, they exist conventionally. They also contemplate the three—themselves as the agent, the actions engaged in, and the objects acted upon—as empty of inherent existence yet conventionally existent, and they dedicate their merit with that awareness. In this way, those who are suitable vessels practice both the method and the wisdom aspects of the path without deprecating either one.

The activities of listening to and teaching emptiness create great merit. The *Gift of the Precious Child Sūtra* (*Āryasatpuruṣ Sūtra*) says (EES 21):

> Mañjuśrī, whoever listens [even] with doubt to this rendition of the teaching [on emptiness] generates much greater merit than a bodhisattva who, lacking skillful means, practices the six perfections for a hundred thousand eons. This being so, what need is there to say anything about a person who listens without doubt!

> What need is there to say anything about a person who imparts the scripture in writing, memorizes it, and also teaches it thoroughly and extensively to others!

Even though someone lacks skillful means—that is, doesn't understand emptiness—and has doubt about it, he plants powerful seeds for liberation on his mindstream by listening to teachings about emptiness. If this is the case, a person who has full confidence in the teachings on emptiness creates that much greater merit. Needless to say, someone who teaches it without error creates extensive merit.

Why does someone who copies or memorizes a scripture create great merit? After all, nowadays we can easily photocopy or digitize Dharma texts without having a virtuous thought! It takes a long time to copy a scripture by manually writing it, and dedicating so much time and effort to writing it meticulously increases our respect for its contents. Copying it slowly provides time to contemplate the scripture's meaning, and memorizing it entails repetition, which is conducive to contemplation. These activities of writing, memorizing, and reciting the scriptures connect us with the precious teachings. Because of this familiarity, when we later hear or read teachings the meaning impacts us more deeply. For this reason, monastics in Tibetan monasteries memorize and recite the scriptures beginning when they are young children.

Contemplating emptiness can prevent unfortunate rebirth. The *Treasury of the One Thus Gone Sūtra* (*Tathāgatakośagarbha Sūtra*) says (EES 21):

> A living being—who, possessing all these [ten great nonvirtues], enters into the doctrine of selflessness and has faith and belief that all phenomena are from the beginning pure—does not take a bad rebirth.

For example, someone has committed a powerful destructive action that will result in an unfortunate rebirth in the next life. Embracing the teachings on emptiness, he generates tremendous faith and respect toward them and with great enthusiasm tries to understand these teachings. Even if he isn't able to understand them fully, having a good understanding can prevent an unfortunate rebirth in the next life.

Many benefits accrue from instructing others on emptiness. However, teaching emptiness should not be done haphazardly, and much care is required. Two principal requirements are necessary: First, a pure motivation, one that is genuinely concerned about the students and wants them to attain awakening is required. This motivation must also be free from the eight worldly concerns, such as seeking material or financial gain, praise, fame, pleasure, or services. Second, the ability to explain the correct meaning of emptiness without error is essential. This requires years of study, contemplation, and meditation.

If, lacking these two requirements, someone gives an erroneous explanation on emptiness or even a correct explanation with an afflictive motivation, his speech becomes the nonvirtue of idle talk. Incorrectly explaining emptiness to someone new to the Dharma is especially grievous because people tend to take to heart the first teachings they hear and, as a result, may hold a distorted view of emptiness for a long time. If an incorrect explanation is given to someone who has studied philosophy, at least that person has the opportunity to use reasoning and discern that it is incorrect. A correct explanation given with a motivation of compassion free from attachment to the happiness of this life is an excellent gift to a student and an excellent offering of our practice to the Buddha.

## REFLECTION

1. What are the qualities of a suitable student to hear teachings on emptiness?
2. What benefits do suitable students accrue from learning about emptiness, and what benefits do qualified teachers gain by teaching the doctrine of emptiness?
3. How can you help yourself become a suitable student who will reap these benefits?

## *Prerequisites for Insight*

Insight and the wisdom realizing emptiness must be specifically cultivated. They will not arise by themselves or by meditating on other unrelated topics such as compassion or serenity. Nevertheless, contemplating other aspects of the path supports our understanding of emptiness. For example, meditating on the defects of saṃsāra or on bodhicitta will increase our joyous effort to learn and meditate on emptiness.

For the practice of insight to flow smoothly, certain prerequisites must be complete. In his *Middle Stages of Meditation* (*Bhāvanākrama II*), Kamalaśīla speaks of three causes to prepare to meditate on emptiness and cultivate insight: relying on a knowledgeable and experienced spiritual mentor, hearing and studying the teachings under his or her guidance, and properly contemplating what was taught.

The first prerequisite—choosing and relying on a qualified spiritual mentor—was discussed in chapters 4 and 5 of *The Foundation of Buddhist Practice*. The second prerequisite is fulfilled by listening to your spiritual mentors' teachings on emptiness as explained in authoritative sūtras, commentaries, and treatises. The Buddha said that one who hears another will be released from aging and death. "Hears another" indicates that the profound view of emptiness is generated by first hearing its meaning from an external spiritual mentor and thinking about the meaning to ensure we have understood it correctly. Without hearing an unmistaken explanation of emptiness from a qualified spiritual master, the profound view will not be generated in your mind no matter how powerful your concentration, how many books you read, how strong your faith in the guru and Three Jewels is, or how many retreats you have done.

To gain a correct understanding of the definitive meaning of emptiness, rely on the treatises of great sages, such as Nāgārjuna. Since distorted understandings of emptiness abound, take care to follow the wise and to develop wisdom in accord with their explanations.

Having heard and studied correct explanations of emptiness, settle the view by contemplating it deeply. A correct inferential understanding of emptiness is an essential prerequisite to cultivating insight on emptiness. Simply saying "All phenomena are empty" does not mean you have understood emptiness. Doing stabilizing meditation for years on your idea of emptiness, without having discerned the correct view, does not generate insight realizing emptiness. Therefore, the upcoming chapters and volumes contain a detailed explanation of how to determine the correct view of emptiness, followed by how to generate insight into emptiness.

Hearing and studying bring the wisdom arising from hearing; contemplating what you have learned and discussing and debating it with others induce the wisdom arising from thinking. By employing complete forms of reasoning, examine how the person exists and decisively conclude that a truly existent self—the object of negation—does not exist. Then meditate to unite serenity and insight and gain the wisdom arising from meditation. With this integrate your understanding of emptiness with your mind to effect deep transformation.

# 2 The Nālandā Tradition

BUDDHISM IN INDIA was the result of the Buddha's three turnings of the Dharma wheel in which he established the basic principles of his teaching. During the first turning, he explained the four truths—how we enter the cycle of existence under the control of afflictions and polluted karma, and how to free ourselves by practicing the path and achieving cessation. Although the Buddha said this, we need to explore whether it is actually possible to cease saṃsāric duḥkha and attain liberation. The Buddha discouraged blind belief and instead encouraged investigation by reasoning and logic.

The Nālandā tradition, which began in India, is named after Nālandā University near Rajgir. This tradition, which stresses the use of reasoning and logic, was later transmitted to Tibet, Mongolia, China, Korea, Japan, and Vietnam. It takes as a starting point the Buddha's advice to his followers, "As the wise test gold by burning, cutting, and rubbing it, so, bhikṣus, should you accept my words—after testing them, and not merely out of respect for me." The Nālandā masters took him at his word and scrutinized his teachings, classifying them into those that were definitive and those requiring interpretation.

The Nālandā tradition has brought great benefit to the world. People in the East and in the West are practicing Buddhadharma, and scientists have interest in it. In the East in general, people have great faith in Buddhism and many recite prayers and the *Heart Sūtra*. But when I ask them what the meaning of the *Heart Sūtra* is, they don't know. To preserve Dharma, people have built many monasteries and temples filled with beautiful statues on the altar, but teaching the meaning of the Dharma is most important so that people will understand and practice the teachings and benefit from doing this. This is the true way to preserve the Buddhadharma.

To show the importance of the Nālandā tradition and my gratitude toward the great masters who comprise it, I wrote a homage expressing my admiration for seventeen Nālandā masters entitled "Illuminating the Threefold Faith: An Invocation of the Seventeen Great Scholar-Adepts of Glorious Nālandā." Although a praise to eight great Indian masters already existed, this praise to the seventeen masters includes other sages whose writings we rely on. They are some of the major scholar-adepts whose views we will examine in the following chapters. Although not all of them lived at Nālandā University, Nālandā's way of study and practice was present in the other large Buddhist universities. Each of these masters specialized in a particular area of the Buddhadharma and all were knowledgeable and realized practitioners of the three higher trainings—the higher trainings of ethical conduct, concentration, and wisdom.

## *Illuminating the Threefold Faith: An Invocation of the Seventeen Great Scholar-Adepts of Glorious Nālandā*[5]

1. Lords of Lords, arisen from the compassionate wish to benefit wandering beings,
you have attained sublime protection, abandonment, and realization,
and liberate sentient beings through teaching dependent arising.
I bow to you, Conqueror, Sun among Teachers.

2. I call to mind esteemed Nāgārjuna, who, as the Conqueror prophesied,
introduced the Middle Way of the Universal Vehicle and was skilled in clarifying
the meaning of suchness, free of extremes, as intended in the Mother of Conquerors (Perfection of Wisdom sūtras),
through the profound, logical presentation of dependent arising.

3. I call to mind the Bodhisattva Āryadeva,
his principal spiritual child, the most learned and accomplished,

who traversed the ocean of Buddhist and other philosophies,
who is the glorious crowning jewel among all holders of Nāgārjuna's treatises.

4. I call to mind esteemed Buddhapālita,
who clarified the ultimate meaning of dependent arising—the thought of Ārya [Nāgārjuna],
essential point of the profound, existence as mere designation and name—
and has ascended the utmost state of accomplishment.

5. I call to mind Ācārya Bhāvaviveka, erudite master
who introduced a philosophical view
that refutes such extremes as truly existent production
while accepting commonly verified knowledge and external objects.

6. I call to mind Candrakīrti, who promulgated the complete path of Sūtra and Tantra,
who was skilled in expounding the profound and vast Middle Way,
in which appearance and emptiness eliminate the two extremes
through dependent arising and the merely conditional [nature of things].

7. I call to mind the Bodhisattva Śāntideva,
skilled in teaching a host of fortunate disciples
the truly marvelous path of great compassion
through versatile means of reasoning, profound and vast.

8. I call to mind the great Abbot Śāntarakṣita,
who introduced the nondual Middle Way to suit disciples' mental dispositions,
was well versed in differentiating the reasonings of the Middle Way and reliable cognition,
and disseminated the teaching of the Conqueror in the Land of Snows (Tibet).

9. I call to mind esteemed Kamalaśīla,
who thoroughly explained the stages of meditation on the Middle Way view, free from extremes,
and the union of serenity and insight according to Sūtra and Tantra;
he flawlessly clarified the Conqueror's doctrine in the Land of Snows.

10. I call to mind esteemed Asaṅga,
whom Maitreya inspired and looked after,
who was adept in disseminating all Mahāyāna discourses,
and revealed the vast path and, as the Conqueror prophesied, blazed the trail of Yogācāra.

11. I call to mind esteemed Ācārya Vasubandhu,
who, by maintaining the system of the *Seven Treatises of Abhidharma*, and the nonduality [of Yogācāra],
clarified the philosophies of Vaibhāṣika, Sautrāntika, and Vijñānavāda;
foremost safe, renowned as a second Omniscient One.

12. I call to mind esteemed Dignāga,
the logician who gave us the discerning insight of fine discrimination
by thoroughly opening one hundred doors of logic
to reveal the system of the Buddha's scriptures through empirical reasoning.

13. I call to mind esteemed Dharmakīrti,
who fathomed the vital points of Buddhist and non-Buddhist modes of logic,
granted conviction in the vast and profound paths of Sautrāntika and Yogācāra through reasoning,
and was adept in expounding the marvelous ways of Dharma.

14. I call to mind esteemed Vimuktisena,
who interpreted the Perfection of Wisdom that came from the Asaṅga brothers

in accordance with the Middle Way, free from the extremes of existence and nonexistence,
and who lit the lamp illuminating the meaning of the *Ornament [of Clear Realization]*.

15. I call to mind esteemed Haribhadra,
who clarified the three Mothers,[6] supreme Perfection of Wisdom scriptures,
in line with Maitreyanath's pith instructions,
and who the Conqueror prophesied would expound the meaning of the Mother.

16. I call to mind esteemed Guṇaprabha, excelling in stability and learning,
who integrated the intentions of a hundred thousand categories of Vinaya,
and in accordance with Mūlasarvāstivāda,
thoroughly and unmistakenly explained the prātimokṣa.

17. I call to mind esteemed Śākyaprabha, ideal Vinaya holder,
master of the treasure of the three trainings'[7] qualities,
who, to ensure the longevity of the flawless Vinaya teachings,
thoroughly explained what the vast scriptures meant.

18. I call to mind Jowo Atiśa, kind Lord
who caused the Sage's teaching to flourish in the Land of Snows,
who expounded doctrines vast and profound—complete teaching of the Conqueror—
in the context of paths of persons of three capacities.[8]

19. Making such invocations with an unflinchingly pure mind
to you, exceedingly fine sages, ornaments for the world,
and sources of stupendous, elegant teachings,
inspire me to ripen my mind so that I may attain liberation.

20. Through understanding the meaning of the two truths, the ground reality of how things are,
I ascertain by way of the four truths just how beings arrive in and leave saṃsāra;
thus valid cognition engenders a firm faith in the Three Jewels.
Inspire me to be enduringly grounded in the path to liberation.

21. Inspire me to master renunciation, the mind intent on liberation—
total pacification of duḥkha and its causes;
and the uncontrived bodhicitta rooted in compassion,
the boundless yearning to protect wandering beings.

22. Inspire me to gain conviction with effortless ease
in the profound points of all paths of the Perfection Vehicle and Vajrayāna,
by listening to, contemplating, and meditating on
the meaning of the commentaries of the great pioneers.

23. May I, in successive births, perfectly obtain a human life endowed with the three trainings,
and serve the doctrine as the great pioneers did
by safeguarding and promoting scriptures and insights
through explanation and practice.

24. May all Saṅgha communities be strengthened by noble, learned practitioners
who devote their time to hearing, contemplation, teaching, and practice
and have totally given up wrong livelihood;
may the entire world be forever adorned with such beings.

25. Due to these invocations may I traverse all grounds and paths of Sūtra and Tantra
and quickly attain the state of an Omniscient Conqueror
who spontaneously fulfills the two purposes;
may I work for sentient beings as long as space endures!

*Colophon*

*Thus the foremost sages of the Noble Land of India mentioned above have composed numerous excellent, meaningful treatises and grant insight to those who think critically about the profound and vast teachings of the Fully Awakened Supramundane Victor, the Buddha. To this day, even after nearly 2,550 years have passed, those treatises survive intact for us to study, contemplate, and meditate on. Therefore, I am grateful to those masters who were the cream of sages and aspire to follow them in my practice with unflinching faith.*

*At the present time, when the world has made great progress in the fields of science and technology and we are distracted and preoccupied by the hustle and bustle of our lives, it is extremely important that followers of the Buddha have faith based on an understanding of what he taught. These texts were composed by such renowned masters as the Six Ornaments and Two Supremes, as well as by Buddhapālita and Ārya Vimuktisena, and others, who analyzed his teachings closely with unbiased and inquisitive minds seeking the reasons [that underlie] them and who developed faith supported by an understanding of those reasons. For those reasons, these excellent texts concerning the profound and vast are indispensable. With this in mind, I commissioned a new thangka painting depicting the seventeen scholar-adepts of Nālandā. I added nine other masters of the vast and profound lineages to [those portrayed in the] traditional painting of the Six Ornaments and Two Supremes.*

*Consequently, I was moved to compose an invocation with wholehearted respect for these supreme sages, and some of my aspiring Dharma friends encouraged me. This is how it came about that I, the Śākya Bhikṣu Tenzin Gyatso, who am in the back row of those studying the works of these sages, have developed unfeigned conviction in the superb work of these sublime masters and have composed this text "Illuminating the Threefold Faith," an invocation of the seventeen great and renowned sages of Nālandā.*

*It was completed at Thekchen Chöling, Dharamsala, Kangra District, Himachal Pradesh, India, on the 1st day of the 11th month of the Iron Snake year in the seventeenth Tibetan "rabjung" [sixty-year cycle], corresponding to 15th December 2001 of the western calendar, 2,545 years, according to the Theravāda system, after the Buddha passed away.*

*May Peace Prevail.*[9]

## *Commentary on "Illuminating the Threefold Faith"*

The verses of praise begin with the Buddha, who, because of his unique philosophical position, is unparalleled in speech. Next is Nāgārjuna (1), who explained the perfection of wisdom teachings, elucidated dependent arising, and was the trailblazer of the Madhyamaka system. Āryadeva (2) was his disciple, as was Buddhapālita (3), who clarified the Prāsaṅgika view. Then comes Bhāvaviveka (4), another student of Nāgārjuna,[10] who disagreed with some of Buddhapālita's assertions by maintaining that things have some objective existence on the conventional level. This prompted a debate among Madhyamaka philosophers that has lasted many centuries.

Candrakīrti (5) emphasized the importance of explaining all phenomena as dependent arisings to avoid the two extremes of nihilism and absolutism. This is the basis for understanding appearance and reality. Candrakīrti also explained the entire teaching of Sūtra and Tantra. Then comes Śāntideva (6), the author of *Engaging in the Bodhisattvas' Deeds*, the most profound and extensive explanation of bodhicitta. In my childhood, I had some interest in bodhicitta but felt it would be very difficult to achieve. I admitted as much to my tutor Tagdrag Rinpoche, who advised me not to feel discouraged and confided that he had some experience of bodhicitta. After going into exile, I received teachings on Śāntideva's text from Khunu Lama Rinpoche and, as a result, came to understand that if I make an effort, I too could feel some closeness to bodhicitta.

Next is Śāntarakṣita (7), to whom we are grateful for establishing the tradition of study in Tibet based on reason and logic. He also ordained the first monks in Tibet, instituting the monastic community there. As the abbot of Nālandā, he began the Yogācāra-Madhyamaka system, which united the Madhyamaka tradition of Nāgārjuna and Āryadeva, the Yogācāra tradition of Asaṅga and Vasubandhu, and the logical and epistemological thought of Dignāga and Dharmakīrti. He is followed by his student Kamalaśīla (8), who wrote the *Stages of Meditation*, an important text that instructs us in proper meditation techniques as well as the cultivation of bodhicitta by the seven cause-and-effect instructions.[11]

Asaṅga (9) was founder of the Yogācāra, or Cittamātra (Mind Only), school. Vasubandhu (10), his younger brother, specialized in Abhidharma. Vasubandhu was originally a proponent of the Fundamental Vehicle, but later adopted the Universal Vehicle (Mahāyāna). Asaṅga knew that his younger brother was very intelligent and was concerned he might misuse his intelligence to deprecate the Mahāyāna, so he sent a messenger to Vasubandhu saying that he was seriously ill and asking Vasubandhu to come and help.

Arriving at Asaṅga's dwelling, Vasubandhu inquired about the cause of his brother's sickness, to which Asaṅga responded that he had a serious illness of the heart that arose because of Vasubandhu. He went on to explain that because Vasubandhu had discredited and defamed the Mahāyāna, Asaṅga was concerned that Vasubandhu would fall to an unfortunate rebirth. This pained him so much that, as a result, he had a heart ailment that might prove fatal. Alarmed, Vasubandhu asked his brother to teach him the Mahāyāna. Listening to Asaṅga's exposition, Vasubandhu applied his penetrating wisdom to gain conviction in the Mahāyāna teachings and meditated on them.

Vasubandhu then became worried that he might take an unfortunate rebirth as a result of previously deprecating the Mahāyāna. Confessing his error to Asaṅga, Vasubandhu considered cutting out his tongue to atone for his destructive speech. Asaṅga told him that that would not purify his negative speech and instead counseled, "Previously you skillfully used your speech to criticize the Mahāyāna. Now you must use it to wisely and effectively propound the Mahāyāna." Vasubandhu then went on to write several texts from the Yogācāra viewpoint.

Vasubandhu's student, Dignāga (11), was a master of logic. He was followed by another logician and epistemologist, Dharmakīrti (12). Both of them used reasoning to demonstrate the truth of the Buddha's teachings, and Dharmakīrti in the second chapter of his *Commentary on Reliable Cognition* used reasoning to prove the Buddha is a reliable authority. Although Vimuktisena (13) was Vasubandhu's disciple, he explained the perfection of wisdom from the Madhyamaka point of view.

Haribhadra (14) too was a celebrated commentator on the perfection of wisdom. Many students in the monasteries today memorize his commentary, *Clear Meaning*. I remember a group of nuns from Kopan Monastery in Nepal who had memorized it, and I commented to them that they had surpassed me by doing so.

Guṇaprabha (15) and Śākyaprabha (16) were both masters of Vinaya, the monastic discipline. Finally, Atiśa (17) was the kind spiritual mentor who caused the Conqueror's teaching to flourish in the Land of Snows during the time of the second dissemination. The first dissemination began when Śāntarakṣita and Guru Padmasambhava brought Buddhism to Tibet in the eighth century, but it was severely curtailed and damaged under the reign of King Langdarma (r. 838–41). Atiśa was invited to Tibet to revitalize the Buddhadharma there.

The praise concludes, "May I be inspired to mature my mindstream and attain liberation. May I be inspired to establish the root of the path to liberation. May I be inspired to perfect an uncontrived awakening mind of bodhicitta. May I be inspired to quickly and easily develop conviction about the profound paths of the perfection of wisdom and the Vajrayāna." May we work with joyous effort to accomplish these aims.

In the colophon I stressed the importance of examining and analyzing the Buddha's teachings with an unbiased and inquisitive mind. Don't be satisfied simply with performing rituals and reciting prayers, but try to understand the Buddha's teachings on the two truths and the four truths of the āryas. Haribhadra said there are dull and intelligent followers of the Buddha; the intelligent question and investigate what they have heard and read, whereas the dull accept the teachings on faith. If you follow the Nālandā tradition and rely on reasoning and logic, the Buddha's teachings will last long in the future; but if you simply fall back on having faith, that is unlikely to happen.

Training in the Nālandā tradition with its extensive use of reasoning and logic is compatible with the scientific method. For almost forty years I have engaged in dialogue with modern scientists to our mutual benefit. Both science and Buddhism emphasize investigation to discover the truth.

The Buddha's teachings of course developed further in Tibet. King Songtsen Gampo (c. 604–49) adopted an Indian model to create a system for written Tibetan. When Śāntarakṣita (725–88) came to Tibet in the eighth century at the king's invitation, he encouraged the translation of Buddhist literature into Tibetan so that Tibetans could study in their own language and set up a translation department at Samye Monastery.

Dignāga's and Dharmakīrti's extensive writings on logic and epistemology were translated into Tibetan. Later Tibetan scholars such as Chapa

Chokyi Senge (1109–69), the abbot of Sangphu, and Sakya Pandita (1182–1251) elaborated on these themes.

Marpa Lotsawa (1012–97) transmitted many tantric teachings from India to Tibet, and his disciple Milarepa (1052–1135), who is said to have attained full awakening in that very life, was one of Tibet's greatest meditators. Tsongkhapa (1357–1419) was a brilliant scholar and meditator. The accomplished logician Gyaltsab Dharma Rinchen set out to challenge Tsongkhapa. Attending one of Tsongkhapa's teachings in a state of inflated confidence, he took a seat next to Tsongkhapa on the throne. Ignoring him, Tsongkhapa continued to teach. Hearing Tsongkhapa's profound presentation, Gyaltsab took off his hat, and he then conceded Tsongkhapa's superiority by sliding off the throne and sitting at Tsongkhapa's feet. Although Tsongkhapa had visions of meditation deities—Mañjuśrī in particular—he emphasized study of the classical texts. He never used his mystical experiences to validate his understanding of the teachings, but relied on extensive reasoning.

Among the dedication verses at the end of his *Great Exposition on the Stages of the Path* (*Lamrim Chenmo*), Tsongkhapa wrote:

> In regions where the supreme, precious teaching has not spread,
> or where it has spread but then declined,
> with my heart deeply moved by great compassion,
> may I illuminate this treasure of happiness and benefit.

Taking this to heart, I have tried to serve humanity and feel that I have not let the Buddha down.

## *Reliable Guides and Explanations*

The Buddha explained the ultimate nature differently according to the dispositions, interests, capacities, and needs of the particular audience. To help us discern the Buddha's definitive meaning, we should rely on his sagacious followers. The Buddha clearly prophesized a sage named Nāgārjuna, who, by employing reasoning, would destroy the two extremes of existence (absolutism) and nonexistence (nihilism). Nāgārjuna's many texts—the most important of which is *Treatise on the Middle Way*—speak extensively about emptiness. His student Āryadeva wrote *The Four Hundred* to supplement his teacher's treatise. After introducing some preliminary topics, Āryadeva critically examines the tenets of non-Buddhist as well as Buddhist tenet systems that do not see emptiness and dependent arising as complementary. *Commentary on "Treatise on the Middle Way"* (*Buddhapālita-Mūlamadhyamakavṛtti*) by Buddhapālita (470–550) is a short but profound text that stresses that it is not possible to reify functioning things beyond their being merely conditioned—that is, aside from being produced by causes and conditions, there is no inherent essence in functioning things. In his *Heart of the Middle Way* (*Madhyamakahṛdaya*) and its extensive autocommentary *Blaze of Reasoning* (*Tarkajvālā*), Bhāvaviveka (c. 500–570) develops his own unique interpretation of Nāgārjuna. Śāntideva's *Engaging in the Bodhisattvas' Deeds* delves deep into the meaning of emptiness.

Atiśa, the scholar-adept who brought the New Transmission of teachings to Tibet, recommended that, of the plethora of Indian sages who wrote about emptiness, we follow the texts of Candrakīrti. Atiśa praised Candrakīrti as someone who correctly understood the thought of Nāgārjuna, and therefore of the Buddha. In his *Introduction to the Two Truths* (*Satyadvayāvatāra* 15–16ab), Atiśa says:

> Through whom should emptiness be realized?
> Through Candrakīrti, the student of Nāgārjuna,
> who was prophesized by the Tathāgata
> and who saw truth, the reality.
> Through the quintessential instructions transmitted from him,
> reality, the truth, will be realized.

The great masters of all four Tibetan Buddhist traditions agree that the Prāsaṅgika view as explained by Nāgārjuna and Candrakīrti is the most sublime, although they may call it by different names and describe it somewhat differently. I recommend that you hear, read, study, reflect, and meditate on the works of the above sages. Relate their teachings to your own perceptions, conceptions, and emotions and examine how you perceive and conceive things. Then you will notice the impact that even a small understanding of emptiness has on your mind.

Until the time of Rendawa Zhonnu Lodro (1349–1412), the Sakya master who was one of Tsongkhapa's closest teachers, the Middle Way view was not widely known. It seems that people did not place special emphasis on the Middle Way, or perhaps did not have a special interest in it, even though Nāgārjuna's teachings were present in Tibet. While the Middle Way view was taught as one feature of the broader Sūtra practice and was seen as necessary for Tantric practice, emptiness was not emphasized as a major subject for study and meditation, and in the early centuries of Buddhism in Tibet, not many treatises elucidated and analyzed its subtle nuances.

Because of Rendawa's special interest in the Middle Way view, people began to understand its importance, and from that time onward studying it became a prominent aspect of Buddhism in Tibet. Rendawa's student, Tsongkhapa, was likewise highly interested in emptiness and wrote extensively on it. Masters from other Tibetan Buddhist traditions began to write on it as well. In fact, the topic of emptiness became so popular at that time that people said, "In Tibet, when you teach, teach emptiness; when you meditate, meditate on emptiness; when you travel, reflect on emptiness."

I talk about emptiness a lot; I'm compelled to do so because without emptiness, nothing works. The realization of emptiness is the only thing that will overcome self-grasping ignorance. Without it, bodhicitta can't be truly effective and we can't progress through the five paths to awakening. Understanding emptiness enables us to know that liberation is possible and to prove the existence of the Three Jewels. The ability to study, contemplate, and meditate on emptiness makes our human life meaningful. As our understanding of emptiness increases, we naturally will see the greatness and kindness of the spiritual mentors who teach it.

For these reasons, the study and practice of works by Nāgārjuna, Āryadeva, Buddhapālita, Bhāvaviveka, and Candrakīrti, as well as the commentaries by Tsongkhapa and other Tibetan luminaries, is of foremost importance. People from the West and other countries are intelligent and can understand emptiness when it is taught to them. Skillfully introducing suitable vessels to the doctrine of the emptiness of inherent existence encourages them to use their intelligence and cultivate wisdom and leads them on the right path.

The philosophers and yogis of India valued poetry, and many of their compositions were written in verse. This allows for diverse interpretations of the words and meanings, which have been debated for centuries. Some of these sages wrote autocommentaries on their metered root texts, whereas others wrote the short root text and left it to others to expand the meaning in commentaries. As a result, there is a wealth of literature that approaches the subject matter from a variety of perspectives.

Sometimes we may wish that the Buddha and the Indian sages would tell us the "one right meaning" of their words that we can latch on to and that will pacify our uneasiness about ambiguity. But the purpose of the Buddha and the sages was to provoke us to think and to sharpen our ability to investigate and test the teachings with reasoning. As a result of that lengthy process, we will gain firm and clear wisdom that goes beyond intellectual knowledge.

While learning the various tenet systems, you will encounter many points of debate. The purpose of the debates is not philosophical argument. Simply proving one's intellectual prowess and refuting others' views does not lead to liberation. Rather, the debates help to clarify your own views. When Prāsaṅgikas refute Svātantrikas' view of emptiness, look inside yourself and see if you hold the Svātantrika view and subtly grasp inherent existence. In meditation, investigate how things actually exist, and examine the view of each tenet system to determine which is the most profound and comprehensive. This is a challenging process that requires much reflection. Having found the correct view, meditate and realize it.

I encourage you to study a variety of Indian commentaries as well as the sūtras that they explain. Some people believe that studying just the debate manuals written by their own monastic college is sufficient to know a subject. They say this out of great respect for the lineage, thinking that the previous masters were so astute that they figured everything out. They see their job as students as simply imbibing and duplicating in their own minds what the main master from their monastic college taught. Some people may even go so far as to think, "I only need to study what my own teacher taught because he or she is the Buddha and knows everything." These narrow viewpoints limit the individual's perspective and cause the tradition to stagnate. All of us need to learn, investigate for ourselves, and use our own intelligence to understand the teachings. Studying widely and looking at a topic from a variety of angles sharpens our faculties and expands our comprehension. It also breathes new energy into our debates and into the tradition as a whole.

# 3 | Introduction to the Philosophical Tenet Systems

IN HIS *Commentary on Bodhicitta* (BV 70), Nāgārjuna tells us:

> A happy mind is tranquil indeed;
> a tranquil mind is not confused.
> To have no confusion is to understand the truth;
> by understanding the truth one attains freedom.

The main purpose of discussing selflessness, emptiness, and insight is to see reality so that we can attain the freedom and peace of liberation and full awakening and help others do the same. To do this, we must investigate the process through which our unwanted duḥkha comes about and how to reverse it. In *Saṃsāra, Nirvāṇa, and Buddha Nature,* we traced the origin of duḥkha to karma—our intentional actions—and from karma back to afflictions such as attachment, anger, jealousy, arrogance, and so on. The root of all afflictions is the ignorance that grasps persons and phenomena to exist inherently—that is, as able to set themselves up and exist under their own power independent of all other factors.

This ignorance can be eradicated by the wisdom that perceives phenomena as they actually are, as empty of inherent existence. The way to generate this wisdom is the topic of this and the next two volumes. As we embark on this exploration of how our mind misapprehends the way phenomena exist, let's be curious and open to consider ideas we may not have heard before. In addition, let's continually maintain a sincere motivation to question, analyze, and learn in order to support our long-term goal of buddhahood.

By realizing the truth of how persons and phenomena actually exist, our mind will become tranquil and free from the pain of ignorance. Beyond fear, anxiety, and insecurity, an unruffled mind imbued with great compassion and wisdom is capable of benefiting others, especially by guiding them to nirvāṇa and full awakening.

Our inquiry into the nature of reality begins with a general overview of the assertions of Buddhist and ancient Indian non-Buddhist philosophical tenet systems. These systems developed as a result of learned adepts questioning, "Who am I?" and "How do things exist?" In these tenet systems, they lay out what they believe is the source of unwanted duḥkha and the wisdom that will undercut that source.

Having heard that the Madhyamaka (Middle Way) view is considered supreme, we may want to immediately jump to it rather than plod through learning other tenet systems first. However, there is great value in studying these other systems, because we may discover that we hold views similar to theirs. In that case, we need to examine if our views are correct. Another benefit of studying other systems is that by taking their positions and trying to defend them, we come to see where they lack evidence and reason, and in that way, gradually sharpen our wisdom and refine our own view.

## *The Value of Studying the Tenet Systems*

During his forty-five years of teaching the Dharma, the Buddha instructed a vast variety of people who had different mental capacities and dispositions. A skillful teacher, he taught whatever would be most effective for guiding a particular person from his present level to awakening. For this reason, the Buddha's method of explaining the ultimate nature—emptiness or selflessness—varied according to his audience. Since emptiness is the opposite of how we ordinarily perceive things to exist, the Buddha had to prepare people so that they would understand its meaning correctly without distorted conceptions or extreme views. He taught people the correct view in stages, according to their aptitude at that time. When speaking to some people, the Buddha negated a permanent, unitary, and independent self. To others, he refuted a self-sufficient substantially existent person but affirmed the person's inherent existence, while to another group he negated the inherent existence of both persons and phenomena. To some people the Buddha taught truly existent external objects and to others he explained that external objects exist but lack true existence. If we do not understand the Buddha's skill in teaching people according to their aptitude, we risk thinking that the Buddha was either confused or that he contradicted himself.

In ancient India, Buddhist practitioners who followed a diversity of sūtras lived in close proximity to one another and debated and discussed the views put forth in these sūtras. Over time, practitioners who had common assertions loosely identified as a group and, later, as proponents of a system of thought. In this way, the names Vaibhāṣika, Sautrāntika, Yogācāra, and Mādhyamika came to identify groups of people with similar views. Although these four systems are not an exhaustive treatment of all Buddhist tenets, they are a helpful tool for understanding the principal ideas that were popular in Buddhist India and the diversity of thought in what was called "Buddhism." Knowledge of these four systems is integral to much of Tibetan Buddhist thought and will help you understand the writings of Buddhist sages throughout history.

While these groups are often called "philosophical systems" or "schools," they did not propound a rigid catechism of tenets that all their proponents adhered to. Not everyone in one system lived in the same place in India, and if someone wanted to study the tenets of a particular system, they did not have to go to a specific monastery to do so. People with various beliefs lived together and debated among themselves as well as with non-Buddhists. Monastics in a single community did the Vinaya ceremonies together: their differing tenets did not interfere with the harmony of the saṅgha.

The Buddha did not announce that he was teaching a particular tenet system; the idea of tenet systems arose later among the Indian sages and became more systematized in Tibet. In his *Heart of the Middle Way* and its autocommentary *Blaze of Reasoning*, Bhāvaviveka extensively explains the tenet systems. Two Indian masters—the second Āryadeva (eighth or ninth century) in *Compendium of the Essence of Wisdom* (*Jñānasārasamuccaya*) and Jetāri (c. 940–980), a pandit from Vikramaśīla, in *Sugatamatavibhaṅgakārikā* and its extensive autocommentary—wrote about the Indian tenet systems. Āryadeva presented Buddhist as well as non-Buddhist systems, whereas Jetāri explained the four main Buddhist systems. In their works, both of these masters suggested that these tenet systems form a progressive series that gradually leads a student to the most accurate view of the basis, path, and result.[12] Śāntarakṣita (725–88), who wrote *Compendium of Principles* (*Tattvasaṃgraha*), a huge compilation of the views of Buddhist and non-Buddhist tenets, recommended studying the lower and higher tenet systems. His student Kamalaśīla elaborated on that in his commentary to that text.

Tibetan masters agreed with this presentation of progressive tenet systems and composed a genre of texts concerning philosophical tenets (*siddhānta*). These texts are widely taught in Tibetan monasteries and now in Dharma centers and monasteries outside Tibet and India. Among contemporary scholars in the four Tibetan traditions—Nyingma, Kagyu, Sakya, and Gelug—there are some differences in presentations of the tenet systems, although the overall meaning and presentation is similar.[13] Tibetan scholars filled out certain tenets in each system, adding definitions and, in some cases, inferring what followers of a particular system would say about a topic. For example, a Buddhist system in India may not have explicitly asserted inherent existence, but by examining its tenets scholars inferred that it did. This is because asserting partless particles, a foundation consciousness (*ālayavijñāna*), or a mental consciousness that carries the karmic seeds is done within the assumption that phenomena inherently exist.

Tibetan philosophers also contributed to the development of the systems by elaborating on the assertions of their Indian predecessors. For example, the Yogācāra system described in current tenet texts is more detailed than the presentations in Asaṅga's and Vasubandhu's treatises, which themselves fleshed out the meaning of sūtras such as the *Sūtra Unraveling the Thought* and the *Descent into Lanka Sūtra*. Later Tibetan and Chinese masters described various types of latencies and elaborated on other topics that were not spelled out in these sūtras and treatises. For that reason, Tibetan and Chinese assertions about Yogācāra differ in some aspects.

The doxographical approach in which later sages classify the statements of prior sages into systems has both advantages and shortcomings. Regarding the benefits, it allowed Tibetans to organize and systematize the enormous amount of Buddhist literature that came to Tibet into a comprehensible form. It enables us to easily identify the important points of each tenet system and see how they interrelate to other points to form a cohesive system. Setting up tenet systems in a certain order was done to gradually lead disciples to what is considered the highest and most accurate view. Together, the presentations of these systems form a pedagogical tool that helps students become acquainted with the major views that they will examine in more depth and meditate on as their Dharma practice progresses.[14]

Regarding the shortcomings, by strictly classifying various positions into one system, the diversity of viewpoints and debates within each system is obscured, and the tenets of each system become codified, although they weren't like that in ancient times. In addition, interestingly, the author of each tenet text belongs to the tenet system that they acclaim to be the highest.

One other result of establishing tenet systems that has both benefits and drawbacks is that it allows an author to set up straw men to refute positions that they disagree with and to clarify the position of their own system. These artificial debates can be very helpful for students' understanding, even when they are not historically accurate. For example, Bhāvaviveka reputedly held certain beliefs that later scholars severely rebuked, but since he had died centuries before the tenet texts were compiled, he had no opportunity to affirm that he actually held those positions or to defend them if he did.

In this volume, we will focus on the organization of the tenets systems according to the Gelug tradition. In general, they are four in number: the Vaibhāṣika, Sautrāntika, Yogācāra, and Madhyamaka. The order of the schools should not be seen as the historical sequential development of Buddhist thought, and the views of a codified system may not always coincide with the actual beliefs of their so-called founders or chief proponents. Sometimes the tenets in a particular system are those of scholars with similar but not identical views to the founder, some tenets may be inferred from what that system's chief proponent said, and some assertations are elaborations on what the proponent said. Nevertheless, by presenting an amalgamation of different tenets into what appears to be a summary of religious doctrine for each school, Tibetan scholar-adepts could differentiate and clarify the subtle points regarding emptiness according to the Prāsaṅgika view, as they understood it, by refuting the tenets of the lower schools.

Theravāda is not included in the four tenet systems described in Tibetan tenet texts, although most of its tenets may be found among the four tenet schools. Buddhism spread to Sri Lanka in the third century BCE. Since Sri Lanka was far from the large Buddhist monastic universities in northern India, Buddhism there developed in a comparatively isolated way and later came to be called the "Theravāda tradition." It is incorrect to equate the Theravāda with the Vaibhāṣika or Sautrāntika schools.[15] There is no mention in the Pāli commentaries or subcommentaries (*ṭīkā*) of the four tenet systems as mentioned in classical India and later formulated in Tibet.

Tsongkhapa, whose followers began the Gelug tradition, lived at a time when the ultimate nature of phenomena was widely discussed and debated. From circa 800 to 1000, Śāntarakṣita's Yogācāra-Svātantrika Madhyamaka views were prominent in Tibet and were considered the most accurate presentation. After Patsab Nyima Drak (1055–1145?) and others began to translate Candrakīrti's works, Śāntarakṣita's view was questioned and no longer seen as the pinnacle view in the period between 1100 and 1400. With Dolpopa Sherab Gyaltsen's (1292–1361) presentation of other-emptiness, more debates arose. Tenet texts became invaluable aids as Tibetans debated these various views.

You may wonder why there are so many different views of emptiness and just want someone to tell you which one is right. Or you may learn the tenet systems according to one tradition and then get confused on discovering that another tradition has a different explanation. I sympathize with your bewilderment, and I also believe this diversity of views makes Buddhism very rich. Each tenet system presents a model of the world according to its unique perspective on conventional and ultimate truths. We are challenged to understand how the assertions of each system form a cohesive whole and to investigate deeply using reasoning to determine which system makes the most sense to us. Our minds will become more flexible because we'll also understand that various systems and traditions may each define the same word differently. This forces us to study other views instead of criticizing them based on our misunderstanding of the meaning of their words and concepts.

Many of the writings of later masters were in response to the assertions of earlier masters. Studying the tenet systems and knowing a little about the history of Buddhist philosophy shows us the context in which different positions arose and various masters wrote their treatises. For example, Nāgārjuna's radical refutation was largely in response to the substantiality propounded by the Sarvāstivādins. Dignāga's and Dharmakīrti's writings emerged in a climate of intense debate between Buddhists and non-Buddhists. Bhāvaviveka's assertions countered those of Buddhapālita, while Candrakīrti defended Buddhapālita's position and refuted that of Bhāvaviveka.

Study of the various tenet systems prompts us to investigate the nature of reality more deeply, instead of assuming that the superficial appearances to our mind are true. Each system presents a progressively more refined view, and while that of the Prāsaṅgikas is considered the most accurate, that does not mean that it is the best view for everyone at this moment. The assertions of other Buddhist systems may be more suitable for a particular individual at this time. As you study the tenet schools, see which one is the most comfortable for you right now and adopt that one. As time goes on, you can refine your view. How do you discern which system to accept? Investigate which system challenges you and helps you do away with mistaken grasping without destroying your faith in conventional existence, the law of karma and its effects, and the importance of practicing the method aspect of the path.

To those new to the study of tenets, the terminology may seem daunting, and you may be inclined to dismiss tenets as intellectual machinations that have little to do with life. But if you look closer, you'll find that when you understand the terminology better, these teachings can aid in understanding your mind, uncovering and dispelling erroneous conceptions, disarming disturbing emotions, and penetrating the nature of reality.

For example, Buddhists refute the view held by many non-Buddhists that the person is essentially permanent but superficially impermanent. Initially we may not understand what this means, but if we think about it we will see that sometimes we view people as having an unchanging essence but also as changing over time. We have to ask ourselves if a person can have both a fixed nature and a transient nature. Are there two selves—one that is permanent and the other that changes with time? In this way, we flesh out our misconceptions and familiarize ourselves with seeing people and things more in accord with the way they exist.

If you are new to tenets, in the first reading, become familiar with the words. In the second reading, remember the concepts. In subsequent readings, investigate the meaning. When you have understood the tenets systems well, meditate on their views to gain insight into how things exist.

Two of my students who engaged in a long retreat were working hard to understand emptiness, so I suggested several great works for them to read. At that time there were not as many books on emptiness in English as there are now, and most were written by scholars for scholars. One day they came to see me and said that they felt burdened by all the reading and wanted to meditate more and study less. I told them about Asaṅga, who was a third-ground bodhisattva when Maitreya instructed him to keep studying. To make sure they understood my point, I held up three fingers and said firmly, "third ground." As they were leaving, I told them they didn't need to read every Madhyamaka book, but at least to continue studying Nāgārjuna, Candrakīrti, and Tsongkhapa. They looked relieved and years later returned to report the progress they had made in understanding emptiness.

## *Buddhist Tenet Systems and Their Sages*

We begin with a brief outline of the Buddhist tenet systems and the Indian sages that expounded them, and in the next chapter we will explore their views on the nature of reality.

The Fundamental Vehicle tenet systems are:

1. Vaibhāṣika, which may be subdivided into three branches according to their location: Kashmiri, Aparāntaka, and Magadha.
2. Sautrāntika, which has two branches: (1) Scripture Proponents, who follow Vasubandhu's *Treasury of Knowledge*, and (2) Reasoning Proponents, who follow Dharmakīrti's *Seven Treatises on Reliable Cognition.*

The Mahāyāna (Universal Vehicle) tenet systems are:

1. Yogācāra (Cittamātra, Mind Only), which has two branches: Scripture Proponents and Reasoning Proponents.
2. Madhyamaka (Middle Way), which has two branches: (1) Svātantrika Madhyamaka (Autonomist), which has two subdivisions: Yogācāra-Svātantrika Madhyamaka and Sautrāntika-Svātantrika Madhyamaka, and (2) Prāsaṅgika Madhyamaka (Consequentialist).

The Vaibhāṣikas follow the tenets expressed in the *Great Detailed Explanation* (*Mahāvibhāṣāśāstra*), a treatise written by Arhat Nyepe and other arhats. It condenses the meaning of the Seven Abhidharma Treatises that only Vaibhāṣikas consider to be the words of the Buddha. Other well-known Vaibhāṣikas are Vasumitra, Dharmapāla, Buddhadeva, and Saṅghabhadra.

Vasubandhu (c. 316–96) wrote the famous *Treasury of Knowledge* (*Abhidharmakośa*). Although he is reputed to hold Yogācāra views, this text is associated with the Vaibhāṣika school. He later wrote a commentary on it, the *Explanation of the Treasury of Knowledge* (*Abhidharmakośabhāṣya*), which is studied by both the Vaibhāṣikas and the Sautrāntika Scripture Proponents.

The great sage Dharmakīrti (c. 600–660) studied with Īśvarasena, a disciple of Dignāga (c. 480–540). Dharmakīrti wrote *Seven Treatises on Reliable Cognition*, which are said to explain the positions of the Sautrāntikas and Yogācāra, although it seems that Dharmakīrti himself was a Yogācāra Reasoning Proponent. Sometimes great sages gave explanations that differed from their own personal beliefs because those were the views more suitable for their disciples.

Historically, the Mahāyāna tenet systems began with Nāgārjuna, the great Indian sage (c. second century CE) who discovered and then propagated the Perfection of Wisdom sūtras in India. This magnificent scholar and practitioner wrote six great treatises on emptiness, the most significant of which is *Treatise on the Middle Way* (*Mūlamadhyamakakārikā*, also known as *Root Wisdom* or *Fundamental Wisdom*),[16] in which he set forth what came to be known as the Madhyamaka view of emptiness as explained in the Perfection of Wisdom sūtras. Nāgārjuna's spiritual heir Āryadeva (c. 170–270), who understood Nāgārjuna's thought completely, further explained this view in his work *The Four Hundred* (*Catuḥśataka*).

Asaṅga (c. 310–90) was himself a Mādhyamika, but he elaborated on and extensively taught the Yogācāra view and thus was known as the "great charioteer" of this view. This view must have been present in Nāgārjuna's time because Nāgārjuna refuted it in his *Commentary on Bodhicitta* (*Bodhicittavivaraṇa*). When explaining the Yogācāra view, Asaṅga refuted the existence of external objects and asserted that an object and the consciousness apprehending it had the same substantial cause. Asaṅga also wrote an Abhidharma commentary, the *Compendium of Knowledge* (*Abhidharmasamuccaya*), from the Yogācāra viewpoint.

By the eighth century in India, Madhyamaka, Yogācāra, and the logico-epistemological views of Dignāga and Dharmakīrti were among the prominent philosophical views. The great sage Śāntarakṣita (c. 725–88) synthesized these three, creating the Yogācāra-Madhyamaka system (later known as the Yogācāra-Svātantrika Madhyamaka in Tibet), which was the last major development in Indian Buddhist thought before Buddhism in India was destroyed in the late twelfth and early thirteenth centuries. When Buddhism first went to Tibet, Śāntarakṣita's view was seen as the highest explanation of Madhyamaka because he was the first abbot ordaining monks in Tibet as well as the first prominent teacher of Buddhist philosophy there.

Since Nāgārjuna and Āryadeva did not clarify whether external objects existed, Bhāvaviveka (500–570) refuted the Yogācāra view of no external objects and established that external objects exist conventionally. Śāntarakṣita asserted that external objects do not exist conventionally and that the mind ultimately lacks inherent existence. Śāntarakṣita's student, Kamalaśīla (c. 760–815), further explained this view. Other prominent followers of the Yogācāra-Svātantrika system were Vimuktisena, Haribhadra, Jetāri, and Lavapa. Because Bhāvaviveka accepted that external objects exist conventionally, his system became known as the Sautrāntika-Svātantrika Mādhyamika. Jñānagarbha was a proponent of this system, although Tibetans usually identify him as Yogācāra-Svātantrika Madhyamaka.

Another branch of Madhyamaka is the Prāsaṅgika Madhyamaka. Buddhapālita (c. 470–540) wrote a commentary on Nāgārjuna's *Treatise on the Middle Way*, using many consequences in support of Nāgārjuna's view. Objecting to the way in which Buddhapālita refuted the Sāṃkhya view of arising from self, Bhāvaviveka asserted that phenomena exist by their own character and have inherent existence on the conventional level.

Candrakīrti (600–650) supplemented and expanded Nāgārjuna's explanations, asserting that external objects exist conventionally and that all phenomena lack inherent existence. He also asserted that syllogisms are not necessary and consequences are sufficient to establish the correct view.[17] Although Candrakīrti asserted some tenets that seem to accord with the Vaibhāṣika and Sautrāntika schools—such as the existence of external objects conventionally (which is accepted by both Fundamental Vehicle schools) and the nonexistence of apperception[18] (which is accepted by Vaibhāṣikas)—his reasons derive from his views on emptiness, which differ from the reasons used by the lower systems. Candrakīrti did not always agree with Dignāga's and Dharmakīrti's system of logic and epistemology and set out other tenets that formed part of the Prāsaṅgika-Madhyamaka system in Tibet.

Although Candrakīrti's writings were infrequently studied during his lifetime or for two or three centuries afterward, he later became known as the chief upholder of the Prāsaṅgika view; Bhāvaviveka was the chief upholder of the Svātantrika view. Śāntideva (eighth century) also expounded the Prāsaṅgika-Madhyamaka view. However, this distinction into two branches of Madhyamaka only occurred later in Tibet, at the time of Tsongkhapa, so it is in retrospect that the Indian masters are designated as being Svātantrika Mādhyamikas or Prāsaṅgika Mādhyamikas. The names of these systems derive from their preferred manner of establishing the correct view—Bhāvaviveka by using autonomous syllogisms (*svatantra-prayoga*) and Buddhapālita and Candrakīrti by using consequences (*prasaṅga*). However, the actual reason for the division into two systems was Bhāvaviveka's acceptance that phenomena exist by their own character conventionally.

Although Mādhyamikas later refuted specific assertions in the two *Knowledges*,[19] it does not appear that they wrote their own Abhidharma texts. Rather, apart from specific assertions in the two *Knowledges* that contradicted Madhyamaka tenets, the Prāsaṅgikas accepted these texts. Examples of the portions they refuted are the definition of the ignorance that is the root of cyclic existence and the wisdom needed to eradicate it.

From India, the Yogācāra and Madhyamaka systems spread to North and East Asia. In China the Yogācāra view became very popular, although the Madhyamaka view still exists among some Chinese Buddhists. The Prāsaṅgika view was widespread in Tibet, and all Tibetan traditions follow it, although the vocabulary they use to explain it may differ.

Atiśa (982–1054), a prominent teacher who brought the teachings to Tibet during the second dissemination of Buddhism in Tibet, mainly referred to Bhāvaviveka's texts *Heart of the Middle Way* and *Blaze of Reasoning*. Although Atiśa recommended that people follow Candrakīrti's view, it was only during the time of the Kadam geshes that Patsab Nyima Drak began to translate Candrakīrti's *Supplement to the Middle Way* (*Madhyamakāvatāra*), *Clear Words*, and *Commentary on the Bodhisattva Yogic Deeds of the Four Hundred* (*Bodhisattvayogācāracatuḥśatakaṭīkā*) from Sanskrit into Tibetan. Patsab gave the first draft of the translation of the *Supplement* to the Kadam Geshe Sharawa to comment on. Although Sharawa did not understand Sanskrit, he pointed out certain passages that needed to be checked. When Patsab compared these comments to the original Sanskrit, he saw that he indeed needed to revise those sections. For this reason, Patsab praised Sharawa's understanding of the Middle Way.

The admiration went the other way too. Sharawa publicly praised the revised translation and expressed gratitude for Patsab Lotsawa's contribution in bringing Candrakīrti's work to Tibet. The Tibetan translators who worked from the original Sanskrit texts were very learned and courageous people. They remained faithful to the original Sanskrit and developed a consistent vocabulary, resulting in modern scholars praising the accuracy of their translations. Of course the philosophical language they used was too complex for the average reader, but their efforts enabled serious students to connect to the thought of the past, to great Indian sages, and to the Buddha himself.

Patsab taught the followers of the Kadam school, which originated with Drömtönpa, Atiśa's foremost Tibetan disciple. The Kadampas influenced the teachings of the New Transmission traditions in Tibet—the Sakya, Kagyu, and Gelug traditions. Unless otherwise noted, the explanation of emptiness given in the subsequent chapters is according to the Prāsaṅgika-Madhyamaka view as presented by the great masters of the Nālandā tradition in India.

## REFLECTION

1. What is the purpose of studying the tenet systems?
2. Review the four principal tenet systems and the scholar-adepts who are their proponents.

# 4 | Overview of Buddhist and Non-Buddhist Tenet Systems

TIBETAN TENET TEXTS begin by briefly covering non-Buddhist tenet systems and then introduce Buddhist systems, beginning with those propounding a coarse view and progressing to those with more refined views of both conventional and ultimate truths.

## *The Worldly Person and the Yogi*

Some of the tenet systems that flourished in ancient India exist today, others do not. Meanwhile new views have appeared. In this chapter, I will mention some of the most important ones. These summaries of non-Buddhist and Buddhist tenet systems are brief and, for the purpose of this book, will focus on their view of ultimate reality. They will give you a foundation for the explanations and discussions in later chapters and volumes and spark your interest in the nature of reality. There are several excellent books on the tenet systems that have been translated into English; please study them for a more comprehensive view.[20]

When beginning to study the tenet systems, some people comment that some of their assertions are nonsensical and think that there is no need to spend much time refuting these views because their defects are so obvious. However, there are several reasons to study and refute these views. First, some of these erroneous views may exist unnoticed within our minds. Only by stating them clearly and examining their validity do we ferret out our own misunderstandings. Second, we may meet people who hold these views. By understanding these views and their refutations, we can help others gain the correct view of reality. Third, those who propound these "silly" views are sophisticated people, not fools. If they came here to teach us, we may very well be convinced by their views. Since our intelligence is limited, it behooves us to develop it, lest we listen to a proponent of incorrect tenets and adopt them ourselves.

Our purpose is to attain full awakening in order to liberate ourselves and others from saṃsāric duḥkha. To do this, we must cut the self-grasping ignorance that is the root of saṃsāra by realizing the ultimate nature of reality. This is our reason for learning philosophy. Śāntideva distinguishes two types of people—worldly people, or those who are not philosophically inclined, and yogis, who rely on philosophical analysis. Here "yogi" does not necessarily refer to a meditator but to someone who grounds their understanding of the world in a philosophical perspective. The Tibetan word for yoga is *naljor* (T. *rnal 'byor*), which means to join or unite one's mind with a chosen virtuous object; "yogi" and "yoginī" refer to an individual who is familiar with a specific virtuous object and fuses his or her mind with it. In a way, this could apply to modern education too, where a diligent student tries to gain mastery over the field—to fuse her mind with it. Such a person does not relate to the world in a naïve way.

Perspectives of worldly beings are undermined by yogis, and among yogis, those who are more advanced philosophically undermine those whose tenets are more superficial. Science is a discipline of inquiry, and although the scientific method and the philosophical method differ, both use critical analysis. So, according to Śāntideva's definition, scientists could be called a type of "yogi" because they engage in investigation and analysis, and some of their findings undermine ordinary appearances. For example, worldly beings see the world composed of discrete objects that are seemingly solid. Scientists know there is more space than mass in these objects. They know that our ordinary perception of the world is a projection, and that reality is more complex than what appears to our senses.

To introduce some of the vocabulary used in tenet systems: in general, "phenomena" refers to all existents. But when speaking of the "self of phenomena" and the "selflessness of phenomena," it refers to all phenomena other than persons, specifically the aggregates (form, feeling, discrimination, miscellaneous factors, and consciousness) that are the basis of designation of a person. The lack of inherent existence of the I is the selflessness of persons (*pudgalanairātmya*); the lack of inherent existence of the aggregates is the selflessness of phenomena (*dharmanairātmya*).

The basis of designation (basis of imputation) is the collection of parts in dependence on which the designated or imputed object is designated. For example, a car is designated in dependence on the collection of its parts—the engine, wheels, axle, and so forth—which is its basis of designation. Similarly, a person or I is designated in dependence on its basis of designation, the five psychophysical aggregates.

The word "self" has multiple meanings, depending on the context. Sometimes "self" refers to the person or I. At other times it refers to the object of negation—the nonexistent object fabricated and grasped by ignorance—as in the terms "self-grasping ignorance," "self of persons," "self of phenomena," and "selflessness." While all Buddhist systems say the object of negation is self, how they define "self" varies. It may be self-sufficient substantial existence, the subject and object being substantially different, true existence, ultimate existence, inherent existence, and so forth.

Similarly, the Tibetan word *'dzin* may be translated as "grasp"[21] or as "apprehend." While we mistakenly grasp inherent existence, we can accurately apprehend a table. In the context of investigating the ultimate nature, we speak of self-grasping ignorance, ignorance, or self-grasping. For the Prāsaṅgikas these terms come to the same point.

It is easy to confuse the meaning of a word in one system with its definition in another. For example, Prāsaṅgikas understand "ultimate truth" as the final mode of being of persons and phenomena, the actual way they exist. For Vaibhāṣikas "ultimate truth" does not refer to the ultimate mode of existence of phenomena. Rather, an ultimate truth is an object that when physically broken up into parts or mentally dissected, the awareness apprehending it is not cancelled. Thus they say that directionally partless particles and temporally partless moments of consciousness are ultimate truths, whereas tables and people are not.

Just because two terms or phrases contain similar words does not mean that the word has the same meaning in both of them. For example, for Prāsaṅgika-Mādhyamikas, an ultimate truth does not ultimately exist, and a consciousness apprehending a rabbit's horn (which does not exist) is a reliable cognizer with respect to its appearing object (the appearance of a rabbit's horn), but it is not a reliable cognizer. These puzzling uses of words will be clarified later.

REFLECTION

1. Review some of the basic vocabulary used in the study of emptiness, such as phenomena, aggregates, basis of designation, self, ultimate truth, selflessness, dependent arising, and so on.
2. Remember the meaning of each term.

## *Non-Buddhist Tenet Schools*

Non-Buddhist schools are sophisticated philosophical systems. Although the brief description below does not do justice to them, it gives you some idea of their approaches to saṃsāra, its origin, liberation, and the path. In later chapters, we will examine some of their assertions in more detail. Most non-Buddhist tenet systems assert an independent creator and/or a permanent cosmic principle from which the world originates. Since the person we see is transient and ephemeral, these schools also assert a permanent self—an *ātman* or soul—that is separate from body and mind and endures from one life to the next.

Vaiśeṣikas (Particularists) and Naiyāyikas (Logicians) assert an inherently existent self that is separate from the mind and the body with its physical senses. The self is a real, findable, all-pervasive entity. A practitioner realizes this self by purifying the mind through rituals and fasts and thereby ceases to create either destructive or constructive karma. The self then separates from the body and, not taking another rebirth, is thereby liberated.

Sāṃkhyas (Enumerators) assert that the consciousness is a permanent self. They also assert a fundamental nature or primal substance (*prakṛti, pakati*) that is unborn, unchanging, and partless. This fundamental nature is a cause of other phenomena but itself has not been produced by anything. It is similar to the idea of a universal substance out of which everything is created and which thus pervades all phenomena. Saying that everything already exists in the fundamental nature yet still arises from it, Sāṃkhyas assert that things are produced from themselves—that is, they already exist within the cause.

Theistic Sāṃkhyas say that the creator Īśvara together with the fundamental nature create phenomena. Saṃsāra occurs because one does not understand that everything—including the misery of saṃsāra—is a manifestation of the fundamental nature. When one realizes this, all manifestations absorb back into the fundamental nature and conventional phenomena no longer appear to the yogi's mind. The self now abides alone; this is liberation.

Mīmāṃsakas (Analyzers or Ritualists) state that defilements abide in the nature of the mind and therefore are impossible to eradicate fully. Many people nowadays have a comparable view, saying, for example, that we human beings are inherently selfish and true altruism is impossible. A somewhat similar view is to say that our mental states arise from or in the brain and that our genetic makeup determines our habitual mental states. Anger, for example, is therefore programmed into us on a genetic or physical level and is impossible to eliminate.

Mīmāṃsakas say omniscience is impossible because phenomena are infinite, so a person could never know them all. This view is also shared by some people today who state that it is impossible for ordinary beings to become omniscient because only a creator God is capable of that; others say because the human brain is finite, it cannot know all of infinity.

Some Nirgranthas (Jains) advocate a path of asceticism that consumes all karma. One is then born in a place that resembles the Christian concept of heaven, where one is free from saṃsāra. In almost every culture there have been groups that assert ascetic practices or extreme physical hardship as the path to heaven or liberation. Some walk across fire; others go naked in freezing weather. Some engage in self-flagellation or extreme fasting. When I was teaching in Mundgod, South India, in 2002, I saw some Indians whipping themselves. I don't know if they were doing this to attain liberation or for some other reason; in either case, a crowd would gather around to stare at them.

From a Buddhist viewpoint, most of the non-Buddhist schools fall to the extreme of absolutism. The Cārvākas (Materialists), however, tend toward the extreme of nihilism, because they assert that only things we can directly perceive with our senses exist. They do not accept inference as a reliable way to know objects. Although they do not reject that a seed produces a sprout because that causal relationship is evident to our senses, they do reject causality that is not evident to the senses, such as the law of karma and its effects and the causality involved in rebirth. Believing that neither the person nor the mind continues after death, they deny the existence of past and future lives because the rebirth process isn't knowable with our physical senses. Instead they assert that the mind is a byproduct of the body, and/or the body and mind are one entity. Since the body no longer functions after death, they believe the mind also ceases. This view is similar to scientific reductionism, in which only things perceivable by the senses or measurable by scientific instruments are said to exist.

To this, some people add the belief that many elements of our personality are controlled or heavily determined by genetics. Such a view can leave people feeling disempowered, as if their mental or physical state were predetermined. It also discounts the fact that everything depends on multiple causes and conditions and that we can make choices in our lives.

## *Buddhist Tenet Systems*

Vaibhāṣika and Sautrāntika are considered Fundamental Vehicle tenet systems, while Yogācāra and Madhyamaka are Universal Vehicle (Mahāyāna) tenet systems. However, a practitioner of one vehicle may follow the tenet system of the other vehicle. A Fundamental Vehicle practitioner who seeks arhatship may hold the tenets of any of the four tenet systems. Similarly, a practitioner of the Universal Vehicle may follow any of the four tenet systems. In addition, someone may change the tenet system they follow, and a follower of any of the tenet systems may change their practice vehicle.

The tenet systems vary in terms of their definition of the ignorance that is the root of saṃsāra and the conceived object of that ignorance. They also differ in terms of their assertions regarding selflessness, afflicted obscurations, and cognitive obscurations.

When observing your mind, you may discover that you hold some non-Buddhist views that you hadn't recognized before. As a child you may have learned that there is a creator God who himself was not created but who created the universe and the beings in it. Prayers to God may have comforted you as a child. You may have learned that you have an immutable soul that is the essence of who you are. Although you may have already come to disbelieve such things intellectually, those beliefs may have been deeply imprinted in your mind, and when crises loom they are emotionally appealing. You may know the words of Buddhist tenets but find that deep inside your mind you have non-Buddhist views.

In your study and exploration of the tenet systems, first think as the Vaibhāṣikas do—many of their assertions make sense to us. After a while, if you see some weaknesses in them, adopt the Sautrāntika tenets. If these later become unsatisfactory, explore the Yogācāra assertions. If that system makes sense to you, stay with it. If not, delve into the Yogācāra-Svātantrika or Sautrāntika-Svātantrika Madhyamaka systems, which are fascinating. But if you find logical inconsistencies in them, look into the Prāsaṅgika view. Whatever system you settle on, use reasoning to clearly evaluate its assertions.

## *Vaibhāṣika*

All Buddhist tenet systems (schools)—and many non-Buddhist systems as well—speak of ultimate truths and conventional truths and ultimate and conventional existence, although what they mean by these terms varies widely. Vaibhāṣikas[22] define an ultimate truth as a phenomenon that if physically or mentally separated into parts, the consciousness apprehending it does not stop. Directionally partless particles (the smallest unit of matter), partless moments of consciousness (the smallest units of consciousness), and unconditioned space are examples of ultimate truths because they cannot be further subdivided physically or mentally and thus do not lose their identity under any circumstances. Tables and people, on the other hand, are conventional truths because when broken up into parts, they are no longer recognizable as tables and people. Mind in general is an ultimate truth and substantially existent because when it is broken into smaller moments, it can still be apprehended because each of those small moments is mind.[23]

Vaibhāṣikas also differentiate substantially established (*dravyasiddha*), which refers to all phenomena, and substantially existent (*dravyasat*). They say all knowable objects are substantially established because they have their own entity that is not dependent on thought. Since phenomena are divided into the two truths, ultimate truth is equivalent to substantially existent, and conventional truths are equivalent to imputedly existent.

According to the Svātantrikas and below, all imputedly existent phenomena need to have substantially existent phenomena as their basis of imputation. Imputedly existent phenomena are called "self-isolates" (T. *rang ldog*) and substantially existent phenomena are called "illustration isolates" (T. *gzhi ldog*). The self-isolate person is the general person, the I that we think of when we say "I'm happy" or "I'm cold." It is imputed on the aggregates. This imputedly existent self has the characteristics of the aggregates—for example, both are impermanent. When the person is mentally separated into parts—the five aggregates—the consciousness apprehending the I ceases. This self-isolate self is the self on which self-sufficient substantial existence is negated when meditating on selflessness.

But when Vaibhāṣikas look more closely and ask just what this self is, they point to something substantially existent, such as the mental consciousness, the collection of aggregates, or each individual aggregate. This is the illustration-isolate person that is found when the person is searched for. Most Vaibhāṣikas consider the illustration-isolate person to be the mere collection of the physical and mental aggregates that are a person's basis of designation. However, some Vaibhāṣikas say that each of the five aggregates is a person, and others assert that the mental consciousness is the person. In short, the self-isolate self is imputedly existent and is not substantially existent; the illustration-isolate self—in this case, the mental consciousness and so forth—is substantially existent.

Vaibhāṣikas speak only of the selflessness of persons. The coarse selflessness of persons is the lack of a permanent, unitary, and independent person; the subtle selflessness of persons is the nonexistence of a self-sufficient substantially existent person (the meaning of these terms will be explained below). They do not assert a selflessness of phenomena.

All Buddhist and non-Buddhist schools that speak of karma must account for how karma goes from one life to another. Kashmiri Vaibhāṣikas say that the continuum of the mental consciousness carries it, whereas the other Vaibhāṣikas assert that acquisition (*prāpti*) or non-wastage (*avipraṇāśa*), which are abstract composites, prevent the loss of the result of an action. Acquisition is likened to a rope that ties up goods and non-wastage is like an IOU, a voucher, or a seal that ensures a lender will not experience the loss of what he has loaned.

According to Vaibhāṣikas, when a buddha or arhat dies, his or her consciousness discontinues. Thus they do not speak of four buddha bodies, nor do they accept the existence of pure lands created by buddhas. In addition, they say that the Buddha is not omniscient—that is, he does not effortlessly know all phenomena simultaneously—but is all-knowing in that when he consciously directs his mind toward something, he can know it individually.

Usually "thing" (*bhāva*) is defined as that which is able to perform a function and is equivalent to products and impermanent phenomena. Vaibhāṣikas, however, say "thing" refers not just to impermanent phenomena but to all phenomena because even permanent phenomena perform functions. For example, permanent space performs the function of allowing things to exist in it. This is the only Buddhist system that asserts this.

## *Sautrāntika*

Sautrāntikas define the two truths differently from Vaibhāṣikas. For Sautrāntikas an ultimate truth is a phenomenon that is able to bear reasoned analysis in terms of having its own mode of existence without depending on imputation by terms and concepts. Ultimate truths are real objects that don't depend on the mind imputing them. Ultimate truths are equivalent to things, products, truly existent phenomena, the impermanent, and specifically characterized phenomena (phenomena that are ultimately able to perform a function). In speaking of ultimate truths in this way, Sautrāntikas emphasize the importance of functionality and being directly perceivable. Tables, persons, and mindstreams are ultimate truths, whereas in the other tenet schools they are considered conventional truths.

According to Sautrāntikas, conventional truths are phenomena that exist only by being imputed by a conceptual consciousness; they are not able to ultimately perform a function. They are equivalent to permanent phenomena, uncompounded phenomena, false existents, and generally characterized phenomena (phenomena that are ultimately unable to perform a function). They are known only by conceptual consciousnesses. These include conceptual appearances, unconditioned space, and true cessations.

Sautrāntikas assert directionally partless particles and temporally partless moments of consciousness. Sautrāntika Scripture Proponents, like Vaibhāṣikas, say these are ultimate truths because they cannot be further divided, whereas Sautrāntika Reasoning Proponents say they are ultimate truths because they are ultimately able to perform a function. However, some people say that only Sautrāntika Scripture Proponents assert partless particles and that Sautrāntika Reasoning Proponents, who follow Dharmakīrti, do not.

In the Sautrāntika system "imputedly existent" (*prajñaptisat*)[24] and "imputed" have different meanings. To say an object is "imputedly existent" means that to identify it depends on identifying something else. A person, Tashi, is imputedly existent because he can be identified only by perceiving his body, voice, or mind. Similarly, a forest is identified by apprehending many trees. "Imputed," on the other hand, refers to whatever is established by being merely imputed by thought without having its own objective nature. An example is permanent space.

To say something is substantially existent means that to identify it doesn't depend on identifying something else. Here "substantially existent" means self-sufficient in that the object doesn't depend on another object for it to be identified. Cars and stars are known in this way. We see them directly with our eyes. The mind and mental factors are likewise substantially existent because, according to the Sautrāntikas, apperception—a type of self-perceiving consciousness—directly perceives them. To know anger in our own mind, we don't need to perceive something else first, whereas to know an hour—which is not substantially existent—we have to first perceive the change in another object.

In *Succinct Guide to the Middle Way* (*Dbu ma'i lta khrid phyogs bsdebs*), Tsongkhapa says (SRR 76):

> Thus the meaning of substantial reality and nominal [imputed] reality is the following: When a thing appears to the mind, if it does so in dependence on the perception of another phenomenon that shares characteristics different from said object, then the object is said to be nominal reality. . . . That which does not depend on others in such a manner is said to be substantially real.

Self-sufficient substantial existence is the same as substantially existent for Sautrāntikas up to and including Svātantrikas. In and of itself, substantial existence is not an object of negation. However, a self-sufficient substantially existent person is. The self-isolate person is imputedly existent;

it is not a self-sufficient substantially existent person, which is the object of negation when Svātantrikas and below refute the subtle self of persons. A self-sufficient substantially existent person does not exist.

When a self-sufficient substantially existent person is negated, the selflessness of person is realized. The absence of being a self-sufficient substantially existent person can be realized with respect to any phenomenon. If the base is the person, then the person not being a self-sufficient substantially existent person is realized. If the base is a phenomenon other than the person, then that phenomenon not being an object of possession of a self-sufficient substantially existent person is realized. For this reason, all schools that assert the absence of a self-sufficient substantially existent person as the subtle selflessness of persons agree that any phenomenon can be the base of the selflessness of persons. Prāsaṅgikas agree with this, except for them it is called the "coarse selflessness of persons."

Sautrāntikas, like Vaibhāṣikas, assert only a selflessness of persons, not a selflessness of phenomena.[25] According to Sautrāntikas, the appearing object of a direct perceiver—including direct perceivers that are uninterrupted paths and liberated paths on the paths of seeing, meditation, and no-more-learning—must be an impermanent object. Selflessness, however, is a permanent phenomenon. Thus they say that these path consciousnesses, which are yogic direct perceivers, do not directly realize selflessness. Rather, they directly perceive the aggregates and indirectly know that the aggregates lack a self-sufficient substantially existent person.

The common assertion of almost all Buddhist tenet systems is that the selflessness of persons is the absence of a self-sufficient substantially existent person and of an I that makes the aggregates mine—the possessor of the aggregates. "Self-sufficient" (T. *rang rkya ba*) means that the person is different from the mental and physical aggregates. However, that is not the case; the person and the aggregates are related: the aggregates are one nature with the person, and because of that we can identify the person by cognizing their body, speech, or mind. Here a substantially existent person would be perceivable without anything else appearing to the mind. That means that without apprehending the body, speech, or mind of a person, we could still perceive a person. That clearly is not the case. To cognize a person, at least one of the aggregates needs to appear. Because a person can be identified only by perceiving some other phenomenon, such as the body, a person is dependent on and related to the aggregates. Thus, the person exists imputedly, not substantially.

The lower Buddhist tenet systems, Svātantrika Madhyamaka and below, negate self-sufficient substantial existence on the general self—the self that is imputed on the aggregates. The general self has the characteristics of the aggregates in that the person walks, talks, knows things, and feels emotions just like one or more of the aggregates does. It is the self that we refer to in everyday conversation when we are not analyzing what the I is.

A person is not substantially existent because his or her body, speech, or mind must be identified in order to identify the person. The person also is not self-sufficient because it is not the controller of the body and mind. However, the person appears to be self-sufficient substantially existent: the I appears to be independent of the body and mind and to control them like a master who tells the servants what to do. The I says, "Walk outdoors," directing the body to walk. The I states, "I will think about this later," telling the mental aggregates what to do. The body and mind seem to depend on the person who orders them about, and the person appears to be different from the aggregates. A yogi, however, realizes that the person does not exist self-sufficiently; it is not an independent controller of the body and mind because it depends on the aggregates. Since there is no self-sufficient person, nothing can be possessed by such a person, so both the I and the mine lack self-sufficient substantial existence.

In short, a self-sufficient substantially existent person is one that appears to be different from the aggregates but is also the controller of the body and mind. It appears to be the self-sufficient substantially existent owner and user of the aggregates that are grasped as mine. This sense of I is false because the I depends on the aggregates and does not exist separate from them. There is no person that authoritatively bosses the body and mind around, even though we sometimes feel there is.

Although the lower systems negate a self-sufficient substantially existent person, they say that the person does exist and point to a personal identity—an illustration of the person—that is the person. Many of these schools say that the mental consciousness is the personal identity because the mental consciousness goes from one life to the next. Others say the collection of the aggregates, the continuity of consciousness, or a foundation consciousness is the personal identity. All of these schools say that the personal identity substantially exists. In the case of saying the mental consciousness is the personal identity, the mental consciousness substantially exists because its appearance to a consciousness doesn't depend on another phenomenon appearance. The mental consciousness appears and is cognized without being imputed, and for this reason it is substantially existent. Although the mental consciousness is a composite of different mind moments, it is not imputed because all those mind moments are of a similar type (that is, they are all moments of mind). In short, while the lower systems negate the substantial existence of the person, they assert that the personal identity—such as the mental consciousness or the collection of the aggregates—is substantially existent. The personal identity does not have all the characteristics of the person. For example, the mental consciousness does not have physical characteristics although the person does.

Objects of possession of the self include the body and mind as well as external objects such as chairs and cups. To meditate on the lack of self-sufficient substantial existence in relation to these objects, we reflect that they are not objects of possession of a self-sufficient substantially existent person.[26] However, the body and mind themselves are substantially existent because they can be identified without another phenomenon first appearing to the mind.

Regarding the second meaning of substantial and imputed existence described above, Asaṅga, in his *Compendium of Ascertainments (Nirṇaya-saṃgraha)*, says:

> Anything whose definition (or characteristic) is designated without relating to others and without depending on others, in short, is to be known as *substantially existent*. Anything whose definition is designated in relation to others and dependent on others, in short, is to be known as *imputedly existent*, not substantially existent.

This explanation is accepted by all Buddhist schools. For the lower schools, the substantial existence mentioned here is the subtle object of negation in the meditation on the selflessness of persons. Prāsaṅgikas, however, say that this meaning of substantial existence is coarse and that the selflessness of the lower schools does not negate enough, because the person is also empty of inherent existence.[27]

In short, according to the view common to all four tenet systems, the view of a personal identity grasps an independent or self-sufficient substantially existent I in our own continuum. Here "independent person" does not refer to an inherently existent person, which is the unique object of negation of the Prāsaṅgika Madhyamaka school. Rather it indicates a person who is the owner or the enjoyer of the psychophysical aggregates. Just as a king rules over his subjects, this I rules over the body and mind, which are subservient to it. The I seems to be independent of the aggregates, like the boss of the body and mind.

A clear indication that we have this feeling of an independent I is, for example, when we see someone with an attractive body or an intelligent mind, we think, "If it were possible to exchange my body with his and my intelligence with hers, I would readily agree." Here, the I seems to be separate and independent from the body and the mind. It appears to be their owner, and this owner can benefit by exchanging its body for a more attractive one or its mind for a more intelligent one. Such an independent, self-sufficient substantially existent I does not exist; when searched for, it cannot be found as one of the aggregates or separate from the aggregates.

### REFLECTION

1. What would a directionally partless particle be like? Why doesn't such a thing exist?
2. What are the two ways that Sautrāntikas use the terms "substantially existent" and "imputedly existent"?

## *Yogācāra (Cittamātra)*

Yogācārins are defined as proponents of Buddhist tenets who use reasoning to refute external objects and assert that dependent phenomena are truly existent. The Yogācāra school[28]—also called Cittamātra (Mind Only), Vijñānavāda, and Vijñaptivāda—has two branches: Yogācāra Scripture Proponents who mainly follow Asaṅga and Yogācāra Reasoning Proponents who principally follow Dignāga and Dharmakīrti. The main sūtras Yogācārins refer to are the *Sūtra Unraveling the Thought [of the Buddha]* (*Saṃdhinirmocana Sūtra*) and the *Descent into Laṅkā Sūtra* (*Laṅkāvatāra Sūtra*). In addition, the Yogācāra Scripture Proponents rely on Asaṅga's *Compendium of the Mahāyāna* (*Mahāyānasaṃgraha*) and Vasubandhu's *Thirty Stanzas* (*Triṃśikā*) and the commentary on it by Sthiramati (c. 510–70).

Following Asaṅga's *Five Treatises on the Grounds*,[29] Yogācāra Scripture Proponents assert eight consciousnesses: the five sense consciousnesses, mental consciousness, plus a foundation consciousness (*ālayavijñāna*) and an afflicted consciousness (*kliṣṭamanas*). The foundation consciousness is a neutral, undefiled, enduring mental consciousness that exists throughout one's life and into future lives. It is the storehouse for all latencies and karmic seeds. Because it is stable and exists while one is awake, asleep, and in the intermediate state between births, it is able to carry karmic seeds and other latencies from one life to the next. For this reason, the foundation consciousness is said to be the person. The afflicted consciousness views the foundation consciousness and, not seeing its nature, mistakenly holds it to be a self with a self-sufficient substantially existent nature.

Yogācāra Reasoning Proponents adhere to Dharmakīrti's *Seven Treatises on Reliable Cognition*.[30] They assert the usual six consciousnesses (visual, auditory, olfactory, gustatory, tactile, and mental consciousnesses) that cognize their corresponding objects (forms, sounds, etc.) through their associated sense faculties (eye, ear, etc.), as do the other tenet schools, and assert that karmic seeds and latencies are deposited on and carried by the mental consciousness. Thus they assert the mental consciousness to be the person.

The Yogācāra Scripture Proponents have a unique way of presenting phenomena and their deeper mode of existence. All conventional things that we interact with on a daily basis—books, trees, and so forth—arise due to the latencies placed on the foundation consciousness. Although these things appear to be external objects unrelated to our minds, this is a false appearance. In fact, they arise from the same latency as the consciousness that perceives them, and they exist simultaneously with their perceiving consciousness. This is very different from other systems that assert external objects and say that the consciousnesses perceiving them are caused by the object and its corresponding sense faculty. In other words, according to these Yogācārins, the flower and your mind perceiving it arise from the same latency on the foundation consciousness. There is some similarity between these Yogācārins and scientific views regarding the lack of objectively existent external matter. More discussion on this topic between Buddhists and scientists would be interesting.

Yogācārins hold the second turning of the Dharma Wheel and the teachings of the Perfection of Wisdom sūtras to be interpretable and the third Dharma Wheel to be definitive. To explain the teaching propounded in the second turning, "All phenomena are empty of inherent existence," they developed the classification of three natures (*trisvabhāva*) and then described the meaning of naturelessness (*niḥsvabhāva*) for each of them. All knowable objects have these three natures.

1. The dependent or other-powered nature arises depending on the power of others, specifically the latencies that produce them. Because the dependent nature arises from causes, it does not last more than a moment.
2. The imputed or imaginary nature includes our imputations and concepts about things. These do not exist by their own characteristics but exist for thought. Unconditioned space is an example of the existent imaginary nature and a self of persons is an example of the nonexistent imaginary nature.
3. The consummate or thoroughly established nature is twofold: (1) the emptiness of external objects—that is, the emptiness of subject and object arising from different substantial entities, and (2) the emptiness of an object existing by its own characteristics as the referent of its name. In short, the consummate nature is the nonexistence of the imaginary nature in the dependent nature.

A flower, for example, is a dependent nature because it is dependent on the latencies that produced it. Although the flower appears to us to be "out there," separate from the mind perceiving it, this is false. Its being a separate entity from the consciousness perceiving it is its imputed nature. Negating this type of existence in terms of the flower is the flower's consummate nature.

Each nature is natureless in its own way:

- Dependent natures are *production natureless* (*utpatti-niḥsvabhāvatā*) because they arise from causes that are a different nature than themselves and do not arise from causes that are the same nature as themselves. (To be one nature, two phenomena must exist at the same time, whereas a cause and its effect are sequential.) They are also *ultimate natureless* (*paramārtha-niḥsvabhāvatā*) because the ultimate nature is the ultimate object of meditation that brings about the purification of obscurations, and dependent natures are not this.
- Imputed or imaginary natures are *character natureless* (*lakṣaṇa-niḥsvabhāvatā*) because they don't exist by their own characteristics. Existent imaginaries such as unconditioned space exist only by the force of conception.
- Consummate natures are *ultimate natureless* (*paramārtha-niḥsvabhāvatā*) because they are the ultimate nature of phenomena that is perceived by the ultimate purifying consciousnesses and do not exist as the self of phenomena.

A *conventional truth* is an object found by a reliable cognizer that is a correct knower distinguishing a conventionality. Dependent natures—such as a table, person, and emotions—and existent imaginaries—such as permanent space—are conventional truths. Conventional truths are falsities in that they appear to be external objects that are different entities than the consciousnesses perceiving them. They do not exist in this way because the object and the perceiving consciousness arise from the same substantial cause, a latency on the foundation consciousness.

An *ultimate truth* is an object found by a reliable cognizer that is a correct knower distinguishing an ultimate—emptiness, consummate phenomena, selflessness, and suchness.

Yogācāra defines true existence as being established by way of its own uncommon objective mode of existence without being posited by conceptuality. Dependent natures—especially the mind—and consummate natures are truly existent. They have their own objective mode of existence that does not depend on being imputed by thought. Imaginaries do not truly exist because they are merely imputed by conception.

For Yogācārins, the selflessness of persons is the lack of a self-sufficient substantially existent person. They also assert selflessness of phenomena from four approaches, which come to the same point: (1) an object's emptiness of existing by its own characteristics as the referent of a term, (2) an object's emptiness of existing by its own characteristics as the object clung to by a conceptual thought, (3) an object's emptiness of being a different entity from the consciousness perceiving it, and (4) an object's emptiness of being external to the mind. Some scholar-adepts condense these four into two approaches to the selflessness of phenomena: (1) an object's emptiness of existing by its own characteristics as the referent of term and concepts, and (2) an object's emptiness of being an external object and a different entity from the consciousness perceiving it.

When on the dependent nature (for example, a flower) the imaginary natures (the flower's existing by its own characteristics as the referent of a name, and the flower and its apprehending consciousness being distinct entities) are negated, that is the consummate nature (emptiness, the ultimate reality).

If dependent natures did not exist by their own characteristics, arising and ceasing would not be feasible and dependent phenomena would not exist. Similarly, if the consummate did not exist by its own characteristics (*svalakṣaṇa*), it would not be the ultimate nature of phenomena.

Vaibhāṣikas and Sautrāntikas assert substantially existent partless particles that do not have any directions (such as east, west, front, and back) and partless moments of mind that do not have earlier and later parts. Yogācārins call this into question, saying that while it may be hard to further subdivide something physically, all particles must have directional parts and sides because physical particles meet side by side to form larger objects. Without directional parts, these particles could not join together to form coarser objects, such as a chair. Instead, all the particles would merge into one another and occupy the same space, becoming one particle. Similarly, moments of mind that lack parts, such as a beginning, middle, and last part, would conflate into one moment, and a continuum could not exist. Mādhyamikas agree with Yogācārins' refutation of partless particles and partless moments of mind.

Studying the Yogācāra view is a good steppingstone that broadens our view and facilitates understanding Madhyamaka views later. Vaibhāṣika and Sautrāntika schools speak only of the selflessness of persons, whereas Yogācāra adds the selflessness of phenomena. In doing so, it spurs us to examine not only how the person exists but also how the aggregates, which are the basis of designation of the person, exist. In asserting that there are no external objects and that phenomena and their apprehending consciousnesses are one nature, Yogācāra draws us into examining the role the mind plays in the existence of phenomena. Although subject and object being one nature is refuted by the Prāsaṅgikas, contemplating the Yogācāra view enables us to see that the appearances of objectively existent external objects to our sense consciousnesses are false and that things exist in relation to the mind. This approach reduces clinging to attractive and repulsive objects because these are seen as illusory; they are not objective external objects as they appear to be but are one nature with the mind perceiving them.

Furthermore, the Yogācāra assertion that phenomena are empty of existing by their own characteristics as the referent of terms stimulates us to explore the role of language and concepts in the existence of phenomena. Understanding these two Yogācāra approaches to the selflessness of phenomena prepares us for the Madhyamaka view.

### REFLECTION

1. Why do some Yogācārins assert a foundation consciousness? What is its function?
2. What is their belief about external objects? Does that view make sense to you?
3. Review the three natures and their non-natures.

## *Madhyamaka*

Mādhyamikas are holders of Buddhist tenets who assert that all phenomena do not truly or ultimately exist. They are of two types: Svātantrikas and Prāsaṅgikas, the differences between them being the topic of much discussion. Contrary to the Yogācārins, Mādhyamikas assert there is no difference between the mind and the external world in that both are empty of true existence—neither has its own mode of being. When Mādhyamikas say that the mind is unborn, they mean that the mind arises, abides, and ceases, but not ultimately or truly. These functions occur dependent on other factors.

Although a clear distinction is made between Svātantrika Madhyamaka and Prāsaṅgika Madhyamaka in contemporary tenet texts, this was not so in India or in the early years of Buddhism in Tibet. It seems to be a distinction made by Tibetans that was widely accepted by the fourteenth century.

### *Svātantrika Madhyamaka*

Differences exist between the two types of Mādhyamikas in several areas, most prominently in how they assert the object of negation. By seeing how the Svātantrikas define conventional existence, we can understand their object of negation, which is the opposite of that. Conventional existence depends on objects being merely posited through the force of appearing to a nondefective awareness. Ultimate existence (*paramārthasiddhi*), which is negated, is the opposite of this. Ultimate existence is without being posited through the force of appearing to a nondefective awareness. If things existed ultimately, they would exist from their own side by their unique mode of being. Ultimate existence is equivalent to true existence (*satyasat*), existence as its own reality (*samyaksiddhi*), and existence as its own suchness (*tattvasiddhi*).

To conventionally exist, two factors are necessary: the object must be posited through the force of appearing to a nondefective awareness, and it must also exist inherently. For Svātantrikas "posited" means an object is designated by a consciousness through appearing to it. Since the object also exists inherently, the consciousness to which it appears is unmistaken regarding its inherent existence. This nondefective awareness to which an object appears inherently existent can be either a conceptual thought or a nonconceptual perception. In both cases, that awareness is not mistaken with regard to its engaged object.

Both Prāsaṅgikas and Svātantrikas assert that all existents are posited[31] by terms and concepts. However, Prāsaṅgikas add that they are *merely* designated by terms and concepts—"merely" indicating that they do not inherently exist—whereas Svātantrikas do not add "merely" and instead assert that all phenomena exist inherently on the conventional level. That is, Svātantrikas assert that conventionally, phenomena exist by their own characteristics (*svalakṣaṇasiddhi*), inherently exist (*svabhāvasiddhi*), and exist from their own side (*svarūpasiddhi*), although they do not exist ultimately, truly, or perfectly on the conventional level. On the ultimate level, they lack all of the above modes of existence.

To get a glimpse of this difference, observe your mind when meditating on emptiness. You may deeply investigate how the I exists and find only its emptiness of true existence. But part of the mind objects, saying that there must be something that really is me conventionally. You agree that phenomena exist by being designated, but still feel that there must be something in the object that makes it what it is. If there weren't, then either things wouldn't exist at all or they would become whatever your thought imputes them to be. Thus they must have some degree of inherent existence conventionally.

Seeing that functioning things each have their own unique potential to bring their results, Svātantrikas say that when searched for with ultimate analysis—analysis that investigates what an object really is and its deeper mode of existence—phenomena cannot be found and are empty of true existence. But on the conventional level they must have some degree of inherent existence, otherwise any cause could produce any effect. For this reason, Svātantrikas assert that things do exist by their own characteristics but not *solely* by their own characteristics, for they also need to be posited through the force of appearing to a nondefective awareness. That is, things do not exist by their own characteristics except when they are designated by mind through the force of appearing to a nondefective awareness. There is something from the side of the object that supports what it is. That, in combination with being posited by a nondefective mind, is the way phenomena exist. The appearance of inherent existence to the sense consciousnesses is not false, for things inherently exist conventionally.

A conventional truth is an object found by a conventional reliable cognizer—that is, by a direct perceiver or inferential cognizer not affected by an internal or external cause of error, an awareness that is not erroneous with respect to its apprehended object. An ultimate truth is an object found by a reliable reasoning consciousness analyzing the ultimate. An ultimate truth, such as emptiness, is realized nondualistically by an unpolluted awareness—that is, by the pristine wisdom of meditative equipoise.

There are two main subdivisions of the Svātantrika school: Yogācāra-Svātantrika and Sautrāntika-Svātantrika. Like Yogācārins,

Yogācāra-Svātantrikas say that there are no external objects and that all phenomena are the same nature as the mind cognizing them because they arise from the same substantial cause, a latency on the mind. The appearance of things as separate entities from their reliable cognizing consciousness is a false appearance. Also, like Yogācārins, they assert apperception (*svasaṃvedana*). Apperception is a consciousness that is nondualistically aware of the consciousness it observes and experiences. Simultaneous with the consciousness it is observing, apperception is one nature with that consciousness and enables us to remember cognizing an object.[32] Yogācāra-Svātantrikas differ from the Yogācārins in that they do not assert that the mind is truly existent. Nor do they assert a foundation consciousness (the eighth consciousness) or an afflicted consciousness (the seventh consciousness). Instead, they say that the mental consciousness carries the karmic seeds and the latencies that create the appearance of the external world.

The Sautrāntika-Svātantrikas do not accept a foundation consciousness, an afflicted consciousness, or apperception; they accept external objects. They assert that external objects exist by their own characteristics conventionally.

Although Yogācārins' identification of the object of negation differs from the Prāsaṅgikas, the two are similar in that both say the object of negation appears to sense consciousnesses. Svātantrikas, on the other hand, say the object of negation appears only to the mental consciousness, because they accept inherent existence on the conventional level.

The main difference between Svātantrikas and Prāsaṅgikas is that, in brief, by refuting true existence and ultimate existence, Svātantrikas avoid absolutism, and by asserting that phenomena inherently exist conventionally, they avoid nihilism. Prāsaṅgikas, on the other hand, refute true existence, ultimate existence, and inherent existence on both the ultimate and conventional levels. They assert nominal existence, meaning that phenomena exist by being merely designated.

### *Prāsaṅgika Madhyamaka*

Of the various Buddhist tenet systems, Prāsaṅgika has the complete understanding of emptiness. It is this view that we will closely examine in upcoming chapters. Prāsaṅgikas assert that things are empty of inherent existence—that is, they are not self-enclosed entities that exist independent of all other factors; they do not exist under their own power, from their own side, or by their own characteristics because they depend on other factors.

Phenomena exist by being merely imputed or designated by mind. "Merely" excludes their being inherently existent. Although phenomena depend on their basis of designation, they are not their basis of designation and cannot be found within it. Neither can they be found separate from it. For example, a person exists by being merely posited by mind in dependence on its basis of designation, the five aggregates. But a person is not any of the aggregates, nor is it the collection of aggregates; and it does not exist separate from the aggregates. Although a person is not findable when we search for it with wisdom analyzing the ultimate nature, it does exist conventionally. We say "I'm walking" or "I'm thinking," and others understand what is meant. Although phenomena lack a findable essence, they still function. In fact, if they had an inherent, independent essence, they couldn't function at all. They would be frozen phenomena, unable to interact with the things around them. Establishing phenomena's functionality and their lack of inherent existence as being compatible is challenging, but the great Prāsaṅgikas such as Nāgārjuna and Candrakīrti have succeeded in doing that.

Unlike the lower schools, the Prāsaṅgika considers all of the following as equivalent: substantial existence, existence by its own characteristics, inherent existence, existence from its own side, true existence, ultimate existence, objective existence, and so forth. Prāsaṅgikas refute all of them on all phenomena across the board. Nevertheless, phenomena do exist: they exist conventionally by being merely designated by mind. The fact that they arise dependently does not contradict the fact that they are empty of inherent existence. In fact, dependent arising and emptiness of inherent existence come to the same point.

As Candrakīrti explained in the *Supplement*, objects are known from two different perspectives. Those known by worldly conventions without critical examination of how they exist are conventional truths. The fact that these objects are not found under ultimate analysis is their ultimate truth. These two perspectives—of worldly conventions and of ultimate reality—are the bases of differentiating the two truths—the conventional and ultimate truths.

An object found by a conventional reliable cognizer perceiving a false knowable object is a conventional truth. A conventional truth is the object of a mistaken cognizer. It is that with respect to which a conventional awareness comes to be a reliable cognizer distinguishing a conventionality. What does it mean to say that conventional truths are false objects known only by mistaken consciousnesses? They are *false* in that they appear truly existent although they are not. They are known by *mistaken consciousnesses* in that inherent existence appears to these consciousnesses although inherent existence does not exist. They are *truths* in the perspective of a veiler—the veiler being the ignorance grasping inherent existence. However, they *are not true* because they do not exist as they appear to the principal consciousness perceiving them. When subjected to ultimate analysis, they cannot be found.

An ultimate truth is an object with respect to which a reasoning consciousness comes to be a reliable cognizer distinguishing the ultimate and which is found by that reliable cognizer. Ultimate truths are found by a nonmistaken consciousness, consciousnesses that know objects' deeper mode of existence. Ultimate truths are emptinesses; they are true in that they exist as they appear to the mind directly perceiving them. To this mind, emptiness appears without the dual appearance of subject and object and without the appearance of inherent existence.

## REFLECTION

1. How do Svātantrikas define ultimate truth and conventional truth?
2. How do Prāsaṅgikas define these?
3. What does it mean when Prāsaṅgikas say that things exist by mere designation?

# 5 Comparing Assertions

EACH TENET SYSTEM has its own definitions of conventional and ultimate truths and its own notions of what selflessness and the object of negation are. Although keeping all of these clear in your mind, let alone understanding what they mean, is initially daunting, as you study and reflect on this material, it will become clearer. The chart below summarizes the definitions of the two truths and gives a short explanation according to each system.

### Conventional and Ultimate Truths

| SYSTEM | CONVENTIONAL TRUTH | ULTIMATE TRUTH |
|---|---|---|
| Vaibhāṣika | A phenomenon that if separated into parts physically or mentally, the consciousness apprehending it ceases (that is, the perception of it ceases); for example, a pot. | A phenomenon that if physically or mentally separated into parts, the consciousness apprehending it does not stop; for example, directionally partless particles, temporally partless moments of consciousness, and unconditioned space. |
| Sautrāntika (Reasoning Proponents) | A phenomenon that exists only by being imputed by a conceptual consciousness; for example, unconditioned space. It is also a phenomenon that is not able to ultimately perform a function. | A phenomenon that is able to bear reasoned analysis in terms of having its own mode of existence without depending on imputation by terms or conceptual consciousness; for example, a table. It is a phenomenon that is able to ultimately perform a function. |

| | | |
|---|---|---|
| Yogācāra | An object found by a prime cognizer that is a correct consciousness distinguishing a conventionality. It is a conventional object of observation suitable to generate afflictions; for example, a computer. | An object found by a prime cognizer that is a correct knower distinguishing an ultimate. It is a final object of observation of a path of purification; for example, the emptiness of a person. |
| Svātantrika Madhyamaka | An object that is realized dualistically by a direct reliable cognizer that directly realizes it; for example, a shoe. It is an object found by a conventional reliable cognizer (that is, a direct perceiver or inferential cognizer not affected by an internal or external cause of error). | An object that is nondualistically realized by a direct reliable cognizer explicitly cognizing it; for example, the emptiness of true existence of a bank. |
| Prāsaṅgika Madhyamaka | An object with respect to which a conventional consciousness becomes a reliable cognizer distinguishing the conventional and which is found by that reliable cognizer; for example, a bicycle. It is an object found by a conventional reliable cognizer perceiving a false knowable object. | An object with respect to which a reasoning consciousness becomes a reliable cognizer distinguishing the ultimate and which is found by that reliable cognizer; for example, the emptiness of inherent existence of an apple, the unfindability of a pot in its basis of designation. |

In the Vaibhāṣika and Sautrāntika systems, the two truths are different sets of unrelated objects. In the Yogācāra and Madhyamaka systems, the two truths are one nature and nominally different. For Vaibhāṣikas, a cup and the partless particles that compose it are unrelated, and for Sautrāntikas, phenomena that perform functions and those that do not are unrelated. Yogācārins say there are no phenomena external to the mind, whereas all the other systems except Yogācāra-Svātantrika Mādhyamikas assert external objects. For Mādhyamikas, the cup is a conventional truth and the cup's emptiness of inherent existence is an ultimate truth. The cup and its emptiness are one nature because they exist simultaneously, and if one exists, so does the other. However, they are nominally different because they are not the same thing and can be distinguished conceptually.

## *Levels of Selflessness of Persons*

After first hearing or reading these various views, we may wonder what all the fuss is about and why there are so many categories and definitions. The purpose of studying tenets is not to make us confused—although it may initially seem to have that byproduct! Rather, it is to help us figure out how things exist, and eliminate the ignorance that is the root of saṃsāra.

Throughout the ages people have questioned, "Who am I?" Arriving at the correct answer to this question is crucial because our concept of self lies at the center of our worldview, and everything we encounter is referenced in terms of ourselves. Be it a person, an idea, or an event, our primary concern is how it will affect Me. Depending on this, we act, creating karma that will influence our future experiences. If our initial concept of self is incorrect, everything that follows will also be erroneous.

The tenet systems have different ways of defining the object of negation—what does not exist that we mistakenly grasp as existent. How a system identifies the object of negation influences how it identifies the self-grasping that holds that object of negation as true and the selflessness that is realized by understanding that the object of negation does not exist. The sequence of the tenet schools is arranged in terms of the depth of their understanding of these issues. By progressively understanding each level of the object of negation, the self-grasping that holds it as true, and the realization that knows that object of negation to be nonexistent, we approach an ever more subtle understanding of reality—how persons and phenomena actually exist.

As each successive level of selflessness is realized, one part of grasping a false self is chipped away. Nevertheless, each of the lower systems leaves something that can act as a basis for further grasping. All Buddhist schools refute the existence of a permanent, unitary, and independent self, the coarsest mistaken notion of self. They then refute a self-sufficient substantially existent person. However, the lower schools leave the inherent existence of the person and all other phenomena untouched. Only by refuting this do we arrive at a full understanding of reality. After fleshing out the residual grasping not refuted by the lower systems, we see the subtlety of the Prāsaṅgika view.

Beginning with the coarsest, the following are the different levels of self of persons that are objects of negation.

### *Permanent, Unitary, and Independent Self*

The first level of the object of negation is a permanent (unchanging), unitary (partless, monolithic), and independent (autonomous) self or soul (*ātman*). This is an unchanging soul or absolute self that continues after death. The person and the aggregates are of two completely different natures: the aggregates are impermanent—the body dies, the mind changes—but the person is permanent. The relationship between the self and the aggregates is like a person carrying a burden. An independent soul or self "picks up" a set of aggregates at the beginning of each rebirth and "sets them down" at death. This unchanging self continues throughout the entire series of saṃsāric rebirths. The mind grasping this is the misconception of a permanent, unitary, and independent self or soul. Most non-Buddhist religions assert such a self, whereas all Buddhist tenet schools refute it.

### *Self-Sufficient Substantially Existent Person*

The next level of the object of negation to establish the selflessness of persons is a self-sufficient substantially existent person. Here, the I and the aggregates appear to be different and exist separately. Grasping a self-sufficient substantially existent person does not regard the I as being designated to the aggregates. The person is like a shepherd, and the mind and body are like the sheep that the shepherd controls. The shepherd and sheep are distinct; the shepherd is in charge and the sheep follow his directions. Here the aggregates appear to be dependent on the I, but the I directs the aggregates and appears to be independent of them. We may feel this when we don't want to get out of bed in the morning and think, "Okay, body, time to get up!" or "I'll try to be more mindful." Realizing the nonexistence of such a person counteracts grasping a self-sufficient substantially existent person.[33]

Grasping a self-sufficient substantially existent person has both acquired and innate forms. Acquired grasping comes about from studying incorrect philosophies, whereas the innate grasping has existed beginninglessly and is carried from one life to the next. Almost all proponents of Buddhist tenets assert the lack of a self-sufficient substantially existent person.[34] The acquired grasping is abandoned at the path of seeing, whereas for bodhisattvas, the innate grasping and the afflictions that arise due to it are abandoned beginning on the fourth ground. They are completely eradicated on the eighth bodhisattva ground. The explicit mention of grasping a self-sufficient substantially existent person being abandoned on the fourth ground has the purpose of asserting that there are innate levels of this grasping and the afflictions it engenders that are the portion of the afflictions to be abandoned on the fourth ground. Similarly, another portion of the innate grasping of a self-sufficient substantially existent person and the afflictions it engenders are to be abandoned on each of the subsequent grounds up to the eighth.

If a self-sufficient substantially existent person existed, then whatever we wished for in terms of our aggregates would happen because a self-sufficient substantially existent person could control the aggregates. If we wished to exchange our polluted body for the body of a buddha with its thirty-two signs and eighty marks, our wish would immediately come true. If we wished to exchange our confused mind for the omniscient mind of a buddha, that, too, would happen.

The mode of apprehension of the innate grasping of a self-sufficient substantially existent person holds the person to be the controller of the aggregates. This is the self that is negated in the common four truths—the four truths accepted by all the Buddhist schools. Coarse true duḥkha arises from its origin, grasping a coarse self—a self-sufficient substantially existent person. True cessation is the nirvana brought about by abandoning the coarse afflictions that arise from grasping a self-sufficient substantially existent person. The true path realizes the absence of such a self. This is the coarse selflessness. It is called "coarse" because in comparison to grasping an inherently existent person and the selflessness of an inherently existent person, it is coarse.

The uncommon four truths are those propounded by the Prāsaṅgika Mādhyamikas, and they center around inherent existence. True duḥkha is the aggregates produced by true origins, which are the afflictions and karma created by grasping inherent existence. The true path refutes inherent existence on both the person and all other phenomena. The nonaffirming negation that the true path realizes is the emptiness of inherent existence. This is subtle emptiness.

### *Inherently Existent Person*

The subtlest degree of the object of negation regarding the person is its inherent, ultimate, or true existence. The false I appears to set itself up and exist under its own power, without depending on any other factors such as causes and conditions, parts, or being designated by term and concept.

Prāsaṅgikas say the I exists *by being merely imputed or designated by name and concept in dependence on the aggregates*. Sautrāntikas say the I is *imputed to the aggregates* and doesn't exist independent of them. But what they mean by this differs from the Prāsaṅgika meaning. Sautrāntikas assert that in order to identify a person, the body, voice, or mind of the person must be perceived; Prāsaṅgikas agree with that but go deeper, saying that the existence of the person depends not only on causes and conditions and parts (the aggregates) but also on the mind that conceives and designates the person.

Only Prāsaṅgika Mādhyamikas assert the inherent existence of the person as an object of negation. They say the lack of a self-sufficient substantially existent person is the coarse selflessness of persons and realizing this alone cannot remove the afflicted obscurations. Why? Because someone could realize with a direct perceiver that there is no self that is the controller of the aggregates but still grasp a self that exists independently, from its own side, truly, and inherently. Only by identifying this subtle object of negation and then refuting it can we realize the deepest level of selflessness of the person.

Of the two types of afflictions—the innate afflictions that go from one life to the next and the acquired afflictions that we learn from false philosophies—holding a permanent, unified, and independent self is an acquired affliction. We learn this view when we are taught that there is a permanent, unified, and independent soul. Grasping a self-sufficient substantially existent person has both innate and acquired aspects, as does grasping the inherent existence of persons and phenomena. Acquired afflictions and views are easier to overcome, whereas innate afflictions and views require more effort and time to eradicate.

## *Levels of Selflessness of Phenomena*

The Yogācāra and Madhyamaka systems also assert grasping a self of phenomena. That is a type of ignorance. The nonexistence of such a self of phenomena is the selflessness of phenomena. Yogācārins speak of two basic misconceptions or grasping regarding phenomena. One is grasping the subject and object of a cognition to be different entities. The other is grasping phenomena to exist by way of their own character as the referent of terms and conceptual thoughts about them. The emptiness of these two objects of negation, according to the Yogācārins, is the selflessness of phenomena.

Mādhyamikas say the true existence or ultimate existence of phenomena is the object of negation of the selflessness of phenomena. The emptiness of true or ultimate existence of phenomena is the selflessness of phenomena, according to this school.

Within the Madhyamaka school, there are further distinctions. Svātantrika Mādhyamikas define true or ultimate existence as existing without being posited through the force of appearing to a nondefective awareness—that is, to a consciousness that is not mistaken with respect to its engaged object that appears inherently existent. This awareness has no superficial causes of error, such as a defective sense faculty or the mental consciousness holding erroneous views. Phenomena's objective existence, without their being posited by the force of appearing to a nondefective consciousness, is the object of negation for Svātantrikas. The emptiness of such true or ultimate existence of phenomena is the selflessness of phenomena. Nevertheless, Svātantrikas hold that phenomena are indeed established inherently and by their own characteristics on the conventional level because there must be something inherently findable conventionally that is the object; if there were not, anything could be anything.

Prāsaṅgika Mādhyamikas put forth the subtlest view of selflessness, the final thought of the Buddha, as described by such luminaries as Nāgārjuna, Buddhapālita, Candrakīrti, and Śāntideva. They assert that inherent existence—a findable, independent nature that exists without depending on being designated by term and concept—is the object of negation of meditation on emptiness. This false object appears to our senses, deceiving the mental consciousness so that it grasps phenomena to exist in this manner. The absence of phenomena's existing inherently, in their own right, from their own side, and by their own characteristics is the deepest meaning of emptiness.

All of these schools have their sources in Buddha's word, as found in the sūtras. The Buddha set forth these varying views as skillful means. To help us understand their meaning, they are classified as interpretable (provisional) and definitive teachings, to be explained below. To understand emptiness properly, study of the definitive teachings is necessary.

## Self, the Object of Negation: The Self Refuted on Persons and Phenomena

| TENET SYSTEM | COARSE SELF OF PERSONS | SUBTLE SELF OF PERSONS | COARSE SELF OF PHENOMENA | SUBTLE SELF OF PHENOMENA |
|---|---|---|---|---|
| Vaibhāṣika | Permanent, unitary, and independent self | Self-sufficient substantially existent person | - | - |
| Sautrāntika | Permanent, unitary, and independent self | Self-sufficient substantially existent person | - | - |
| Yogācāra | Permanent, unitary, and independent self | Self-sufficient substantially existent person | - | Subject and object as different entities; external phenomena; phenomena existing by their own characteristics as the basis of names; phenomena existing by their own characteristics as the basis of conceptions |
| Yogācāra-Svātantrika Madhyamaka | Permanent, unitary, and independent self | Self-sufficient substantially existent person | Subject and object as different entities; external phenomena | True existence of persons and phenomena |
| Sautrāntika-Svātantrika Madhyamaka | Permanent, unitary, and independent self | Self-sufficient substantially existent person | - | True existence of persons and phenomena |
| Prāsaṅgika Madhyamaka | Self-sufficient substantially existent person | Inherently existent person | - | Inherent existence of phenomena |

## REFLECTION

1. What are the qualities of a permanent, unitary, and independent person?
2. Did you learn a view comparable to this as a child?

3. If so, what do you think of that view now? Does a permanent soul or self exist?

---

## *What Is the Middle Way?*

Each tenet school has its own way of explaining the basis, path, result, object of negation, and Middle Way view. In future chapters, some of these differences will be explored to flesh out the Prāsaṅgikas' unique interpretation of the Middle Way view. The Middle Way is valued because it is free of the extremes of absolutism and nihilism; the former superimposes a way of existence that phenomena don't have—inherent existence—and the latter deprecates the way phenomena do exist. The extreme of absolutism is also called "the extreme of permanence," since if phenomena existed inherently, functioning things would have a permanent essence. A person, for example, would be permanent and unable to change, making awakening impossible. The extreme of nihilism is also called "the extreme of annihilation," since if phenomena existed in that manner, the continuum of functioning things would be totally severed when those things disintegrated. For example, when a person dies, there would be no mental continuum or rebirth in the case of ordinary beings.

Someone may be philosophically nihilistic or ethically nihilistic. A philosophical nihilist thinks that phenomena do not exist; an ethical nihilist deprecates the law of karma and its effects and believes that our actions do not have an ethical dimension that influences our future lives. Many people who initially are philosophically nihilistic become ethically nihilist, whereas those who are ethically nihilistic may or may not be philosophically nihilistic. In the following sections, nihilism chiefly refers to philosophical nihilism.

As you read each school's assertion in the statements below describing how it avoids the two extremes and establishes the Middle Way, think deeply: Which assertions feel most comfortable at first glance? Which makes the most sense when you apply reasoning?

Cārvākas avoid absolutism by saying that no phenomenon exists beyond what is perceived by our senses. They avoid nihilism by saying that all phenomena are manifest to our senses.

Sāṃkhyas avoid absolutism by asserting that phenomena are manifestations of the fundamental nature. They avoid nihilism by stating that the fundamental nature—a real substance from which all phenomena manifest—is unchangeable.

Sāṃkhyas are absolutists in that they hold that the cause continues to exist at the time of its result. Vaibhāṣikas avoid this extreme of absolutism by asserting that a cause must cease for its effect to arise. They avoid nihilism by saying that an effect arises after the cessation of its cause—after the bud ceases, the flower arises. They also avoid nihilism by saying that past and future are substantial entities (T. *rdzas*). The past of an object exists after its present existence, and the future of an object exists before its present existence. For Vaibhāṣikas, everything is substantially established (T. *rdzas su grub pa*).

Sautrāntikas avoid absolutism by asserting that conditioned phenomena disintegrate moment by moment; things change and transform into something else in each new moment. They also avoid absolutism by saying that permanent phenomena, such as unconditioned space, are not substantial entities. They avoid nihilism by asserting that the continuity of most products—such as the self and the six elements—isn't severed and exists continuously. In this way, the self continues from one life to the next. They also say that objects exist by their own characteristics as referents for terms and concepts—that is, there is something in a table that makes it suitable to be called a "table" and for our mind to think of it as a table. Furthermore, they assert that external objects are composed of partless particles and are truly existent.

Yogācārins avoid absolutism by asserting that dependent phenomena do not exist by their own characteristics as the referent of words and thoughts. They also avoid absolutism by asserting that imaginary phenomena are not truly existent. They avoid nihilism by saying that dependent and consummate phenomena are truly existent. If they weren't, they would not exist at all.

Svātantrika Mādhyamikas avoid absolutism by saying that nothing truly or ultimately exists without being posited by the power of appearing to a nondefective awareness. They avoid nihilism by asserting that all phenomena exist inherently and exist by their own characteristics conventionally. If they did not, they would not exist. That is, things exist from the side of the object conventionally; this appears to a nondefective awareness that posits the phenomena. In that way, phenomena exist.

Prāsaṅgika Mādhyamikas say that what Svātantrikas assert to avoid nihilism makes them fall to the extreme of absolutism. Prāsaṅgikas avoid this fault by asserting that all phenomena are not established from their own side or under their own power either ultimately or conventionally. When sought among their bases of imputation, phenomena cannot be found. They avoid nihilism by asserting that phenomena exist conventionally by being merely designated by terms and concepts in dependence on their bases of designation. Although things exist as mere designations, they are still able to perform functions. If they didn't exist in this way, either they would be permanent or they wouldn't exist at all.

### How Each Tenet System Establishes Its Middle Way View

| TENET SYSTEM | HOW IT AVOIDS ABSOLUTISM | HOW IT AVOIDS NIHILISM |
|---|---|---|
| Cārvāka (non-Buddhist) | Phenomena do not exist beyond what is perceivable by our senses. | All existents are manifest to our senses. |
| Sāṃkhya (non-Buddhist) | Phenomena are manifestations of the fundamental nature—a real substance from which all phenomena manifest. | The fundamental nature is unchanging. |
| Vaibhāṣika | (1) All products are impermanent and disintegrate moment by moment. (2) For an effect to arise, its causes must cease. | (1) An effect arises after the cessation of its causes. (2) All phenomena are substantially established. |
| Sautrāntika | (1) Conditioned phenomena disintegrate in each moment; things momentarily disintegrate and transform into something else. (2) Permanent phenomena such as unconditioned space are not substantial entities. | (1) The continuity of many products, such as the self, isn't severed and exists continuously. (2) Objects exist by their own characteristics as referents for terms and concepts. |
| Yogācāra | (1) There is no external matter composed of partless particles. (2) Dependent phenomena do not exist by their own characteristics as the referent of words and conceptual consciousnesses. (3) Imaginary phenomena are not truly existent. | (1) Dependent and consummate phenomena are truly existent. (2) Ultimate truths are ultimately established and exist inherently. |

| | | |
|---|---|---|
| Svātantrika Madhyamaka | Phenomena do not truly or ultimately exist without being posited by the power of appearing to a nondefective awareness. | All phenomena are established from their own side, exist by their own characteristics, and exist inherently on the conventional level. |
| Prāsaṅgika Madhyamaka | All phenomena do not exist from their own side, under their own power, or inherently. They lack inherent existence even conventionally. | Phenomena exist conventionally by being merely designated by terms and concepts in dependence on their basis of designation. |

You may have noticed that what one school asserts as its way of avoiding the extreme of negating too much (nihilism), the next school says is actually the extreme of adding too much (absolutism). Thinking about the views of these schools in progressive order gradually leads our mind to the correct view. Although each successive tenet system negates the unique position of the lower ones, understanding the views of the lower tenet systems serves as the basis to understand the views of the higher systems. As we gradually accept the positions of the higher systems, we must be careful not to denigrate the lower ones.

After you finish reading and reflecting on this volume and the next two volumes on emptiness, you may want to come back to this section. Chances are you will see much deeper meaning in it then.

## *Gradually Leading Us to the Correct View*

The Buddha is a skillful teacher who leads us through a sequence of objects of negation and assertions regarding the Middle Way view in order to counteract our distorted views and ignorance. He does this by explaining a steady progression away from substantial, true, and inherent existence and toward dependent, imputed existence. A short summary will illustrate how he did this.

Vaibhāṣikas say that ultimate truths substantially exist because the awareness knowing them isn't cancelled when they are physically broken or mentally divided into parts, whereas conventional truths imputedly exist in that they cannot be perceived when mentally or physically broken into smaller parts. Nevertheless, all of these are substantially established because they have their own autonomous entity that is not dependent on conceptuality.

Sautrāntikas take this a step further, saying that ultimate truths, which are impermanent, functioning things, are substantially existent because they perform functions, and conventional truths are not because they are imputed by term and thought; but all are truly existent because they exist in reality in just the way they appear.

Yogācārins take yet another step, saying that dependent and consummate phenomena are truly existent because they are not merely imputed by the consciousness apprehending them and exist by their own uncommon mode of existence. Imaginaries are imputed by conception. But all of these inherently exist in that they have their own mode of being and are findable when the object to which the term is attributed is sought.[35]

Svātantrikas go further, saying that no phenomena truly exist because they don't exist without being posited through the force of appearing to a nondefective mind, but they do exist inherently on the conventional level because they appear to a nondefective mind.

At the end, Prāsaṅgikas say that no phenomenon inherently exists but everything is merely imputed because it exists by being merely designated by term and concept. For them, substantially existent implies something exists as it appears, whereas "imputedly existent" means that it is dependent on being designated by term and concept and does not exist as it appears. Emptiness exists as it appears to a direct perceiver and is therefore true, but it is not truly existent.

The Buddha also presented a progression of objects of negation, examining first how the person exists and then how phenomena exist. He began by first refuting the existence of a permanent, unitary, and independent self, a view held by many non-Buddhists. This view is acquired—it is fabricated by our intellectual mind through incorrect philosophical speculation—and is comparatively easy to refute. Innate afflictions that go from one life to another are more deeply rooted and difficult to remove.

Having refuted a permanent, unitary, and independent self, we are ready to look deeper, so the Buddha introduces the notion that there is no self-sufficient substantially existent person. This is an innate view and is the prominent object of negation of the lower schools for the selflessness of persons. By refuting this, one layer of grasping and the afflictions that depend on it are released.

We also need to be aware of the Buddhist essentialists' assertions regarding substantial existence and imputed existence. In their view, a person is imputedly existent because it cannot be identified without some other phenomena—in this case the aggregates—appearing to the mind. The aggregates, however, are substantially existent because they can be known directly. In general, essentialists speak about two types of cognizers: conceptual cognizers and nonconceptual direct perceivers. This gets us thinking about the role of conception and how unconditioned phenomena come into existence by imputation. These points are developed in the Sautrāntika tenet school.

Incorrect graspings and misconceptions abound. We may hold the idea that smallest partless particles compose larger forms and forms can be reduced to such particles. However, if particles were directionally partless, it would be impossible for them to join together to form larger objects. If they had no sides, either they would merge and become one or they could not touch. In either case, a larger composite would not be created. The Yogācāra school and above refute such particles.

To counteract grasping things as being external, objective, and unrelated to the mind apprehending them, the Buddha teaches the absence of external objects and teaches that the apprehending mind and the apprehended object arise from the same seed on the foundation consciousness.[36] In teaching this object of negation, the Buddha helps us to see that the mind and the object it apprehends are not unrelated to each other. This view is useful because seeing that objects of our attachment and anger are in the nature of the mind dramatically reduces the intensity of our afflictions.

The Buddha also taught that things do not exist by their own characteristics as the referent of terms. Here he challenges us to investigate the relationship between an object and the term imputed to it. We see that terms are useful as conventional devices to communicate with other people, but that the relationship between an object and its name is dependent upon the mind. A name does not exist from its own side in the object.

The Buddha then teaches that phenomena come about in a collaborative manner: something exists from the side of the object, but it also depends on being designated by a nondefective awareness. An object's inherent nature appears to a nondefective awareness and is also posited by mind. Although objects are unfindable when searched for with a reasoning consciousness analyzing the ultimate nature, conventionally they have their own inherent nature. In that way, anything can't be called anything; each object has something in it that warrants its receiving a certain name. This is the Svātantrika view.

By working through all these views, our mind has loosened its belief in many incorrect notions of existence. Yet it still holds on to one bit of security—that conventionally phenomena have an inherent nature and there is something in each phenomenon that exists independent of other factors. Without this, we fear that nothing exists at all. Now the Buddha cuts away even this grasping by saying that all phenomena exist by being merely designated by term and concept. Everything depends on the imputing mind to exist, even the mind itself. Contrary to the Yogācārins, who say that the mind truly exists, the Prāsaṅgikas assert that the mind exists by being merely designated. Contrary to the Svātantrikas, who say that all phenomena have their own inherent nature conventionally, Prāsaṅgikas say they lack such a findable nature both ultimately and conventionally.

Just as a tangled ball of yarn cannot be untangled quickly by pulling at just one place, our mind cannot instantaneously drop all misconceptions and grasping at once. After all, the mind has held these erroneous views from beginningless time! The guidance of a skillful teacher, the Buddha, is needed to gradually lead us to the correct view through the progression of the four tenet systems.

Why is negating a permanent, unitary, and independent self not enough? Because we still hold on to the self as a controller of the aggregates, and many afflictions arise due to this grasping.

While refuting a self-sufficient substantially existent person helps to reduce the strength of the coarse afflictions, it nevertheless is insufficient to eradicate all afflictions. This is because grasping at the basis of the self—the mental and physical aggregates—as inherently existent still remains. Without negating the inherent existence of the aggregates, we will continue grasping the inherent existence of the I imputed in dependence on them.[37] This grasping leads to attachment and anger. Grasping at agreeable objects as inherently existent, we seek to procure and protect them, and attachment arises. Grasping at disagreeable objects as inherently existent, we want to destroy them or distance ourselves from them, and anger arises. Even though we may have realized the lack of a self-sufficient substantially existent person, subtler afflictions that grasp inherent existence[38] still exist in our mindstream.

Viewing objects as existing by way of their own character as the referent of their terms and seeing external phenomena as being unrelated to the perceiving mind, we believe that things exist objectively "out there." This sets the stage for attachment, anger, and other afflictions to arise. Dismantling these views, as the Yogācārins do, reduces our emotional reactivity to external objects.

But negating the objective existence of the external world is not sufficient because it doesn't stop grasping the true existence of the internal mind and mental states. We continue to be fixated on truly existent emotions and perceptions. The Mādhyamikas counteract this by negating true existence across the entire spectrum of phenomena, internal and external. However, the way the Svātantrika Mādhyamikas do this is not sufficient; they leave a degree of objective reality by saying that phenomena exist from their own side. They still hold on to an objectified locus in phenomena that makes them what they are. As long as we hold on to anything whatsoever as existing from its own side, we cannot cut the root of cyclic existence and will continue to grasp the aggregates, and thus the person, as inherently existent. This, in turn, perpetuates afflictions. Nāgārjuna says (YS 51–52ab):

> As long as there is an [objectified] locus,
> one is caught by the twisting snake of the afflictions.
> Those whose minds have no [objectified] locus
> will not be caught.
> How could the deadly poison of the afflictions fail to arise
> in those whose minds possess an [objectified] locus?

As long as we consider phenomena and persons as having an objectified locus that is their true essence, afflictions will continue to arise. Only when the full meaning of selflessness is realized directly can that basis for self-grasping ignorance be cut. Thus Prāsaṅgikas take the Madhyamaka refutation a step further than Svātantrikas by saying there is not the tiniest bit of an objectified locus in any phenomena and that things exist by being merely designated in dependence on their basis of designation. Here, "merely" excludes inherent existence. In this view, there is nothing left to grasp because inherent or objective existence is negated on all external and internal phenomena, including the person and the mind.

Everything is empty of inherent existence and yet exists nominally and dependently.

A similar understanding is growing among scientists. Newtonian science took for granted an objective external world that exists separate from the observer. The findings of quantum physics cast doubt on this and make it difficult to ground reality in objective matter. Some scientists are considering that perhaps things are not completely separate and unrelated to the perceiver after all.

Although you see the inconsistencies in the tenets of the lower schools, you may initially feel uneasy with the Prāsaṅgikas' radical idea of emptiness. Go slowly and continue to deepen your understanding of that system. In time, your inquiry and analysis will deepen your understanding.

Personally speaking, I'm inclined to the Prāsaṅgika view of emptiness; it helps avert attachment, anger, and other afflictions and at the same time confirms that we human beings have a common, shared world that arose due to causes and conditions.

In short, all Buddhists agree that ignorance is dispelled by wisdom, but tenet systems differ on what the object of that ultimate wisdom is. The layout of the tenet systems articulates the various diversions we could easily fall into as well as the correct direction to follow when eliminating ignorance and cultivating wisdom. To understand emptiness, question how the people and environment and even your self exist. Reflect on the mechanism with which we construct our self-identity and the world around us, and how ignorance reifies these. In this process, you will counteract wrong views and familiarize yourself with correct ones.

## REFLECTION

1. Why does each tenet system want to portray itself as the Middle Way? What is it the middle between?
2. Review how each tenet system asserts itself as the Middle Way.
3. How does the sequence of tenet schools from lowest to highest lead students to the actual Middle Way view?
4. What are the advantages of provisionally adopting the view of each tenet

school beginning with the Vaibhāṣika, investigating it and noticing both its strong and its weak points, and then progressing to the next tenet school and doing the same?

---

## *Definitive and Interpretable*

As we know, the Buddha gave a variety of teachings to different audiences in the forty-five years after attaining awakening. In doing so, he took into consideration their dispositions and interests because his ultimate intention was to lead them to fully realize the emptiness of inherent existence, banish all saṃsāric duḥkha, and attain full awakening. Nāgārjuna comments that the Buddha gave seemingly contradictory statements to different audiences in order to skillfully lead the variety of listeners to nirvāṇa (MMK 18.8):

> Everything is real, and is not real;
> both real and unreal;
> neither unreal nor real—
> this is the Lord Buddha's teaching.

On some occasions the Buddha said that the aggregates are like a burden and the person is the carrier of that burden, implying that the person is separate from the aggregates. To another group he said there is no permanent, unitary, independent self that is different from the aggregates. Sometimes he said the self is self-sufficient substantially existent; at other times he said a self-sufficient substantially existent person does not exist. In some sūtras, he stated that external phenomena do not exist but the mind truly exists, and in still others, he negated the true existence of all phenomena.

Aware of the Buddha's compassion and skill as a teacher, we are left with the task of discerning the definitive (*nītārtha, nītattha*) and the interpretable or provisional (*neyārtha, neyyaattha*)[39] with respect to the meaning (subject matter) and the scriptures. In terms of the meaning, we must discern whether the subject matter that is expressed is to be understood definitively or provisionally, and in terms of scriptures—the words and means of expression—we must also distinguish definitive and interpretable. This issue is important because our philosophical understanding impacts our meditation, and meditation on the correct view is essential to cut the root of saṃsāra.

Each philosophical tenet system has its own criteria for discerning what is the Buddha's teaching and what is not. The way they do this reflects their unique understanding of the object of negation, selflessness, and ultimate truth.

Some Vaibhāṣikas and Sautrāntikas assert that all statements of the Buddha can be taken literally and are definitive and that no sūtra passage requires interpretation. They accept as literal and definitive sūtras explaining that conditioned phenomena are impermanent, that things conditioned by ignorance are duḥkha in nature, and that selflessness is the lack of a self-sufficient substantially existent person. In this context "sūtra" does not necessarily refer to whole texts but to passages, or even a few words, spoken by the Buddha.

Some later Vaibhāṣikas assert there are both definitive and interpretable meanings. Citing the Perfection of Wisdom sūtras as interpretable, they say the Buddha did not really mean that all phenomena have no inherent nature; rather, he was refuting non-Buddhist assertions concerning the fundamental nature and production from self.[40] In the same vein, some Sautrāntikas accept the Perfection of Wisdom sūtras as the Buddha's word but say these sūtras cannot be taken at face value and require interpretation. For example, they assert that when the Buddha said that products do not exist, he was referring to their disintegration in each moment.[41]

Only in the Yogācāra and Madhyamaka systems do we see a well-defined method to differentiate definitive and interpretable teachings of the Buddha. The Yogācārins assert that definitive sūtras are those whose explicit teachings can be accepted literally—for example, the *Sūtra Unraveling the Thought* (*Saṃdhinirmocana Sūtra*). Interpretable sūtras are those whose explicit teachings cannot be accepted literally—for example, the *Heart Sūtra* (*Prajñāpāramitāhṛdaya Sūtra*). Because Yogācāra Scripture Proponents say dependent phenomena and consummate natures truly exist and exist by their own characteristics, whereas imaginaries do not, they assert as definitive the sūtras that assert a foundation consciousness, explain their view of the three natures, and whose literal content refutes external objects.

Yogācārins base their way of distinguishing definitive and interpretable meanings and sūtras on the *Sūtra Unraveling the Thought*, which says the first and second turnings of the Dharma wheel are interpretable and the third is definitive. The first turning is interpretable because there the Buddha said that all phenomena exist by their own characteristics; the second turning is interpretable because there the Buddha said that no phenomenon exists by its own characteristics. The third turning of the Dharma wheel is definitive because there the Buddha clearly laid out which phenomena exist by their own characteristics and which do not.[42] Expressed in another way, the first turning presents the selflessness of persons but not the selflessness of phenomena, because it doesn't refute that phenomena exist by their own characteristics as bases of names and concepts. The second turning literally sets forth the non-true existence of all phenomena but doesn't differentiate that some phenomena truly exist and others do not. The third turning differentiates the true existence of dependent and consummate natures and the non-true existence of imaginaries.

Yogācārins differentiate words and meanings as definitive or interpretable by discussing the four reliances and the four reasonings. They differentiate the sūtras as definitive and interpretable through the four thoughts and four indirect intentions. An in-depth study of these four sets of four and the reasons that both groups of Yogācārins employ them to differentiate definitive and interpretable sūtras and meanings reveals a great deal about their view of emptiness.[43]

Mādhyamikas refer to the *Teaching of Akṣayamati Sūtra* (*Akṣayamatinirdeśa Sūtra*) to discern definitive and interpretable. It says (MP 809):

> What are definitive sūtras? Which require interpretation? Sūtras setting forth the establishment of conventionalities are called "requiring interpretation." Sūtras setting forth the establishment of the ultimate are called "definitive. . . ."
>
> Those sūtras teaching [about various objects] by way of various words and letters are called "requiring interpretation." Those teaching the profound, difficult to view, and difficult to realize are called "definitive." Those teaching, for instance, [the inherent existence of] an owner when there is no [inherently existent] owner and teaching those objects indicated by various words

> [such as] self, sentient being, life, nourisher, being, person, progeny of Manu, child of Manu, agent, and experiencer are requiring interpretation.
>
> Those sūtras teaching the doors of liberation—the emptiness of things, signlessness, wishlessness, no activity, no production, no creation, no sentient being, no living being, no persons and no controller—are called "definitive." This is called "reliance on definitive sūtras and non-reliance on those requiring interpretation."

The sūtras requiring interpretation are those whose subject matter is the diversity of conventionalities, such as everyday objects. Those that are definitive speak about the absence of inherent existence of those objects, saying "no sentient being" and so forth. For Prāsaṅgikas, the interpretable may or may not be taken literally, but its main subject matter is not the final mode of existence, emptiness.

An example of a sūtra whose meaning is not to be taken literally is the one where the Buddha said that one's mother and father are to be killed. He said this to help relieve the crippling grief and remorse of someone who had killed his own parents. Clearly, this cannot be taken at face value but needs to be interpreted and understood in context. In this case, the Buddha was referring to killing not biological parents but the second and tenth of the twelve links of dependent origination—formative action and renewed existence. By "killing" these, saṃsāra ceases and nirvāṇa is attained.

Similarly, in the *Guhyasamāja Tantra*, the Buddha says that the Tathāgata is to be killed, and by killing the Tathāgata, one will attain supreme awakening. Obviously this cannot be taken literally but must be understood in a tantric context as controlling the life and vitality (T. *srog tshol*). The winds in the body are related to the mind. When the winds are uncontrolled, distractions arise. By controlling the winds through the practice of life and vitality, distractions are stopped. With much practice, this meditation stops the functioning of the coarse winds and coarse consciousnesses, enabling the extremely subtle mind to manifest. Meditators then employ this mind to realize emptiness, purify the mind of all defilement, and attain full awakening.

An example of a sūtra whose meaning is literal but whose subject matter is not the final mode of existence is a sūtra explaining the lack of a self-sufficient substantially existent person. While the person does lack such a mode of existence, that is not its final, deepest nature. Similarly, the statement "forms are impermanent" is literally correct, but impermanence is not the ultimate nature of forms. The meaning of both these statements is provisional.

The Buddha's sūtras on the twelve links of dependent origination—"from ignorance polluted actions arise"—are also interpretable. A cause produces an effect on the conventional level. On the ultimate level both the cause and effect are empty of true existence. Because there is a deeper meaning—the emptiness of inherent existence—to be understood, these sūtras are provisional.

According to the Svātantrikas, sūtras of definitive meaning are those that explicitly teach the ultimate truth as their main topic and can be understood literally. Such sūtras are definitive because the ultimate can be established by a reliable cognizer and cannot be interpreted to be other than the ultimate. Sūtras that cannot be taken literally or that mainly teach conventionalities require interpretation.

According to Prāsaṅgikas, definitive scriptures are those whose main and explicit subject matter is the emptiness of inherent existence. They are called "definitive" because they teach the emptiness of inherent existence—the subtle selflessness of all existents, the ultimate truth beyond which there is no more profound meaning to be discovered—and refute the elaboration of inherent existence. Within the sphere of reality, all phenomena become undifferentiable in that their ultimate nature is equally free of inherent existence. A sūtra's meaning is said to be definitive when it cannot be interpreted to mean other than the deepest mode of existence, emptiness, which is the final view to be settled and the final nature of phenomena. Passages of definitive meaning cannot be interpreted to mean other than what is expressed because their meaning has been validly proven and realized.

Sūtras of interpretable meaning mainly and explicitly discuss conventionalities—all phenomena other than emptiness, such as sentient beings and karma—and describe how these arise, function, and cease. These sūtras are considered interpretable because they require interpretation to know the final mode of existence of conventionalities. Prāsaṅgikas say that conventionalities are falsities because they appear one way and exist in another. For example, money appears to exist "out there," with its own inherent value, while in fact it is merely designated in dependence on paper and ink. It has worth only because we have attributed value to it. Interpretable sūtras do not challenge the seeming inherent existence of phenomena.

The word "interpretable" or "provisional" implies "to be led to" or "to be drawn out." That is, provisional scriptures lead to understanding the final mode of existence. Their meaning must be drawn out because it is not the ultimate nature. The process of interpretation leads the literal meaning of the sūtra around to a different meaning, one that is emptiness.

In the *Heart Sūtra*, Avalokiteśvara speaks inspired by the blessing of the Buddha, "There is no eye, no ear . . . ." He is not refuting the existence of eyes, ears, and other conventionalities. If he did, someone could say that if eyes and ears did not exist, his words were also nonexistent, in which case they could not prove his point. Earlier in the sūtra Avalokiteśvara said, "the emptiness of inherent existence of the five aggregates also." That qualification of "no inherent existence" is to be carried over to the other negations in the sūtra, such as "no eye, no ear . . . ," so the meaning is that there is no inherently existent eye, no inherently existent ear, and so forth. Therefore the *Heart Sūtra* is definitive.

Since Svātantrikas negate inherent existence only ultimately but accept it conventionally, they say statements such as "all phenomena are empty of inherent existence" cannot be accepted literally and are interpretable. For it to be definitive, this statement would have to be qualified to read "all phenomena are *ultimately* empty of inherent existence." The *One Hundred Thousand Stanza Perfection of Wisdom Sūtra* has the qualification "ultimately" and thus is considered definitive, whereas the *Heart Sūtra* lacks this qualification and is said to be interpretable.

To review: both Svātantrikas and Prāsaṅgikas accept that the *Heart Sūtra* mainly and explicitly teaches emptiness. However, for Svātantrikas it is an interpretable sūtra because it is not acceptable literally. This is because the sūtra literally states that the aggregates and so forth are empty of inherent existence, whereas Svātantrikas assert that they are empty of inherent existence only on the ultimate level but not conventionally. For Prāsaṅgikas, the sūtra is definitive because phenomena do not exist inherently on either the ultimate or conventional level, and this emptiness is phenomena's final mode of existence.

While Svātantrikas say there are instances of both interpretable and definitive meanings in the second turning of the Dharma wheel, Prāsaṅgikas say sūtras of the second wheel are definitive because all phenomena lack inherent existence both ultimately and conventionally. In addition, Prāsaṅgikas carry over the qualification "no inherent existence" that is found in one sūtra to all sūtras of the same class. For them, the second turning of the Dharma wheel consists of definitive sūtras, and there are instances of definitive passages in the first and third turnings of the Dharma wheel where emptiness is explicitly taught.

The *Sūtra Unraveling the Thought* and the *Teaching of Akṣayamati Sūtra* employ different criteria to discriminate definitive and interpretable teachings of the Buddha. If we were to determine what is definitive and what is interpretable only according to what a sūtra says, there would still remain the question of what makes that sūtra authoritative. If citing another sūtra were required to validate the first sūtra, we would soon have an infinite regression. Thus we cannot rely entirely on scripture to make this differentiation, and since the Buddha is not here now, we cannot ask him. We must use reasoning and analysis to discern what is definitive. When a sūtra statement concerning the ultimate nature is subjected to critical analysis and does not contradict reasoning, it is said to be definitive. If a statement does not pertain to the ultimate nature—or even if it does, if it is not supported by reasoning—it requires interpretation. With this in mind, Nāgārjuna wrote the *Treatise on the Middle Way*, where his primary approach was reasoning.

In summary, according to the Prāsaṅgikas, interpretable and definitive can refer to either a scripture or its meaning. Scriptures that speak mainly and explicitly about the emptiness of inherent existence are definitive because emptiness is the final mode of being of all phenomena and understanding it leads directly to liberation. All other topics are provisional because they are not the deeper nature of reality and lead to liberation only indirectly. Passages that speak of emptiness are definitive, even when the term "inherently" is used as a qualification in some but not all occasions in that scripture.

All of the Buddha's teachings lead to liberation. Interpretable teachings indirectly steer us toward the correct view, and definitive teachings directly point out the ultimate nature of reality. For that reason, we should respect both sūtras of definitive meaning and those of interpretable meaning. Deprecating provisional sūtras would be an error because following their teachings—especially those concerning bodhicitta and renunciation of saṃsāra—leads us toward the realization of the emptiness of inherent existence. As a follower of Nāgārjuna and a Madhyamaka practitioner, I respect and revere the *Sūtra Unraveling the Thought*, which presents an alternative explanation on the meaning of emptiness, even though my faith and conviction are directed toward the teachings on dependent arising and emptiness expressed in the Perfection of Wisdom sūtras.

Similarly, we should respect the teachings of other religions because they benefit sentient beings and are therefore valuable. Nevertheless, our faith, conviction, and practice should be directed toward the tradition and path that we follow. In the following chapters, when explaining the ultimate truth, I will rely upon the definitive teachings of the Prāsaṅgika Madhyamaka system, which is considered the supreme, definitive view.

### REFLECTION

1. Why did the Buddha teach a diversity of views, some of which seemingly contradict each other?
2. Why is differentiating definitive and interpretable sūtras important to our Dharma practice?
3. What do Yogācārins consider definitive and interpretable sūtras?
4. What do Prāsaṅgikas consider definitive and interpretable sūtras?

## *Proving the Definitive Meaning*

We cannot simply claim that the definitive teachings as understood by the Prāsaṅgikas are supreme, but must offer some logical proof that all phenomena are empty of inherent existence that others can verify for themselves.

When engaging with the world, we have the sense that things exist out there, independent of our perception or conception. But when we search for the actual object—the real referent of our words—we cannot find something that exists from its own side or under its own power. If phenomena possessed inherent existence, they would have an objective basis that grounds their reality. However, when we closely examine the nature of things, we see that their identities depend on factors other than themselves. If they were not dependent on other factors and were self-enclosed entities in and of themselves, they could not impact one another. In that case, causes could not produce effects.

A similar reasoning used in quantum physics can apply to material phenomena. To our naïve everyday perception, the flower in front of us seems to be "out there," something different from me. I can touch it and see it. It is there in front of me, waiting for me or someone else to come along and see it. But when you examine "What exactly is that flower?" and start reducing the flower to its constitutive elements on the molecular level and then to subatomic particles, we come to a point where there are simply subatomic particles without any difference between organic and inorganic phenomena. When you deconstruct even the notion of subatomic particles, nothing can be found. This approach from quantum physics is helpful to deconstruct the solidity of the objects that we perceive.

Yogācārins apply the process of deconstruction to the external material world, but stop there. They still reify the internal world of experience and maintain the view that it is truly real. Mādhyamikas continue the examination and extend the same type of analysis to our inner mental world of experience and consciousness. The mind is immaterial, so we can't examine its spatial dimensions. It is a continuum, and when deconstructed there is only a series of minute temporal points; there is nothing to identify as a mindstream.

The Yogācāra rejection of the external world of matter can almost be seen as a kind of nihilism. Because they cannot find an objective basis of the material world, they negate the external, material world even conventionally. Mādhyamikas, however, do not ground their notion of reality on some kind of objective basis. The reality and existence of things is understood only within the framework of conventional day-to-day experience. From that perspective, both the mental world of experience and the external world of material phenomena exist. Mādhyamikas do not make one more or less real than the other.

The essentialists—those who assert true existence—use the principle of dependent arising as the premise to argue that phenomena possess a real, specific, true nature. For them, dependent arising is proof of true existence. Nāgārjuna responds by saying that the reason they use to prove true existence—dependent arising—actually proves the exact opposite—emptiness. The fact that things arise from causes and conditions and depend on other factors shows that they do not possess any truly existent nature of their own.

According to the essentialists, if things didn't truly exist, they wouldn't exist at all. Nāgārjuna retorts that in a system that does not accept emptiness, there is no way to establish the existence of karma and its effect, the four truths, dependent arising, and so on. If all phenomena were not empty of true existence, none of these things would be tenable; they could neither arise nor cease. In contrast, in a system that upholds the emptiness of true existence, all these phenomena are possible.[44] In fact, emptiness and dependent arising come to the same point. In this way, Nāgārjuna demonstrates through reasoning that the meaning of the Perfection of Wisdom sūtras cannot be interpreted otherwise but is definitive. He also shows that the sūtras that disagree with this require interpretation and cannot be understood literally.

How, then, do we understand sūtras that contain statements such as "everything is mind only"? Nāgārjuna explains that they were spoken to allay the fears of some disciples; in *Precious Garland* he said (RA 394–96):

> Just as a language teacher makes [some students]
> read from a diagram of the alphabet,
> likewise, the Buddha taught the Dharma
> in accord with his disciples' abilities.
>
> To some, the Dharma he taught is
> for the purpose of stopping negativity.
> To some, it is aimed at the practice of virtue.
> And to some, he taught one that is based on duality.

To some, the Dharma he taught is not based on duality,
and to some, he taught a profound Dharma that terrifies the timid.
Its essence is wisdom and compassion,
and it is the means to attain full awakening.

As these verses show, the Buddha teaches the Dharma according to the aptitude, receptivity, and needs of the specific disciples. In general he begins by teaching ethical conduct—abstaining from destructive actions and engaging in constructive ones. Then he teaches the most basic level of no-self. When disciples are prepared, he teaches them the Yogācāra presentations of the nonduality of subject and object. Finally, to those of advanced mental faculties, the deepest meanings of emptiness and bodhicitta are revealed. This skillful method of introducing students to teachings requiring interpretation first, followed by teaching on the definitive meaning when they are receptive to it, protects students from falling into nihilism by misunderstanding emptiness.

Tsongkhapa himself struggled to maintain the balance between negating inherent existence on all phenomena and at the same time maintaining the everyday reality of cause and effect. In the earlier part of his life, he held a view that considers everyday reality to be a mere illusion and the meditation on emptiness to be constituted by disengagement from phenomena. Just as reality is indescribable and indefinable, in the same way the meditation on emptiness is one of nonjudgment and disengagement, he thought. Later in his life Tsongkhapa refuted this view and realized that although phenomena are empty of inherent existence, they function in the world and exist conventionally like illusions.

### *Avoiding Confusion*

We may easily mistake the meaning of words when reading Madhyamaka texts on emptiness. For example, sometimes both "things" (*bhāva*) and "non-things" (*abhāva*) are negated. Here, "thing" refers to inherent existence, and "non-thing" to total nonexistence. In this case Mādhyamikas are refuting the two extremes. They are not saying all impermanent and permanent phenomena don't exist at all.

Similarly, sometimes Madhyamaka texts negate existence and nonexistence. We may become confused because these are a dichotomy and if one is negated, the other must be asserted. However, in this context "existence" means inherent existence and "nonexistence" refers to total nonexistence. Refuting "existence" and "nonexistence" undermines the two extremes.

## *The Three Doors of Liberation*

Definitive sūtras speak of the three doors of liberation (*vimokṣa*, *vimokkha*). These are selflessness seen from three perspectives: the entity, cause, and result of conditioned phenomena. The first, *emptiness* (*śūnyatā*, *suññata*) door of liberation, is the lack of inherent existence of the entity or nature of any phenomenon—for example, a sprout or a person. Meditation on this leads to realization that the entities of phenomena lack inherent existence, and this leads to the pacification of grasping the entities of phenomena as inherently existent.

The *signless* (*ānimitta*, *animitta*) door of liberation is the emptiness that is the absence of inherent existence of the cause of anything—for example, the emptiness of a seed in relation to the sprout. Meditation on this leads to the realization that causes do not inherently exist and this pacifies grasping the causes of a conditioned thing to be inherently existent. Here "sign" means cause.

The *wishless* (*apraṇihita*, *appaṇihita*) door of liberation is the lack of inherent existence of the effects of any phenomenon. Meditation on this leads to the realization that effects do not inherently exist and frees us from the effects of saṃsāra. "Wish" means the objects that are wished for, both those in saṃsāra and in nirvāṇa, and the wishlessness is their lack of inherent existence. There are no inherently existent objects to be sought, hoped for, or attained. Although we seek the cessation of duḥkha and its causes and the attainment of the path and cessation, none of these exist from their own side, and neither do we.

The three doors of liberation can be understood in multiple ways. First, emptiness is the emptiness of a phenomenon, let's say an apple. Signlessness is the lack of inherent existence of its causes and conditions—the apple seed, water, fertilizer, and so forth. Wishlessness is the lack of inherent existence of its results—applesauce or an apple pie. These too do not exist inherently.

The three doors of liberation can be contemplated in terms of saṃsāra and nirvāṇa: the entity, causes, and effects of saṃsāra lack inherent existence.

Nirvāṇa is permanent and its entity is empty. The true paths that are causes of the attainment of nirvāṇa are impermanent, and they too lack inherent existence. The nature of both saṃsāra and nirvāṇa are empty. The causes of our saṃsāra—afflictions and polluted karma—are empty of inherent existence, as is the wisdom that brings about nirvāṇa. The wise do not try to eliminate inherently existent afflictions or attain inherently existent nirvāṇa, for they know these do not exist. Nor do the wise conceive of an inherently existent person who practices the path and later becomes an inherently existent buddha. Meditation on each of the three doors of liberation leads us to realize the emptiness of inherent existence and pacifies grasping at inherent existence.

In addition to things, their causes, and effects being empty, the relationship between these—the activity of arising from causes and the activity of producing effects—are also empty.

The three doors of liberation are related to other topics. They include the eight profound meanings stated in the *Heart Sūtra* when Avalokiteśvara says:

> Śāriputra, like this all phenomena are merely empty, having no characteristics. They are not produced and do not cease. They have no defilement and no separation from defilement. They have no decrease and no increase.

*Empty, having no characteristics* speaks of the emptiness door of liberation: phenomena lack both an inherently existent general nature and an inherently existent specific nature. A lamp's general nature is, for example, its impermanence, and its specific nature is its function to light up an area. The four characteristics—*not produced and do not cease, no defilement and no separation from defilement*—pertain to the signless door of liberation because they speak of the cause (and effect) of the thoroughly afflictive, saṃsāra, and the thoroughly pure, nirvāṇa. The cause and effect in terms of saṃsāra are true cause and true duḥkha; the cause and effect in terms of nirvāṇa are true path and true cessation. The remaining two—*no decrease and no increase*—speak of the wishless door of liberation. The faults that we wish to decrease and the excellent qualities we want to increase lack inherent existence.

The three doors of liberation are also related to the basis, path, and result. Grasping the basis of our saṃsāra—the five aggregates, eighteen constituents, ignorance, afflictions, and so forth—as inherently existent blocks the emptiness door to liberation. Realizing the emptiness of these opens the emptiness door to liberation.

Holding the path to freedom as having inherently existent signs or characteristics blocks the signless door to liberation. Realizing that they lack such signs of inherent existence and using this realization to cease craving and clinging to an inherently existent path opens the signless door to liberation.

Believing the results of liberation and full awakening to be inherently existent blocks the wishless door to liberation. Abandoning the wish to attain inherently existent liberation or awakening opens the wishless door to liberation.

In addition, the three doors can be related to the sixteen aspects of the four truths. The explanation of this is slightly different in the *Ornament of Clear Realizations* and the *Treasury of Knowledge*. The *Ornament* explains that the three doors are paths of antidotes. Paths of antidotes are exalted knowers that are able to destroy the superimpositions that are their objects of negation, in this case the superimposition of inherent or true existence. In the mindstreams of ārya bodhisattvas, the door of emptiness relates to the last two aspects of true duḥkha: empty and selfless. It is an antidote to the view of self because it directly realizes the absence of a permanent, unitary, independent self (empty) and the absence of a self-sufficient substantially existent self (selfless). The door of signlessness is the pristine wisdom that directly realizes the four aspects of true cessation—cessation, peace, magnificence, and definite emergence—and the four aspects of true paths—path, suitable, accomplishment, and way of deliverance. As such, it is an antidote to grasping inherent existence. The door of wishlessness is the antidote to the wish for birth in the three realms of saṃsāra. It is the pristine wisdom that directly realizes the lack of inherent existence of the first two aspects of true suffering—impermanence and duḥkha—and of the four aspects of true origins—cause, origin, strong producer, and condition.

Although three doors of liberation are mentioned, in fact the view of emptiness—the absence of inherent existence—is the door to liberation that takes priority over the others. When we know that all phenomena lack self—inherent existence—and employ that wisdom to extinguish craving for things, we no longer crave for or apprehend signs of inherent existence in anything. The *Requisites for Awakening* (*Byang chub kyi tshogs*)[45] explains (LC 3:194):

> Because [phenomena] do not inherently exist, they are empty.
> Further, because [phenomena] are empty, what use are signs?
> Inasmuch as they have overcome all signs,
> why would the wise wish [for such phenomena]?

The aspiration for liberation, bodhicitta, faith, and ethical conduct are among the many qualities needed to attain awakening, but the realization of the three doors of liberation are the incomparable cause for awakening because they cut the root of saṃsāra completely.

The three doors of liberation are also explained in the Pāli tradition. The liberations are ārya paths that realize nirvāṇa—the signless, wishless, and empty doors of liberation. These three are one nature but are differentiated depending on the aspect of nirvāṇa they focus on. Signlessness sees nirvāṇa as being free from the signs of conditioned phenomena. Wishlessness sees nirvāṇa as completely devoid of clinging and desire. The emptiness door of liberation sees nirvāṇa as empty of a self or any kind of substantial identity.

Because there are three liberations, there are three doors of liberation (*vimokṣamukha*, *vimokkhamukha*) through which one leaves the world and enters liberation. These three doors correspond to insight into the three characteristics. Insight into impermanence is the door to the signless liberation because it removes all signs of conditioned phenomena—specifically the aggregates—so that the undeclining, undisintegrating nature of nirvāṇa can shine forth. By knowing impermanence, we know all conditioned things to be limited and circumscribed by their arising and ceasing. They do not exist before they arise, and they do not go beyond disintegrating. The signless element is nirvāṇa in which all signs of conditioned things—such as their arising and ceasing—are absent.

Insight into duḥkha is the door to wishless liberation, since directly knowing the unsatisfactory nature of conditioned phenomena stops any wish or desire for them. Contemplation of duḥkha leads to a sense of urgency to be free from conditioned things and the mind enters into nirvāṇa viewed as the wishless element. The wishless element is nirvāṇa because in nirvāṇa there is no desire, greed, or clinging that wishes for conditioned existence.

Insight into selflessness is the door to empty liberation, since it reveals that no conditioned phenomenon has a substantial identity and therefore it is unreasonable to think nirvāṇa, the unconditioned, is encumbered by a solid identity. Contemplating that conditioned things are not I or mine leads to seeing them as foreign, and the mind enters into nirvāṇa viewed as the empty element, which derives its name because it is empty of self.

In all three cases, the correct understanding of the conditioned cuts through mental fabrications to reveal the unconditioned, nirvāṇa. Thus the way to realize the unconditioned is through understanding the conditioned correctly—as impermanent, duḥkha, and not self. Nirvāṇa is not some isolated, absolute entity; rather it is realized by seeing with wisdom conditioned phenomena as they really are.

## *Nāgārjuna's Homage*

Like the three doors of liberation, Nāgārjuna's homage to the Buddha in *Treatise on the Middle Way* explores the emptiness of causes and their effects:

> I prostrate to the perfect Buddha,
> the best of all teachers,
> who taught that that which is dependent arising
> is without ceasing, without arising,
> without discontinuation, without permanence,
> without coming, without going,
> without difference, without identity,
> and peaceful—free from [conceptual] fabrication.

Here Nāgārjuna identifies emptiness as the absence of eight characteristics of conditioned things: ceasing, arising, discontinuation, permanence, coming, going, difference, and identity. These eight absences are not qualities of an absolute or permanent entity that neither arises from causes nor produces effects. Rather, they pertain to the very things that conventionally have causes and effects, that come and go, that are the same (identical) or different, and so on. Conditioned phenomena and their eight characteristics all exist conventionally, but ultimately cannot be found by analytical wisdom.

In what sense do things arise? How can we understand causation? In his text, Nāgārjuna explains that on the conventional level, when we say something arises from something else—for example, peach trees arise from peach seeds—we do so in the context of everyday convention. We do not examine whether the peach tree arises from a cause that is identical to itself, a cause that is inherently distinct, both, or causelessly. We simply observe a peach tree growing from a peach seed and say, "This thing arises from that thing."

But when we move beyond the limits of conventional truths and search for some kind of inherent, objective arising or production of the peach tree, we have to consider what kind of cause could produce an inherently existent peach tree. Such a cause has to be either identical to its effect or completely distinct and unrelated to it. The non-Buddhist Sāṃkhyas assert the former, saying the result is already in the cause at the time the cause exists. Buddhists refute this, saying that if the result is present in the cause while the cause exists, then a fully formed adult elephant would exist in the womb in a mother elephant, and a peach tree with leaves and branches would exist in a peach seed. The alternative is that an effect arises from a cause that is completely unrelated to it. In that case, the adult elephant would have no relationship at all to the embryo in the mother elephant and a peach tree would be totally unrelated to the seed from which it grew.

On the conventional everyday level, there is no problem with talking about causes and effects being different. We know the elephant embryo and the adult elephant are not the same thing but are causally related to each other. But when we search with ultimate analysis, asking "How exactly does an effect arise from a cause? At what specific moment does the cause become the effect?" the process of production becomes amorphous.

Nāgārjuna presents two arguments to refute that an effect arises from a cause that is inherently different and other than it. The first points out that the very idea of "other" presupposes something that has its own unique, inherent nature that is unlike anything else. But if something does not possess its own self-nature—if it is not an inherently existent thing—then how can we posit something that is different from it? If something is not inherently real, how can we posit something that is inherently other than it? This is one way in which the notion of an objectively real difference between self and other is undermined.[46]

Nāgārjuna's second argument states that the very idea of arising becomes untenable if we assert that cause and effect are inherently different or inherently other. A cause precedes its effect, and the effect follows its cause. But when we look at the activity of something arising, we see that two processes are occurring simultaneously: the ceasing of the cause and the arising of the effect. When the effect is arising the cause is ceasing; when the cause is ceasing the effect is arising.

The cessation of the cause is an activity of the cause, and the arising of the effect is an activity of the effect. While the seed is ceasing, the sprout is arising. If these two simultaneous activities existed inherently, the two agents that are doing these two activities—the seed and the sprout—should also exist at the same time. But this is impossible because the seed must cease for the sprout to arise. Such faults appear if we assert inherently existent causes and effects. Through these two arguments, Nāgārjuna undermines any notion of something arising from another thing that is a totally unrelated other.

Commenting on Nāgārjuna's homage, Candrakīrti says that these eight attributes of dependent phenomena are negated from the perspective of unpolluted wisdom—the āryas' wisdom of meditative equipoise that directly and nonconceptually realizes emptiness. This wisdom is free of subject-object duality and free of conceptual fabrications. The only content or object of that wisdom is the emptiness of inherent existence; veiled truths do not appear to this nonconceptual wisdom. For that reason, Candrakīrti says that the negation of the eight characteristics of dependent phenomena has to be understood from the perspective of emptiness, not on the conventional level. While conventionally things arise and cease, are identical or different, come and go, these activities do not exist on the ultimate level, nor do the agents of these activities exist in the perspective of the wisdom realizing the ultimate nature.

Understanding this is important. Dzogchen contains the practice of searching for the nature of mind—what the mind is, where it comes from, what its shape and color are, and so on. This is a skillful way to lead beginning meditators to approach understanding the nature of mind, for they come to understand that the mind has no form, no shape, no color; it cannot be touched or smelled or tasted. These meditators have not realized the ultimate nature of the mind, which is the absence of inherent existence; they have only realized the mind's lack of conventional qualities such as color and shape. We have to clearly distinguish the conventional and ultimate natures of the mind and understand that realizing the ultimate nature of the mind involves negating its (fabricated) inherent existence, not its form or location.

## REFLECTION

1. What are the three doors of liberation? How are they similar? How are they different?
2. What was the Buddha's purpose in teaching them?
3. What are Nāgārjuna's two arguments refuting inherently existent causes and effects?

# 6 Cognizing Subjects and Cognized Objects

As mentioned before, a direct perceiver of emptiness has the power to cleanse our mind from all defilements. Generating this kind of wisdom mind involves gaining the correct understanding of the meditation object—in this case emptiness—as well as the types of minds that can perceive it, be they conceptual consciousnesses or direct perceivers. These are the topics of the present chapter.

## *The Steps to Understand Emptiness*

Practitioners gradually pass through several stages of knowledge while progressing from ignorance to the correct realization of emptiness. We begin with wrong awareness, progress to doubt inclined to the right understanding, followed by correct assumption, then inference, and finally a direct perceiver of emptiness.

We ordinary people have a wrong awareness that grasps both persons and other phenomena to exist inherently; this is the opposite of how they actually exist. This erroneous mind doesn't disappear by itself; the first step to removing it is to listen to correct teachings on emptiness. Contemplating these teachings arouses doubt. Doubt inclined to the wrong conclusion rejects emptiness, but if we continue to study and reflect on emptiness, it will gradually give way to doubt that thinks phenomena may or may not be empty. After more study and reflection, doubt inclined to the right conclusion thinks, "I'm not sure, but phenomena lacking inherent existence makes sense." Continuing to learn and discuss, you reach a correct assumption that phenomena lack inherent existence. Although you are now going in the right direction, your understanding is shallow, and the reasoning proving emptiness is not adequately clear to your mind. You know the words to explain emptiness and intellectually you may believe that all phenomena are empty of inherent existence because they are dependent arising, but it doesn't impact your mind very much.

The step of correct assumption may last a long time, as you must continue to learn, question, and analyze in order to refine your understanding of emptiness. After some time you will gain the correct understanding of emptiness and have a correct inference, which irrefutably knows through valid reasoning that all persons and phenomena lack inherent existence. Inference is a conceptual consciousness that realizes emptiness by means of a conceptual appearance of emptiness. This realization, which may occur before or after entering a path, has a powerful effect on the mind; it shakes how you view the world because you understand that the world and the sentient beings in it don't exist the way they appear to.

Practitioners who have not already developed concentration at the level of serenity now put effort into that. When cultivating serenity, their object of concentration can be any of the objects explained in the scriptures.[47] After gaining serenity, they continue to meditate, alternating analytic and stabilizing meditation on emptiness. As time goes on, emptiness becomes more and more familiar to their minds, to the point where, by engaging in minimal analysis, the analysis itself leads to pliancy and serenity. They then meditate on emptiness with a mind that is the union of serenity and insight; this marks the beginning of the path of preparation. Through continual meditation, emptiness becomes clearer until eventually the conceptual appearance is worn away and they directly and nonconceptually perceive emptiness. At this point, they enter the third path, the path of seeing. Though a conceptual consciousness and a direct perceiver are very different, the former can lead to the latter, since in this case they are both mental consciousnesses and have the same apprehended object, emptiness.

Now the process of eliminating the afflictions begins, starting with the acquired afflictions, which are eliminated at the beginning of the path of seeing. Through familiarization with the view of emptiness on the fourth path, the path of meditation, the innate afflictions are eradicated. Those following the paths of śrāvakas and solitary realizers reach the fifth path, the path of no-more-learning of their vehicles, when all afflictive obscurations have been uprooted. Those following the bodhisattva path abandon all afflictive obscurations at the eighth bodhisattva ground on the Mahāyāna path of meditation. They attain the Mahāyāna path of no-more-learning, buddhahood, when the cognitive obscurations have been completely overcome.[48]

*Realization of emptiness* can refer to a range of mental states, from a correct inference to a nonconceptual direct perceiver. Both of these mental consciousnesses are reliable cognizers that know emptiness correctly. Realization does not occur suddenly in a flash to a completely unprepared person. The rare practitioners who experience sudden awakening have done considerable practice in many previous lives and left strong imprints on their mindstreams for understanding emptiness. When these imprints ripen in this life, it may appear that their realization is "sudden," but in fact it was cultivated gradually over many lifetimes.

*Awakening* has different meanings according to various Buddhist traditions. Zen masters explained to me that in their tradition, awakening includes the first glimpse of emptiness, which is a conceptual realization. Awakening is neither a final attainment nor a stable realization, and when the person arises from meditation on emptiness, dualistic appearances and afflictions appear again. A long time may pass before having another glimpse of emptiness. Only when their realization of emptiness is stable, direct, and nonconceptual do they begin the process of removing afflictions from the root.

In the Theravāda tradition, awakening has four stages: stream-enterer, once-returner, nonreturner, and arhatship. A practitioner becomes a stream-enterer upon having the direct perceiver of nirvāṇa.[49] This introductory realization is deepened and integrated into their minds during the stages of once-returner and nonreturner and finally becomes the stable and profound realization of an arhat.[50]

In the Tibetan tradition, gaining the realization of emptiness does not mean one is awakened. "Awakening" refers to having attained the path of no-more-learning of whichever vehicle one follows. Although texts speak of the awakening of a śrāvaka or solitary-realizer arhat, in the Sanskrit tradition, in general "awakening" refers to buddhahood.

## REFLECTION

1. Contemplate the steps to realize emptiness with a direct perceiver, beginning with a wrong view, progressing to doubt and then correct assumption, followed by inference and finally direct perceiver.
2. What changes occur from one step to the next?
3. What does it mean to realize emptiness? What minds do that?
4. What are the various meanings of "awakening"?

---

## *The Process of Cognition*

In any process of cognition, there is the subject—the consciousness that apprehends—and the object—what is apprehended. When examining how things exist, identifying the varieties of subjects and objects and differentiating the accurate from the mistaken is crucial. Some background regarding Buddhist ideas of cognition will be helpful to do this. In addition to the following sections, we recommend reviewing chapters 2 and 3 in *The Foundation of Buddhist Practice*, the second volume of the *Library of Wisdom and Compassion*.

### *Subjects—Consciousnesses Knowing an Object*

Among subjects—the minds that know or experience an object—there are nonconceptual consciousnesses (*nirvikalpaka*) and conceptual consciousnesses (*kalpanā*). Nonconceptual consciousnesses know their objects without the medium of a conceptual appearance (generic image, *artha-sāmānya*), while conceptual consciousnesses know their objects by means of a conceptual appearance.[51] In general, direct perceivers are knowers that are free from conceptuality (*kalpanā-apoḍha*) and nonmistaken (*abhrānta*). There are three kinds of direct perceivers that are nonconceptual consciousnesses: (1) Sense direct perceivers (visual, auditory, olfactory, gustatory, tactile, and mental direct perceivers). These are, for example, the visual consciousness apprehending yellow and the auditory consciousness apprehending a melodious sound. (2) Mental direct perceivers—for example, clairvoyance and clairaudience. (3) Yogic direct perceivers—mental consciousnesses, developed through meditation, that directly know more subtle phenomena, such as impermanence and emptiness. This is the Sautrāntika view; Prāsaṅgikas gloss "direct" as meaning not dependent on a reason, and so consider the second moment onward of inferences to be direct perceivers even though they are conceptual.

Conceptual consciousnesses are mental consciousnesses that know their object indirectly, by means of a conceptual appearance. These consciousnesses think, imagine, plan, remember, visualize, impute, designate, learn ideas and concepts, and so forth. Often, for a conceptual appearance to arise, first a sense consciousness perceives raw sense data directly. A conceptual consciousness gives a name to that object, and the name and concept are mixed with what we see. The appearing object to the conceptual consciousnesses is a conceptual appearance of that thing, not the actual object. It may be a visual image when we remember something we saw, or it may be an image of a sound, tactile sensation, feeling, abstract object, and so forth.

One conceptual consciousness may give rise to another one. When planning where to put a table in a room, we imagine it being against the wall, in the middle of the room, turned this way or that. Each one is a new conceptual appearance known by a new moment of consciousness.

For example, a visual direct perceiver directly sees the blue color of the sky. Later when we remember the sky's color, we do not see it directly. Instead a conceptual appearance of blue appears to our mental consciousness. This conceptual appearance is not the actual blue color, yet it appears to be the same as the blue color. For this reason, conceptual consciousnesses are considered mistaken, even though they may understand their object properly. The conceptual appearance is only an approximation of the blue we saw, a mixture of each moment of the shades of blue we saw in the sky that forms a conglomerate general image of the blue sky.

Imagining an apple is very different than actually tasting one. A conceptual consciousness does not perceive the distinct qualities of a particular apple; rather an abstract aspect of an apple that seems to be an apple appears to our mind. When we eat an apple, we directly perceive its color, shape, smell, taste, and tactile qualities by means of our sense direct perceivers.

All the qualities of a flower do not appear simultaneously to a conceptual consciousness in the same way they do to a direct perceiver. While the color, shape, impermanence, and so forth of a flower appear simultaneously to a visual direct perceiver, a conceptual consciousness must think about each of these traits one by one. Conception knows the qualities of the flower individually and indirectly; it does not perceive the flower and its attributes as clearly as a direct perceiver does.

Both sense consciousnesses and conceptual consciousnesses (thoughts) may be either erroneous (*viparyāsa*) or nonerroneous (*aviparīta*). A visual consciousness correctly seeing the color of a flower in a garden and an inferential cognizer of emptiness are nonerroneous. Seeing flowers in the sky under the influence of drugs and asserting a permanent, unified, and independent soul are erroneous. A reliable visual consciousness and an inferential understanding of not-self discounts these.

Although direct perceivers know their objects more vividly than conceptual consciousnesses, both types of consciousness have their roles. Many of the advances human beings have made are due to our ability to think and reason, which involve conceptuality. Learning the Dharma involves conceptual consciousnesses; auditory direct perceivers hear the sound of words, but conceptual consciousnesses attribute meaning to them, enabling us to discuss and exchange ideas. Before attaining a yogic direct perceiver of emptiness, it is necessary to hear or read teachings, study, think about, and discuss or debate our understanding of emptiness. These activities all involve conceptual consciousnesses. Only by meditating over time with a correct conceptual understanding of emptiness will we be able to diminish the conceptual appearance of emptiness and perceive emptiness directly. To make this point, the *Kāśyapa Chapter Sūtra* gives the analogy of a fire created by two sticks rubbed together that in turn burns the sticks:[52]

> Once the fire has arisen, the two sticks are burned. Just so, Kāśyapa, if you have the correct analytical intellect, an ārya's faculty of wisdom is generated. Through its generation, the correct analytical intellect is consumed.

If the stick of correct thought rubs against the stick of wrong thought, the fire of wisdom will arise and consume both thoughts. The stick of correct thought is needed to start the fire, but once the fire begins, it is no longer needed and is destroyed. Although thought is initially necessary to learn the correct view of reality, the union of serenity and insight that directly perceives emptiness goes beyond thought.

## REFLECTION

1. What is a conceptual appearance?
2. What is the difference between how a conceptual consciousness knows an object and how a direct perceiver knows it?
3. Consider your day. Make examples of direct perceivers and conceptual consciousnesses knowing objects.

---

### *Objects—Phenomena Known by a Consciousness*

One perception or conceptual consciousness has different types of objects. Knowing these enables us to better understand the process of cognition and is essential for comprehending the relationship between emptiness and dependent arising. Among the various types of objects are appearing objects, observed objects, apprehended objects, and conceived objects. The presentation below is according to the Sautrāntika system; Prāsaṅgikas agree with it unless otherwise noted.

The **appearing object** (*pratibhāsa-viṣaya*) is the object that appears to that consciousness. The appearing objects of sense direct perceivers include color, shape, sound, smell, taste, texture, temperature, and so forth.

The appearing object to a conceptual consciousness is a conceptual appearance of the object. Conceptual appearances are considered permanent phenomenon. A conceptual consciousness is mistaken with respect to its appearing object because the conceptual appearance of a table appears to be a table, although it is not. For this reason, thought consciousnesses, which are always conceptual, are mistaken with respect to their appearing object because they mistake a conceptual appearance of the object for the actual object.

The **observed object** (*ālambana*) is the basic object that the mind refers to or focuses on while apprehending certain aspects of it. It is equivalent to the focal object (*viṣaya*).[53]

The **apprehended object** (object of the mode of apprehension, *muṣṭibandhaviṣaya*) of a consciousness is equivalent to its **engaged object** (*pravṛtti-viṣaya*) and its **object of comprehension** (*prameya*). This is the main object with which the mind is concerned, the object that the mind is getting at. This is the object that is apprehended. For direct perceivers, the appearing object and the apprehended object are the same. For a conceptual consciousness thinking about a table, the appearing object is a conceptual appearance of a table, and the apprehended object is a table. This mind is mistaken with respect to its appearing object because it knows the object via a conceptual appearance, but is not erroneous with respect to its apprehended object. According to the Prāsaṅgikas, an ignorant mind grasping the table as truly existent is erroneous with respect to both its appearing and its apprehended object because the table is not inherently existent. Although a casual visual consciousness seeing the table is not erroneous with respect to its apprehended object, the table, it is mistaken with respect to that object because it appears truly existent.

The **conceived object** (*adhyavasāya-viṣaya*) is the principal object of a conceptual consciousness. The appearing object of a conceptual consciousness thinking about a flower is the conceptual appearance of a flower; its conceived object is the same as its apprehended object—a flower.

Let's apply these different types of objects to a common situation. Jane and her friends go out to an Italian restaurant and order lasagna. Although we may think of eating as a single experience, actually a lot is going on. When the plates of lasagna are served to them, they see the red of the sauce, the white of the noodles, and the green of the salad with their visual consciousness. These are the observed objects of their visual consciousness. The smell of the lasagna is the observed object of their olfactory consciousness. The various tastes are the observed objects of their gustatory consciousness and the smoothness of the noodles is the observed object of their tactile consciousness. The consciousnesses directly perceiving these attributes are reliable sense direct perceivers, and their apprehended objects are the same as their observed objects—the color and shape for the visual consciousness, the taste for the gustatory consciousness, and so on.

A week later Jane and her friends return to the same restaurant. While looking at the menu and thinking about what to order, they remember the lasagna they ate the previous week. The color and shape, taste, and so on of the lasagna are known through conceptual consciousnesses. The appearing object of the taste is a conceptual appearance of the taste that appears to the mental consciousness knowing the taste of the lasagna. The apprehended object is the taste of the lasagna, and because this is a conceptual consciousness, its conceived object is also the taste of the lasagna.

It may happen that some exaggeration slips in. If Jane is very hungry, when she remembers the qualities of the lasagna from last week, the mental factor of distorted attention exaggerates its delicious taste, appealing smell, and colorful appearance. As a result of this exaggeration, attachment arises. Attachment is a conceptual consciousness; it is erroneous because the lasagna appears to be really fantastic, although it is not.

Not everything that appears to a sense consciousness is its appearing object. When a visual consciousness sees a table, the subtle impermanence of the table—its quality of changing moment by moment—also appears to that consciousness, but since impermanence is a subtle object, the visual consciousness cannot apprehend it. Thus subtle impermanence appears to that visual consciousness, but it is not its appearing object; the table is. If the person later thinks about subtle impermanence and correctly infers its existence, their mental consciousness apprehends it via a conceptual appearance; the conceptual appearance of subtle impermanence is the appearing object of that thought, and subtle impermanence is its apprehended object. If, through meditation, they remove the veil of the conceptual appearance, they will know subtle impermanence with a yogic direct perceiver. At that time subtle impermanence is both the appearing and apprehended objects of that consciousness. For view of the personal identity, according to the Prāsaṅgikas the observed object is the I and mine in your own continuum, and the apprehended object is an inherently existent I and mine.

## REFLECTION

1. What is a conceptual appearance?
2. As you go about your day, be aware when you are directly perceiving an object and when you are thinking about it.
3. What is the difference in your experience between knowing an object

with a direct perceiver and knowing it with a conceptual consciousness by means of a conceptual appearance?

4. Does your mind go from a direct perceiver to a conceptual consciousness of the object quickly? Do you sometimes think you're directly perceiving an object when you're actually thinking about it?

5. What are the benefits and disadvantages of a direct perceiver? What are the benefits and disadvantages of a conceptual consciousness?

---

Of our many conceptual consciousnesses during the day, some are useful and some aren't. The conceptual mind involved in reading this book enables you to learn ideas that will lead you to deeper understanding and wisdom. But the mind ruminating about a problem or judging other people's seeming faults easily turns the mind to nonvirtue. On these occasions, observe that although the object is not actually present, the conceptual mind has been so drawn into it that attachment, anger, or another destructive emotion easily arises. This accounts for many of our distractions during meditation.

These terms and distinctions among subjects and objects may initially seem confusing, but becoming familiar with them will clarify your understanding of the object of negation in the meditation on emptiness. The following chart encapsulates some of the key elements regarding objects according to the Sautrāntika system, which accepts inherent existence.

### Consciousnesses and Their Objects

| CONSCIOUSNESS | OBSERVED OBJECT | APPEARING OBJECT | APPREHENDED OBJECT | CONCEIVED OBJECT |
|---|---|---|---|---|
| Visual consciousness perceiving blue | Blue | Blue | Blue | — |
| Memory or thought of blue * | Blue | Conceptual appearance of blue | Blue | Blue |
| Thought of a permanent self (wrong conceptual consciousness of a nonexistent) * ^ | Self | Conceptual appearance of a permanent self | Permanent self | Permanent self |

| | | | | |
|---|---|---|---|---|
| Visual consciousness perceiving moving scenery when riding in a vehicle (wrong consciousness) ^ | Scenery | Moving scenery | Moving scenery | — |
| Conception of a rabbit's horn (wrong consciousness) * ^ | Rabbit's ear | Conceptual appearance of a rabbit's horn | Rabbit's horn | Rabbit's horn |
| Thought apprehending truly existent aggregates (wrong consciousness)* ^ | Aggregates | Conceptual appearance of truly existent aggregates | Truly existent aggregates | Truly existent aggregates |
| Visual consciousness of an adult apprehending the reflection of a face in a mirror | Reflection of a face | Face | Reflection of a face | — |
| Conceptual mental consciousness knowing the reflection of the face in the mirror as a face is false * | Reflection of a face | Conceptual appearance of a reflection of a face | Nonexistence of a real face in the mirror | Nonexistence of a real face in the mirror |

* Thought consciousnesses are mistaken with respect to their appearing object because they confuse the actual object with the conceptual appearance of it.

^ Wrong consciousnesses are erroneous with respect to their apprehended object because they do not apprehend or know it correctly.

## REFLECTION

Identifying the objects of the various types of consciousness you have during the day helps you determine the type of minds that know an object and thus to assess if those cognizers are accurate.

1. When gazing at a garden and enjoying the colors of the flowers, what is the appearing object to your visual consciousness? What is the apprehended object?
2. Close your eyes and think about the flowers. Be aware that a conceptual

appearance of the flowers appears to your mind, not the actual flowers. How does that differ experientially from seeing the flowers directly?

3. When you find yourself becoming irritated, stop and investigate, "What is the appearing object? What is the apprehended object?" If you're remembering an incident in the past, be aware of how anger arises even though the incident is not happening now.

4. Look at one of the dishes on your lunch plate. Close your eyes and imagine its taste.

5. Taste that food. Is the conceptual appearance of the taste to your conceptual consciousness the same as the actual taste? Was it better or worse?

---

Applying these teachings to your daily life can be fun and will enhance your understanding of your outer and inner environment. It brings the teachings home and enables you to understand them through your personal experience.

Let's now bring inherent existence into the discussion and speak from the viewpoint of the Prāsaṅgika system. The objects of consciousness are basically the same, but whether they are considered mistaken or erroneous differs.

In the Prāsaṅgika system, all phenomena mistakenly appear to be inherently existent to all sense and mental consciousnesses of sentient beings, except for an ārya's meditative equipoise on emptiness. The appearance of an inherently existent table, inherently existent taste, inherently existent sound, and so forth to the five sense consciousnesses is false, and those consciousnesses are mistaken with respect to their appearing objects because these things appear inherently existent although they are not. From the viewpoint of the Svātantrikas and below, the appearance of inherent existence is an accurate appearance. For them those sense consciousnesses are not mistaken with respect to either their appearing object or their apprehended object because inherently existent objects exist.[54]

Prāsaṅgikas say a visual consciousness apprehending yellow is mistaken with respect to its appearing object because the yellow *appears* to exist inherently although it does not exist in that way. Nevertheless, this visual consciousness realizes its apprehended object, yellow, and is a direct reliable cognizer of yellow. Regarding conceptual mental consciousnesses, there are those that do not grasp inherent existence and those that do. In the case of the former, the appearing object is the conceptual appearance of inherently existent yellow to a consciousness remembering the yellow you saw yesterday. The apprehended object and conceived object are yellow. That mind is mistaken in two ways: first, it conflates the conceptual appearance of yellow with the color yellow; second, yellow appears inherently existent although it is not. However, that consciousness is not erroneous because it knows yellow and can differentiate it from blue, red, and other colors.

But let's say you saw the perfect color yellow to paint your house and start thinking with attachment about how beautiful your house will be and how much your neighbors will admire it. This conceptual mind grasps that yellow color as inherently existent. It is mistaken with respect to its appearing object because it's a conceptual consciousness and because its object appears inherently existent. It's also erroneous with respect to its apprehended object because it grasps inherently existent yellow although inherently existent yellow does not exist. Similarly, a mind grasping the I as inherently existent is mistaken with respect to its appearing object because the I appears to exist inherently although it does not, and it is an erroneous consciousness because an inherently existent I does not exist at all. This means that attachment, anger, jealousy, arrogance, and so on—which all depend on grasping inherent existence—are erroneous consciousnesses.

Although all minds have apprehended objects, their apprehended objects do not necessarily exist—for example, a permanent self apprehended by the mental consciousness grasping the self as permanent. When we pull the corner of our eye while looking at the moon, a double moon is both the appearing object and the apprehended object of that visual consciousness, even though a double moon does not exist.[55]

Let's look again at Jane's lasagna dinner. While she was eating, the appearing object, observed object, and apprehended object of her visual, olfactory, gustatory, and tactile consciousnesses were the color and shape, smell, taste, smooth texture, and warmth of the lasagna. However, these appear to exist inherently, and thus these sense consciousnesses are mistaken. Jane may or may not grasp these objects as inherently existent. If she doesn't, her mental consciousness is still mistaken because the taste and so forth appear to exist inherently, but that conceptual consciousness is not erroneous because it doesn't hold them as inherently existent. But if Jane is very attached to delicious lasagna and starts planning how she can take some extra orders of lasagna home, then her mental consciousness is erroneous because attachment is based on self-grasping ignorance. In addition, since attachment is based on distorted attention that exaggerates or projects unfounded good qualities on an object, that mind is also erroneous. Note the difference between appearing inherently existent and being grasped as inherently existent. Also note that sense consciousnesses do not grasp inherent existence although inherent existence appears to them. Only the mental consciousnesses grasp inherent existence.

### Consciousnesses and Objects according to the Prāsaṅgikas

| CONSCIOUSNESS | OBSERVED OBJECT | APPEARING OBJECT | APPREHENDED OBJECT | CONCEIVED OBJECT |
|---|---|---|---|---|
| Visual consciousness perceiving truly existent blue | Blue | Truly existent blue * | Blue | — |
| View of a personal identity | I and mine in one's own continuum | Conceptual appearance of truly existent I and mine * | Truly existent I and mine in one's own continuum ^ | Truly existent I and mine in one's own continuum ^ |
| Wisdom directly realizing emptiness of a truly existent I and mine | I and mine in one's own continuum[56] | Emptiness of true existence | Emptiness of true existence | — |
| Wisdom conceptually realizing the emptiness of a truly existent I and mine in one's own continuum | I and mine in one's own continuum | Conceptual appearance of the emptiness of a truly existent I and mine * | Emptiness of I and mine in one's own continuum | Emptiness of I and mine in one's own continuum |

* These consciousnesses are mistaken.

^These consciousnesses are erroneous with respect to their apprehended objects.

### REFLECTION

1. When there is not a strong emotion in your mind and you think "I'm reading this book," what kind of consciousness is that? What are its appearing and apprehended objects? Are either of them mistaken or erroneous?
2. When you feel guilty or angry at yourself, is that a direct perceiver or a conceptual consciousness?
3. Do you appear truly existent at that time?
4. Do you grasp a truly existent I that is bad because you made a mistake?
5. Is that an accurate or erroneous mental state?

## *Syllogisms and Consequences*

Reasonings—especially syllogisms and consequences—are important when delving into the meaning of emptiness. Please refer to chapter 2 of *The Foundation of Buddhist Practice* to review the parts of a syllogism and the three criteria necessary to prove the thesis. A person who is receptive and understands the three criteria will understand the thesis because they know (1) the reason applies to the subject, (2) the pervasion (whatever is the reason must be the predicate), and (3) the counterpervasion (whatever is not the predicate must not be the reason).

In the syllogism, "Consider the subject, the I; it is empty of true existence because it is a dependent arising, like a mirage," the thesis that is understood is that the I is empty of true existence. To understand this, we must establish the three criteria in our mind. The world contains many people who know that things arise dependent on causes and conditions. All of us know that flowers grow from seeds, but we still hold flowers to be truly existent. To disprove true existence by the above syllogism, we must first clarify the meaning of dependent arising, specifically understanding causal dependence—how the I depends on causes and conditions that have the ability to produce it. The I also depends on parts: the body and mind of the person. This establishes the first criterion, the presence of the reason in the subject of the syllogism—the person is a dependent arising.

Then we clarify the meaning of the predicate—empty of true existence. What constitutes true existence? What would it look like if the self were truly existent? After that, we check the pervasion: Is whatever arises dependently necessarily empty of true existence? With analysis, we discover that yes, if something arises dependently, it necessarily lacks true existence.

To test the counterpervasion, we examine if whatever is the opposite of the predicate is necessarily the opposite of the reason—that is, is whatever is not empty necessarily not a dependent arising? Here, too, the response is yes, if something is not empty of true existence, it cannot arise dependently. Now we can draw the conclusion that the self is indeed empty of true existence because of being a dependent arising.

This brief description may sound intellectual and dry, but when we are aware of how things appear to us and how we grasp them as truly existent, these reasonings challenge our deeply held assumptions and beliefs as well as our ordinary cognitions. We must go slowly, preparing ourselves properly by being aware of how things appear to us and how we apprehend them. We must also understand the various terms, their meanings, and their relationships in order to investigate if a syllogism is correct.

Sometimes a person holds a wrong view very strongly, and their confidence in this view needs to be dislodged before they can generate a correct understanding. This is done by presenting the person with a consequence—a statement in which his beliefs contradict each other. Consequences operate as a *reductio ad absurdum* by showing internal inconsistencies in the other's view. For example, the ancient brahmins strongly believed the sound of the Vedas was permanent. To show them the fallacy of this belief, we present the consequence, "Sound is not a product of causes because it is permanent." This person already knows that sound is a product of causes, and now he is faced with the fact that it can't be if it is permanent. This makes him reflect if sound is indeed permanent or not.

The Svātantrikas and below not only assert that the self is inherently existent but also support that belief by giving the reason that it is a dependent arising. To them, dependent arising indicates inherent existence, and they assert that if phenomena didn't exist inherently, they wouldn't exist at all. To cause them to doubt their adherence to inherent existence, Prāsaṅgikas may present them with the consequence, "The self is not a dependent arising because it exists inherently." Because these Buddhists believe that the self is a dependent arising, they feel uncomfortable saying that it cannot be dependent because it exists inherently. That makes them examine their belief that the I inherently exists.

Prāsaṅgikas say that the dissonance provoked by this consequence will cause those who are receptive yet still adhere to inherent existence to understand that the I is empty without having to state the syllogism: Consider the self; it is empty of inherent existence because it arises dependently. Seeing the undesirable consequence of their previous view, someone who already has some doubt about that view will abandon it and gain a right understanding. However, when a person strongly holds a wrong view, a consequence followed by a syllogism is necessary to help him gain the right understanding. The consequence is used to disprove the wrong view, and the syllogism is used to establish the correct one.

To be receptive to a consequence, someone must have certain qualifications. Although she has a wrong view, she is open-minded and willing to investigate that view. A person who accepts that a sprout inherently exists, but understands the two pervasions that whatever arises dependently is empty of inherent existence and whatever is not empty of inherent existence does not arise dependently, is on their way to a correct understanding. When hearing the consequence—the sprout is not a dependent arising because it inherently exists—she will feel uncomfortable asserting inherent existence because she knows the sprout is a dependent arising.

A person who is completely closed-minded is not receptive, and presenting them with a consequence will bring either resistance or a blank look. Likewise a person who is cynical or stubborn and has no wish to think deeply or reconsider his opinions is not receptive. Consequences and syllogisms do not move the minds of such people, so it is better not to waste time debating with them.

Sages advocate that we begin to contemplate emptiness by examining the nature of things that are commonly known as deceptive in the world, such as mirages, dreams, reflections, hallucinations, and holograms, because it is easier to see that they don't exist as they appear. We can later apply this to other phenomena where understanding the discrepancy between how something exists and how it appears is more difficult.

A mirage appears to be water, but it is not; its appearance is false. This appearance arises depending on sand, sunshine, the angle at which it strikes the sand, our distance from the sand, and so forth. Understanding that the silvery sparkle on the sand falsely appears to be water is not an understanding of the mirage's lack of inherent existence, although it is a step in that direction.

From there, we move to the syllogism: Consider a person; he does not inherently exist because he arises dependently, like a mirage. Contemplating that the water in the mirage is a false appearance helps to understand the thesis of the syllogism, that the person does not inherently exist.

# 7 The Importance of Realizing Emptiness

## *Who Am I?*

The Buddha counseled us to recognize true duḥkha, abandon true origins of duḥkha, actualize true cessations, and cultivate true paths. Because this is done by a person, the self, questions relating to the existence and nature of the self become important. The self is the agent who experiences suffering and happiness, engages in constructive and destructive actions, practices the path, and attains nirvāṇa. What is the nature of this being—this self or I? This was an important issue for both Buddhist and non-Buddhist schools in ancient India and continues to be so today. Many philosophical systems have arisen on this topic.

When we examine the causal process of happiness and duḥkha, it is evident that these experiences arise in relation to multiple causes and conditions—both internal factors such as our sense faculties and our way of interpreting events, and external factors such as sense objects. What is the nature of these factors that give rise to our experiences of pain and pleasure? Do they actually exist? In what way do they exist? This, too, was the focus of major reflection in ancient India.

In our own experience, when we ask "What is this I?" we notice an innate, natural, instinctual sense of self. If our hand is hurt, we automatically say, "I am hurt." Although our hand is not us, we instinctively identify with that experience and feel "I am hurt." Here the sense of I arises in relation to our body.

The sense of I also arises in relation to the mind. When there is a grumpy mood, we say, "I am grumpy," and when delight is present, we exclaim, "I am delighted."

However, this I isn't completely identifiable with our body, because if we could exchange our old, wrinkled, sick body with a fresh, youthful, healthy body, we would do so. In the depth of our heart we feel that there is a self who would benefit from this exchange. Similarly, if we were given the opportunity to exchange our afflictive, ignorant mind with a buddha's fully awakened one, we would eagerly do this. This suggests that we do not completely identify with our mind either. This willingness to exchange our mind for another person's mind indicates a belief in the depth of our heart that there is a separate person, an I, who would benefit from this exchange. On one hand, the sense of I arises in relation to our body or our mind; on the other hand, we do not completely identify with either our body or mind.

In our naïve, ordinary sense, there is a feeling of self, of a being who is intricately involved with the body and mind and is the master who can control them. Yet the I feels independent of both the body and mind, with its own distinct identity. In the case of those who believe in rebirth, this sense of a separate self extends across lifetimes with an independent self taking birth in one life and then another. Even those who do not believe in multiple lives think the same person experiences childhood, adolescence, adulthood, and old age. Although the body and mind constantly change, we have the sense of an I that endures over time when we say, "I was young and now I'm old." We believe there is a person that holds the continuums of body and mind over time.

Because of the problematic identity of the self, many non-Buddhist schools posit a self or soul (*ātman*) that has an absolute status; it is unchanging, unitary, and autonomous. Buddhist schools in general reject the notion of such a self, soul, or eternal principle. They espouse that the self or person is dependent on its mental and physical aggregates, and only on the basis of the continuum of the physical and mental aggregates can we say that the person exists through time. When the body and mind become old, we say that the person becomes old. Aside from the body and mind, we cannot find an autonomous person that ages.

The Buddha was clear that the conception of a permanent, unified, and independent self is a metaphysical construct, an artificial conjecture that exists only in the minds of people who have intellectually thought about it. Our innate sense of self does not feel that we exist in this way. While unliberated sentient beings have an erroneous innate sense of a real self, this conception of self as unchanging, monolithic, and autonomous is not it.

In addition, our naïve sense of the self being a master over the body and mind is also false. The self does not exist as an independent controller or master of the aggregates. In this way, the Buddha rejected self-existence and embraced selflessness—"not-self," as translated by Pāli translators. Various tenet systems contain different assertions concerning the meaning of selflessness, the self that is negated, and the conventionally existent self that is born, dies, practices the path, and attains liberation.

The *Heart Sūtra*, a popular Mahāyāna sūtra, speaks of realizing the emptiness of *even* or *also* the five aggregates, depending on the translation. This indicates the wide range of phenomena that are empty. The five aggregates on which a person depends are empty of inherent existence. Since they are empty, so too is the person that depends on them. Since the I is empty of inherent existence, the mine is also empty of inherent existence. Just as the aggregates and the self are empty because they are designated in dependence on their parts, so too all other conditioned phenomena are also empty. Because all conditioned phenomena are empty, all unconditioned or uncompounded phenomena that are necessarily imputed in relation to conditioned things are also empty. Finally, even emptiness, the ultimate nature of all phenomena, is empty of inherent existence. Just as sentient beings in saṃsāra are empty of inherent existence, so too are buddhas who dwell in nonabiding nirvāṇa.

Does this mean nothing exists? Does this mean that when we sit in the hot sun, the person getting sunburned is nonexistent? Of course not! Although persons and other phenomena cannot be found when analyzed, someone who experiences and what is experienced still exist.

Understanding the nature of reality is challenging. How do we identify and refute what doesn't exist and still establish what does? In response, ancient Indian philosophical traditions developed various theories. Some accept the concept of an eternal soul or self; others assert a primordial substance out of which everything arises. Buddhists reject such notions. Meanwhile, some Buddhist schools accept the selflessness of persons and phenomena, although others do not accept a selflessness of phenomena. Among the Buddhists that accept the selflessness of both persons and phenomena, some accept true existence and others do not. Among those who reject true existence, some maintain some notion of inherent existence conventionally, whereas others reject inherent existence even conventionally. For this reason, there is a great deal of discussion about the nature of reality.

## *The Root of Saṃsāra*

In general, two types of ignorance exist: ignorance that does not understand karma and its effects, and ignorance that misunderstands the ultimate nature (self-grasping ignorance). Although both cause cyclic existence, the self-grasping ignorance is the *root* of cyclic existence. This ignorance is not just the lack of wisdom regarding the final nature; it is an active misconception of it. The way ignorance apprehends persons and phenomena is totally opposite to the way they exist; it apprehends the opposite of what the wisdom realizing the ultimate nature perceives. While ignorance grasps phenomena as inherently existent, wisdom perceives them to be empty of inherent existence. This ignorance is the first of the twelve links of dependent arising. In *Seventy Stanzas on Emptiness* (VV 64–65), Nāgārjuna explains:

> That which conceives things produced
> from causes and conditions to be real (inherently existent)
> was said by the Teacher (Buddha) to be ignorance.
> From it, the twelve links [of dependent origination] arise.
>
> Through knowing well that things are empty
> because of seeing reality, ignorance does not arise.
> That is the cessation of ignorance,
> whereby the twelve links cease.

Nāgārjuna asserts that the root of saṃsāra is the ignorance grasping inherent existence and the antidote that eliminates it is the direct realization of the emptiness of inherent existence. Because this ignorance is of two types—grasping a self of persons and grasping a self of phenomena—there are two types of selflessness: the selflessness of persons and the selflessness of phenomena. Here "person" refers to the beings of the six classes (gods, demigods, humans, animals, hungry ghosts, and hell beings), as well as to āryas, arhats, bodhisattvas, and buddhas. The person is the one who wanders in saṃsāra, cultivates the path, and attains liberation and awakening.

Meanwhile, Candrakīrti says the view of a personal identity (*satkāyadṛṣṭi*) is the root of saṃsāra (MMA 6.120):

> Seeing with his mind that all afflictions and defects
> arise from the view of a personal identity . . . .

Since Candrakīrti identifies the view of a personal identity as the root of saṃsāra and Nāgārjuna identifies the ignorance grasping true existence as the root, are there two roots? No, these two are not considered two separate roots of saṃsāra, for they apprehend their objects in the same erroneous way—as existing inherently, truly, or independently. The difference between them is that ignorance is the mistaken superimposition of a self of persons and phenomena, whereas the view of a personal identity superimposes inherent existence on our own I and mine, not on other people or phenomena.[57] Tsongkhapa says (FEW 56–57):

> The view of a personal identity is the root of all other afflictions. If it were something other than ignorance, there would be two discordant roots of saṃsāra; therefore, both [grasping the inherent existence of persons and of phenomena] should be taken as ignorance.

Ignorance must be eliminated in order to attain nirvāṇa. Only the wisdom directly realizing emptiness has the power to eradicate this ignorance because it refutes the existence of the object ignorance holds as true—inherent existence, existence from its own side, existence by its own characteristics, and so on. While loving-kindness, meditation on impermanence, and other meditations are useful in counteracting specific afflictions and are necessary to attain awakening, they cannot eradicate ignorance. Thus gaining the correct view of emptiness and realizing it nonconceptually is of crucial importance.

In the *Precious Garland*, Nāgārjuna explains that the self-grasping of phenomena—specifically the aggregates—is the cause of the self-grasping of persons (RA 35):

> As long as there is grasping at the aggregates,
> so long the grasping at I will exist.
> Further, when grasping at I exists,
> there is action, and from it there also is birth.

Based on grasping the body and mind as inherently existent, grasping the I that exists in dependence on them as inherently existent arises.[58] Thus the self-grasping of phenomena is the root of *all* afflictions. However, we cannot say the same about the view of a personal identity, for it is the effect, not the cause, of the self-grasping of phenomena. Nevertheless, both graspings must be eliminated to attain liberation.

Self-grasping of persons pertains to grasping both ourselves and others to be inherently existent. Grasping ourselves to exist inherently is the view of a personal identity (as I and mine). Sometimes "view of a personal identity" is translated as "view of the perishing aggregates." This translation undercuts two erroneous views. First, by saying the aggregates are perishing, it negates the idea of an unchanging soul and emphasizes that the person and aggregates are momentarily impermanent. Second, "aggregates" indicates plurality, which negates the notion that the person is one indivisible monolithic unit and affirms that the person depends on the collection of its physical and mental aggregates.

The view of a personal identity is an afflictive "wisdom": it is an ascertaining consciousness that misapprehends its object. According to the Prāsaṅgikas, the observed object of the view of a personal identity is the mere I, the conventionally existent person. The apprehended and conceived objects are a truly existent I, and this consciousness is erroneous with respect to them because it grasps a truly existent I, which does not exist at all, as existent.

Yogis begin by examining how the self exists. Could the self that they think and feel exists objectively, the self that is the object of self-grasping ignorance, exist? By investigating with reasoning how the self exists, they conclude that it cannot truly exist. The mind that erroneously grasps an objective self cannot be manifest at the same time as the wisdom that sees the nonexistence of an objective self, because those two minds are contradictory. Wisdom has the power to overcome ignorance because wisdom is a correct mind, whereas ignorance is erroneous. By repeated familiarization with the wisdom realizing the emptiness of an objective self, self-grasping, the afflictions that depend on it, and their seeds are gradually eliminated and saṃsāra is brought to an end.

## *How Ignorance Grasps Its Object*

Ignorance grasps persons and phenomena as inherently existent—that is, as existing from their own side, independent from all other factors. This view is erroneous because, in fact, everything exists dependent on other factors, including imputation by thought and name. The *Questions of Upāli Sūtra* (*Upālipariprcchā Sūtra*) says:

> Here the various mind-pleasing blossoming flowers
> and attractive shining supreme golden houses
> have no [inherently existent] maker at all.
> They are posited through the power of thought;
> through the power of thought the world is imputed.

Although all phenomena exist by being imputed, designated, or posited by the mind, ignorance apprehends them as existing in exactly the opposite way—as existing under their own power, with their own inherent nature. According to the Prāsaṅgika Mādhyamikas, the observed object of the self-grasping of phenomena is phenomena such as our eye, leg, house, emotions, and so forth. The observed object of the self-grasping of persons is the mere I, the person that exists conventionally, the dependently designated self, the I that is observed when we generate the mere thought "I." This I is bound in saṃsāra; it cultivates the path and will attain liberation.

The conceived object and apprehended object of the two self-graspings is inherent existence—an inherently existent I, inherently existent aggregates, and so forth. Let's say you have intense anger toward Tashi. If you examine your mind, you'll notice the idea that Tashi is an objective person who is the target of your displeasure. The conceived object of this self-grasping is an inherently existent Tashi. At that time, pause and reflect, "Who or what exactly is Tashi? Is he his body? His mind? A soul that is completely separate from his body and mind?" If Tashi existed inherently as he appears to, you should be able to find who Tashi really is. And if you did, the conceived object of ignorance would exist and ignorance would be a reliable cognizer.

But the more you search for the "real" Tashi, the more it becomes evident that you cannot isolate something that is him. In fact, the opposite occurs: you can't find a real Tashi that you're mad at, and the intensity of your anger decreases.

Self-grasping ignorance is a deceptive mind that has tricked us since beginningless time. It has two levels: innate (*sahaja*) and acquired (*parikalpita*). All beings revolving in saṃsāra have innate ignorance, the root of saṃsāra. Acquired ignorance comes from learning incorrect philosophical or psychological theories. Acquired ignorance depends on engaging in incorrect analysis, whereas innate ignorance grasps its object without any analysis. Phenomena appear inherently existent and, assenting to that appearance, innate ignorance grasps them as existing inherently. To combat ignorance, investigation and analysis are essential. We must use our intelligence to examine how ignorance holds its object and whether things exist in the way ignorance apprehends them to exist. Only through rigorous analysis can we become convinced that phenomena do not exist the way they ordinarily appear to us and that their actual mode of existence is not something reified, objective, and "out there," unrelated to the mind. There is another way of existing, but it is not apparent to our obscured, distracted mind.

Ignorance is the source of all other afflictions. In *The Four Hundred*, Āryadeva says (CŚ 135):

> Just as the tactile sense [pervades] the body,
> likewise confusion is present in all [afflictions].
> Therefore, by overcoming confusion
> one will also overcome all afflictions.

Here confusion (*moha*) is synonymous with ignorance. The tactile sense faculty pervades all parts of the body, while the other sense faculties—visual, auditory, olfactory, and gustatory—exist in specific areas: the eyes, ears, nose, and tongue, respectively. The tactile sense is analogous to innate ignorance that pervades and lies at the root of the other afflictions, whereas the other sense faculties resemble the other afflictions that depend on ignorance. Afflictions such as anger and attachment have their own specific functions that do not overlap with each other, although they both are informed by ignorance. The other afflictions do not function on their own but exist in dependence on innate ignorance.

By eliminating ignorance, all the afflictions that depend on it are stopped, just as by uprooting a tree, its branches and leaves die. In the *Treatise on the Middle Way*, Nāgārjuna says (MMK 18.4):

> When thoughts of I and mine
> are extinguished in regard to internal and external things,
> the appropriators [of the aggregates—afflictions and karma] will stop;
> and through its extinguishment, birth will be extinguished.

"Thoughts of I and mine" refers to the wrong view of a personal identity that grasps I and mine. When this is extinguished, afflictions and polluted karma cease. Without afflictions and polluted karma, birth in saṃsāra—the eleventh of the twelve links of dependent origination—cannot occur.

Āryas still create karma, but not the karma that leads to rebirth in saṃsāra. Their unpolluted karma results in liberation and awakening. Ārya bodhisattvas are "born"—that is, they manifest—in our world by the force of wisdom and compassion, not ignorance.

### REFLECTION

1. What is the view of a personal identity?
2. How is it similar to and how does it differ from self-grasping ignorance?
3. What is the root of saṃsāra? What does it mean to be the root of saṃsāra?

## *The Development of Afflictions in Daily Life*

Although afflictions often arise quickly in our mind, seeming to come out of nowhere, they develop through a sequential process. To have the notion of I, one or more of our mental or physical aggregates must appear. Based on this appearance, a valid sense of I arises. This I exists by being merely designated in dependence on the aggregates. Observing this mere I, ignorance erroneously grasps it to exist inherently. That grasping is the view of a personal identity grasping I (*ahaṃkāra*).

Based on that, the view of a personal identity grasping mine (*mamakāra*) arises when we think, "This is *my* body. These are *my* thoughts." The object of the grasping at mine is the sense of "myness," the I that makes things mine; it is not the body or the thoughts themselves. Grasping the body or thoughts to be inherently existent is self-grasping of phenomena, not self-grasping of persons. Tsongkhapa says (FEW 43):

> . . . the observed object of an innate awareness thinking "mine" is that very "mine." It should not be held that your own eyes and so forth are the observed object.

The body, intelligence, table, and so forth are *examples* of "mine" because in ordinary language we say, "This body is mine. This table is mine." But the observed object of grasping "mine" is the mine that is the owner, and not the body, intelligence, or table.

Once the I is grasped as inherently existent, attachment, anger, and other destructive emotions quickly follow, because we want to give this I pleasure and protect it from pain. These mental factors arise very quickly, one right after the other. If our mindfulness is sharp, we can observe this process and thwart it. Otherwise, these afflictions control us.

Grasping the inherent existence of I and mine are erroneous minds. They are not present every time we use the conventions "I" and "mine." When we casually and calmly say "I'm walking" or "This is my book," grasping I or mine is not present. This way of apprehending I and mine differs greatly from the self-grasping that is present when we arrogantly think "*I* am famous," or greedily say "This is *mine*."

## REFLECTION

1. Observe how you relate to people and your surroundings when afflictions are present in your mind; for example, when you crave a certain food, crave love, or are very angry or upset.

2. Observe how you relate to the same people and objects when afflictions are not manifest in your mind.

3. Reflect that this difference is due to the presence or absence of the self-grasping ignorance that underpins all afflictions. Get a sense of how things appear to you when grasping true existence is and is not present.

4. Reflect that this true-grasping is an erroneous mind as well as the source of all afflictions and make a determination to uproot it.

---

## *Inappropriate Attention and Distorted Conceptions*

Based on ignorance, distorted conceptions (inappropriate attention, *ayoniśo-manaskāra*) superimpose attractiveness or ugliness on objects that we believe to truly exist. Other types of distorted conceptions project permanence on impermanent things, purity on impure things, and pleasure on things that are unsatisfactory by nature.

When we apprehend an object that appears attractive, we become attached to it; when we apprehend an object that appears disagreeable, we generate aversion; and when we apprehend a neutral object, we remain indifferent. These and other disturbing emotions depend on ignorance and do not operate separately from it.

Both virtuous attitudes and afflictions arise depending on this mental factor of attention. Appropriate attention leads to virtuous attitudes and emotions—such as compassion and equanimity—while inappropriate attention (distorted conception) produces disturbing ones, such as animosity and arrogance. A practitioner who cultivates the appropriate attention that sees saṃsāric pleasures as impermanent and unsatisfactory and views nirvāṇa as blissful will easily generate the determination to be free. Someone who habitually interprets others' actions as suspicious and malicious will go through life with fear, mistrust, and anger. Since distorted conception misinterprets sense data, projects and exaggerates positive or negative qualities, imputes motivations on others, and so on, it's important to monitor our mind vigilantly.

The observed object of both love and attachment is sentient beings. Appropriate attention sees sentient beings as kind, subject to duḥkha, and possessing buddha nature. From it, empathy, love, and compassion arise. Inappropriate attention sees sentient beings as permanent and desirable, which leads to clinging to them. In both cases, sentient beings appear truly existent. Both love and attachment are *mistaken* consciousnesses in that sentient beings appear truly existent to them. However, love is not a *wrong* or *erroneous* consciousness because conventionally it sees sentient beings in a realistic manner. Attachment, anger, and other afflictions are erroneous consciousnesses because they view their objects in a distorted way, based on distorted conception projecting qualities such as permanence, beauty, ugliness, pleasure, and suffering on them.

Here we see the difference between two types of *innate awarenesses* (T. *blo lhan skyes*): those that are conventionally correct and those that are not. With the first, their objects exist conventionally and cannot be refuted by reasoning. These include minds of love and forgiveness, consciousnesses apprehending apples or persons, and reasoning examining impermanence. With the second, their objects can be refuted by reasoning and do not exist even conventionally. These include attachment, anxiety, resentment, and true-grasping.

Virtuous mental factors and conventional reliable cognizers are not abandoned by the wisdom realizing emptiness, because distorted conception doesn't operate on them. Our understanding of emptiness and dependent arising will purify them of the influence of distorted conception and ignorance, which enables them to operate more fully and to develop completely.

## *Conceptualizations and Elaborations*

This leads us to the topic of conceptualizations and elaborations, which also spur the arising of afflictions. Nāgārjuna said (MMK 18.5):

> Through ceasing karma and afflictions there is nirvāṇa.
> Karma and afflictions come from conceptualization.
> These come from elaborations.
> Elaborations cease by [or in] emptiness.

In the first line, Nāgārjuna defines nirvāṇa as the complete cessation of karma and afflictions resulting from the application of the antidote, the wisdom realizing emptiness. How does nirvāṇa, the state of true freedom, come about? By ceasing the first-link ignorance, its branches (the afflictions) cease, as do second-link formative actions (karma). In this way, resultant rebirth in saṃsāra comes to an end. Where do afflictions and karma come from? Conceptualizations (*vikalpa viparyāsa*) involving distorted concepts in which we focus on the imagined attractive or unattractive aspects of objects. Conceptualizations are fueled by elaborations (mental fabrications, proliferations, *prapañca*, *papañca*), which here principally refers to the ignorance grasping inherent existence. The cessation of these four—karma, afflictions, conceptualizations, and elaborations—is nirvāṇa.

The fact that different people have very different reactions to the same object demonstrates that afflictions arise from our own subjective conceptualizations, not from the side of the object. We cannot account for the arising of attachment on the basis of that object being desirable or attractive in and of itself. Nor can we account for the arising of anger on the basis of the object being objectively distasteful or threatening, because one object can arouse various emotions in different people as well as opposite emotions in the same person at different times. For Jeff football is interesting, for Lucy it is boring. When Sarah is hungry, she craves food, but after she has eaten her fill, the same food is unappetizing. This shows that our subjective conceptualizations and interpretations are powerful conditions that give rise to these emotional reactions.

When speaking of an object being attractive or unattractive, we must see it in relation to a specific person or group of people. "This person is attractive" actually means "I find them attractive." "This place is repugnant" actually indicates "To me it is disgusting." The qualities of attractiveness and unattractiveness are dependent on the perspective of the individual experiencing them. Our subjective conceptualizations are the main factors that give rise to our emotional reactions.

We can see this clearly by observing the people we encounter in our daily lives. Some individuals are very self-centered, referencing all objects and events to themselves. A short phrase or small event misinterpreted by their inappropriate attention can instantly trigger strong emotional reactions in these people.[59] They cannot tolerate what they perceive to be criticism and flare up in anger when hearing words that are not offensive to all others. We also know people that are more relaxed and not very self-centered. We can tease them, and they laugh and aren't offended. They admit their faults and weaknesses without trying to conceal them. An individual's conceptualizations and interpretations determine how they experience a person, object, or situation. Their emotional reactions arise primarily from these, not from the objects themselves.

A speaker at a conference I attended told me that people who excessively use the first person pronouns I, me, and mine have a greater risk of having a heart attack. Another scientist explained that when we develop hostile feelings toward someone, 90 percent of the negativity we see in that object is our own mental projection. Although this scientist is not a Buddhist, his view resonates with the Buddhist explanation of how afflictions arise. The Buddha pointed out that the attractiveness and unattractiveness that provoke the arising of attachment and anger are predominantly a function of our own, often erroneous, conceptualization. We tend to see a person, object, or situation as either 100 percent attractive or 100 percent repugnant, whereas few, if any, things are like that.

## REFLECTION

1. Remember a disturbing situation in your life. Recall what you were thinking and feeling. Examine how your attitudes created your perception and experience.
2. Examine how your attitude affected what you said and did in the situation. How did your behavior either calm or agitate the situation?
3. Was your attitude realistic? Was it seeing all sides of the situation or was it viewing things through the eyes of "me, I, my, mine"?
4. Consider other ways you could have viewed the situation and how that would have changed your experience of it.
5. Determine to be aware of how you're interpreting things that happen in your life and to cultivate beneficial and realistic ways of looking at things.

Conceptualizations come from *elaborations*, the chief of which is grasping persons and phenomena as inherently existent. The word "elaborations" has various meanings according to the context, and there are several types of elaborations.

- The elaboration of inherent existence is the object of negation.
- The elaboration of grasping true or inherent existence (T. *bden 'dzin gyi spros pa*) is the root of saṃsāra and the chief culprit.
- The elaboration of afflictive states of mind is derived from grasping inherent existence.
- The elaboration of dualism is subject and object appearing to be separate (T. *gnyis snang gi spros pa*).
- The elaboration of the appearance of inherent existence (T. *bden snang gi spros pa*).
- The elaboration of conventionalities (T. *kun rdzob kyi spros pa*) is the multiplicity of conventional truths. In the perspective of a direct cognizer of emptiness, conventional truths do not exist because they are not the ultimate nature. However, conventionally they exist.
- The elaboration of the object (T. *chos chan gyi spros pa*) concerns an object and its properties—for example, emptiness is a property or attribute of a person; arising and ceasing are characteristics of impermanent phenomena. This kind of relationship exists to a conceptual mind; to a direct perceiver of emptiness, only emptiness appears.
- The elaboration of conceptuality (T. *rtog pa'i spros pa*) refers to any concept or thought that knows its object by means of a conceptual appearance.
- The elaborations of the eight extremes are inherently existent arising and disintegration, annihilation and permanence, going and coming, and sameness and difference. These also are objects of negation.
- The elaboration of the coarse winds and minds (*rlung sems rags pa'i spros pa*), spoken of in Tantra, includes all winds and minds except the fundamental innate clear light mind and the subtlest wind that is its mount.

Nāgārjuna describes emptiness as the total dissolution of all elaborations. Some elaborations do not exist because they are opposite to the ultimate nature of reality—for example, the elaborations of inherent existence and the elaborations of the eight extremes. These elaborations are objects of negation that are refuted by reasoning. Other elaborations exist—for example, the elaboration of conventionalities, the elaboration of the object, and the elaboration of conceptuality. Although these elaborations exist, they too are not the ultimate nature of reality.

None of these elaborations—be they existent or nonexistent—are present in āryas' meditative equipoise on emptiness. It is by the non-seeing of elaborations that āryas in meditative equipoise are said to realize emptiness directly. That does not mean, however, that the valid characteristics of dependently arising phenomena are to be negated or that they do not exist conventionally. Rather, they are not perceived by āryas in meditative equipoise when the mind is totally fused, single-pointedly and directly, with emptiness. However, they *do* conventionally exist in dependently originated phenomena.

Therefore, we need to distinguish between emptiness, which is the ultimate nature of reality, and *having the nature of* emptiness. Conventional phenomena, such as our parents, the table, and the government, are not emptiness, but they have the nature of emptiness in that they are empty of inherent existence. In the perspective of the meditative equipoise that perceives emptiness directly and is totally fused with emptiness, these conventional phenomena do not exist because they are not perceptible to someone in that meditative equipoise.

To review the causal sequence of saṃsāra: the elaboration of grasping inherent existence gives rise to distorted conceptions—erroneous thought processes—which, in turn, provoke afflictions. Afflictions lead to the creation of actions that bring rebirth in saṃsāra and its attendant duḥkha. To give a rough analogy, self-grasping ignorance and its elaborations are like the unscrupulous boss of a company producing faulty products; conceptualizations and distorted concepts are like the salespeople who exaggerate the qualities of the product; afflictions are like our signing the contract; and karma is all the actions we take afterward.

What ends this chain of events? The realization of the emptiness of true existence. Bringing an end to elaborations involves dismantling all grasping of an objectified basis (T. *yul gyi ngos nas yod pa*) of persons and phenomena, all grasping of persons and phenomena as having an inherent, independent essence.

Emptiness is free from all such elaborations, and the direct realization of emptiness gradually eradicates all grasping of any objectified basis that could serve as the basis for grasping inherent existence. This involves negating all inherent existence and inherent characteristics even on the conventional level.

In general, conceptualizations and conceptuality (*kalpanā*)[60] are synonymous and refer to thought—a mind that knows its object via a conceptual appearance.[61] In Nāgārjuna's verse above, "conceptualizations" has a negative connotation, but in the conventional world, thoughts can be helpful. After all, learning and reflecting on the Buddha's teachings takes place in the context of language and thought. There are different types of conceptualizations; some are helpful on the path and others are not. Some examples of conceptualization are:

- Virtuous conceptualizations. The wisdom understanding emptiness on the levels of learning, thinking, and the initial phase of meditating is conceptual. It does not know emptiness directly but is an essential step to realize emptiness directly. Understandings on the method side of the path—including the aspiration to attain liberation, love, compassion, and bodhicitta—are all conceptual consciousnesses in sentient beings. Only in the continuum of buddhas are these nonconceptual.
- Conceptualizations involving distorted conceptions. These include the four distorted conceptions seeing the impermanent as permanent, the foul as pure, the unpleasant as pleasant, and that which lacks a self as having one.[62]
- Discursive thought or discursiveness, which is an impediment to developing serenity.
- Afflictions. All afflictive views and emotions are conceptualizations. They do not see their objects correctly and are erroneous.
- The conception, or grasping, of true existence (T. *bden 'dzin gyi rnam rtog*). As the root of saṃsāra, this is the most detrimental type of conceptualization.
- The conception of ordinariness (T. *tha mal pa'i rnam rtog*) is found in the context of Tantra.

The various meanings of "conceptualization" and "conception" challenge us to be aware of the various contexts in which these terms are used. Certain types of conceptions are helpful and necessary on the path to buddhahood.

However, at the culmination of the path all conceptions must be transcended, for buddhas know all phenomena directly and nonconceptually.[63]

According to the Tibetan translation of Nāgārjuna's verse, the cessation of elaborations—especially grasping inherent existence—is brought about *by* emptiness. Here the instrumental case is used, indicating that elaborations are ceased *by* the wisdom that realizes emptiness. Ignorance *grasps* the inherent existence of all phenomena, whereas the wisdom realizing emptiness *negates* the inherent existence of phenomena and perceives its opposite—the emptiness of inherent existence. Both ignorance and wisdom focus on the same object, but they relate to it in a dramatically opposed manner.

While giving an oral commentary on the *Treatise on the Middle Way*, Khunu Lama Rinpoche, a great Buddhist master as well as a Sanskrit scholar, explained that in Sanskrit this final line can be read in the locative case as well—that is, elaborations cease *within* emptiness. This latter reading has profound meaning because all elaborations and defilements arise within the empty nature of the mind. The ultimate creator of all phenomena of both saṃsāra and nirvāṇa is the mind. All afflictions are created by mind and must finally be cleansed within the nature of the mind itself. At the time a meditator has a nondual experience of emptiness, all elaborations and defilements dissolve back into that reality—into the emptiness of the mind. The emptiness into which all afflictions have been extinguished through the antidote of wisdom is the true cessation of duḥkha and its origins; it is nirvāṇa. In this sense, all elaborations are extinguished in the sphere of reality.

The result—buddhahood—is also a state of mind. The mind plays a tremendously important role in the process of purification and perfection. The *Sublime Continuum* (*Ratnagotravibhāga Śāstra*, *Uttaratantra Śāstra*) states that all pollutants of the mind are adventitious—they can be separated from the mind—and all the awakened qualities of the Buddha's omniscient mind exist as potentials in the minds of sentient beings.

A statement in Sakya literature says that within the basis, which is the causal mind-basis-of-all,[64] all phenomena of saṃsāra and nirvāṇa are complete. The mind-basis-of-all is, in some sense, the fundamental innate mind of clear light. At the level of ordinary beings, this foundation consciousness is called the "causal continuum." Within that causal continuum, all phenomena of saṃsāra are complete in the form of their natural characteristics, all phenomena of the paths and grounds are complete in the form of their qualities, and all awakened qualities of the Buddha's omniscient mind are complete in the form of their potentials. This beautiful and comprehensive picture summarizes the essence of the Sakya approach to the basis, path, and result.

The Nyingma's Dzogchen, the Mahāmudrā of the Kagyu, the Sakya Lamdre's view of the union of profundity and clarity, and the Gelug understanding of *mind isolation* according to the Guhyasamāja Tantra—in all of these, the emphasis is on realizing the ultimate nature of the mind. Although in meditative equipoise there is no difference between the mind's emptiness and the emptiness of external objects, contemplation on the emptiness of mind is emphasized in meditative practices in all four traditions of Tibetan Buddhism because it has such a dramatic impact on the mind of the practitioner.[65]

## REFLECTION

1. Recall an event that disturbed you.
2. Try to identify the fundamental elaboration—self-grasping—that arose and grasped the people and elements of the situation to exist objectively "out there."
3. What were the distorted conceptions, such as seeing impermanent things as permanent, that arose?
4. What other distorted conceptions (inappropriate attention) were active in interpreting the elements of the event?
5. What affliction(s)—such as attachment, anger, jealousy, arrogance, and so forth—arose?

## *Ceasing Saṃsāra*

Self-grasping ignorance is an erroneous mind. Since its conceived and apprehended objects—the self (inherent existence) of persons and the self of phenomena—do not exist, cultivating the wisdom that sees things as they actually are reduces and eventually completely eradicates it. Candrakīrti outlines the process whereby yogis enter into emptiness and actualize liberating wisdom by first refuting the conceived object of the view of a personal identity (LC 3:120–21):

> Yogis who wish to enter reality and who wish to eliminate all afflictions and faults examine the question, "What does this saṃsāra have as its root?" When they thoroughly investigate this, they see that saṃsāra has as its root the reifying view of a personal identity, and they see that the self is the object observed by that reifying view of a personal identity. They see that not observing the self leads to eliminating the reifying view of a personal identity, and that through eliminating that, all afflictions and faults are overcome. Hence, at the very beginning they examine only the self, asking, "What is the self that is the object of grasping self?"

Tsongkhapa confirms the necessity of refuting the conceived object of self-grasping (FEW 56–7):

> . . . without rejecting the object of the grasping of a self of persons, a realization of selflessness cannot occur. . . . Furthermore, because the two graspings of self operate mainly within observing functioning things—persons and phenomena—you need to delineate that just those bases, with respect to which the error is made, do not exist in the way that they are grasped.

Having identified the object of negation, yogis go about refuting it. By familiarizing their minds with the direct realization of emptiness, they eradicate the acquired and innate afflictions, and the entire structure of saṃsāra begins to crumble. The *Sūtra on the Secrecies of the Tathāgata* says (FEW 56):

> Śāntimatī, it is like this. For example, when the roots of a tree are cut, all the branches, leaves, and twigs dry. Śāntimatī, similarly,

> when the view of a personal identity is pacified, all [root] afflictions and auxiliary afflictions are pacified.

Although not all the Buddha's teachings directly speak of selflessness, they directly or indirectly lead to this realization. The elimination of wrong views and afflictions cannot be accomplished simply by making aspirational prayers. We must cultivate the wisdom that directly opposes their false and erroneous perspectives. Just abiding in a state of nonconceptuality and non-mentation does not eliminate these obscurations. Although defilements may not arise in a nonconceptual state, there is nothing in the nonconceptual content of that experience that contradicts or reduces their power.

Disturbing elaborations are overcome by realizing that inherent existence does not exist at all. This is accomplished by the probing awareness (*yuktijñāna*) analyzing the ultimate. Probing awarenesses are of two types: (1) conceptual (inferential) probing awareness that realizes emptiness in dependence on a reason, and (2) the nonconceptual pristine wisdom of an ārya's meditative equipoise that directly and nonconceptually perceives emptiness. The latter probing awareness is not actively analyzing emptiness, but having previously done in-depth analysis, it has given rise to a union of serenity and insight focused on emptiness.

Both types of probing awareness harm the elaboration of inherent existence, but the pristine wisdom of an ārya's meditative equipoise on emptiness eradicates the elaboration of conceptuality because it perceives emptiness directly, not through the medium of a conceptual appearance. This meditative equipoise is free from the elaboration of dualistic appearance, because that wisdom and its object (emptiness) are experienced as undifferentiable, like water poured into water. Conceptual probing awareness, however, still has the appearance of subject and object; this wisdom has eliminated only a portion of elaborations.

Many people associate conceptual knowledge with intellectual knowledge, but in Buddhadharma, analysis is not about intellectual acrobatics and juggling a proliferation of words. It involves a process of observing how things appear to the mind, how ignorance grasps them to exist, and then investigating whether or not things actually exist in that way. A conceptual probing awareness realizing emptiness contradicts belief in inherent existence and has a powerful effect on our mind.

## *Emptiness Is a Nonaffirming Negative*

To identify the apprehended object—the object realized—by the wisdom realizing emptiness, we must understand nonaffirming negatives (*prasajya-pratiṣedha*) and how they differ from affirming negatives (*paryudāsa-pratiṣedha*). An affirming negative negates one thing while asserting another. In the expression "an unhappy event," happiness is negated, but an event is asserted. A nonaffirming negative, on the other hand, is a simple negation: it excludes something without implying anything else. An example is "no sugar." Here, sugar is negated and nothing else is implied or asserted in its place.

Nonaffirming negatives are absences; as such, they are permanent phenomena. Most essentialists say that permanent phenomena cannot be known by direct perceivers, be they sense, mental, or yogic direct perceivers. Mādhyamikas, however, say that the emptiness of true existence can be directly perceived by a yogic direct perceiver.

According to Mādhyamikas, the apprehended object of the wisdom realizing emptiness is a nonaffirming negative. It is simply the negation of inherent existence. Other than that mere negation, nothing else is apprehended or affirmed. Although we are used to thinking in terms of affirmative or "positive" phenomena that we can point to and see, emptiness is the mere refutation of inherent existence. Here "positive" and "negative" don't refer to virtue and nonvirtue; these terms indicate that something is put forth in an affirming or negating way. Making a positive statement, "There is a chicken," influences the mind in one way—it starts to think about all the attributes of the chicken and what it does. But "There is no elephant here" leaves us with the simple negation of an elephant.

The purpose of cultivating the correct view of emptiness is to undermine any objectified basis—any inherently existent phenomenon—that can give rise to afflictions such as greed, anger, and so on. Being able to refute inherent existence and focus on that simple negation has liberating power.

For example, if you are afraid that a snake is in your bedroom, and your friend searches everywhere in the room and, not finding a snake, tells you

"There is no snake here," just that simple statement has the power to dispel your fear. However, if your friend says, "There is no snake, but I saw a scorpion," your fear is not quieted. Similarly, the wisdom realizing emptiness knows just the absence of inherent existence—it has dismantled any objective basis that you could hold on to and doesn't project anything else. Realizing a nonaffirming negative can have a strong impact on your mind. Consider people who walked past the twin towers of the World Trade Center in New York every day and suddenly one day the towers are no longer there. Those people know the absence of the towers.

As a simple negation that implies nothing in its place, emptiness is said to resemble empty space. Unconditioned space, which is the mere negation of physical obstruction, is also a nonaffirming negative. Although both emptiness and space are mere negations that don't affirm something in their place, they are not the same. Space is the mere negation of physical obstruction, and emptiness is the mere negation of inherent existence. The two must be differentiated in meditation. Apprehending the latter leads to liberation; apprehending the former does not.

The Second Dalai Lama explains that just the phrase "free from elaboration," or "without elaboration," is a nonaffirming negative. Those words negate the elaboration of inherent existence but do not establish anything positive in its stead. During meditative equipoise on emptiness, only this nonaffirming negative appears to the mind, and that mind knows emptiness nondualistically. At that time there is no grasping true existence of emptiness, nor is there the thought "This is emptiness." The perception of emptiness energizes the mind, giving it power and strength. This is completely different from a weak mind that focuses on nothingness. Meditating on nothingness does nothing to harm self-grasping ignorance, whereas an invigorated mind realizing emptiness contradicts ignorance.

In my own case, although I lack a direct realization of emptiness and haven't had even a meditatively derived realization,[66] by repeatedly analyzing if phenomena exist the way they appear and by reflecting on the reasons disproving inherent existence, sometimes an unusual experience occurs. Although these experiences may be brief, within that state of meditation, there is no grasping.

As with a direct perceiver of emptiness, the apprehended object of an inference realizing emptiness is also a nonaffirming negative—the emptiness of inherent existence, the ultimate truth. Whereas the appearing object of a mind directly perceiving emptiness is emptiness itself, the appearing object of an inferential realization of emptiness is the conceptual appearance of emptiness in which emptiness appears mixed with the conceptual appearance of emptiness. There is debate whether the object that is the base of emptiness—the person, the body, the mind, and so forth—also appears to an inferential realization of emptiness. Most scholar-adepts think that it does not.[67] It definitely does not appear to a direct perceiver of emptiness.

## *Realizing the Selflessness of Persons and Selflessness of Phenomena*

Because there is a multiplicity of phenomena, there is a multiplicity of phenomena to grasp as inherently existent. These can be subsumed in two: grasping the person as inherently existent and grasping other phenomena as inherently existent. The significance of this division is to emphasize the distinction between the subject—the person who is bound in saṃsāra and attains liberation—and the object—the aggregates that are the basis of designation of the person and other phenomena that a person uses or enjoys. Because grasping is twofold, selflessness is also twofold: the selflessness of persons and the selflessness of phenomena. Tsongkhapa clarifies (FEW 40):

> . . . the mode of grasping inherent existence—the object of negation—is to grasp [that objects] are not posited through the force of beginningless conceptuality but are established objectively, by their own entity. The conceived object of that grasping is called self or inherent existence. The nonexistence of that with a person as the substratum is called the selflessness of persons, and the nonexistence of that regarding [other] phenomena, such as an eye, ear, and so forth as the substratum, is called the selflessness of phenomena. Hence, we can implicitly understand that grasping inherent existence with respect to persons and [other] phenomena are the self-graspings of the two selves.

Vaibhāṣikas and Sautrāntikas confine themselves to refuting only the self of persons, which they say is a self-sufficient substantially existent person. However, by refuting this, a practitioner decreases clinging to oneself, but not to the aggregates and other objects. In the Yogācāra and Madhyamaka systems, selflessness applies both to the person and other phenomena. Realizing the selflessness of both has a stronger impact because it dismantles grasping both the subject and object of the afflictions as inherently existent. When attachment arises for an object—let's say a new device—there is the component of the subject, "*I* want this," and the object, "*This device* is wonderful!" Both the subject of the affliction—I—and the object of the affliction—the device—appear to exist in and of themselves, and ignorance grasps them as existing in this way. The understanding of emptiness gained through deconstructing the false appearance of both subject and object has a powerful effect on the mind.

To attain arhatship or buddhahood, the realization of both selflessnesses is necessary. A yogi begins by focusing on the most serious troublemaker, the view of a personal identity in his own continuum—grasping an inherently existent I and mine—and investigates if the I exists in this way. If it does, it should be either identical to the aggregates or totally separate and unrelated to the aggregates. Through analysis we understand that both options are impossible and conclude that an inherently existent I does not exist. If the I does not exist inherently, neither can the aggregates that are the basis of designation of that I. For example, if a cart is burned, its parts—the wheels, axle, and so forth—are burned. If inherent existence is refuted on the I, it is also refuted on the mine—what is possessed by the I, for example, the five aggregates.

The conventional self that exists is merely designated in dependence on the aggregates, which are its basis of designation. This conventional self or mere I is the base on which ordinary beings project and grasp inherent existence. The self and the aggregates have the relationship of appropriator and appropriated, or "clinger" and "clung to." That is, the self "takes," "appropriates," or "clings to" the mental and physical aggregates, and the aggregates are what are taken, appropriated, or clung to by the self. While this language may give us the idea that there is a real self that exists by itself and later takes on the aggregates, this is not the case. Rather, the terms "appropriator" and "appropriated" indicate a mutually dependent relationship. We cannot posit an I that is the appropriator without positing aggregates that are appropriated, and vice versa.

Because Vaibhāṣikas and Sautrāntikas do not assert a selflessness of phenomena and believe the aggregates exist inherently, they realize neither the selflessness of phenomena nor the subtle selflessness of persons. Because they believe the aggregates to exist inherently, they will continue to hold the self designated in dependence on them to also exist inherently. This occurs because the mode of apprehension of the self-grasping of phenomena and self-grasping of persons is the same: they both grasp inherent existence.

Yogis first realize the selflessness of persons followed by the selflessness of phenomena. Because the I is an abstract composite imputed in dependence on the aggregates, realizing that it doesn't exist independently or under its own power is easier than realizing the aggregates are empty of such existence. However, to realize the emptiness of the person, strong self-grasping of the aggregates cannot be manifest in our mind. If someone strongly grasps the aggregates as inherently existent, they won't question whether the person, which is imputed in dependence on those aggregates, exists inherently.

The awareness that inferentially realizes the emptiness of persons and the awareness that inferentially realizes the emptiness of phenomena are not the same consciousness, because these conceptual consciousnesses have different objects. Although the consciousness realizing the selflessness of persons does not realize the selflessness of phenomena either explicitly or implicitly, through its force it can induce a consciousness that does realize the emptiness of phenomena such as the aggregates. That is, although the mind realizing the emptiness of the person does not think "The aggregates are empty," it can induce a mind realizing this when attention is turned to the aggregates. Tsongkhapa says (CTB 175):

> If a selflessness of phenomena is established by a reliable cognizer in terms of one phenomenon, then when you analyze whether or not another phenomenon inherently exists, you can realize its non-inherent existence on the basis of your previous reasoning.

This applies to inferential reliable cognizers of emptiness that arise through reasoning, not direct reliable cognizers. When you have an inferential reliable cognizer of the emptiness of one phenomenon, just by turning your mind to another phenomenon and wondering how it exists, you can realize its emptiness as well because you've already understood the reasoning. This does not mean that at the precise moment you realize the emptiness of the person, you also realize the emptiness of the aggregates. Rather, after realizing the emptiness of the person, when you consider the aggregates, you immediately realize their emptiness. For example, when you realize there is no elephant in this room, you don't simultaneously realize there is no elephant's trunk here. But when you turn your mind to consider the elephant's trunk, you immediately know that it is nonexistent because an elephant in this room is nonexistent. Similarly, you realize there are no inherently existent aggregates of a person because there is no inherently existent person to begin with. The *King of Concentration Sūtra* says (YDB 194):

> Through one all are known
> and through one all are seen.

Āryadeva agrees (CŚ 191):

> [One who sees] the emptiness of one phenomenon
> is said [to see] the emptiness of all.
> That which is the emptiness of one [phenomenon]
> is the emptiness of all.

Āryadeva affirms that an inferential cognizer of the emptiness of the I immediately generates an inferential cognizer of the emptiness of other phenomena merely by directing the mind to those things while holding the question "Is this inherently existent or not?" The inherent existence of each and every phenomenon does not need to be refuted individually. If that were the case, it would be impossible to realize the emptiness of all countless phenomena.

If we taste one drop of ocean water, we know the rest is salty. The emptiness of inherent existence is the ultimate mode of existence of all phenomena. It doesn't appear in different ways, as do blue and red. Emptiness is like the space in different receptacles: we speak of the space inside a pot and the space inside a cup separately, but when we apprehend the space inside the pot, we know what the space inside a cup looks like. Similarly, by knowing the emptiness of inherent existence of Susan, we'll know the emptiness of Trinley by merely directing the mind to him. The process of reasoning that induced the initial cognition of Susan's emptiness doesn't need to be repeated. The *Sūtra Requested by Gaganagañja* (*Gaganagañjaparipṛcchā Sūtra*) says (YDB 194):

> Whoever through one phenomenon knows through meditation
> that all phenomena are inapprehensible like illusions and mirages—
> hollow, deceptive, and ephemeral—
> will before long reach the essence of awakening.

This verse corroborates the same principle when it comes to knowing all phenomena are like illusions in post-meditation time. By tasting one drop of honey in a bottle, you thereby know that the remaining honey is sweet.

Unlike realizing emptiness inferentially, when meditators directly perceive the emptiness of one phenomenon, they simultaneously realize the emptiness of all phenomena. As the ultimate nature of all phenomena, the emptiness of each thing appears the same to the mind of meditative equipoise directly perceiving emptiness.

### REFLECTION

1. What is a nonaffirming negation? Why do masters insist that the ultimate truth is a nonaffirming negation?
2. What is the self of persons according to the four tenet systems? What is the self of phenomena?
3. What are the selflessness of persons and selflessness of phenomena? Are they emptiness?

## *Characteristics of Reality*

Although the full experience of suchness—the way things really are—is beyond words and concepts, it can be expressed through language and thought. This description doesn't impute false characteristics on reality; it simply uses conventional terms to describe them. Nāgārjuna mentions five characteristics of the way things really are (MMK 18.9):

> Not understandable from another [person], void, and
> not captured by verbal phantasms,
> not conceptualized, without distinctions;
> that is the characteristic of things as they really are.

1. The way things really are *cannot be fully understood* by depending on another person's teachings or description of it. Reality has to be realized by our own purified wisdom. A person with the visual impairment of vitreous floaters sees falling hairs where there are none. Someone who doesn't have this appearance can tell him that there are no falling hairs, and through that, the person with vitreous floaters knows the hairs aren't real. However, he doesn't know their absence in the same way that the person without this visual impairment does. When the visual impairment is resolved, he will know by his own experience that there are no falling hairs.

   Similarly, ordinary beings can hear a correct explanation of the way things really are and in that way understand the ultimate by means of a conceptual appearance. However, they do not understand it the way āryas who directly perceive emptiness do. When their wisdom shatters their ignorance, ordinary beings become āryas and realize emptiness directly by themselves.
2. The way things really are is *devoid* of false appearances. Just as vitreous floaters do not exist in the eyes of someone without that visual impairment, likewise reality is devoid of inherent existence.
3. Reality is *not expressed by verbal fabulations*; it cannot be fully captured by words.
4. It is *without* the distraction of *conceptualizations* and thought.
5. It is *without distinctions*; all phenomena equally lack inherent existence. Ultimately there is no individuality; reality cannot be differentiated into separate objects.

Words and concepts may give us an idea of the way things really are, and in that way we can intellectually understand the ultimate nature. However, we must never mistake words and concepts for the actual experience of emptiness. Nor should we dismiss the benefits that derive from conceptual analysis of the ultimate nature in helping us to gain direct experience.

## *The Object of Attainment*

Between our present mind and our future buddhahood lie two obscurations: the afflictive obscurations (*kleśāvaraṇa*) and the cognitive obscurations. The afflictive obscurations are the afflictions—wrong views and disturbing emotions that cause saṃsāra and their seeds. The cognitive obscurations (*jñeyāvaraṇa*) are the aspect of the mind that continues to mistakenly perceive all internal and external phenomena dualistically (T. *gnyis snang 'khrul pa'i cha*)—that is, as inherently existent—as well as the latencies that cause this dualistic aspect (T. *gnyis snang 'khrul pa'i bag chags*). Cognitive obscurations are not consciousnesses. The aspect that continues to perceive inherent existence is a quality that is concomitant with the consciousness, whereas the latencies are the cause of these dualistic perceptions or appearances.[68]

Nirvāṇa is the passing beyond sorrow—the extinguishment of duḥkha and its origins, the afflictive obscurations. This is liberation, the object of attainment for śrāvakas and solitary realizers. For bodhisattvas the object of attainment is nonabiding nirvāṇa (*apratiṣṭha-nirvāṇa*), the elimination of both the afflictive and cognitive obscurations. The purified emptiness, or suchness, of the mind in which all defilements have been extinguished is both the object of attainment—the *dharmakāya* (nature truth body) of a buddha—and the object of meditation. This is called "nonabiding nirvāṇa" because having eliminated afflictive obscurations, a buddha does not abide in saṃsāra, and having additionally eliminated the self-centered attitude and cognitive obscurations, a buddha does not abide in personal peace.

The afflictions that cause saṃsāra, the actions they motivate, the aggregates we take as a result of those actions, the person who performs the actions and experiences their results, and the results that person experiences all appear to ordinary beings to have their own inherent nature. However, they do not exist in this way; they are false, like a hologram that appears to be a person but is not.

Since these things do not have their own inherent nature or essence, what is the actual nature of phenomena that we seek to realize? This is nonabiding nirvāṇa, the extinguishment of grasping at I and mine with respect to all internal phenomena—the sense faculties, body, mind, and mental factors—and external phenomena—forms, sounds, and other sense objects—that is rooted in grasping inherent existence and its seeds. This is attained by removing all mistaken appearances of phenomena as inherently existent through familiarizing ourselves with their emptiness of inherent existence. Nonabiding nirvāṇa is the emptiness of a buddha's mind, the purified state of the natural buddha nature, the nature dharmakāya. Nonabiding nirvāṇa possesses two purities: the natural purity that is the mind's primordial emptiness of inherent existence and its purity from adventitious defilements—its final true cessation—that is attained by practicing the path.

What happens to the seeds of polluted karma when someone becomes an arhat or a buddha? According to the upper tenet systems—the lower tenet systems have a different idea—the seeds of nonvirtuous karma in the mindstream of someone who has become a śrāvaka or solitary realizer arhat or an eighth-ground bodhisattva have become powerless and no longer exist; nothing nonvirtuous remains in their mindstreams. Seeds of previously created virtuous karma become unpolluted seeds of virtuous karma.

# 8 Objects of Negation

CORRECTLY IDENTIFYING the object of negation—the false mode of existence that ignorance grasps as real—is the most important step when meditating on emptiness. If we do not properly identify the object of negation, we may meditate on selflessness and think we have realized emptiness, but in fact we may understand only the lack of a self-sufficient substantially existent person, not the full emptiness of the person. Alternatively, we may have an experience of vacuity and mistake this for the emptiness of inherent existence.

It is wise to banish all romantic ideas that the ultimate nature of all phenomena will automatically appear to you in a flash as an amazing experience that will instantly free you from all duḥkha forever. Instead let's deepen our understanding of ignorance and what it grasps as true so that our meditation on emptiness will bear fruit.

## *Objects Negated by the Path and Objects Negated by Reasoning*

Objects of negation are of two types: those negated by the path and those negated by reasoning. "Negated" has different meanings in these two phrases. Regarding objects negated by the path, "negated" means abandoned or eradicated; but when speaking of objects negated by reasoning, "negated" means disproved or refuted.

*Objects negated by the path* are mental obscurations, which can be subsumed in the afflictive obscurations and cognitive obscurations. Afflictive obscurations primarily interfere with attaining liberation, and cognitive obscurations primarily hinder attaining the omniscience of a buddha. The objects negated by the path are existent phenomena. If they weren't, sentient beings would not have to work to eliminate them.[69]

*Objects negated by reasoning* are nonexistents that we erroneously believe exist. The chief of these is inherent existence. Although the ignorance that grasps inherent existence, which is a mental factor, exists, its conceived and apprehended object—inherent existence—has never existed. Grasping inherent existence is a consciousness and is an object negated by the path, whereas its conceived object—inherent existence—is an object negated by reasoning. When inherent existence is negated, the awareness grasping it gradually weakens and ceases.

If inherent existence existed, it could not be refuted by reasoning. We cannot prove as nonexistent things that in fact exist. Even though inherent existence does not exist at all, refuting it is essential because to eliminate the erroneous consciousness that grasps it, we must first disprove the object that consciousness apprehends.

Why is self-grasping ignorance a wrong consciousness? Why is the object it apprehends nonexistent? If things existed inherently, as ignorance apprehends them, when we searched for what they really are we would be able to find something. When we analyze what the name "apple" actually refers to—what the inherent nature or true essence of the apple really is—it should become clearer. Among the parts of the apple—the skin, pulp, and core—we could point to something that is indeed the apple. However, instead of the apple becoming clearer to our mind when we analyze it, the apple seems to vanish.

Ignorance apprehends phenomena as existing independent of all other factors. If ignorance apprehended things correctly, then everything would exist in its own self-enclosed manner, unrelated to everything else. However, when we examine how things exist, it becomes apparent that they are dependent—on their causes and conditions, on their parts, and even on the mind that conceives them and gives them a name. Something that is dependent cannot be independent—the two are contradictory. Thus ignorance is a wrong consciousness.

Refuting inherent existence is not like erasing writing on a white board; we are not making something that exists nonexistent. Instead, it is like proving that the bogeyman—a mythical creature fabricated by adults to frighten children to be good—doesn't exist; we realize that something we believed existed has, in fact, never existed. When we realize the bogeyman doesn't exist, we stop being afraid of him; we see that he never existed at all and that all along our ignorance had blindsided us and we were terrified of a monster that didn't exist. Similarly, when we realize inherent existence does not exist, we gradually stop being under the control of our ignorant grasping that it does exist.

Refuting inherent existence and establishing the emptiness of inherent existence is not destroying something that exists. Everything has always lacked inherent existence. No one made phenomena empty of inherent existence; that has always been their ultimate nature. We understand this truth for the first time upon refuting inherent existence. Furthermore, realizing emptiness does not create something new that didn't exist before, such as constructing a bicycle. It's like removing the cataract-like mental obscurations so that you can see clearly.

We may wonder: "Why are so many words needed to prove that a nonexistent doesn't exist? If it exists, we cannot refute it, and if it does not exist, we don't need to refute it; so of what use are all these refutations and proofs?" Let's look at the example of the bogeyman again. Although the bogeyman doesn't exist, a child who believes he does trembles in fear. If we hold the child's hand and take him around the house to look for the bogeyman, when we can't find him anywhere, the child will understand there is no bogeyman and his fear will vanish.

The mind is very powerful and misconceptions can make us terrified when there is nothing to fear. Ignorance has blindsided us into believing that the I and all other phenomena exist inherently, and as a result our attachment and anger, having grown out of ignorance, have caused us eons of duḥkha in saṃsāra. When we refute and familiarize ourselves with the nonexistence of the object of this grasping, ignorance gradually ceases, the afflictions arising from it gradually cease, polluted karma is no longer created, and our saṃsāra comes to an end.

Words alone do not overcome true-grasping, but they can teach us how to do this. Although the words of the teachings also lack inherent existence, they can function to generate the understanding in our minds that inherent existence does not exist. Here it becomes evident that attaining liberation or awakening doesn't involve going somewhere else; it is a matter of changing our mind.

In addition to our innate grasping, the mind is home to a plethora of acquired wrong views. Some of these wrong views are held by non-Buddhists, others by adherents to the lower Buddhist tenet systems. All of them are rooted in grasping inherent existence. For example, in asserting the existence of a permanent, unitary, independent self, non-Buddhists do not begin by apprehending the self as permanent or perceiving it as one monolithic whole. Rather, they grasp the self as existing from its own side. By not recognizing that the inherent existence apprehended by this innate grasping does not exist, they then make up beliefs to explain how karmic seeds can go from one life to the next. The notion of a permanent self that is one partless whole and is independent of causes and conditions is one such fabricated belief.

Proponents of the lower Buddhist tenet systems recognize the fallacies of that belief, so they instead assert that a foundation consciousness or the mental consciousness is the self. In this way, self-grasping constantly seeks a way to make itself prevail and feel secure.

Because of our deep-seated belief in inherent existence, we cling to people and things that appear to be attractive from their own side, have aversion to disagreeable people who appear hateful in and of themselves, are arrogant about our seemingly inborn talents, and become jealous of those who have opportunities we do not. If we were to correctly identify the grasping consciousness that is the root of all these disturbing emotions and refute its conceived object, all other wrong views would be gradually destroyed. The antidote for each individual affliction—for example, meditating on the ugly aspects of an object to counteract attachment and on fortitude to subdue anger—temporarily overcomes only that disturbing emotion and does not damage the others. Using these antidotes is comparable to cutting down one obtrusive branch and then another, with new ones growing from the trunk. Realizing the emptiness of inherent existence and familiarizing our mind with it over time is like uprooting a poisonous tree; nothing more can grow from its trunk.

## *The Importance of Correctly Identifying the Object of Negation*

Correctly identifying the object of negation by reasoning is essential for our meditation on emptiness to be effective. Śāntideva affirms (BCA 9.139ab):

> Without having identified the object [of negation] that is imputed, the absence of that object cannot be apprehended.

The word "emptiness" in Buddhism designates something completely different from the word's ordinary meaning. The emptiness is not like the emptiness of our stomach or the emptiness of our bank account. It is a mode of existence that is the absence of incorrect ways of existence that ignorance projects on persons and phenomena; in the context of the Prāsaṅgikas, this is inherent existence, which is synonymous with existence by its own characteristics, existence from its own side, and so on.

The first step in refuting inherent existence is to have an idea of what it would be like if it in fact existed. This process is called "identifying the object of negation." For example, to expel a thief from your house, you must first know what he looks like.

Even great masters such as Tsongkhapa initially had difficulty in identifying the subtlest object of negation. His early writings such as *The Golden Rosary* (*Legs bshad gser phreng*) show that like many of the early Tibetan Buddhists, he believed that since nothing can be found when analyzed with reasoning, nothing exists conventionally. He thought that sages assert dependent arising and conventionalities only when talking to others—that is, discussion of conventionalities is done for the sake of others, not because oneself asserts their existence.

By asking questions to Mañjuśrī, the Buddha of wisdom, Tsongkhapa later saw the error in that view. In the "Three Principal Aspects of the Path," he emphasized that if we think emptiness is an independent, absolute truth such that dependent arisings and emptiness are incompatible, then we have not understood emptiness correctly. As long as dependent arising and emptiness are seen as alternating realities that do not converge, we lack the correct view.

Identifying the object of negation—inherent existence—is a subtle process that takes time, especially since conventionally existent phenomena and inherent existence appear to us completely mixed. Teasing these apart is delicate; it is easy to veer toward negating too much or not negating enough. Tsongkhapa reminds us (LC 3:126):

> Just as, for example, to ascertain that a certain person is not here, you must know the person who is not here, so in order to

> ascertain the meaning of "selflessness" and "lack of [inherent] nature," you must also identify well that self and nature that do not exist. This is because, if the conceptual appearance of that which is to be negated does not appear well, then also the negative of that will not be unmistakenly ascertained.

To catch a terrorist, we have to know what he looks like. If we have no idea whether he is tall or short, fat or thin, our efforts to locate him will not bring any results. Similarly, if we have no conceptual image of what inherent existence would be like, it will be hard to tell it does not exist. Of course we could say the words "There is no inherent existence," but that would be like saying "There is no terrorist here" when the terrorist is standing next to us but we don't recognize him. If we refute too much or not enough, if we negate the wrong object, or if we remain in blank-minded meditation, our efforts will not bring the desired result of liberation or awakening. For this reason, proper identification of the object of negation is crucial.

Changkya Rolpai Dorje (1717–86), a sage from eastern Tibet, says that some dialecticians, people skilled in philosophical debate, insist on consistency and are obsessed with giving a rational account of everything. They claim to be intelligent scholars and good practitioners, but they leave intact the solidity of what they perceive in front of them. They think the object of negation is something external that can be identified without questioning the way the I appears in the everyday functioning of the ignorant mind. It seems as if they are negating something with horns that is completely unrelated to their own apprehension of I. This is because they haven't correctly identified the inherent existence that appears to them in their daily perceptions and thoughts as being the object of negation. Changkya says:[70]

> Among today's thinkers, there seem to be
> some caught in the web of words:
> "self-substantial," "ontologically real," and so on.
> They only invent monsters
> with horns to negate, leaving intact
> our vivid, coarse, apparent world.

It is crucial to recognize that the solid, concrete, objective reality of an object appearing to us is the very object of negation. Doing this can be unnerving because it involves challenging our everyday, habitual perceptions. The object of negation must be tied to the way we see ourselves. If it isn't, negating an inherently existent I won't have any effect on us. When our meditation on emptiness is successful, we discover that how we have been thinking of ourselves and all other phenomena from beginningless time until now has been completely wrong. We do not exist in the way we thought we did. At that time, it's almost as if we are no longer able to posit the self. It seems as if things barely exist—they do not have their own essence but exist dependently, like illusions.

Nāgārjuna identifies emptiness as the meaning of dependent arising, thus pointing out the necessity of not only negating inherent existence but also establishing dependently arising conventional truths. In other words, the object of negation is not all existence whatsoever, only inherent existence. In the case of persons, the I exists in dependence on the body and mind. This I meditates, eats, creates karma and experiences its results, practices the path, and attains awakening, and it does all these without existing under its own power. This sense of I is a valid innate conception; on its basis we seek happiness and not suffering. This valid sense of I is not the object of negation, and negating it would lead to the extreme of nihilism. Grasping the reified I is the troublemaker, and its conceived object is the object of negation. Identifying it takes time and finesse.

## REFLECTION

1. What are objects negated by the path and objects negated by reasoning?
2. Why is correctly identifying the object of negation important in order to realize emptiness?

## *What Is Not the Object of Negation*

In *The Four Hundred*, Āryadeva says (CŚ 398):

> If things existed inherently,
> what good is it to perceive emptiness?
> Seeing by way of conceptions binds;
> this is refuted here.

The first two lines warn that if phenomena existed inherently, inherent existence would be the nature of phenomena and could not be refuted. In that case, emptiness could not be realized. "Conceptions" refer to conceptions of inherent existence that superimpose existence from their own side onto persons and phenomena.

Of the three types of phenomena—evident, slightly obscure, and very obscure—emptiness is a slightly obscure phenomenon.[71] Ordinary beings cannot initially directly apprehend slightly obscure phenomena with their sense consciousnesses. They can initially be known only through reasoning, by means of an inference. Only after correctly ascertaining the emptiness of true existence conceptually, and then repeatedly meditating on it until the conceptual appearance of emptiness is worn away, can ordinary beings realize emptiness directly and become āryas. If all conceptual consciousnesses—even inferences that are correct conceptions of emptiness—were erroneous, then teachers and students could not use conceptual consciousnesses to teach and listen to explanations on emptiness. Cultivating the correct view of emptiness would then be impossible.

Not all conceptual consciousnesses grasp true existence. A mental consciousness envisioning the layout of a building and the mind designing a scientific experiment do not necessarily grasp true existence, and their apprehended objects are not objects of negation. If we are not clear about this point—that the object of negation is the conceived object of self-grasping ignorance, not the objects of all conceptual consciousnesses—we may spend a long time doing blank-minded, nonconceptual meditation that doesn't engage with any object whatsoever, mistakenly believing that it will lead to liberation.

The object of negation being discussed here is not wrong objects learned through the study of faulty philosophies. The conceptual consciousnesses holding those objects are acquired afflictions and are not the root of saṃsāra. Although refuting directionally partless particles, apperception, a permanent creator, a primal substance, one universal mind, and so forth are steppingstones to gain the correct view of emptiness, refuting these does not discredit the conceived object of innate ignorance. However, when we correctly negate the conceived object of ignorance, all the false objects posited by non-Buddhists and the lower Buddhist tenet systems are negated, and the process of gradually uprooting all incorrect conceptions begins. Just as uprooting a noxious weed decimates its stalks, leaves, and flowers, uprooting the root of saṃsāra damages all the wrong conceptions and afflictions that grow from the innate self-grasping ignorance.

Furthermore, the object of negation is not the object of sense consciousnesses or of mental direct perceivers. Training ourselves to think that the inherently existent things that appear to our senses do not exist is a skillful method to help us recognize the mistaken quality of our sense perceptions. However, this does not directly refute the object of negation. Objects apprehended by the five sense consciousnesses are not the object of negation because the object of negation is apprehended, conceived, and grasped by a conceptual mental consciousness grasping inherent existence. It is the *conceived object* of this erroneous *mental* consciousness that grasps true existence that is to be refuted by reasoning. This reasoning consciousness is a special mental consciousness, a pristine wisdom (*jñāna*) that is either an inference or a direct mental reliable cognizer. Emptiness is not perceivable by the sense consciousnesses. Only a special type of mental consciousness—the pristine wisdom of meditative equipoise—can perceive emptiness directly. Tsongkhapa said (LC 3:212):

> Therefore, the awarenesses whose mode of apprehension is to be eradicated by reasoning are only conceptual mental consciousnesses, and moreover, are the two graspings of self [of persons and of phenomena] or those conceptual consciousnesses that mistakenly superimpose further attributes on objects imputed by those two graspings of self.

## *The Valid Sense of I*

Before refuting the inherent existence of the I, it is important to differentiate the valid sense of I and the view of a personal identity, and their objects. This will clarify how the view of a personal identity reifies the valid I by superimposing inherent existence on it. It will also help us discern the object of negation and the valid I that exists.[72]

The psychophysical aggregates are the basis of designation of the self; they are the basis of our innate sense of self. The notion "I" comes about as a result of some experience; it arises in relation to one of our aggregates. We say "I'm sick" when our lungs are tight and "I'm full" when our stomach is full. We comment "I'm happy" or "I'm sad" in relation to the feeling aggregate. "I'm clever" and "I know what's going on" are said referring to our aggregate of discrimination, and "I'm angry" or "I have compassion" come in reference to the aggregate of miscellaneous factors. We say "I'm thinking" in dependence on the mental consciousness and "I'm hearing" in dependence on the auditory consciousness. In short, the thought "I" arises only in relation to our body and mind.

At these times, we're not thinking "I am my body," "I am my feelings," or "I am the one who is thinking." Rather, there's just the sense of a conventionally existent I. This is a valid mind apprehending the mere I, the I that is merely designated in dependence on the aggregates. The I *appears* inherently existent to this valid I-apprehending mind; however, that mind does not *grasp* the I to exist inherently.

Self-grasping arises after this. Something may happen in our environment that triggers it, or internally we may think of a troubling or desirable situation. At that time, the appearance of an inherently existent I becomes more vivid—the I seems to have its own essence and exist under its own power, independent of all other factors. It seems that there is a real I that is being threatened or wants something very badly. This I is the apprehended and conceived object of the view of a personal identity. At this time, the view of a personal identity, which is a form of self-grasping ignorance, has arisen, and it grasps that independent I.

It's at this point that the trouble begins, because based on this self-grasping, afflictions such as craving, belligerence, conceit, and so forth arise. Sometimes a virtuous mind arises supported by the view of a personal identity—for example, when we have faith in the Three Jewels or experience compassion for a homeless person. In either case, polluted karma is created and the ripening of the karmic seeds will perpetuate saṃsāra. However, the experience in saṃsāra will be happy or suffering depending on if the causal karma was virtuous or nonvirtuous.

### *Inherent Existence*

Ignorance superimposes inherent existence on both persons and other phenomena. What is inherent existence? We cannot define what it is because it doesn't exist. However, we can talk about what it would be like if it did exist. As we closely examine our own perceptions and thoughts, we'll gradually be able to identify how inherent existence *appears* to our mind and how ignorance *grasps* this appearance as true. Several ways of describing the object of negation follow. As you ponder them, you will see that they revolve around a common theme. In his *Commentary on the "Four Hundred,"* Candrakīrti says (LC 3:213):

> "Self" is an essence of things that does not depend on others; it is an inherent nature.

Commenting on the statement that all phenomena are without their own power—that is, they cannot set themselves up—and therefore there is no self, Candrakīrti points to four terms equivalent to self (LC 3:212):

> This refers to existing essentially (T. *rang gi ngo bo*), inherently (T. *rang bzhin*), autonomously (T. *rang dbang*), and without depending on another (T. *gzhan la rag ma las pa*).

These terms have varying English translations, but their meanings come to the same point:

- Inherent, intrinsic, or essential existence (*svabhāvasiddhi*, T. *rang bzhin gyis grub pa*): existence able to set itself up (T. *tshugs thub tu grub pa*).
- Existence by its own entity (*svarūpasiddhi*, T. *rang gi ngo bo nas grub pa*): having its own inherent nature.
- Existence by its own power, autonomous existence (T. *rang dbang du*

*grub pa*): a phenomenon appears to its apprehending consciousness as not depending on others—that is, not dependent on merely being posited by conceptuality—and it is taken to exist in that way. A phenomenon has a mode of abiding that is able to set itself up by its own entity right with the object. Its nature has an essence, its own unique mode of existence.
- Existence without depending on another (T. *gzhan la rag ma las pa*): existence without depending on merely being posited by conceptuality.

Ignorance apprehends persons and phenomena as if they existed as self-enclosed phenomena without being posited by a conventional consciousness. Tsongkhapa says (LC 3:212–13):

> What exists objectively in terms of its own essence without being posited through the power of a subjective mind is called "self" or "inherent nature." . . .
>
> In the case of reification by ignorance, there is, with regard to objects, be they persons or other phenomena, a grasping (T. *bzung*) that those phenomena have ontological status—a way of existing—from their own side (T. *rang gi ngos nas*), without being posited through the force of an awareness. The conceived object that is thus apprehended by that ignorant grasping, the independent ontological status of the phenomena, is identified as a hypothetical self or inherent nature.

If the conceived and apprehended objects of the innate self-grasping ignorance existed, they would exist from their own side, in and of themselves, under their own power, and without being posited by a conventional consciousness. Self is something that has its own essence and is able to set itself up. Self-enclosed, it does not depend on anything else. It exists by its own entity, truly, ultimately, and independently. Self refers to any nature or state that objects could have in which they do not rely on anything.

The ignorance that grasps such a self is erroneous because nothing can be established independent of the power of thought. Although things appear to exist "out there" objectively, and we assent to that appearance and grasp them as truly existent, that view is incorrect because phenomena do not exist in that way.

My guru, Kyabje Ling Rinpoche, described the object of negation to be the basis of designation and the designated object appearing undifferentiable. In other words, the object of negation is the designated object mixed with the basis of designation or inside the basis of designation. In the case of the view of a personal identity, it is an I that seems independent but still mixed with the aggregates.

The object of negation has also been described as what exists beyond what is merely designated by concept and term. That is, the conventional object—for example, the I—exists by being merely designated by concept and term, but ignorance grasps as existent something that goes beyond that—an I that has its own mode of being, its own independent essence.

Another description of the object of negation in terms of the I is: the meditator has already negated that the aggregates are the I, but an I that appears to be independent of the aggregates still seems to exist from the side of the aggregates.

Tsongkhapa says (FEW 40):

> . . . the mode of apprehending true existence—the object of negation—is to conceive [that objects] are not posited through the force of beginningless conceptuality but are established objectively by way of their own entity.

In *Seventy Stanzas on Emptiness* (*Śūnyatāsaptati*), Nāgārjuna says that ignorance grasps dependently arising phenomena as having a final reality of their own. Nāgārjuna uses causal dependent arising to reject the object of negation: things having a final reality of their own (ŚS 64–65):

> The Buddha said:
> grasping that things truly arise
> from causes and conditions is ignorance,
> and from that, the twelve links [of dependent origination] arise.
>
> When you realize that things are empty,
> you see properly and are not confused.

> That stops ignorance,
> and from that, the twelve links stop.

All conditioned phenomena are empty because they arise by the power of causes and conditions. The coarse form of causal dependence is not difficult to understand: we get an education so that we can work and earn a living. We save for the future so that we will have enough to live on when we are unable to work. Even animals understand this level of causality: they know that if they eat they will not feel hungry!

What allows for a cause to produce a result? Anything that is a cause is impermanent by its very nature, changing in each and every moment. Thus its arising is sufficient for it to disintegrate. As it ceases, something new arises—its result. If causes or results existed from their own side, they would have their own unchanging essence, would not be affected by other factors, and could not change. If things existed inherently, they would be frozen, unable to be influenced by causes and conditions. If the environment were an objective entity, it would not be influenced by carbon dioxide levels, earthquakes, and the increase in human population.

In the chapter "Questions from Upāli" in the *Ratnakūṭa Sūtra*, the Buddha clearly states that causes are not being emptied by means of emptiness—that is, causes are not negated or made nonexistent by emptiness. Rather, causes themselves are empty. As long as we assume that phenomena have some kind of objective reality of their own and think that not finding the conventional phenomenon when we search for its true essence is the meaning of emptiness, we have not arrived at the full understanding of emptiness. Rather, the basis of designation of a term has no inherent existence. For example, the basis of designation that has been designated "truck"—the wheels, axle, hood, and so forth—is totally devoid of inherent reality. There is not a findable, inherently existent truck in that collection of parts. Nevertheless, we can drive the merely designated truck.

Āryadeva explains ignorance and the object it grasps by explaining its antidote (CŚ 136):

> When dependent arising is seen,
> ignorance will not occur.

> Thus every effort has been made here
> to explain precisely this subject.

By identifying the wisdom of dependent arising as the antidote to ignorance, Āryadeva points out that ignorance grasps phenomena as devoid of dependence and as having an independent reality of their own. This is another way to express the object of negation.

In summary, a self of persons or phenomena would be something that existed objectively, apart from being posited by mind. Although things are designated in dependence on their basis of designation, they are not their basis of designation. There is nothing in any of the five aggregates or in the collection of the aggregates that is a person. However, a person exists; we know that from our own experience. The only way a person can exist is by being merely designated in dependence on the aggregates that are its basis of designation.

As we contemplate this, we get the sense that a person does not exist under their own power or from their own side. However, when we observe how things appear to us, they do not appear to be dependent on conceptuality; they appear to exist from their own side, objectively. This is the object of negation: that aside from our conception and name of an object, there is something in the basis of designation that is that object.

Since inherent existence does not exist at all, only hypothetical definitions and descriptions of it can be given. A coiled rope appears to be a snake, and we may think it is one. But when we analyze to find the snake on that base, no snake is found. Similarly, the person appears to be an inherently existent, independent entity, but when we analyze to find this real person, it is not found.

## REFLECTION

1. Describe the I that is the object of negation in the meditation on the emptiness of the person.
2. Describe the conventional I that exists.
3. Why is it important to differentiate between those two?

## *Self of Persons*

Having seen how a valid sense of I arises and how self-grasping quickly solidifies it, making it seem to inherently exist, let's look at the various levels of misconception and grasping concerning the I. Some of these wrong conceptions are acquired due to incorrect ways of thinking in this life, whereas others are innate and have been with us from beginningless time. Understanding the various levels of wrong conceptions and their erroneous objects helps us identify the ignorance that is the root of saṃsāra and the object of negation that it grasps.

Regarding the I, the erroneous conceptions grasping it, from the coarsest to the subtlest, are (1) the misconception of the person as permanent, unitary, and independent from causes; (2) grasping the I to be self-sufficient substantially existent; and (3) grasping the I to exist inherently.

Each of these errs in how they view the relationship of the I and the aggregates and superimposes a false mode of existence on the self. Although what is superimposed does not exist, there are different levels of superimpositions; some are subtler and more difficult to identify than others. They are like layers of an onion peeled away until nothing remains. We will begin examining the coarsest, since it is the easiest to recognize and to negate.

### *Permanent, Unitary, and Independent Self*

The first, grasping at a permanent, unitary, independent self (*ātman*), is an acquired wrong view that holds the self and the aggregates to be totally separate and unrelated to each other in that they have contradictory characteristics: the self is seen as permanent, whereas the aggregates are impermanent; the self is one, whereas there are many aggregates, and so forth. "Permanent" means the self is unchanging; it neither arises nor passes away. "Unitary" means that the I does not depend on parts; it is one monolithic object. "Independent" signifies that it does not depend on causes and conditions. The self is like a porter and the aggregates are the burden he carries; the two are completely different entities. This view does not arise in our minds innately; it is acquired by studying erroneous philosophical views. All Buddhist schools refute the existence of such a self.

How did the view of such a self come about? We notice that, from birth until the present, our body has grown and our mind has matured. But our sense of self feels constant. We say "When I was in my mother's womb" with the feeling that we are the same person now as then. Since people in ancient India accepted rebirth, they said that there must be something that goes from one life to the next and carries the karmic seeds. They concluded that a permanent self maintains the continuity of the person. Although the body and mind consist of parts, the self must be a unitary whole. Furthermore, while the body and mind are subject to causes and conditions, the self that transmigrates is beyond that; it is independent.

Most non-Buddhist religions have a similar idea of a permanent, unitary, and independent soul. Some people believe that a soul—the unchanging essence of a person—goes to heaven or hell after death. Some believe the soul remains in an undecided state until just before the Day of Judgment when it will be reunited with the body. Others believe this self is immutable and does not experience birth and death, although the aggregates change. This permanent self is trapped in the aggregates, where it suffers from creating karma and experiencing its result. Liberation is attained when the self transcends conditioned existence and either reunites with its creator or dwells in eternal bliss.

You may have been taught a similar view of the self or soul as a child, or you may have absorbed such a view simply through cultural conditioning. Because this conditioning is deep, portions of it may remain in your mind, and you may unconsciously think you have a soul that is your unchanging essence in this life and beyond. It is helpful to identify this belief in the mind and then investigate if it is possible for such a self or soul to exist.

Related to this conception of an unchanging self is the notion of an external, permanent creator of sentient beings and the universe. Buddhists employ several reasonings to negate the possible existence of such an independent creator:

- A permanent creator cannot create because creation involves change from what was to something new, and a permanent creator is fixed.
- If the creator succeeded in creating, it would be impermanent. As an impermanent thing, the creator would arise from causes and conditions and produce results. This contradicts the basic notion of an independent creator.
- Why did the creator create? It must have had a motivation, in which

case it is not independent of causes and conditions but is influenced by them.

- Some people say the creator is permanent but is temporarily impermanent while it creates. But something cannot be both permanent and impermanent, because these are contradictory qualities. Also a permanent creator cannot change to become an impermanent one and then change again to become unchanging.

*Self-Sufficient Substantially Existent Self*

The next level is grasping a self-sufficient substantially existent I, of which exist an acquired form and an innate form. Here the I appears to stand on its own, as if it could be identified without one or more of the aggregates having to be identified by the mind. The relationship between a self-sufficient substantially existent person and the aggregates is like that of a controller and the controlled—the person is the controller and the aggregates are what the person controls.

Here, the aggregates are seen as different from the person, yet having concordant characteristics with the person. This is noticeable when we think "My body falls ill so often. I wish I had the body of a deva." It seems as though the I could exchange its body for another, more preferable body, as if the body were a commodity that is different from the person possessing it. An example of seeing the person and the mind as different occurs when thinking, "My mind is full of afflictions. I wish I had the mind of a buddha!" The self seems to be the possessor of the mind, and the mind is like merchandise that can be exchanged. Holding the self and aggregates to be different in this way is grasping a self-sufficient substantially existent person. This is the self that the lower schools assert to be the object of negation when realizing the selflessness of persons.

Grasping a self-sufficient substantially existent person is present when we say "I can lose weight anytime I want," as if the I were the boss of the body that is overweight and the mind that likes to snack. Sometimes we may think "I can stop drinking, no problem," or "I'll be able to remain single-pointed on the object of meditation once I make up my mind to do so." In these cases, it seems as if the I is the mental consciousness that rules over the body and mind, which are its subjects.

How does grasping a permanent, unitary, independent self differ from grasping a self-sufficient substantially existent self? The non-Buddhists who assert the existence of a permanent, unified, and independent self assert that the I and the aggregates are different natures and have discordant characteristics. Different natures means two things can exist at different times and different places. Discordant characteristics means that some of their characteristics are dissimilar. For example, non-Buddhists believe the I is permanent, partless, and independent, whereas the Buddhists who refute a self-sufficient substantially existent person consider the person to be impermanent, composed of the aggregates that are its parts, and dependent on causes and conditions. In short, seeing the self as a self-sufficient substantially existent person does not entail seeing the person and the aggregates as having discordant characteristics, whereas the conception of a permanent, unified, and independent self does.

Although the lower schools—the Svātantrikas and below—believe that they are refuting the subtle self-grasping of persons, according to the Prāsaṅgikas, they are not. The Prāsaṅgikas differentiate two levels of innate self-grasping of persons—innate self-grasping of a self-sufficient substantially existent person and innate self-grasping of an inherently existent person. They say that the lower systems refute only a self-sufficient substantially existent person while leaving grasping an inherently existent I intact.[73]

Tsongkhapa asserts that grasping the self-sufficient substantial existence of the I exists in the minds of both those whose awarenesses have and have not been affected by tenets; this means that it has an acquired form that is learned in this lifetime and an innate form that comes from previous lives. However, grasping the person and the aggregates to have discordant characteristics—as in conceiving the self to be permanent, unified, and independent—exists only in the minds of those who have learned incorrect philosophies. This indicates that it is an acquired, not an innate, affliction (FEW 245):

> Apprehension that persons are substantially existent in the sense of being self-sufficient also exists among those whose awarenesses are not affected by tenets, but apprehension that persons exist as other than the [mental and physical] aggregates in the sense of having a character discordant with them does not exist among those whose awarenesses are not affected by tenets.

In the *Supplement*, Candrakīrti says that at the fourth ground ārya bodhisattvas eliminate the ignorance that is a coarse self-grasping. This ignorance is the innate self-grasping of a self-sufficient substantially existent person; it is considered coarse in comparison to the ignorance grasping an inherently existent person.

Realizing the lack of a self-sufficient substantially existent person is similar to the meditation having the aspect of grossness and peacefulness—which is common to both Buddhists and non-Buddhists—in that it temporarily suppresses the manifest afflictions explained in the two Knowledges (the *Treasury of Knowledge* and *Compendium of Knowledge*). But it cannot suppress even the manifest afflictions dependent on grasping inherent existence that are considered afflictive obscurations by the Prāsaṅgikas, let alone uproot any afflictions, be they those explained in the two Knowledges or those asserted by the Prāsaṅgikas. Since grasping the inherent existence of persons and phenomena is the root of saṃsāra, practitioners who have realized the lack of a self-sufficient substantially existent person are still far from cutting the root of saṃsāra and attaining liberation. Here we see not only the benefits of realizing the lack of a self-sufficient substantially existent I—its temporary suppression of manifest coarse afflictions—but also its limitations in that it does not free us from saṃsāra.

However, the meditation realizing the absence of a self-sufficient substantially existent person and the meditation having the aspect of grossness and peacefulness do differ in that the former is capable of suppressing the manifest afflictions up to and including the fourth formless realm, whereas the latter can suppress manifest afflictions only up to the third formless realm.

The Svātantrikas and below assert that the person is imputedly existent in that one of the aggregates must be known in order to identify the presence of a person. For example, we see a person's body or hear their voice, and in that way know a person is there. They refute a self-sufficient substantially existent person who can be known without first knowing one of the aggregates.

Unlike the Prāsaṅgikas, the lower schools assert something that is the person—that is, something that is findable when we investigate what the person is. Some of these schools say the mental consciousness is found and is the person; others say the collection of aggregates is the person. In their systems, the mental consciousness and the aggregates are substantially existent, so although they say the self-isolate person—that is, the person in general—

is imputedly existent, the illustration-isolate person—what is found when the person is searched for (the mind or the collection of aggregates)—is substantially existent. In the refutation of the self-sufficient substantial existence of a person, the substantial existence of the self-isolate person is negated, not the illustration-isolate person, which is substantially existent.

While refuting a permanent, unitary, and independent self and a self-sufficient substantially existent self are steppingstones to the realization of the emptiness of inherent existence of persons and phenomena, these are not the conceived objects of the innate ignorance that is the first link of dependent origination. By accepting that the mental consciousness, the collection of aggregates, or so on is the person, Svātantrikas and below do not accept that the I is merely designated in dependence on the collection of aggregates, and thus they do not negate an inherently existent person.

To understand the lack of a permanent, unitary, independent self and a self-sufficient substantially existent I, it is not necessary to first realize the emptiness of inherent existence or the selflessness of phenomena. However, the direct, nonconceptual realization of the emptiness of inherent existence completely overcomes all the other misconceptions and graspings.

### *Inherently Existent Self*

The third level of erroneous grasping is grasping the self as inherently existent. Prāsaṅgikas negate inherent existence on both the person and other phenomena such as the aggregates. We may learn an acquired form of grasping the inherent existence of the person by studying incorrect tenets, but the innate form is more insidious; it has kept us chained in saṃsāra since beginningless time. It exists in animals, babies, and all ordinary beings, whether or not they know language or hold philosophical tenets.

How does the innate self-grasping ignorance view the relationship of the self and the aggregates? Innately, we do not conceive the I and the aggregates to be unrelated, as shown in the examples of saying "I'm sick" when our stomach hurts and "I'm thinking" when the mind is thinking. Seeing the self and the aggregates as totally different is an acquired view.

We also do not innately see the person and the aggregates as completely the same, as shown by the examples of being willing to exchange our body or mind with that of another person. If our ordinary innate mind saw the self and the aggregates as completely the same, these thoughts would not arise. Therefore, seeing the I and the aggregates as identical is also an acquired view.

When we say "*I'm* sick," our sense of self is identified with the body, although there is not the thought "I am my body." Similarly, when we say "*I* don't want to be reborn in unfortunate states," the sense of self is closely related to the mind, although we're not thinking, "I am my mind." These are not the subtle innate self-grasping. The Fifth Dalai Lama clarifies (HSY 133):

> Sometimes the I will seem to exist in the context of the body. Sometimes it will seem to exist in the context of the mind. Sometimes it will seem to exist in the context of feelings, discriminations, or other factors. At the end of noticing a variety of modes of appearance, you will come to identify an I that exists in its own right, that exists inherently, that from the start is self-established, existing indistinguishably with mind and body, which are also mixed like milk and water. This is the first step, ascertainment of the object of negation in the view of selflessness. You should work at it until deep experience arises.

The sense of self does not arise in a vacuum but is based on the body and mind. After "I" has been validly designated in dependence on the body and mind, grasping that I as inherently existent may arise. The subtle self-grasping of the person takes the mere I as its observed object, not the body or mind. That is, the observed object of the view of a personal identity is the conventionally existent I, and the view of a personal identity erroneously apprehends it as inherently existent.

The innate view of a personal identity grasps the self as mixed in with the aggregates yet able to stand on its own. As the Fifth Dalai Lama said above, the self appears blended with the aggregates but still distinct from them. When we are in physical danger, we easily experience a strong sense of I focused on the body: "I'm going to get hurt." When we think of all the destructive karma we have accumulated, we may experience a strong sense of I based on the mind: "I'm going to be born in an unfortunate birth." The way the I appears in both of these situations is not the subtlest object of negation, because the I appears identified with one of the aggregates, whereas the I that is the subtlest object of negation appears mixed with the aggregates but still a self-enclosed entity.

As mentioned above, the mere I, the conventional I that exists—not the aggregates—is the observed object of the view of a personal identity. This view thinks "I" and holds that I to exist by its own characteristics. Its conceived object, which is the object of negation, is an inherently existent I that does not exist at all. However, its observed object, the mere I, is not refuted, for it exists conventionally. It is the self that creates karma, is reborn, and becomes a buddha.

The notions of a permanent, unified, and independent self, a self-sufficient substantially existent person, and an inherently existent person differ in terms of how they view the relationship of the I and the aggregates. The non-Buddhists who grasp a permanent, unified, and independent self assert the I and aggregates are different natures and totally unrelated. Buddhist essentialists—from the Vaibhāṣikas up to and including the Svātantrika Mādhyamikas—refute a permanent, unified, and independent self as well as a self-sufficient substantially existent person. Here the self is the controller of the aggregates, such that the aggregates depend on the person but the person does not depend on the aggregates. Prāsaṅgika Mādhyamikas refute the previous two notions of the person as well as an inherently existent person. An inherently existent person is one in which the I and the aggregates are neither completely the same nor totally unrelated. The I is mixed in with the collection of the body and mind but exists in its own right and is able to stand on its own. Prāsaṅgikas are the only ones who refute all three wrong views of the self.

Only the Prāsaṅgikas negate an inherently existent self; the lower Buddhist schools proclaim that the I must have some inherent essence from its own side because if it didn't, it would be only an arbitrary name. There must be some objective nature or essence that allows us to have a sense of identity as the doer of actions and the experiencer of results. The Prāsaṅgikas, however, refute even this, saying the I exists merely nominally.

In other words, all Buddhist systems agree that the I is dependent on the aggregates, but everyone except the Prāsaṅgikas states that when the I that travels from one life to the next is sought within the aggregates, something can be found that is the person. Unlike the Prāsaṅgikas, the lower systems do not understand that because the I is dependent, it lacks inherent existence. In fact, they believe that the I must inherently exist or it would not exist at all.

In your meditation, be aware of the various ways in which self-grasping can grasp the person. Try to identify if you grasp a permanent, unified, and independent I; at other times see if you can detect grasping a self-sufficient substantially existent person. Also be aware of when you grasp an inherently existent person. Becoming familiar with the above descriptions of these three will help you to do this. However, it takes time to identify these wrong views of how the person exists, so be patient.

In the meditation on emptiness, identifying the appearance of an inherently existent I is the first and most difficult step. It doesn't work to sit down and say to yourself, "What is my conception of the I?" That is like asking a thief to stand up and declare his activities. He won't do it. Yet without having a clear idea of the false self we naively believe exists, how can we realize its emptiness?

As beginners it's difficult to identify the inherently existent I that is the object of negation. Start with observing your sense of I when you feel a strong emotion. For example, one day a group that I (Chodron) was teaching had an interview with His Holiness. When we entered the room, His Holiness greeted each of us individually and then a monk directed us to a row of seats in a semi-circle. Since I was first, he indicated to me to move down the row to make room for the others. Following directions, I went to the last chair, and when the monk told us to be seated I sat down. His Holiness finished greeting people and then approached me, and leaning over, gently said, "I think that's my chair." How embarrassed I was! The object of negation was showing itself in living color!

To identify the object of negation, one corner of our mind must discreetly and unobtrusively observe how the sense of I manifests in our lives. We may have any or all of the above notions of the self at different times during the day. So we must quietly observe how the I appears to exist in various situations—for example, when we are unjustly blamed or when we are highly praised. What is the sense of I when we crave to have something? When we criticize ourselves? When others ignore us or shower us with attention? When someone says our name?

When we observe the sense of I that exists when a strong emotion is present, how do we differentiate the apprehended objects of coarse and subtle self-grasping in our own experience—coarse self-grasping of persons being grasping a self-sufficient substantially existent person and subtle self-grasping of persons being grasping an inherently existent person? Most of our glaring anger, for example, probably involves grasping the self as self-sufficient substantially existent in addition to grasping the self as inherently existent. Grasping inherent existence is the source of all afflictions. It may lead to grasping a self-sufficient substantially existent person, which then gives rise to the manifest affliction. However, it is extremely difficult to tease apart the conceived objects of the two types of self-grasping in our actual experience.

In your practice, first identify and then refute a permanent, unitary, and independent I by reflecting that it is impossible for a permanent, unitary, independent self to exist. Since this is a coarse notion of self created by incorrect philosophies, it is comparatively easy to disprove. The idea of a self-sufficient substantially existent person is more subtle, and the idea of an inherently existent person is the subtlest and therefore the most difficult to identify and refute. If you refute the existence of an inherently existent self, all other graspings of self are automatically overcome.

Once you have identified how the false, inherently existent I appears, investigate if such an I can actually exist. Here, reasoning and analysis are critical. Inquire how the I exists until you are convinced that it cannot exist inherently. At that time, rest the mind in the absence of such an inherently existent self.

## REFLECTION

1. When you were a child, were you taught that there is a permanent soul and a permanent creator?
2. Review the reasons that disprove these. Do the reasons make sense to you? Does one part of your mind still find attractive or comforting the idea of a permanent creator of the universe and the permanent soul that is your essence?
3. Review the characteristics of a permanent, unitary, independent self, a

self-sufficient substantially existent person, and an inherently existent person.

4. Can you identify in your experience when you are grasping at any of these?

---

*Grasping Mine*

The view of a personal identity involves grasping both I and mine as inherently existent. Just as casually saying "I'm walking" does not involve grasping the inherent existence of I, casually thinking "my body" or "my mind" is not grasping mine to be inherently existent. However, when a strong destructive emotion such as attachment or anger arises, grasping inherently existent I or mine is involved. At that time we think, "Don't you treat *me* like that!" "This is *mine*," or "*My* child was admitted to a prestigious school."

Grasping mine implicitly grasps the I. The view of a personal identity grasping mine arises in relation to things that belong to us—our body, mind, possessions, and so forth. However, these things are not its observed object; it focuses only on the sense of mine—the feeling of "myness" or ownership[74]—not on the things that are mine. Technically speaking, mine is neither a person nor a phenomenon in the context of the division of persons and phenomena as the basis of the two selflessnesses. It is just the sense of mine. However, implicit in thinking "mine" is the notion of a person. For that reason, grasping mine as inherently existent is part of the self-grasping of persons, and within that, the view of a personal identity.

The body, mind, and possessions are illustrations of things that are mine, but they are not the mine that is the observed object of the view of a personal identity. Grasping the body and mind as inherently existent is grasping the self of phenomena, whereas grasping the body and mind as inherently mine is grasping the self of persons. Grasping mine takes our body, mind, and other external things and views them as mine while holding that mine to exist inherently. We think, "These are *my* eyes. This is *my* house. These emotions are *mine*."

In the above examples, grasping inherent existence is involved, whereas casually clarifying ownership—for example, saying "Is this pen yours or mine?"—does not involve self-grasping.

Not all grasping of a self of persons is the view of a personal identity. The view of a personal identity refers just to grasping one's own self, whereas grasping a self of persons applies to grasping any person as inherently existent. When we grasp Tashi, Sally, and Fluffy the cat as inherently existent, this is self-grasping of persons but not the view of a personal identity.

REFLECTION

Observe what happens when you superimpose inherently existent "my" or "mine" on someone or something.

1. Recall an object in a store before you bought it—for example, a car on the showroom floor. If it were damaged, would you be disturbed?
2. What would your reaction be if it were damaged after you purchased it, once it became "mine"? You park your new car and do an errand. When you return, it has a big dent in the side.
3. Consider your expectations when you think of *my* child (spouse, parent, or sibling). Do you hold those same expectations and judgments for another person's child? They are both children. Why does the term "my" change your feelings and judgments so drastically?
4. What would happen if you left the designation "my" aside and just looked at people and things without imputing ownership?

### *Self of Phenomena*

When inherent existence is superimposed or projected onto persons, it is called "self of persons"; when it is superimposed onto the psychophysical aggregates and other phenomena, it is called "self of phenomena." The terms "self-grasping of persons," "self-grasping of phenomena," "selflessness of persons," and "selflessness of phenomena" are given accordingly.

Non-Buddhist tenet systems generally do not talk about the selflessness of phenomena. Vaibhāṣikas and Sautrāntikas speak of the selflessness of persons, but not the selflessness of phenomena. Yogācārins and the Svātantrika Mādhyamikas speak of both, but they assert that realizing the selflessness of persons is sufficient to attain liberation, whereas realizing both the selflessness of persons and of phenomena is necessary to attain full awakening. How they define the self and selflessness of phenomena differs from the Prāsaṅgikas. Understanding their assertions helps us get at the more subtle Prāsaṅgika view.

To review, Yogācārins speak of four approaches to grasping a self of phenomena: (1) grasping the subject and object of a perception to be different substantial entities, (2) grasping phenomena to exist by their own characteristics as the referents of names and terms, (3) grasping external objects, and (4) grasping phenomena to exist by their own characteristics as the basis adhered to by thoughts. All four come to the same point, although they have different approaches. Realizing the absence of all four is realizing the selflessness of phenomena according to the Yogācārins. Their ideas will be explained in more depth in a future volume.

Svātantrikas speak about grasping phenomena as truly existent, ultimately existent, or existent as its own reality. To them, these three mean a phenomenon exists exclusively as self-instituting without being posited by the force of appearing to a nondefective consciousness. "Nondefective consciousness" means a consciousness that is not erroneous with respect to its engaged object. For example, it does not have superficial causes of error, such as faulty sense faculties, being in a moving vehicle, or holding wrong views. Svātantrikas say that phenomena exist inherently and are posited by the force of appearing to a nondefective awareness, but ignorance grasps them as existing without being designated by a nondefective awareness.

Svātantrikas negate true existence and ultimate existence—as their school explains the meaning of these terms—but they hold that phenomena are indeed established by way of their own character and exist inherently on the conventional level. For Prāsaṅgikas, "true existence," "inherent existence," "existence from its own side," "ultimate existence," "substantial existence," and so forth are synonyms. However, these terms have different meanings according to the lower tenet systems, so when discussing the assertions of each system, it is necessary to clarify the meaning of the terms we use.

All of the above terms refer to the object of negation of the Prāsaṅgikas. For them, inherent existence is something that can set itself up and exists without being merely designated by name and concept. For example, when we look at a building, it seems to exist objectively, independent of our mind. When we think of the CEO of a company or the president of a country, they seem to have some inherent power or quality that makes them that. We forget that "CEO" or "president" is merely a name that has been temporarily designated to a person as a result of societal consensus.

Prāsaṅgikas say that all phenomena exist by the force of mind—by being merely designated by mind in dependence on a basis of designation. However, things appear to the six consciousnesses to exist by their own nature, to have their own inherent essence or true reality. Innate ignorance assents to these false appearances and grasps phenomena to exist inherently as they appear.

All four Buddhist tenet systems have their source in Buddha's word, although they differ in which sūtras they consider definitive and interpretable. A skillful teacher, the Buddha set forth different views of emptiness according to the capabilities of his audience in order to lead us gradually to the subtlest and most complete view. In the next volume, we will explore the ways he sets forth for refuting the various objects of negation.

## *The* Heart Sūtra

The *Heart Sūtra* concisely expresses the meaning of all the Perfection of Wisdom sūtras in its four famous and profound phrases: "Form is empty. Emptiness is form. Emptiness is not other than form. Form is not other than emptiness." The meaning of these four phrases illustrates the noncontradictory nature of emptiness and dependent arising. The key to understand this is to avoid negating too much or too little in the meditation on emptiness.

The sūtra uses form as an example; its fourfold approach applies to the other aggregates—feelings (discriminations, miscellaneous factors, and consciousnesses) are empty. Emptiness is feelings (and so forth). Emptiness is not other than feelings (and so forth). Feelings (and so forth) are not other than emptiness. These four phrases concern all impermanent phenomena, which together comprise the five aggregates. They can also be applied to permanent phenomena, thereby including all existents.

Observing what is negated and what is affirmed in this passage from the *Heart Sūtra* will give us a better idea of what is and isn't the object of negation. While it is easy to say that inherent existence is negated and the conventional world of dependent arising is affirmed, we ordinary beings are not skilled in actually doing this.

*Form Is Empty*

Although some translators render this first phrase as "form is emptiness," this is incorrect. Form is not emptiness because form is a conventional truth and emptiness is an ultimate truth, and what is one truth cannot be the other. Emptiness is an attribute of form; it is form's ultimate nature. Said in another way, form's emptiness is form's lack of inherent existence.

"Form is empty." When we perceive form, it appears as if form itself constitutes its own ultimate reality. If the form we perceive is its ultimate reality—if form were inherently existent—then when we subject form to critical analysis that seeks its true or ultimate reality, form should be able to withstand that analysis. The reasoning analyzing the ultimate should be able to identify something that definitely is form. However, this is not the case. Form is unfindable through such an analytic process. This doesn't mean form doesn't exist. Rather, it is empty of the inherent existence that our ignorance erroneously projected on it. Form does not exist in its own right; it doesn't exist under its own power, independent of other factors. This emptiness of inherent existence of form is the ultimate nature of form.

Form arises due to the assembly of its causes and conditions. Because form is dependent on other factors, it does not exist independently. Dependent and independent existence are mutually exclusive, and because independent existence is synonymous with inherent existence, form is empty of inherent existence. It has never and will never exist inherently because its very nature is dependent.

*Emptiness Is Form*

What then is form? The *Heart Sūtra* says, "Emptiness is form." This doesn't literally mean emptiness is form; it indicates that what we call "form" is a dependent arising and is utterly empty of independent existence. Because it arises dependent on other factors, it lacks inherent existence. Its emptiness of inherent existence allows for form to arise dependent on other factors that are not it. A form arises from a multiplicity of causes and conditions, and in turn it becomes a cause or condition for other things. A form is part of a vast interconnected array of interdependent functioning things that exist within emptiness, within their being empty of true existence.

When the sūtra says "form is empty; emptiness is form," the meaning is "emptiness, therefore form; form, therefore emptiness." In other words, because form is empty, the only way it can exist is dependently. It is not possible for something that is not empty to exist. And because form's emptiness exists, form exists. Form and form's emptiness depend on each other. They are mutually dependent.

The *Kāśyapa Chapter Sūtra* from the *Heap of Jewels Sūtra* (*Ratnakūṭa Sūtra*) lists many ways in which something can be empty. One is "other-emptiness," as in the temple being empty of monastics. The temple being empty of monastics is other-emptiness because the basis of emptiness, the temple, is empty of some other thing, the monastics. But the manner of being empty in "form is empty" is self-emptiness—empty of self-nature. Emptiness of self-nature does not mean form is devoid of form. Form is form, and the reality of form being form is not rejected. Rather, form is devoid of an inherent nature; it is empty of being an inherently existent form. Emptiness does not imply nonexistence. Rather, the fact that things are empty of inherent existence allows for them to arise dependent on causes and conditions. Emptiness and dependent arising are compatible.

We may think that form has some sort of objective existence or existence from its own side and that it is now being made empty of objective existence. In the *Perfection of Wisdom Sūtra in 25,000 Lines*, the Buddha states, "Form is not made empty by emptiness. Form itself is empty." In the chapter "Questions from Upāli" in the *Ratnakūṭa Sūtra*, the Buddha clearly states that causes are not made empty by emptiness, nor are they being negated by emptiness. Rather, causes themselves are empty. That means that there is no objectified basis that is the referent of the term "form" or "cause." All phenomena are totally devoid of any inherent reality in and of themselves.

"Emptiness is form" indicates the conventional existence of form. The expression "the dawning of emptiness as the meaning of dependent arising" is the meaning of "emptiness is form." That is, the fact that phenomena lack inherent existence indicates that they exist conventionally. Conversely, the expression "the dawning of dependent arising as the meaning of emptiness" is the meaning of "form is empty."[75] Because phenomena arise dependently, they lack inherent existence.

The conventional reality of form is that it is a dependent arising. It comes into being as a result of causes and conditions. In a dependently arising world, the law of causality is feasible, and cause and effect can be posited. Form's nature as a dependent arising is possible only because it is empty of inherent existence. "Emptiness is form" tells us that form arises within the emptiness of inherent existence; the ultimate nature of all phenomena, emptiness, is the basis that allows for the form and everything else to exist. The world of diverse objects is an expression or manifestation of emptiness. If emptiness were not phenomena's ultimate nature—if phenomena existed inherently—they would be frozen in time and unable to arise or function because they would be independent of all other factors, such as causes and conditions. Dependent arising is possible only in a world that is empty of inherent existence, and the emptiness of inherent existence is possible only in a world that exists dependently.

Emptiness is not an absolute reality like Brahmā, God, or a cosmic energy or primal substance that is an underlying reality at the heart of the universe out of which the world of multiplicity arises. Emptiness is not an independent reality somewhere far away out of which the diversity of phenomena arise. Emptiness is right here, right now. It is our very nature and the nature of everything around us.

From the Madhyamaka viewpoint, emptiness is the absence of the elaboration of inherent existence. It is not an emptiness that is totally devoid of any basis, because emptiness can be understood only in relation to individual phenomena. Emptiness depends on a conventionally existent phenomenon whose ultimate nature it is.

Emptiness is a nonaffirming negation; it is not an affirmative phenomenon that we can find. It is not an independent, absolute reality because it depends on phenomena whose ultimate nature is empty. We can speak only of the emptiness of specific objects; emptiness is not an external, independent, absolute energy.

Since emptiness can only be known in relation to individual phenomena, if an individual thing ceases, its emptiness also ceases. Although that emptiness is not a product of causes and conditions, because the basis upon which it is understood no longer exists, the emptiness of that thing also no longer exists. When the cup breaks into pieces, the emptiness of the cup no longer exists. However, since the pieces exist, the emptiness of the pieces exists.

Depending on the conventional object we choose as the basis of our meditation on emptiness, our meditation may be more or less powerful. When we meditate on emptiness in deity yoga, the basis of our meditation is a pure object—the form of a deity—and we meditate on its emptiness. In Mahāmudrā and Dzogchen, the mind is the basis of meditation, and we focus on its emptiness. Meditating on the emptiness of the mind, the I, or the form of a deity will have a stronger impact on us than meditating on the emptiness of a candle.

### *Emptiness Is Not Other Than Form, and Form Is Not Other Than Emptiness*

All of the Buddha's teachings were given within the framework of the two truths—conventional (veiled) and ultimate. These two sentences indicate the relationship between the two truths. Although understanding the nature of reality in terms of the two truths was common to many systems of thought in ancient India, both Buddhist and non-Buddhist, the subtlest explanation speaks of them not as two separate independent entities, but as two aspects of one phenomenon.

Conventional truths—which include form and the other four aggregates—are the truths of everyday worldly conventions. This is the level of reality that is ascertained by mere appearance to our ordinary consciousnesses. Conventional truths are not established by the reasoning analyzing the ultimate, nor are they in the purview of that wisdom. They constitute the world of multiple and diverse phenomena. Ultimate truths, on the other hand, are those arrived at through a reasoned analysis of the ultimate. When we search for the deeper mode of existence of phenomena, we find their emptiness of inherent existence. This is their suchness (*tattva*), their ultimate mode of existence, the ultimate truth.

"Emptiness is not other than form" indicates that the emptiness of form is form's ultimate nature. It is not separate and unrelated to form. Emptiness does not exist apart from the individual objects that are empty. Emptiness cannot be independent from the basis on which it is ascertained.

Similarly, "form is not other than emptiness" means that form and other veiled truths exist within the reality of emptiness and are in the nature of emptiness. Form—and veiled truths in general—and its emptiness cannot be separated: if one exists, so does the other; if one ceases, so does the other. The two truths are inseparable. They are one nature but nominally different.

We must contemplate the emptiness of feelings and so forth as well as the emptiness of form. When the *Heart Sūtra* says "perfectly looking at the emptiness of inherent existence of the five aggregates also," the word "also" indicates the person who is designated in dependence on the five aggregates. That person—I, me—is also empty of inherent existence. In your practice, it is helpful to think, "I am empty; emptiness is me. Emptiness is not other than me; I am not other than emptiness." Such meditation will have a powerful effect on your mind.

## REFLECTION

1. Think of a form such as your body. It feels very solid, as if it were independent of causes and conditions and existed objectively from its own side.
2. Does your body exist in the way it appears? Is it independent of causes such as the sperm and egg of your parents?
3. Focus on the thought: My body exists only because the causes of it existed. If those causes didn't exist, my body wouldn't exist. When the causes for each moment of the body cease, a new moment of the body will arise; then it too will cease.
4. This understanding contradicts the feeling that the body is an independent entity that will always be there. Your body is impermanent and empty of inherent existence.

---

The tradition coming from the Nyingma master Mipham (1846–1912) presents these four lines in the *Heart Sūtra* as "the four approaches to understanding emptiness." Here the four lines are related to the refutation of the four alternatives:

*Form is empty* indicates that all phenomena are empty of inherent existence. This counteracts the extreme of existence (the extreme of absolutism), which holds that phenomena are their own ultimate reality (that they exist inherently).

*Emptiness is form* indicates that within emptiness, form and other dependent arisings appear. While phenomena are empty, they also exist dependently; emptiness must be understood in terms of dependent arising. This counteracts the extreme of nonexistence (the extreme of nihilism).

*Emptiness is not other than form* indicates the union of dependent arising and emptiness, the union of conventional appearances and their emptiness. Far from being unrelated, emptiness and dependently arising phenomena exist in relation to each other. This annuls the extremes of both existence and nonexistence, both absolutism and nihilism.

*Form is not other than emptiness* shows that dependent arising and emptiness—appearances and emptiness—are compatible and complementary. This line presents the total elimination of all conceptual elaborations and enables us to transcend the extreme of neither-existence-nor-nonexistence.

The Sakya Lamdre (Path and Fruition) tradition has a similar fourfold approach to emptiness: appearances are established as empty; emptiness is dependent arising; emptiness and appearance are a unity; this union of emptiness and appearance is beyond expression or language.

Usually the wisdom realizing emptiness is presented as the antidote to both grasping inherent existence and the extreme of absolutism, and the understanding of dependent arising as the counterforce to both total nonexistence and the extreme of nihilism. However, if our understandings of emptiness and dependent arising have correctly penetrated the depths, these two understandings will work in the reverse order as well. Understanding emptiness will help us transcend the extreme of nihilism. The fact that phenomena are empty indicates that they are not totally nonexistent; they are empty of just inherent existence. Understanding the appearances of dependently arisen phenomena enables us to transcend the extreme of absolutism; because phenomena exist dependently, they cannot exist inherently. This reverse way of opposing the two extremes is profound and is unique to the Prāsaṅgika approach.

# 9 The Middle Way View

AS A SKILLFUL TEACHER, the Buddha taught people according to their varying aptitudes and dispositions in order to lead them to the correct realization of the ultimate nature. These teachings evolved to become the philosophical tenet schools in ancient India. Some key points the proponents of these systems discussed were the object of negation and the view of selflessness. We will begin this chapter with a review and overview of the positions of the various Buddhist philosophical schools on these and other topics and then show the Madhyamakas' and, within that, the Prāsaṅgikas' unique assertions of the Middle Way.

For some readers, understanding the meaning of so many terms may initially be daunting. But just as a young science student gradually becomes familiar with scientific terms until they seem very natural to him, so too will you become familiar with these philosophical terms.

## *Settling the Object of Negation and the View of Selflessness*

Meditation on emptiness involves ensuring that the apprehended object is a nonaffirming negative that is the negation of inherent existence. The lower Buddhist tenet systems meditate on the selflessness that is the refutation of a self-sufficient substantially existent person. Although nothing else may be affirmed after negating a self-sufficient substantially existent person, that is not the deepest object of negation. It is like a person who wants to have a clean floor thinking "there are no pebbles on the floor" while neglecting to see the dirt there.

Among the various philosophical systems, different assertions exist regarding the observed and conceived objects of the self-grasping of persons. The observed object—the conventional I—is the basis on which self-grasping of persons superimposes a false way of existence and therefore misapprehends the I. The conceived object is a false person that self-grasping apprehends instead. The tenet systems also have different definitions of the self-grasping of persons and the self-grasping of phenomena, as well as what constitutes obscurations to be abandoned to attain liberation and awakening.

Saṃmitīya Vaibhāṣikas say the observed object of the self-grasping of persons is all five aggregates, Yogācārins state it is the foundation consciousness, and Sautrāntikas and Svātantrika Mādhyamikas say it is the mental consciousness. According to Prāsaṅgikas, it is the mere I—the I that exists by being merely designated.

Most systems say the conceived object of the view of a personal identity and of the innate self-grasping of persons is a self-sufficient substantially existent self. Prāsaṅgikas explain that that is the coarse object of negation, whereas an inherently existent self is the actual conceived object to be negated.

Vaibhāṣikas and Sautrāntikas do not speak of self-grasping of phenomena. Yogācārins present four approaches related to self-grasping of phenomena: (1) grasping the subject and object of a perception to be different substantial entities, (2) grasping phenomena to exist by their own characteristics as the referents of names and terms, (3) grasping external objects, and (4) grasping phenomena to exist by their own characteristics as the basis adhered to by thoughts. They accordingly assert four formulations of the selflessnesses of phenomena: (1) the absence of duality of subject and object, (2) the absence of phenomena existing by their own characteristics as referents of names and terms, (3) the absence of external existence, and (4) the absence of phenomena as existing by their own characteristics as the basis adhered to by thoughts.

Svātantrika Mādhyamikas say the self-grasping of phenomena grasps phenomena as ultimately existent. For them ultimate existence and inherent existence are different, and they negate inherent existence only on the ultimate level. Also, the lack of ultimate or true existence of persons for Svātantrika is considered a selflessness of phenomena, not of persons. This is because, unlike the Prāsaṅgikas, Svātantrikas differentiate the self of persons and the self of phenomena not so much by the basis of negation—

the person or other phenomena—but by the object of negation. The self of persons is a self-sufficient substantially existent person, whereas the self of phenomena is the ultimate existence and true existence of all phenomena, including persons. Prāsaṅgika Mādhyamikas, on the other hand, differentiate the selflessness of persons and the selflessness of phenomena in terms of the basis—the person or phenomena other than the person. They assert that ultimate existence and inherent existence are synonymous and say the object of negation for both selflessnesses is ultimate, true, and inherent existence.

These two branches of Madhyamaka also differ in their assertions of the selflessness of phenomena: the Svātantrikas state it is their absence of ultimate existence, whereas Prāsaṅgikas propound a selflessness of persons and phenomena that are the absence of inherent existence of persons and phenomena, respectively. In chapter 5, see the chart of the object of negation—the self refuted on persons and phenomena by each tenet system. Their coarse and subtle selflessnesses of persons and phenomena are the nonexistence of their corresponding object of negation.

Below is a chart regarding what each system asserts as coarse and subtle afflictive and cognitive obscurations. All Buddhist systems agree that overcoming afflictive obscurations is necessary to attain liberation, and all Mahāyāna tenet systems agree that eradicating cognitive obscurations brings full awakening. However, they differ on what they assert the afflictive and cognitive obscurations to be. This depends on how they define selflessness, which in turn accords with their varying assertions regarding the object of negation in the meditation on selflessness. As you explore the assertions of the tenet systems concerning many topics, you will see how their assertions regarding the object of negation influence their other assertions to a great extent.

All schools except Prāsaṅgika say that to attain liberation, realizing only the selflessness of persons—which for them is the absence of a self-sufficient substantially existent person—is necessary. Yogācārins and Svātantrikas assert that to attain full awakening, realizing the selflessness of phenomena as they define it is also necessary. Prāsaṅgikas disagree, proclaiming that the attainments of liberation and full awakening both entail realizing the selflessness of persons and of phenomena, which are the absence of inherent existence. For them, the two self-graspings do not differ in terms of how they grasp the person or phenomena, because both grasp inherent existence.

## Afflictive and Cognitive Obscurations

| | COARSE AFFLICTIVE OBSCURATIONS | SUBTLE AFFLICTIVE OBSCURATIONS | COARSE COGNITIVE OBSCURATIONS | SUBTLE COGNITIVE OBSCURATIONS |
|---|---|---|---|---|
| Vaibhāṣikas and Sautrāntikas | Conception of a permanent, unitary, independent self | Grasping a self-sufficient substantially existent person, afflictions it produces, and their seeds | none | none |
| Yogācārins | Conception of a permanent, unitary, independent self | Grasping a self-sufficient substantially existent person, afflictions it produces, and their seeds | none | Grasping self of phenomena and its latencies (grasping phenomena to exist by their own characteristics as the referents for names; grasping phenomena to exist by their own characteristics as the basis adhered to by thoughts; grasping subject and object as different entities; grasping external existence) |
| Yogācāra-Svātantrika Mādhyamikas | Conception of a permanent, unitary, independent self | Grasping a self-sufficient substantially existent person, afflictions it produces, and their seeds | Grasping subject and object as different entities, grasping external objects | Grasping self of phenomena as truly existent and its latencies |

| | | | | |
|---|---|---|---|---|
| Sautrāntika-Svātantrika Mādhyamikas | Conception of a permanent, unitary, independent self | Grasping a self-sufficient substantially existent person, afflictions it produces, and their seeds | none | Grasping phenomena as truly existent and its latencies |
| Prāsaṅgika-Mādhyamikas | Grasping a self-sufficient substantially existent person, afflictions it produces, and their seeds | Grasping inherent existence of persons and other phenomena, afflictions it produces, and their seeds | none | Latencies of ignorance, subtle dualistic appearance, latencies for grasping the two truths as different entities |

Vaibhāṣikas and Sautrāntikas do not speak of cognitive obscurations but differentiate a buddha's awakening from that of an arhat by saying that in addition to afflictive ignorance, buddhas also overcome nonafflictive ignorance. Afflictive ignorance mainly impedes liberation and consists of grasping a self-sufficient substantially existent person; the three poisonous minds of confusion, attachment, and anger; and their seeds. Nonafflictive ignorance mainly impedes the attainment of the all-knowing of a buddha. This ignorance has four aspects: the ignorance of the profound and subtle qualities of a buddha; ignorance due to the object being far away; ignorance due to distant time; and ignorance due to the object's nature, such as the result of a specific karma that a certain individual has created.

How do we determine which tenet system has the most profound and accurate view? Reasoning is the essential key. We must determine which views hold up when scrutinized with logic and which ones crumble. Something "feeling right" is not sufficient, because to our ignorance, grasping inherent existence feels right! Referring to the sūtras as well as the treatises and commentaries by the great Indian and Tibetan scholar-adepts is extremely helpful, but solely banking on them is not sufficient. We must apply reasoning as the true test of their accuracy. We must be able to negate what does not exist and at the same time establish what does exist.

## *Correctly Identifying the Object of Negation to Avoid the Two Extremes*

Discerning the subtle and coarse objects of negation is not an easy process. Because we are so used to believing that persons and phenomena exist in the way they appear, we ordinary beings generally don't think that is anything to question. Imagine if you can, people born wearing sunglasses: they would be so used to seeing everything as dark that they wouldn't realize there was anything wrong with their perceptions. Similarly, the cognitive obscurations have covered our minds since beginningless time; we have never cognized anything else but inherent existence, so we naturally believe everything exists objectively—independent of our mind. As a result we attribute all our problems and suffering to other people or to external conditions, and we believe all happiness comes from obtaining whatever external object, person, or circumstance that appears desirable and attractive to us.

From beginningless time, we have endeavored to procure everything that we believe will bring us happiness and fight off everything that threatens or interferes with that happiness. Has this strategy worked? If it had, we would no longer be experiencing saṃsāric duḥkha and would instead experience the bliss of nirvāṇa. But this isn't the case. Now is the time to try a different strategy: to examine our mind and see the way it misapprehends and misconceives how the self, other people, and things in our environment exist; to refute the objects of our erroneous consciousnesses; to banish all misapprehensions, erroneous grasping, and false appearances; and to establish realistic and beneficial views.

The crucial first step to gain the correct view of the ultimate nature is to accurately identify the subtlest object of negation—the inherent existence that appears to our mind and that we grasp as true. If we do not have a clear idea of what inherent existence would be like if it existed, we will be unable to investigate it and perceive its absence, and the realization of selflessness, the nonaffirming negative that is the negation of inherent existence, will elude us.

Someone who fails to properly identify the subtlest object of negation, inherent existence, will fall to either the extreme of absolutism (also called "the extreme of existence," "permanence," or "eternalism"), or to the extreme of nihilism (the extreme of nonexistence or annihilation). Adhering to an absolutist view, some people do not negate enough, and grasping inherent existence will continue its dreadful antics in their lives. Adhering to a nihilistic view, other people negate too much and lose faith in the functioning of cause and effect. Some go so far as to insist that nothing exists. Holding such a view, they give themselves permission to ignore ethical conduct, which leads to unfortunate rebirths and continued wandering in saṃsāra in addition to sufferings in this very lifetime.

By negating too much, those who fall to the extreme of nihilism rule out inherent existence plus some more. Because they have not properly identified the object of negation, they mistakenly negate dependently arisen phenomena in addition to whatever they think inherent existence is. By denying the conventional existence and functioning of karma and its results, they abandon the basis for good ethical conduct. This is much more harmful than falling to the absolutist extreme because it leads its proponents to rationalize their destructive actions and the degeneration of their ethical conduct. Someone with an absolutist view may still grasp karma and its effects as inherently existent, but at least they will respect the fact that their actions have an ethical dimension that brings the results of happiness and suffering and will try to live ethically.

Someone who holds an absolutist view, even if they think they have the correct view, has also not properly identified the object of negation. Instead of negating inherent existence, they leave it untouched and refute something else. As a result, their saṃsāra continues on unobstructed.

Although absolutism and nihilism are posited as two opposite extremes, they are in fact based on similar premises. Proponents of both extremes believe that if something exists, it must exist inherently, and if something is empty of inherent existence, it must not exist at all. Those falling to the extreme of absolutism dare not negate inherent existence because they fear that it would mean nothing at all exists. Thus they assert inherent existence. Those falling to the extreme of nihilism think that they have negated inherent existence although they have not. Unable to accept dependent arising as complementary to emptiness, they deny dependent arising and therefore state nothing exists.

Although almost every society contains people who fall to either of the two extremes, at the time of Nāgārjuna in the second century, many Indian philosophers tended toward absolutism. Some of them negated something that had no relation to the actual cause of duḥkha and in its place asserted a path that does not challenge self-grasping ignorance at all. Others accepted inherent existence, even though they refuted something coarser such as a permanent, unitary, independent self or a self-sufficient substantially existent person. To lead these people on the correct path, Nāgārjuna's texts focused on refuting the absolutist views of inherent existence.

Several centuries later, many Tibetan philosophers believed that they held the Madhyamaka view, but these so-called Mādhyamikas had in fact adopted nihilistic views. Some said that the ultimate truth could not be perceived and was not a knowable object; others thought that conventional truths did not exist but were only spoken about to help others. For this reason, the teachings of Rendawa, Tsongkhapa, and others emphasized the refutation of nihilism as well as of absolutism and established the Middle Way. They rejected both total nonexistence and inherent existence. It is interesting to note, however, that both nihilists and absolutists make the same mistake of thinking that if things lack inherent existence, they don't exist at all and that if they exist, they must inherently exist. This demonstrates that both do not correctly identify the object of negation.

When discussing these views, let's remember that we are not simply refuting other people's wrong conceptions; we must examine our own mind and ferret out our own erroneous views and refute them. If we focus on pointing out the flaws of others' views without recognizing the errors in our own, we will remain in saṃsāra, far from liberation and full awakening.

## *Confusing Existence with Inherent Existence and Emptiness with Nonexistence*

Both so-called Mādhyamikas, who negate too much, and absolutists, who do not negate enough, do not see dependent arising and emptiness as complementary. Confusing existence with inherent existence and confusing emptiness with total nonexistence, they fall to the two extremes of absolutism and nihilism. They think that if something is empty of inherent existence, it is totally nonexistent, and if it exists, it must inherently exist. As a result, neither so-called Mādhyamikas nor absolutists can establish cause and effect within emptiness. Nor can they see cause and effect as like illusions because they do not understand that things mistakenly appear inherently existent. Instead they believe that if things appear to inherently exist, they must inherently exist.

People deal with this quandary in different ways. Nihilists deny the existence of dependently arisen veiled truths, whereas absolutists abandon the emptiness of inherent existence, assert something else as the ultimate truth, and fall to the extreme of absolutism. Until people relinquish the tenet systems that have such views, they will continue to confuse existence with inherent existence and emptiness with total nonexistence.

Dependent arising counteracts the extreme of nihilism, for although things are empty, they still exist dependently. Emptiness opposes the extreme of absolutism because, being empty, phenomena do not inherently exist. In the Prāsaṅgika system, it works the other way around too: dependent arising counteracts the extreme of absolutism and emptiness counteracts the extreme of nihilism. This is explained in more detail in the next volume of the *Library of Wisdom and Compassion*. Phenomena exist only nominally, by being merely designated by term and concept.

Saying that functioning things are unreal does not mean that they lack the ability to perform functions. "Unreal" means they lack inherent existence. They are unreal in the sense that a reflection of a face in a mirror is unreal: it appears to exist in one way but exists in another. A reflection appears to be a real face but is empty of a face.[76] In spite of its being false, a reflection still functions: by perceiving it, we wash our face. Similarly, although phenomena falsely appear as inherently existent, they arise from causes and conditions and perform their specific functions.

## REFLECTION

1. How does a tenet school's assertion regarding the object of negation influence how they define the afflictive obscurations and the cognitive obscurations?
2. In what ways are the absolutists and nihilists similar?
3. What is happening in someone's mind when they confuse existence with inherent existence? When they confuse emptiness with nonexistence?

## *Madhyamaka's Unique Quality*

Madhyamaka means Middle Way. This Middle Way view that eschews both absolutism and nihilism is difficult to detect. Tsongkhapa says in the *Middle Exposition of the Gradual Path* (FEW 80):

> The difficult point is that one must, from the depths, be able to induce ascertainment with respect to the negation of an inherent nature, without residue—establishment by way of [the object's] own nature—and be able to posit those very persons and so forth lacking inherent existence as the accumulators of actions, experiencers of effects, and so forth. A composite of these two hardly occurs. Hence the Madhyamaka view is very difficult to find.

Both the so-called Mādhyamikas and the essentialists fail to see the Mādhyamikas' unique quality: that being empty and arising dependently are noncontradictory and mutually supportive.

Buddhadharma speaks of the basis, path, and result. The basis is what we begin with; in this context it is the two truths, which encompass all existents. The paths are the realizations cultivated in our minds. The result is nirvāṇa. For Mahāyāna practitioners the result is full awakening, the state of having the two buddha bodies: the truth body (*dharmakāya*) and the form body (*rūpakāya*).

Attaining the two buddha bodies depends on practicing a path of inseparable method and wisdom. Method refers to the collection of merit by practicing the first five perfections. Method practices involve working with conventional truths, such as sentient beings and virtuous actions. The method aspect leads primarily, but not exclusively, to attainment of the form body. Wisdom refers primarily to the collection of wisdom, specifically the wisdom realizing emptiness. Wisdom practices involve realization of the ultimate truth—the way things actually are. The collection of wisdom leads primarily to a buddha's truth body.

Correct understanding of conventional truths involves ascertaining the functionality of cause and effect. This entails becoming convinced from the depths of our hearts, not just intellectually, that desired effects—from fortunate rebirths to awakening—come from virtuous causes, and undesired effects—from bad rebirths to obstacles on the path—arise from destructive causes.

Correct understanding of ultimate truths stems from studying the definitive texts and ascertaining through reasoning and analysis that each and every phenomenon lacks even the tiniest bit of inherent existence. This conviction must be profound, not simply words that we mouth.

In addition, understanding that the two truths are noncontradictory and mutually supportive is an essential aspect of the Middle Way view. Because phenomena arise dependently and exist only nominally, they do not exist under their own power or from their own side. They are empty of inherent existence. Being empty of inherent existence, they arise dependent on other factors—causes and conditions, parts, and the mind that conceives and names them.

Only the Madhyamaka view can fully explain the two truths in a complementary manner. Those who negate too much or too little confuse inherent existence with existence, and confuse non-inherent existence with total nonexistence. Therefore they mistakenly believe that if phenomena exist, they must exist inherently, otherwise they would not exist at all; and if phenomena lacked inherent existence, they would be totally nonexistent. For someone who has realized the Middle Way view, however, emptiness dawns as the meaning of dependent arising, and dependent arising dawns as the meaning of emptiness. Knowing this, they appreciate the Buddhadharma and respect the Buddha as the teacher of such a marvelous doctrine. Nāgārjuna concludes the *Refutation of Objections* by saying (VV 71–72):

> For those to whom emptiness is possible,
> everything is possible.
> For those to whom emptiness is not possible,
> nothing is possible.
>
> I bow down to the Buddha,
> the unequaled, supreme teacher,
> who taught that emptiness and dependent arising
> hold a single meaning in the Middle Way.

Mādhyamikas are unique in being able to accept the suitability of saṃsāra and nirvāṇa, arising and cessation, bondage and release, and so forth within their being empty of inherent existence. In fact, they say that if these things were not empty of inherent existence, they could not exist or function at all. Nāgārjuna affirms (MMK 36):

> Those who deny emptiness,
> which is dependent arising,
> undermine all
> mundane conventions.

Someone who denies that phenomena are empty also disavows dependent arising, because emptiness and dependent arising are one nature. They are complementary and support each other. By undermining dependent arising, that person also rejects all dependently arisen worldly conventions, such as saying "Put this on the table" or "Who called?"

A person who denigrates emptiness and seeks to establish inherent existence runs into the difficulty of how to establish cause and effect, and the triad of agent, object, and action. If these existed inherently, none of them could function because inherently existent things don't rely on other factors: effects cannot arise from their causes without depending on them; an agent couldn't commit an action with an object without the three depending on one another.

Furthermore, if phenomena weren't empty and therefore weren't dependent, then sentient beings could not be born or die because birth and death depend on causes, or once born they would never die because there would be no cause of death.

Things are produced in dependence on concordant causes—causes that have the potential to produce those results. They are not produced in a confused manner by unrelated causes or by no cause at all. An inherently existent cause cannot produce a result; it needs conditions for the result to come forth. A seed alone cannot give rise to a sprout; it must depend on water, fertilizer, and the correct temperature. If it existed as a self-enclosed entity and had its own inherent essence, it could never produce a sprout, even if the other three conditions were present. These are the kind of logical conundrums that come about if we say that dependently arisen phenomena are not empty.

If things existed inherently, from their own side and under their own power, they would have an essence that was findable under analysis. After searching for this essence by examining all of the object's parts, we would be able to identify it. For example, if we looked through all the parts of a car to find the real car, we would find something that was the essence of the car. But whether the parts of the car are piled in a disorderly heap or arranged to form the shape of the car, we still could not identify one part or the collection of parts to be the essence of the car. And even if we could, such an independent object could not be influenced by other factors, such as their causes and conditions, and therefore could not function or change. In short, for something to exist and function it must depend on other factors, which means it must lack an independent essence.

## REFLECTION

1. People often worry about the economy, but what is the economy? Can you identify one thing that is the real economy or the essence of what the economy really is?
2. The economy has many factors: banks, human beings, the stock market, individuals' spending habits, interest rates, production of goods, supply and demand, governmental rules, international trade, and so on. It is influenced by a multitude of conditions, such as viruses, wars, natural disasters, climate change, politics, and so on.
3. None of those factors alone are the real economy, and if they were a collection of unrelated parts, they wouldn't be the economy.
4. In addition, each aspect of the economy could not function unless the majority of them were present and functioned together. All these aspects depend on one another.
5. Can the economy be changed? Who invented it?

---

By seeing that dependence and emptiness come to the same point, we avoid the extremes of absolutism and nihilism as well as the extremes of permanence and annihilation and the extremes of real and unreal. Here, *permanence* means a cause continues to exist in its effect, and *annihilation* means that the continuity of the cause is completely severed when it ceases. People holding the view of permanence say that each person has a permanent soul that is not produced and does not cease. It goes from one life to the next without changing. Those holding the view of annihilation fear that at the time of death, the continuity of the person is destroyed: the person ceases to exist and becomes nothingness. The argument for the beliefs of permanence and annihilation is this: If the I existed inherently, it would be independent of causes and conditions and would therefore be permanent. In that case, we should be able to see the I before it was produced and after it ceased. Since this is not the case and such a self cannot be found, the I would become nonexistent at death.

Another set of extremes is thinking that things either have a real essence and exist with their own independent nature or that they lack a real essence and are therefore unable to perform functions. Understanding the inseparability of dependent arising and emptiness negates these two extremes, because things exist and perform functions precisely because they lack an independent nature of their own. This is the beauty of the Madhyamaka system.

## REFLECTION

1. Observe your present mood. Does it feel very solid and real? Try to identify exactly what it is.

2. Did it arise without a cause or were there events, memories, or other thoughts that caused it?

3. Is that mood permanent and unchanging? Is it exactly the same as when you began this reflection?

4. Does it have its own immutable essence, or is it like a cloud that forms and then dissolves?

## *Saṃsāra and Nirvāṇa Are Empty and Dependent*

Let's return to the opening verses of chapter 24 of Nāgārjuna's *Treatise on the Middle Way*, which we discussed in the first chapter. This begins with Buddhist essentialists raising an objection to Nāgārjuna's teachings, particularly his principal point that no phenomenon exists inherently or by its own characteristics (*svalakṣaṇa*). The essentialists give a lengthy challenge: If nothing has its own specific characteristics, then nothing has any reality of its own. In that case, making distinctions between specific characteristics that are unique to each object and general characteristics that are shared by several objects would be impossible because there would be no basis for that distinction. When speaking of characteristics, we must assume an entity, a thing that possesses these characteristics. If nothing has inherent existence, there would be no entity that had any of these characteristics. In that case, we wouldn't be able to account for any functions, such as the arising and ceasing of functioning things. The essentialists continue by presenting a lengthy argument that begins with saying that if arising and disintegration are not tenable, then the existence of the four truths, the Three Jewels, and all worldly conventions are undermined.

Nāgārjuna begins his rebuttal to this serious objection by saying that the essentialists do not understand emptiness, its purpose, and its meaning. The purpose of teaching emptiness is to eliminate the afflictions. This is done by undermining any objectified basis that could serve as a basis for grasping—that is, there is no inherent essence possible in phenomena that would enable grasping them as existing by their own characteristics. In that case, there is nothing in phenomena to be grasped as inherently attractive or repugnant. When one sees this reality, there is no longer a support for attachment, anger, or other afflictions to arise.

Within the fact that all phenomena of saṃsāra and nirvāṇa are empty of inherent existence, their existence and functioning can still be established. Duḥkha arises dependent on the assembly of specific causes and conditions. Because dependent arising exists, production from causes and conditions exist, and therefore duḥkha can arise. If dependent arising did not exist, duḥkha would be independent of causes and conditions and, being permanent, it could neither arise nor cease. In that case we would never get a cold even if we were surrounded by people coughing and sneezing, or if we had a cold, we could never recover. However, as a dependently created phenomenon, a cold, like all duḥkha, does not exist under its own power and is empty of inherent existence. Thus when the causes for duḥkha cease, duḥkha also ceases.

Because duḥkha exists, its causes exist, its cessation exists, and the paths leading to those extinguishments of duḥkha exist. Thus the four truths are established. Since the four truths exist, knowing true duḥkha, eliminating true origins, actualizing true cessations, and cultivating true paths also exist. Because these exist, the fruits of the path exist. These fruits, which are successive levels of realization, are stream-enterer, once-returner, nonreturner, and arhat.[77] Since these exist, practitioners who have attained them (abiders) exist, as do people who are approaching those attainments (approachers). These approachers and abiders are part of the Saṅgha. Thus the Saṅgha Jewel exists.

Since the four truths exist, the Buddha's doctrine—the Dharma Jewel, which consists of true cessations and true paths—exists. Since the Saṅgha Jewel and the Dharma Jewel exist, the Buddha who has completed the path also exists. Thus the Three Jewels exist as reliable objects of refuge for those wandering in saṃsāra.

Reflecting deeply on the above argument will lead us to a profound understanding of the Buddhadharma based on the reasoning that all phenomena lack inherent existence and exist dependently. We can then establish the existence of virtuous and nonvirtuous actions and their results—happiness and misery, respectively. All phenomena of the thoroughly afflictive class (those having to do with saṃsāra) and all phenomena of the very pure class (those leading to or being nirvāṇa) can be established. These 108 groups of afflictive phenomena and pure phenomena[78] are either conventional truths or ultimate truths. Thus the two truths exist. In this way, we see that things being empty is what allows for them to exist conventionally and to function. Such understanding makes our refuge in the Three Jewels irrefutable and increases our joyous effort in practicing the Dharma.

In Nāgārjuna's homage in the *Treatise on the Middle Way*, he states that dependent arisings are empty of inherent existence and lack eight characteristics: In terms of characteristics, they are without cessation and arising. In terms of time, they are without annihilation and permanence. In terms of mobility, they lack coming and going. In terms of number, they lack being distinct (multiple) and identical (one and the same). Although these eight characteristics exist on the conventional level, they do not inhere in things as their ultimate nature. Phenomena have characteristics conventionally, but they do not exist by their own intrinsic characteristics in terms of their ultimate nature. From the perspective of the direct realization of emptiness, these characteristics do not exist and do not appear to āryas' minds that are single-pointedly and directly perceiving emptiness.

Because things arise in dependence on other factors such as their causes, parts, and the mind that conceives and designates them, they do not exist under their own power and cannot set themselves up. Lacking any independent essence or nature, they are empty of inherent existence. Something that arises dependently cannot exist inherently. If something were inherently existent, it could not be a dependent arising; it could not arise due to causes and conditions, and therefore it could not function. Since our daily experience confirms that functioning things arise and change into something else, they clearly are dependent and thus lack existence from their own side.

People and things appear to us to have a real essence of their own. A person that we are fond of appears to be a real person, existing right there in front of us. We don't think that they exist simply because the causes for them exist. Rather, they appear to have a real essence, a concrete personality that makes them so loveable. Similarly, someone who has harmed us appears to have their own intrinsic personality that makes them despicable. They, too, don't appear to depend on causes and conditions. We don't consider their family's dynamics, the influence of the society around them, or the karmic seeds that accompanied them into this life.

This accounts for our perplexed reaction when someone acts "out of character." We thought they had a fixed, independent character, and this new behavior or trait doesn't fit with it. We don't think that a person is composed of many different attitudes, views, and emotions, and many of them contradict one another. Societal attitudes toward those who have been convicted of performing harmful deeds demonstrate this. A person is now an inherently existent criminal; in their very nature they are corrupt and irredeemable. We don't want anything to do with them even if we speak about having compassion for them. We don't consider that causes and conditions in their family and society helped to create the person they are now, or if we do admit to damaging influences when they were children, we think they are inherently defective individuals.

Sometimes we even consider ourselves in such a harsh light, especially when we feel shame or guilt. Shame arises based on seeing ourselves as intrinsically damaged and incapable, as if that were our permanent nature and we came into this life that way independent of causes and conditions. Not only do we seem to be inherently existent, so does the shame. We don't consider that this self-image arose due to causes and conditions, that it is a projection of our mind based on ignorance.

By familiarizing ourselves with the doctrine of dependent arising, we can overcome these wrong ideas about ourselves and others. This frees us to understand that each and every living being has the buddha nature and is to be respected and appreciated.

## REFLECTION

1. In your daily life, observe how you think about yourself and others.
2. Do you see yourself and others as fluid individuals changing in each moment, or do you see yourself and others as having fixed personalities that are who you really are?
3. Which view is accurate?
4. How does your feeling about yourself and others change when you alter your view?

---

Phenomena are simultaneously empty of inherent existence and dependently existent. The fact that these two are mutually supportive does not mean things switch back and forth between being empty of inherent existence and existing dependently. A sweater arises dependent on its substantial cause—wool—and conditions such as the people who made it and the implements they used to do so. Being created in this way, the sweater does not exist under its own power; nor does it have an independent nature of "sweaterness"—there isn't a sweater in the wool, the people, or the implements. The sweater came into being because of the functioning of many things that are not sweaters. Because it arose dependent on other factors, it is empty of having its own independent nature. Because a conditioned phenomenon such as a sweater is empty, it will disintegrate and one day become a rag. If it were not empty, it would be static and nothing could influence it, in which case it could neither arise nor cease, or exist for that matter.

If we were to put this in the form of a syllogism as explained in chapter 6, it would be:[79] Consider the sweater; it is empty of inherent existence because it is a dependent arising. *Sweater* is the subject, *empty of inherent existence* is the predicate, *the sweater being empty of inherent existence* is the thesis to be proven, and *dependent arising* is the reason. The *application of the reason* is: the reason (dependent arising) applies to the subject (sweater)—that is, the sweater is a dependent arising. The *pervasion* is: whatever is the reason (a dependent arising) necessarily is the predicate (empty of inherent existence). That is, whatever is a dependent arising necessarily is empty of inherent existence. The *counter-pervasion* is: Whatever is the opposite of the predicate (empty of inherent existence) necessarily is the opposite of the reason (dependent arising). That is, whatever isn't empty of inherent existence is necessarily not a dependent arising. Someone must ascertain all three criteria—the application of the reason to the subject, the pervasion, and the counter-pervasion—to realize that the sweater is empty of inherent existence.

The point—whether we explain it as a syllogism or in ordinary language—is that emptiness and dependent arising are mutually inclusive. Whatever arises dependently is empty; whatever is empty arises dependently. Examples such as a sweater or a football are useful to understand this, but our reflection becomes more interesting when we apply this reasoning to a problem, such as our anger at someone's criticism, and see it as being both empty and arising dependently.

Neither the so-called Mādhyamikas who negate too much nor the essentialists who negate too little can reconcile dependent arising and emptiness, although they deal with this difficulty differently. Those who negate too much sacrifice conventional truths and dependent arising in order to hold their view that emptiness means total nonexistence. Essentialists relinquish emptiness in order to assert the inherent existence of dependent arisings.

The essentialists use the reason of dependent arising to refute emptiness by saying that whatever is a dependent arising must exist inherently; thus, it cannot be empty of inherent existence. Those who negate too much, on the other hand, say that because things are empty, they lack any existence whatsoever; thus dependent arisings do not exist. In this way, both fail to understand the profound view of the Middle Way that the Buddha expounded.

Wrong conceptions, ignorance, and the seeds of ignorance obscure us from understanding emptiness. For example, if we look closely at our body, it is clear that it is composed of filthy substances. We may not like to hear this, but our experience validates this. No one thinks the excrement our body produces is lovely, and no one falls in love with another person's intestines. However, in our ordinary view, we consider our own and others' bodies as desirable and become attached to them. If our mind is so obscured that such disparity between reality and our thoughts exists in a comparatively simple example such as this, needless to say, our mental obscurations make understanding the Middle Way view very difficult.

Avoid being proud, thinking that you are wiser than the ignorant people who negate too little or too much. Many of these people are knowledgeable, have strong faith in the Three Jewels, and practice well. The non-Buddhist teachers as well as Buddhist sages such as Asaṅga, Dharmakīrti, Bhāvaviveka, and so forth are not fools. If you engaged them in a debate, they could very well convince you of their views!

## *Mādhyamikas Are Not Nihilists*

Having the correct view is essential if we want to meditate on emptiness. Without a proper understanding, we will not negate enough or will negate too much, leaving the Middle Way beyond our reach. Falling to the extreme of nihilism is especially dangerous. Nāgārjuna cautions (MMK 24.11):

> By a misperception of emptiness
> a person of little intelligence is destroyed,
> like a snake incorrectly seized
> or like a spell incorrectly cast.

Someone misperceives emptiness and falls to the extreme of nihilism by adopting incorrect reasonings. For example, to identify what a pot actually is, they investigate with ultimate analysis to see if the pot is one with or different from its parts. They see that a pot cannot be found in or among its parts—it is not the bottom, the sides, the inside, or the outside—and they conclude that a pot does not exist. They then investigate: Who am I, the one who analyzes? Here, too, they see that they are not their head, heart, legs, belly, or mind and conclude that they do not exist. Finally they think: If there is no person who analyzes, then no one exists who can determine phenomena as existent or nonexistent. Therefore phenomena are neither existent nor nonexistent.

Another way nihilists negate too much is by discounting reliable cognizers. "Reliable" means nondeceptive and implies that these consciousnesses apprehend their objects correctly. Since phenomena cannot be found under ultimate analysis, nihilists go overboard and think that since a reliable cognizer doesn't apprehend objects, these things do not exist at all. Their confusion arises because they think reliable cognizers of the ultimate also perceive conventionalities. However, conventional truths are beyond the purview of consciousnesses analyzing the ultimate, so the fact that such consciousnesses don't perceive them doesn't mean they don't exist. That would be like saying because the visual consciousness didn't hear the music, the music doesn't exist. Music isn't within the purview of the visual consciousness! By erroneously rejecting reliable cognizers of conventional truths, these people deny conventional existence altogether.

The meaning of nihilism varies in different contexts. By negating conventional existence, some people say virtue and nonvirtue do not exist. They may say: "Everything is a dream; it does not exist in reality. Therefore there is no good and no bad." Such a person is nihilistic in the sense that they do not believe that constructive actions lead to happiness and destructive ones to suffering. In this way, they negate the functioning of karma and its effects.

Another type of nihilism is believing that a previously inherently existent person becomes totally nonexistent at the time of death. Nihilists believe an inherently existent person exists while alive, but the continuity of the person ceases altogether after death. With the cessation of the person, all karma ceases and no effects of their actions are experienced.

A third nihilistic view is denying the existence of past and future lives because we cannot see an inherently existent person coming from a previous life to this life or going from this life to the next. The non-Buddhist Cārvākas (Materialists) of ancient India were nihilists in this sense because they believed that only things that could be directly perceived by the physical senses exist. We meet some people with similar nihilistic views nowadays.

Asserting that rebirth does not exist because we cannot see it with our senses does not disprove the existence of rebirth. There is a difference between not perceiving something with our senses and perceiving its nonexistence. As ordinary beings our senses are incapable of perceiving everything that exists: eagles and cats see things we cannot; dogs detect odors we cannot. If our senses or if inference could prove the nonexistence of rebirth, we would have to accept that. However, they cannot. Saying that we do not perceive something does not establish its nonexistence. Many reasons in favor of rebirth exist; we have discussed some of them in previous volumes.[80]

Another nihilistic belief is that because the mind depends on the body, it is not possible to transform the mind because it is always bound by this material human body. The urge for self-preservation and self-protection is hardwired in our brain. We have no choice but to become hostile and aggressive or to flee in fear when in danger. These qualities as well as the self-centered attitude are in our biological makeup, so the best we can do is mitigate their extreme forms, but freeing ourselves from them completely is neither desirable nor possible. I wonder how someone could prove that the mind is the brain or that the mind is an emergent property of the body.

In the context of discussing the Middle Way, nihilism specifically refers to believing that because phenomena are empty, conventional objects either do not exist or they do not bring the results that they do bring. Based on this view, more nihilistic views proliferate.

Nihilistic views prevent properly positing both conventional and ultimate truths and result in deprecating both. If we do not affix the word "ultimately" when doing ultimate analysis, we may think: A pot does not exist because it is neither one with nor different from its parts. The correct way to investigate is: A pot does not *ultimately* exist because it is neither one with nor different from its parts. Ultimate analysis does not examine the conventional existence of something; it determines if that thing exists on the ultimate level.

Essentialists erroneously think that because Mādhyamikas negate inherent existence, they are nihilists, for, according to essentialists, if phenomena do not inherently exist, they do not exist at all. Mādhyamikas disagree, saying that phenomena are empty of inherent existence, but are not empty of all existence whatsoever. They exist dependently. If they existed from their own side, they could not function at all because they would be independent of all other factors. But functioning things that exist merely on the nominal level are able to produce results because they depend on causes and conditions. The four truths and all the thoroughly afflictive phenomena of saṃsāra and the very pure phenomena of nirvāṇa exist because they are empty of inherent existence and exist dependently. In this way Mādhyamikas affirm conventional existence while negating inherent existence.

The theses and reasons that Mādhyamikas and nihilists put forth to prove their assertions differ considerably. Mādhyamikas do not assert total nonexistence, as nihilists do; they assert non-inherent existence. Whereas Mādhyamikas claim that past and future lives do not inherently exist because they arise dependent on causes and conditions, Cārvāka nihilists declare that past and future lives do not exist because we cannot see anyone coming from a past life to this life or going from this one to the next. Furthermore, Mādhyamikas say that past and future lives are conventional truths, whereas nihilists say they are neither conventional nor ultimate truths because they do not exist at all.

Sometimes the words Mādhyamikas and nihilists use sound similar. For example, both say "phenomena do not inherently exist." But what they mean by these words is different, for nihilists equate non-inherent existence with total nonexistence, while Mādhyamikas equate it with dependently arising existence.

In answer to the essentialists' question "If nothing inherently exists, what is there?" Buddhapālita responds in *Buddhapālita's Commentary on "Treatise on the Middle Way"* (DAE 399):

> . . . time and so forth are established as mere entities that are mutually dependent designations, conventions of this and that with respect to individual appearances of things.

People veering toward nihilism will benefit from studying dependent arising, which reaffirms the conventional existence of phenomena. In addition, they should understand that emptiness is a phenomenon—it is an existent; it is not nothingness. Emptiness is a property of conventionally existent phenomena. All properties of a phenomenon are one nature with that phenomenon, and when that phenomenon exists, so do its properties. For people who understand this, saying that the table exists implies that its emptiness also exists, because these two are inseparable. When meditators realize emptiness directly, they do not fall to nihilism because they know that emptiness is a property of an existing phenomenon.

Someone who misunderstands the meaning of emptiness and refutes it creates the powerful destructive karma of abandoning emptiness, which leads to an unfortunate rebirth. Such karma may be created by thinking, "Emptiness means total nonexistence. Since everything is empty, nothing exists." This is the extreme of nihilism. The karma of abandoning emptiness may also be created by thinking, "All these things appear so real, so they must inherently exist. Therefore emptiness cannot mean the lack of inherent existence." This is the extreme of absolutism.

The disadvantages of holding such views are clear. If we think our duḥkha exists inherently, we see no way out of it. We become depressed and give up hope because the present situation seems so overwhelmingly real and unchanging. On the other hand, if we see our difficulties as empty of inherent existence, we see that they arise dependent on other factors. If those causes are eliminated, the resultant duḥkha can be stopped, and if the causes of happiness are created, happiness will arise. With this view, we feel optimistic and make effort to cease the causes of our pain and create causes for happiness.

## REFLECTION

1. Name some nihilistic views.
2. How does holding one of the views influence someone's behavior and the karma they create?
3. Refute each of the nihilistic views you listed.

## *Emptiness Exists and Is Itself Empty*

Many early Mādhyamikas in Tibet—those who lived during the early phase of the second transmission of the Dharma to Tibet in the eleventh century—said that emptiness was ineffable and could not be perceived by the mind. Since emptiness cannot be perceived by mind, they thought it did not exist. They misunderstood the Perfection of Wisdom sūtras that clarified that emptiness exists (NT 42):

> Whether the tathāgatas appear or not, the reality of phenomena just abides.

Citing a sūtra, Candrakīrti states in his *Autocommentary on the Supplement* (*Madhyamakāvatārabhāṣya*, NT 43):

> Who could say that it [emptiness] does not exist? If it did not exist, for what purpose would bodhisattvas cultivate the path of the perfections? For what purpose would bodhisattvas initiate hundreds of efforts for the sake of realizing such a reality?

In *Clear Words*, Candrakīrti says (NT 44):

> What is this suchness? The entity of suchness does not change and always abides. For that which is not produced in any way because of not being fabricated and because of not relying on another is called "the [ultimate] nature of fire" and so forth.

These quotations show that emptiness is an existent phenomenon. In *Clear Words*, Candrakīrti affirms that emptiness exists conventionally even though it is the ultimate nature of all phenomena. Initially, it may sound strange to hear that emptiness exists conventionally although it is the ultimate nature. Conventional existence is the only kind of existence there is. Ultimate existence is disproven because nothing can bear ultimate analysis. Because emptiness is not fabricated and is the ultimate nature of all phenomena, it always exists, whether the tathāgatas appear in our world or not.

If emptiness were nonexistent, then no one could cognize it, and thus it would be useless for bodhisattvas to cultivate the perfections—especially the perfections of meditative stability and wisdom—in an effort to realize it.

Since emptiness exists, what is its ultimate mode of existence? Is it related to us and our world, or does it exist separate from all phenomena as an inherently existent reality? Emptiness is not nothingness, nor is it merely a linguistic convention. It is a permanent phenomenon that is known by a reliable cognizer—in this case an ārya's meditative equipoise directly and nonconceptually perceiving emptiness. It is our ultimate nature and the ultimate nature of all persons and phenomena around us.

Emptiness exists dependently. It depends on the reliable cognizer that knows it directly. It also depends on its parts. Emptiness is not a partless absolute reality that existed first and from it the universe and sentient beings arose. Emptiness has parts in the sense that there are many emptinesses—the emptiness of the moon, the emptiness of the table, the emptiness of the parts of the table, and so forth. Each thing has its own emptiness that comes into existence when that thing arises and goes out of existence when that thing ceases. The emptiness of the apple comes into existence simultaneously with the apple and it stops existing when the apple ceases.

The *Kāśyapa Chapter Sūtra* makes clear that emptiness should not be reified or seen as truly existent (OR 300):

> That which is emptiness does not empty phenomena, because phenomena themselves are empty. That which is signlessness does not make phenomena signless, because phenomena themselves are signless. That which is wishlessness does not make phenomena wishless, because phenomena themselves are wishless. To so analyze, Kāśyapa, is called the middle path—in the correct analysis of phenomena. Oh Kāśyapa, I say that whoever analyzes emptiness by objectifying emptiness has fallen, fallen far from my teachings.

Saying that emptiness does not empty phenomena and so on indicates that the ultimate nature of phenomena itself is emptiness. It is not the case that phenomena that are not themselves empty are made empty by something else. Someone who objectifies emptiness and holds it to inherently exist as a reality separate from phenomena that are empty lacks the correct view. Similarly, reifying the view of emptiness and clinging to it also misses the point. This doesn't mean we can't think about or discuss emptiness. After all, teachers talk about emptiness when instructing their students. It means holding the view that emptiness exists inherently. Nāgārjuna says (MMK 13.8):

> The victorious ones have said
> that emptiness is the elimination of all views.
> Anyone for whom emptiness is a view
> is incorrigible.

If someone negates true existence and then grasps the emptiness of true existence as truly existent, correcting his view will be difficult. This is like a sick person who took medicine that cured his illness. However, since the medicine was itself not digested completely, it remained in his stomach and made him sick again. In the same way, refuting the true existence of phenomena solves one set of problems by diminishing afflictions, but to turn around and grasp emptiness as truly existent makes one sick with afflictions once again.

Other people do not hold emptiness to be truly existent, but after negating the true existence of emptiness, they say that emptiness doesn't exist. These people confuse emptiness with total nonexistence and fall to the extreme of nihilism, whereas those who hold emptiness as truly existent fall to the extreme of absolutism.

## *Do Mādhyamikas Have Theses?*

Some scholars question whether Mādhyamikas have theses or not. Because Mādhyamikas completely negate inherent existence and because emptiness doesn't affirm anything in the wake of that negation, these scholars think that Mādhyamikas don't affirm any theses in a debate and that they focus solely on refuting others' views. These scholars believe that even if Mādhyamikas were to give any affirming statements about emptiness—such as "emptiness is the nature of all phenomena"—that would mean emptiness is truly existent, which would contradict Mādhyamikas' own beliefs that nothing exists truly. In the past, this radical way of thinking became an issue in Madhyamaka circles in both Tibet and China. It arose from misinterpreting some of Nāgārjuna's statements, for example from *Refutation of Objections* (VV 29):

> If I had any thesis,
> then I would suffer from that fault.
> But as I have no theses,
> I am purely without fault.

When Nāgārjuna says he has no thesis, he says that from the ultimate perspective, where nothing can withstand ultimate analysis. From this perspective, there is no syllogism, no subject, no predicate, no reason, no thesis, or anything else. But that doesn't mean nothing exists. From the conventional perspective, all these things exist, and Nāgārjuna employs conventionally existent syllogisms and consequences to prove his assertions. In that way, he cannot be faulted. Non-ultimately existent words have the power to refute ultimate existence because those words exist and function, precisely because they are empty of ultimate existence. Not realizing that Nāgārjuna was speaking from the perspective of the ultimate, these scholars misinterpreted his words and thought he was saying Mādhyamikas had no theses at all.

Imagine Nāgārjuna debating with one of these scholars who saw everything as inherently existent on the topic of whether phenomena existed inherently or not. In response to everything the scholar said, Nāgārjuna would probably say, "no," indicating that the subject, thesis, and reason of the scholar's argument did not exist from its own side. Not realizing that Nāgārjuna was speaking from the perspective of the ultimate, the scholar would misunderstand and think that Nāgārjuna was a nihilist refuting all existence whatsoever.

We use a reflection of our face in a mirror to check our appearance, even though the appearance of the face is false and no face exists in the mirror. Similarly, we can realize the meaning of a syllogism in which each part lacks ultimate existence yet exists falsely or conventionally. A reflection of a face is not totally nonexistent, nor does it ultimately exist. It arises due to causes and conditions and is dependent, although it is false in that there appears to be a face in the mirror when there isn't. Similarly, the words of a thesis exist and function although they are not ultimately existent. When it is said that

Mādhyamikas have no positions, it means they have no assertions in which they accept ultimately existent phenomena.

Essentialists say Nāgārjuna deprecates existence and is nihilistic. They fail to realize that Nāgārjuna did not say that things are empty of true existence because they cannot perform a function. He did not negate the ability of tables, diplomas, and emotions to perform their respective functions. Rather, he honored functionality and causality by saying that things are empty of true existence because they arise dependently.

Some people say Mādhyamikas assert the existence of things only from the perspective of others—that they speak of conventional objects only because others think they exist, but they do not affirm anything by speaking of conventional things. This is incorrect because Mādhyamikas assert theses for themselves.

If Mādhyamikas had no theses, they could not set forth consequences when refuting others' systems. This is because consequences show the fallacy of the opponents' theses, and by doing that, the right view is implied. By negating true existence, Mādhyamikas automatically prove non-true existence.

People who mistakenly believe that Mādhyamikas have no assertions even conventionally haven't properly identified the object of negation. These people refute the truly existent assertions of their opponents,[81] and then when they apply those same arguments to their own theses, they mistakenly think that they have refuted them as well. Because they have not been able to differentiate true existence from existence, they erroneously think that refuting truly existent assertions is the same as refuting all assertions whatsoever. The Mādhyamikas, however, say that assertions, like all other phenomena, exist conventionally but not ultimately.

Since Madhyamaka is the Middle Way system, it must assert something. Its principal assertion is that nothing is truly existent, yet conventionally everything exists like illusions. Since Mādhyamikas reach this conclusion by refuting wrong views, there must be reliable cognizers that know the theses that are proven and the nonexistence of those that are refuted. Since Mādhyamikas also teach others, they must have theses.

## *Abandoning the Two Extremes*

How do Mādhyamikas abandon the two extremes? They refute absolutism by saying that things are empty of inherent existence and refute nihilism by asserting that they exist dependently. It can also be said that they avoid absolutism by accepting dependent arising and avoid nihilism by asserting that phenomena are empty. In this case, instead of going to the extreme of inherent existence, they assert dependent existence, and instead of going to the extreme of total nonexistence, they assert no inherent existence.

Just the words "dependent arising" refute the two extremes. "Dependent" refutes inherent or independent existence, the extreme of absolutism, and "arising" refutes total nonexistence and the extreme of nihilism. "Dependent" indicates phenomena are empty, "arising" indicates that they exist. Dependent arising means no inherent existence because phenomena arise depending on many factors that are not them. A pear exists dependent on many factors that are not that pear—the pear seed, water, fertilizer, sunshine, and the farmer—and a person exists dependent on a diversity of factors that are not that person, such as her parents.

Dependent arising also means to exist falsely. Existing falsely isn't nonexistence; it means that like illusions, dreams, and holograms, things appear one way but exist in another. They exist nominally, only on the level of appearances, because like clouds in the breeze, they lack any essence. They appear and exist dependent on causes and conditions, parts, and the mind that conceives and designates them. In this way, dependent arising refutes the extreme of nonexistence.

Things can be either inherently existent or non-inherently existent. There is no third choice. These two are a dichotomy, and if something is not one, it must be the other. By refuting inherent existence, non-inherent existence or the emptiness of inherent existence is automatically established.

Inherent existence has never existed. Realizing emptiness does not entail destroying an inherently existent object by making it empty. Because the object never existed inherently, its inherent existence cannot be destroyed. Rather, we are simply realizing that it was never there to start with. Emptiness is right here in every person and object around us. It is our very nature, yet it too is empty of inherent existence.

Grasping something as inherently existent is the extreme of absolutism, and thinking that thing was once inherently existent and now has become totally nonexistent is the extreme of nihilism. An example of the latter is thinking that at present a truly existent person exists—we see and speak with them—but after death there is no continuity of their mindstream and they become totally nonexistent.

At present, because grasping inherent existence is firmly entrenched in our mind, we usually hold the extreme of absolutism, which lies behind the attachment, anger, and other afflictions that besiege us. Still, the danger of falling into nihilism is real. Sometimes we meet people who claim that everything is illusory and has no real existence so there is no need to observe the law of karma and its results. Others claim that since virtue and nonvirtue are merely designated, they are completely fabricated by the ignorant mind and thus ethical standards have no weight.

If we wish to develop the Middle Way view, the Buddha advised us to cultivate its causes by abiding in pure ethical conduct, relying on an excellent spiritual mentor, purifying our negativities, and accumulating merit and wisdom. To do this, we should follow definitive scriptures and the works of great sages such as Nāgārjuna, Āryadeva, and Candrakīrti to understand them. Then the Buddha directed us to study, contemplate, and meditate on emptiness and its compatibility with dependent arising.

## REFLECTION

1. Do you see emptiness as some absolute thing that exists independently?
2. Why is that view incorrect?
3. Try thinking of emptiness as a quality of all persons and phenomena that is here right now.
4. Reflect that although conventional truths and ultimate truths are contradictory, they exist together and are inseparable.

# 10 The Extreme of Absolutism

Among all the teachings the Buddha gave, the teaching on dependent arising is the most profound. It is what marks the Buddha as an unexcelled teacher. Although the Buddha can be praised from many angles and for many of his spectacular qualities, Nāgārjuna, Tsongkhapa, and many other scholar-adepts praise him for revealing the profound message of dependent arising. I, too, have found the impact of his teachings on the compatibility of emptiness and dependent arising to be profound and feel the same reverence for the Buddha as an unsurpassable teacher. Every day I chant the homage to the Buddha from the *Treatise on the Middle Way* to reaffirm my deep spiritual connection to him and his teachings, especially to the teaching on dependent arising.

Because things are dependent, they cannot arise from an unchanging, independent entity or substance. If they did, we could never attain higher spiritual states because that entails change, and change depends on causes and conditions. Absolutist notions cannot stand up to scrutiny by reasoning because they are antithetical to the fact that everything exists by depending on other factors.

During India's classical period,[82] in the great monastic universities such as Nālandā in India, non-Buddhist and Buddhist sages debated with one another. This led to a rich exchange as these sages explored a broad variety of views, testing them with the rigor of reasoning and logic. The writings of many of the great Indian scholar-adepts consisted of analyzing the inconsistencies in many of the non-Buddhist systems as well as the lower Buddhist systems. In this chapter we'll look at a few of these, hopefully whetting your appetite to study such treatises as *Commentary on the "Compendium of Reliable Cognition"* (*Pramāṇavārttika*) by Dharmakīrti and *The Four Hundred* (*Catuḥśataka*) by Āryadeva as we ferret out these beliefs in our own minds and use reasoning to overcome them.

In this chapter we will examine some ideas held by those holding an absolutist position, beginning with some tenets of the lower Buddhist systems and then analyzing some non-Buddhist beliefs. Some of these assertions may be similar to ones you may have learned either from your family, school, or another religion. This is an opportunity to reassess them in light of what you know now about dependent arising and, in doing so, clarify and refine your beliefs.

## *Buddhist Essentialists That Don't Refute Enough*

Like nihilists, Buddhist essentialists also fail to identify the object of negation properly. Although they may negate something, they have missed the mark—for example, by negating a superficial distorted view while leaving inherent existence untouched. Many philosophies fall to the extreme of absolutism because assenting to inherent existence agrees with our innate self-grasping. Asserting a real, unchanging essence that is the person and a permanent divine entity that is in control of the universe is much more emotionally satisfying for some people. Such views are comforting and protect from the fear arising from having limited control over our body, mind, other people, and our environment. All of these factors make us hesitant to challenge our accustomed views and assumptions.

To help us overcome these hindrances, the great masters recommend that prior to delving into emptiness, we engage in practices to purify negativities and accumulate merit. They also emphasize the importance of contemplating the four truths—especially the defects of saṃsāra and the afflictions that cause it—in order to generate renunciation of duḥkha and the aspiration to attain liberation. That strong aspiration for freedom, as well as bodhicitta, gives us the inner determination and strength to challenge the self-grasping ignorance that has imprisoned us since beginningless time.

An example of not negating enough is refuting only a permanent, unitary, independent self and not looking deeper. Although refuting such a self or soul is a necessary beginning, it only touches the surface of the object of negation. The concept of a permanent and eternal soul or self that exists after death and is the essence of a person is an acquired obscuration, one fabricated by incorrect philosophies, such as those propounded by non-Buddhist schools. Refuting only it does not eliminate the culprit causing all our problems. We are still far from realizing the emptiness of inherent existence.

The lower Buddhist schools negate a self-sufficient substantially existent person, but that too doesn't get to the root problem of grasping inherent existence. They too have not identified the full object of negation, which is more subtle. It is worthwhile to spend time trying to identify the object of negation, inherent existence.

To refute inherent existence, we contemplate the unwanted consequences that would come about if persons and phenomena existed inherently. For example, the I would be permanent and unchanging; it wouldn't have components such as the body and mind and would be totally unrelated to the body and mind. Although these unwanted consequences would arise, they are not the meaning of inherent existence. That is, being permanent or independent from the aggregates is not the definition of inherent existence. Inherent existence is more subtle. Nevertheless, seeing the contradictory consequences that would arise if things existed inherently enables us to chip away at that wrong view.

Similarly, if something truly existed, it would have to be partless, but partless minute particles that are the building blocks of the universe and partless moments of mind do not exist—they are notions created by incorrect philosophies. Although they are to be negated, negating them does not destroy the root of our duḥkha, the innate self-grasping ignorance.

Refuting these coarser objects of negation is a steppingstone to realizing emptiness, but only realizing the emptiness of the conceived object of innate self-grasping ignorance will cut all afflictions. For example, if someone is afraid that a poisonous snake is in the room, telling him there isn't an elephant here doesn't calm his fears. Similarly, if someone clearly sees the untrustworthy nature of saṃsāra and wants to be free from it, but spends her time refuting only a permanent soul as asserted by non-Buddhists, partless particles as accepted by Vaibhāṣikas, external phenomena as refuted by Yogācārins, or inherent existence on the conventional level as accepted by the Svātantrikas, she is missing out.

Although some philosophies and psychologies may be comforting, we must persevere and recognize the actual source of saṃsāric duḥkha to eliminate it. In the spiritual supermarket of the modern age, so many beliefs exist. Many are much more glamorous than the Buddhadharma. They promise quick results and attract many followers. Although some of these beliefs may alleviate some problems, they do not identify the deep cause of suffering or show the method to overcome it. They may help the people who practice them live more peacefully in this life—and that is wonderful—but spiritual aspirants seeking liberation or full awakening should not be satisfied with superficial remedies. They must persevere and correctly identify the object of innate ignorance and then refute it.

## *What Do Śrāvakas and Solitary Realizers Realize?*

How do we reconcile that the two Fundamental Vehicle tenet systems, the Vaibhāṣika and Sautrāntika, assert inherent existence with the fact that śrāvakas and solitary realizers who are Fundamental Vehicle practitioners attain arhatship? Not all Fundamental Vehicle practitioners follow Fundamental Vehicle tenet systems; similarly, not all Mahāyāna practitioners follow Mahāyāna tenet systems. Let's unpack the significance of this.

Prāsaṅgikas speak of the coarse and subtle four truths, the coarse being the presentation in the *Treasury of Knowledge* and the *Compendium of Knowledge*, and the subtle being the Prāsaṅgika presentation.[83] The principal differences between the two lie in their assertions regarding the object of negation and the root of saṃsāra. The non-Prāsaṅgika systems assert that the object of negation is a self of persons—specifically a self-sufficient substantially existent person—and the root of saṃsāra is grasping at such self of persons. In addition, the Yogācārins and Svātantrikas negate a self of phenomena, saying that grasping a self of phenomena is the *final* root of saṃsāra.

According to the coarse four truths, the first truth is the duḥkha arising from grasping at a self-sufficient substantially existent person. The second truth is grasping a self-sufficient substantially existent person, the afflictions arising from it, and the karma propelling rebirth created by them. The third truth is the cessation that is the abandonment of this grasping and the afflictions that arise due to it. The fourth truth is the wisdom path that counteracts this grasping and the afflictions stemming from it.

The presentation of the subtle four truths accords with the Prāsaṅgika view in which grasping the inherent existence of persons and phenomena, not grasping at a self-sufficient substantially existent I, is the origin of saṃsāra.[84] The object of negation is the inherent existence of both persons and phenomena. The other three truths are asserted accordingly.

Of the four attributes of true duḥkha in the presentation of the coarse four truths, the attribute of emptiness refers to the lack of a permanent, unitary, independent self or I, and the attribute of selflessness is the lack of a self-sufficient substantially existent person. According to the Prāsaṅgikas, the path directly realizing coarse emptiness and course selflessness can temporarily stop the manifestation of the coarse afflictions, but cannot eradicate those afflictions. Although the manifest coarse afflictions may be temporarily suppressed, those practitioners will still take rebirth in saṃsāra by the force of grasping inherent existence and the afflictions and karma arising from it.

Someone may have directly realized the selflessness of a self-sufficient substantially existent person and still grasp the person and the aggregates as inherently existent. This practitioner has yet to realize the deepest mode of existence of persons and phenomena—their emptiness of inherent existence. Only the wisdom directly realizing this emptiness is capable of abolishing grasping inherent existence and the afflictions it generates. In the *Questions of Adhyāśaya Sūtra* (*Adhyāśayasaṃśōdana Sūtra*), the Buddha makes this point in a dialogue with a disciple (CTB 161):

> "For example, during a magical display, a man sees a woman created by a magician and desire arises in him. His mind becomes ensnared with desire, and he is frightened and ashamed in front of his companions. Rising from his seat, he leaves and later considers the woman to be ugly, impermanent, unsatisfactory, and selfless. O child of a good lineage, what do you think? Is that man behaving correctly or incorrectly?"
>
> "Blessed One, he who strives to consider a nonexistent woman to be ugly, impermanent, unsatisfactory, and selfless behaves incorrectly."
>
> The Blessed One said, "O child of a good lineage, you should similarly view those bhikṣus, bhikṣuṇīs, laymen, and laywomen

> who consider unproduced and unarisen phenomena to be ugly, impermanent, unsatisfactory, and selfless. I do not say that these foolish persons are cultivating the path; they are practicing in an incorrect manner."

Here the Buddha emphasizes that if we contemplate nonexistent objects of attachment as ugly, impermanent, empty, and lacking a self-sufficient substantially existent I, we are missing the point. There's no use contemplating the impermanence and so forth of nonexistents; if we understood that these things did not exist to start with, our attachment to them would vanish. Meditating on the attributes of coarse true duḥkha is like discussing how to dispose of wilted flowers in a hologram or how to shave the moustache off a turtle when such flowers and such a moustache do not exist. To attain liberation, realization of the ultimate mode of existence—the emptiness of inherent existence of both persons and phenomena—is essential. Saying phenomena are unproduced and unarisen indicates that they are not inherently produced and do not inherently arise, although they are produced and arise conventionally.

In the *Sūtra on the Miserliness of One in Dhyāna* (*Dhyāyitamuṣṭi Sūtra*), the Buddha describes the disadvantages of not meditating on subtle selflessness by speaking of someone who, adhering to true existence, meditates on the coarse four truths and thinks, "I know duḥkha, have abandoned all fetters that are its origin, actualized cessation, and cultivated the path. I am now an arhat." However, when he dies, he sees that he will be reborn in saṃsāra and doubts the Three Jewels, which causes him to be reborn as a hell being. Although this does not happen to everyone who mistakenly believes they have realized subtle emptiness, it does happen to some.

In the sūtra, the Buddha then explains how the four truths should be cognized to attain liberation (CTB 163):

> Mañjuśrī, he who sees all products as not produced knows duḥkha thoroughly. He who sees all phenomena as without origin has abandoned the origin of suffering. He who sees them as utterly passed beyond sorrow has actualized cessation. He who sees all phenomena as totally unproduced has cultivated the path.

When the Buddha speaks in such seemingly enigmatic language, he means that one who sees all produced things as lacking inherent arising, all phenomena as lacking truly existent origin, and so forth knows how phenomena actually exist—they are empty of true existence. Only someone who directly realizes the absence of true existence of persons and phenomena can eliminate both the coarse and subtle afflictions as well as their seeds and attain liberation from saṃsāra. This applies equally to everyone, whether they are Buddhist or non-Buddhist and whether they follow the śrāvaka, solitary realizer, or bodhisattva path.

As Fundamental Vehicle practitioners, do śrāvakas and solitary realizers realize the emptiness of inherent existence and attain liberation, or do they meditate on the coarse four truths, in which case they remain far from liberation? Since Fundamental Vehicle arhats have attained liberation, they must have meditated on and realized the emptiness of inherent existence of persons and phenomena. For this reason deprecating the Śrāvaka and Solitary Realizer Vehicles by saying that they do not lead to liberation is a grave error, and doing this is a transgression of the fourteenth root downfall of the bodhisattva ethical code. The *Diamond Cutter Sūtra* (*Vajracchedikā*) agrees:[85]

> [Buddha], "Subhūti, does a stream-enterer think, 'I have attained the fruit of stream-enterer'?"
>
> Subhūti replied, "Bhagavan, no, it is not so. Why? Bhagavan, because one does not enter into anything whatsoever; therefore, one is called stream-enterer. . . . Bhagavan, if that stream-enterer thinks 'I have attained the result of stream-enterer,' that itself would be grasping a self, a sentient being, a soul, a person."

Subhūti responds similarly when the same question is asked about a once-returner, nonreturner, and arhat. Since someone who has directly realized the emptiness of inherent existence does not grasp the self of persons and phenomena, Fundamental Vehicle āryas have definitely realized the emptiness of the person (themselves as the attainers of stream-entry and so forth) and the emptiness of phenomena (the four truths, the fruit of stream-entry, and so forth). The emptiness and the two selflessnesses they realize are the same as those of Mahāyāna practitioners.

Furthermore, in his *Autocommentary on the Supplement* and in *Clear Words*, Candrakīrti sets forth more reasons to support his assertion that śrāvakas and solitary realizers meditate on and realize the emptiness of inherent existence. The *Sūtra of the Ten Grounds* (*Daśabhūmika Sūtra*) says that bodhisattvas outshine śrāvakas and solitary-realizer āryas by the power of their wisdom on the seventh bodhisattva ground.[86] If Fundamental Vehicle āryas did not realize the emptiness of inherent existence, bodhisattvas would outshine them on the first ground. However, first-grounders only outshine śrāvaka and solitary-realizer āryas in terms of their lineage.

Also, Nāgārjuna says in the *Precious Garland* (RA 35) that as long as there is grasping at the aggregates as truly existent, grasping at the person as truly existent remains. Since śrāvaka and solitary-realizer practitioners attain liberation, they must have realized the emptiness of true existence of the aggregates. The *Perfection of Wisdom Sūtra in 8,000 Lines* (*Aṣṭasāhasrikā Prajñāpāramitā Sūtra*) says that those seeking śrāvakas', solitary realizers', and bodhisattvas' awakening should be trained in the perfection of wisdom.[87]

In short, all āryas of the three vehicles realize the same emptiness of inherent existence of persons and phenomena and eliminate the same self-grasping ignorance and the afflictions based on it. All of them realize the subtle four truths.

How do Fundamental Vehicle practitioners realize the subtle four truths and the selflessness of both persons and phenomena if their tenet systems assert that realizing the coarse selflessness of persons is sufficient to attain liberation? To support his position that practitioners of the Fundamental Vehicle realize the same subtle emptiness as the holders of Mahāyāna tenets, Candrakīrti explains that it is important to distinguish a proponent of a Fundamental Vehicle tenet system from a practitioner of the Fundamental Vehicle. Proponents of the Vaibhāṣika and Sautrāntika systems do not realize the emptiness of inherent existence because they accept the inherent existence of all phenomena. However, śrāvaka and solitary-realizer arhats have necessarily realized the emptiness of inherent existence as asserted by the Prāsaṅgikas.[88] This is because some sūtras in the Pāli canon speak of the emptiness of inherent existence. Penetrating the meaning of these passages, śrāvakas and solitary realizers realize suchness and attain liberation. We will examine some of these passages in *Realizing the Profound View*, volume 8 of the *Library of Wisdom and Compassion*.

## *The Fundamental Vehicle and the Universal Vehicle*

Bhāvaviveka says that if the selflessness of phenomena were taught in the Śrāvaka Vehicle, the teachings of the Universal Vehicle would be redundant and therefore useless. However, that doesn't mean he thinks all the Mahāyāna teachings would be senseless. As a scholar-adept, he knows that the Mahāyāna scriptures include much more than discussion of the selflessness of phenomena. They also explain great compassion, the methods to cultivate bodhicitta, bodhisattvas' aspirations, bodhisattva grounds, perfections, the collections of merit and wisdom, the abilities of the Buddha's truth body and form body, and many other topics. To attain the full awakening of a buddha, studying, practicing, and actualizing the complete Mahāyāna teachings and practices are indispensable.

Nor does this mean that Bhāvaviveka thinks it would be useless for Mahāyāna scriptures to teach the selflessness of phenomena if it were taught in the Fundamental Vehicle. What then does he mean? Nāgārjuna says in *Praise to the World Transcendent* (LS 25):

> Without entering signlessness
> there is no liberation, you have declared;
> so you presented this [signlessness]
> in its entirety in the Universal Vehicle [sūtras].

Signlessness—the emptiness of inherent existence, suchness—must be realized to attain liberation. Since śrāvakas and solitary realizers attain liberation, they must have this realization. But in the last two lines, by saying the Buddha presented signlessness in its entirety in the Mahāyāna sūtras, Nāgārjuna implies that it is taught briefly in the Fundamental Vehicle scriptures. What does he mean by this?

First, let's look at what Nāgārjuna does not mean: By saying "in its entirety," he does not mean that bodhisattvas realize the emptiness of all phenomena but śrāvakas and solitary realizers realize the emptiness of only some phenomena. Like bodhisattvas, they cognize the emptiness of all phenomena.

In the Mahāyāna scriptures, the Buddha explains the selflessness of phenomena using numerous reasonings and approaches, such as those Nāgārjuna set out in his *Treatise on the Middle Way*. However, because of the different aptitudes of his followers, the Buddha did not use extensive reasonings to explain emptiness in the Fundamental Vehicle scriptures. Bodhisattvas want to benefit all sentient beings, so they must know and meditate on many and varied reasonings proving non-inherent existence, causing their minds to become very broad with respect to emptiness. The depth and force of a bodhisattva's realization of emptiness is greater due to the way they meditate on emptiness on the path.

Furthermore, owing to the difference in their spiritual goals, bodhisattvas cultivate the realization of the selflessness of phenomena fully while the śrāvakas and solitary realizers do not. Here "fully" means that bodhisattvas' realization of emptiness has the power to eliminate both afflictive obscurations and cognitive obscurations, resulting in their attainment of buddhahood. Because śrāvakas and solitary realizers seek to abandon only afflictive obscurations, meditation on the succinct meaning of the selflessness of phenomena is sufficient to meet their goal of liberation.

## *Examining Our Absolutist Beliefs*

When subjecting views and beliefs to critical analysis, we must remember that our purpose is to understand the ultimate nature, not to criticize or demean the people who hold these views. To do so would contradict the great love, great compassion, and bodhicitta that we practice on the method side of the path.

For many years I have studied, contemplated, and meditated on the Buddha's teachings. I consider myself a staunch Buddhist because my confidence in the Buddha's teachings derives not from blind faith but from reason. At the same time, I respect all spiritual and religious traditions, even though the authors of some Buddhist texts point out contradictions in their philosophies or practices. Over the years I have visited many mosques, churches, synagogues, and Hindu temples and become friends with a wide range of religious leaders and practitioners. By speaking to them as one human being to another, I can genuinely say that their teachings benefit them and their followers. I have felt deeply moved visiting the holy sites of other religions. From my own experience, I know it is possible to have strong and reasoned faith in one's own spiritual tradition and still respect and appreciate other traditions.

When discussing and debating the nature of reality, our purpose is to examine our own deeply held beliefs and assumptions and to discern if they are accurate. We are challenging not only our personal beliefs but also the innate way we apprehend things and our innate feeling of who we are. The purpose of doing this is to free ourselves from duḥkha. It has nothing to do with proclaiming "I'm right and you're wrong" or "My religion is best." In fact, dogmatically clinging to our opinions indicates that our grasping inherent existence is quite strong!

The fundamental and most important theme in Buddhism is dependent arising. If we claim to follow the Buddha's teachings, it is important that our worldview is one in which our own existence as well as the origin of the universe is based on the principle of dependent arising. Inquiring into the origin of the world and the sentient beings in it without positing a permanent transcendent creator has been a prominent part of our Buddhist heritage stemming from ancient India.

Generally speaking, the diversity of world religions falls into two broad camps. One is theistic religions, in which the belief in a creator forms the primary foundation. The other is non-theistic religions, in which the concept of a creator does not form the foundation of the faith. Among non-theistic religions are Buddhism, Jainism, and one branch of the ancient Indian tradition, Sāṃkhya.

Within non-theistic religions, there are again two categories. The first are faiths that deny the concept of an all-mighty creator but accept the notion of an eternal self or soul, which is the True Self and is permanent, unitary, and independent of causes. The second are faiths that deny the existence of such a self or soul. Buddhism is the sole example of this, and this is the principal factor distinguishing Buddhism from other religions and philosophies.

Another way of classifying spiritual traditions is into those that accept liberation (*mokṣa*) and those that do not. Buddhism belongs to the first group. Within the spiritual traditions that accept liberation or salvation, there are those that consider liberation or spiritual freedom to be existence in an externally blissful heaven and those that understand liberation to be a mental state. Here Buddhism belongs to the second group, in which liberation is understood as the actualization of a state of mind that is free from all afflictive obscurations and is no longer reborn under their control.

As we examine some of the diverse philosophical and religious beliefs, please note that I do not hold a foregone conclusion that Buddhism is the best faith or that everyone should become Buddhist. As you know, I have always been a proponent of interfaith dialogue, harmony, and cooperation. Some of the beliefs we will examine exist in multiple religions and tenet systems. We will focus just on the absolutist beliefs without explaining the entire philosophical basis, path, and result of each religion or tenet systems that espouses them.

While doing this investigation, remember that "permanent" means something doesn't change from moment to moment—it doesn't mean that something exists eternally. Also, in all Buddhist systems except the Vaibhāṣika, a functioning thing—sometimes called simply "thing"—is equivalent to product and is produced by causes and conditions.[89]

Something else to keep in mind during our examination are the three principles Asaṅga explained concerning causal dependent arising:

1. Conditioned, compounded phenomena must arise from causes and conditions; they cannot arise without them. Thus the world and the beings in it didn't come into being as a result of a prior intelligence or an external creator that exist outside the interplay of causes and conditions. Anything existing in that way cannot interact with other factors to produce something new. This reasoning will be explained below.
2. The world and the beings in it did not arise from a permanent cause. Not only do conditioned things depend on causes and conditions, but the causes and conditions must also be impermanent. A permanent cause cannot produce results because causes must undergo change in order to produce their results.
3. The world and the beings in it did not arise from a discordant cause. Not only are causes impermanent, but they must also produce concordant results. A result can be produced only by causes that have the potential to produce it, and a cause can produce only results that it has the capacity to produce. Spinach seeds produce spinach, not daisies;

> tulips grow from tulip bulbs, not from light bulbs. Because the potential to produce a certain result exists within a cause, a cause cannot produce just anything in a random fashion. Similarly, a result cannot be produced by just any cause; its production requires its specific causes and conditions.

Many Buddhist sages throughout the centuries have refuted a permanent creator; prior intelligence; a permanent, unitary, independent self or soul; a permanent primal substance out of which everything is created; directionally partless particles; and other absolutist notions. All these ideas rely on the premise that all phenomena must have a stable and permanent basis, otherwise they could neither exist nor function. Buddhist sages state just the opposite: that anything that is permanent, partless, and independent of causes and conditions cannot function; it cannot interact with other things or be influenced by them.

## *A Creator or Prior Intelligence*

In ancient India, as in contemporary times, various views regarding an external, independent creator existed. From the Buddhist viewpoint, many contradictions arise by asserting such a creator. However, from the viewpoint of those accepting a creator, the creator exists even though Buddhists do not accept it. Similarly, Buddhists accept karma and its results even though others may not think this is correct. If we approach a non-believer, she may say neither a creator nor karma exists! Different assertions appeal to different people, and given this situation, it is important to be tolerant and accepting of these differences. Belief in a creator can benefit the followers of theistic religions by encouraging them to keep good ethical conduct, develop love and compassion for others, and practice generosity and forgiveness. However, as Buddhists we must use reason when discerning our own beliefs; we can't say that something exists just because we believe in it.

Some topics such as subtle impermanence or emptiness can be accepted by believers and non-believers, scientists, and those of other faiths. However, some people find it uncomfortable to apply the implications of subtle impermanence and emptiness to their spiritual beliefs. But participants in debates on such topics in ancient India were eager and willing to examine these issues. They were open to change their assertions and beliefs if they were disproven. The arguments below were addressed to such people as well as to Buddhist practitioners. The Buddha and his followers refuted ideas such as an independent creator because they contradict dependent arising, impermanence, and emptiness.

The Buddha encourages us to take responsibility for the state of our mind and the actions we engage in. The Buddhist path is not about worshiping or propitiating external beings, but about cleansing our minds of wrong beliefs and cultivating more realistic and beneficial beliefs and mental states.

Religious systems that accept an external creator do not seem to be based on a detailed analysis of whether or not there is independent existence. Rather, the idea of a creator is an attempt to explain the origin and functioning of the world and the experiences of sentient beings. Since the universe is extensive and causal relations are complex, people think that only a preceding magnificent intelligence could have created it. Dharmakīrti formulated what he considered to be the reasons some spiritual traditions at his time asserted a creator. To express it in the form of a syllogism: consider the external world and the sentient beings in it; they were created by a preceding intelligence because (1) things function in an orderly manner, (2) they have forms, and (3) they bring effects.

Some believe that the universe and sentient beings are an effect of a well-planned act, the product of an external agent, creator, or prior intelligence. This creator is said to be permanent and doesn't change moment by moment, it is self-arisen and doesn't depend on causes and conditions, and it is omnipotent (all-powerful) and omniscient (all-knowing). Buddhist sages respond to such beliefs with the following rebuttals:

- A permanent being cannot create because for creation of something new to occur, the cause must cease for the result to arise.
- A permanent being cannot be omniscient because it perceives different objects in each moment. If the cognized objects change moment by moment, so too must the being or the mind knowing them. An unchanging mental state cannot perceive different objects.
- A creator who is self-arisen and has come into being without causes cannot exist because nothing can arise without causes. A creator that

does not depend on causes cannot exist because it would be permanent and subject to the faults above.

- If nothing existed before creation, what caused creation to occur? From nothing, how can something arise? Causeless production does not exist.
- The creator would be both the cause of rice growing in a rice paddy and the non-cause—that which does not generate a result—of rice growing in that same rice paddy when it lay dormant. If rice grew, the creator would be its cause; if the rice did not grow, the creator would be responsible for that too. That means the creator would change from being a cause to being a non-cause, which contradicts the assertion that the creator is permanent.
- Once the creator made something, that object could not change or cease. Since the creator is permanent, its creations would also be permanent. The creator created human beings, but those beings would be permanent and unchanging.
- A permanent creator could not stop creating. It would create the first moment of the table, the second moment of the table, and so on. Since a permanent creator could not stop creating the next moment of the table, the table would exist forever.
- Some people may say that from the beginning everything existed in the creator in a fully developed form and that the process of creation simply made it manifest. This is similar to the belief of the Sāṃkhyas, who assert that even at the time of a cause (the primal substance and the creator), the result (the universe and sentient beings) exists, but we do not see the result at that time because it has yet to manifest. This assertion leads to many contradictions—for example, that cause and result would exist at the same time. But results cannot exist at the same time as their causes, and causes must cease for their results to arise.
- If a creator existed independently, under its own power, it would exist inherently. In that case, we should be able to find the creator when we search with reasoning analyzing the ultimate. But if we try to identify exactly what this creator is, what can we point to? Nothing exists under its own power. Everything exists dependently, by being merely designated by mind.

To sidestep the above difficulties, some people assert the creator or prior intelligence is impermanent. Buddhists respond:

- If the creator is impermanent, it must have been created by causes. What were the causes of such a creator or intelligence? Who or what created it?
- A creator that depends on causes and conditions is not all-powerful because it cannot control all causes and conditions; it is under the control of causes and conditions.
- A creator that is dependent on causes would have an intention or motivation that would cause it to create. What intention motivated it to create the world and sentient beings? What internal or external factor provoked the creator to change from an inactive state to one that actively creates the world and sentient beings?
- If an independent and perfect being exists, why did it create the world and the sentient beings in it? Why would a perfect and all-powerful being create a world with turbulence and suffering?
- What proof is there that the creator was omniscient from the beginning? If you say the complexity of the world and the human body could only have been created by an omniscient and omnipotent creator, you are assuming that such things could only arise due to the conscious, intentional effort of a creator or prior intelligence to create them. However, other systems of causality—biology, physics, chemistry, karma and its effects, and so on—could account for that.

In *Engaging in the Bodhisattvas' Deeds*, the eighth-century sage Śāntideva adamantly refuted the possibility of a permanent creator. He asked: If the creator were unchanging and independent, what could make it produce anything? If nothing existed before the creator made the world and all phenomena were created by the creator, what spurred the creator to create the world? If there were other causes and conditions, they would be the cause of the world. This is so because once those conditions came together, creation would occur and the creator would have no power to stop it.

But if there were no other conditions sparking creation, the creator would have no power to produce effects. If the creator's desire to create sparked creation, then the creator is not independent because it is under the power of its desires. Śāntideva repeatedly brings us back to the same fundamental points: functioning things arise due to causes and conditions; these causes and conditions are impermanent and have to cease to produce their effects; effects arise due to concordant causes—not just anything can produce anything.

Personally speaking, I believe that the notion of a creator came about primarily to promote human beings' good qualities. Because many people feel comfortable with the idea of a creator in whose hands their fate rests and to whom they can appeal for aid, that belief continues.

Believers see the creator and their relationship with it in a variety of ways. Some people say everything is in God's hands and happens according to his will. They must simply surrender to him. Others believe human beings must also help by acting morally. Salvation will come to those who properly follow God's teachings.

Some Jews explained to me that God is ultimate reality, but each individual also has responsibility to conduct themself in a moral way. These Jews and Christians do not believe that absolutely everything is up to God. Rather, God created human beings, but human beings have the responsibility to create a happier world. A co-partnership between God and human beings exists. So in that sense, they may say human beings are a "small creator"!

## REFLECTION

1. Review Asaṅga's three principles of causal dependence.
2. Make examples of the three principles in your life.
3. Apply these principles to the idea of an independent creator and contemplate the refutations of such a creator.
4. How does this influence your ideas about yourself and the universe?

## *The Origin of the Universe*

Many philosophies and cultures have proposed ideas about the origin of the universe. Here we will briefly touch on two: that of the Sāṃkhyas, one of the oldest schools of Indian philosophy, and that of modern scientists.

The Sāṃkhya system states that the physical world is a manifestation of primal matter (*pradhāna*), which is the subtle undifferentiated total of all material elements in their unmanifest state. When it manifests as various objects, it is called the "material principle" (*prakṛti*). This primal nature has six characteristics: it is the agent of actions; it is unborn and permanent; it is unitary and partless; it is only an object and is not consciousness; it pervades all objects be they animate or inanimate; and it is unmanifest and is a balance of three qualities—activity, which allows things to arise; lightness, which makes them increase and endure; and darkness, which causes them to disintegrate and cease. Some Sāṃkhyas are nontheistic, whereas others say that when the primal matter is spurred by the god Īśvara, it gives rise to the world.

The notion of primal matter resembles what some people today call a cosmic substance or a cosmic radiance from which everything manifests. They say it is a positive phenomenon that exists independent of all else, but from which the world is created.

Examining the idea of the primordial nature without going into the details of the Sāṃkhya system, we can see logical inconsistencies. Something that is permanent is not a cause and therefore cannot act; something that is partless can't give rise to the diversity of phenomena. In the contemporary view of everything arising from a cosmic substance, similar contradictions arise: If the cosmic substance is permanent, it cannot produce all phenomena; if it is impermanent, what triggers it to manifest the diversity of phenomena? And what determines what phenomenon it becomes?

According to Asaṅga's three points regarding causal dependence, searching for an absolute beginning before which nothing whatsoever existed is futile, and positing an external, absolute creator as the origin of the universe is untenable.

Alternatively, many contemporary scientists propose that a Big Bang marked the origin of the universe. Buddhism shares with science the appreciation for empirical evidence and reason to prove theories. Most Buddhists are willing to accept valid scientific discoveries about the origin of this universe. However, if the Big Bang is regarded as an absolute beginning to the universe before which nothing existed, such an assertion presents logical difficulties because nothingness cannot act as a cause from which conditioned things arise.

Similarly, should someone assert a permanent substance out of which the universe was created when the Big Bang occurred, there are also logical contradictions. Permanent phenomena do not come into existence dependent on causes, they are not affected by conditions, and they cannot produce results. If such a permanent substance existed, nothing—not even the Big Bang—could affect it, and thus it could not produce the elements of our universe.

However, if the Big Bang is not posited as an absolute beginning and if a permanent substance is not posited as the cause of the universe, then there is the opportunity to investigate what could have existed before the Big Bang that acted as conditions for the Big Bang to occur. The view of causal dependence opens the door to the arising of the universe due to impermanent causes that are concordant with the resultant universe that has come into being.

Ancient Buddhist scriptures speak of the existence of many universes. Each universe goes through four periods, each lasting for twenty eons: the periods of its evolution, abiding, destruction, and vacuity. While one universe may be evolving, others are abiding, others are being destroyed, and in place of some is a dormant, vacuous state before evolution begins anew. It would be interesting to see if scientific investigation came to the same conclusion.

## *Self and Soul*

Many religions espouse the existence of an indestructible soul that is the essence of a person. Because it is permanent, not made of parts, and not created by causes, this self or soul does not cease and remains unchanging forever. It is the person—what the word "I" ultimately refers to; it is what a person really is. The soul goes from life to life, or goes from this life to heaven or hell, depending on the beliefs of a particular religion. For non-Buddhist religions that accept the law of karma and its effects, a permanent soul is the stable basis that carries karmic seeds from one life to the next. The thought of such an everlasting soul brings a feeling of security and stability to those who fear the I becoming nonexistent at death.

In ancient India, all non-Buddhists asserted the existence of the ātman, whereas the Buddha, by analyzing what this self could be if it existed, concluded that its existence was not possible. He investigated:

- A permanent person could not be born in saṃsāra. The person could not attain nirvāṇa or awakening because that would involve the person changing from a sentient being to a liberated one.
- If the I were a fixed and permanent soul, a person would be unable to change; everything about them would remain the same. However, we see that people change. Learning from our experiences entails change, as does experiencing pain and pleasure.
- If the person were permanent, mental and emotional growth could not occur, and we would be unaffected by helpful or harmful influences.
- A permanent person could not act because action involves change. This would make preparing for future lives and liberation impossible, because creating their causes could not occur.
- If the soul were unaffected by causes and conditions, then destructive actions would not bring suffering and constructive actions would not bring happiness. Furthermore, purification practices would have no effect.

Looking at the second quality of a self, being a partless unity, that too can be negated by reasoning.

- If the person were partless, we wouldn't have two components—a body and a mind.
- We could not say, "One part of me wants to vent my anger but another part of me doesn't want to harm myself and others."
- An infant who grew into a toddler, child, adolescent, adult, and senior citizen could not be referred to by the same name or be considered the same person because that would entail having parts.

Regarding the third quality, being independent of causes:

- Someone would experience suffering and happiness randomly or without any cause.
- There would be no cause for someone to be born.
- Once born, neither illness nor severe injury could cause death.

Some non-Buddhists in ancient India asserted that the self was a permanent, functioning thing—that is, the self is permanent but the body and mind are impermanent. Sometimes we may think that we have an unchanging essence but superficially we change and are influenced by causes and conditions. That is, we feel that we have a solid, permanent core, but we are also influenced by the circumstances around us. Our mind changes and the body ages, but inside we are a permanent self. In that case:

- Nothing can be both permanent and impermanent at the same time because those two qualities are contradictory.
- A person would have two opposite natures or would be two people—one that doesn't change and the other that does.
- If the person were permanent, the body and mind would also have to be permanent because they are the component parts of an unchanging I.

### REFLECTION

1. Contemplate the various statements that refute a permanent soul and a fixed origin of the universe.
2. Can you disprove any of those statements?

## *Misunderstanding Buddha Nature*

The Mahāyāna teaches that each sentient being has the buddha nature (*gotra*), an aspect of the person that can never be removed and is the potential enabling them to become fully awakened buddhas. Some people may misconstrue this to be a soul or self—a permanent essence of a person, or an inherent purity that exists independent of any other factors. They may think of the buddha nature as a truly existent, already awakened essence that they simply have to realize has always been there. For people raised in a theistic religion, this idea may be especially appealing due to its familiarity.

However, this view of buddha nature contains logical inconsistencies. Asserting a truly existent awakened essence would contradict several Buddhist principles: being independent of all other factors, it would not exist by being merely designated by mind. In addition, people could mistakenly think that because they have an inherently pure essence that they are already buddhas but haven't yet awoken to that fact. But if that were the case, we would be ignorant buddhas, which is an oxymoron. An ignorant buddha cannot exist because buddhas have eliminated the two obscurations. Furthermore, if we were already buddhas, we wouldn't need to practice the Dharma in order to gain realizations because we would already have them.

Why, then, do some Buddhist masters say that we are already buddhas? This may be a skillful method that speaks to some people and encourages them to practice the Dharma. It gives a sense of self-confidence and increases enthusiasm on the path. However, such a statement should not be taken literally.

According to Maitreya, the author of *Sublime Continuum* (*Ratnagotravibhāga*, *Uttaratantra*), and Asaṅga, who composed a commentary on it,[90] our buddha nature has two aspects: (1) The *natural buddha nature* is the emptiness of our mind. This emptiness is permanent and is a nonaffirming negative. (2) The *transforming buddha nature* includes all those aspects of mind whose continuity will go on to full awakening—for example, our compassion and the clear and cognizant nature of mind. This is impermanent and is developed and refined by Dharma practice.

In the contemporary spiritual marketplace, some people speak of our "higher self" or "true self." The description is rather amorphous, but it seems that this higher self is a pure essence that is our true nature. It has always been within us and we just need to discover it. This idea is similar to a mistaken view of buddha nature. Although people may espouse this idea as a way of encouraging others to feel they have an innately good essence, such a personal essence would be permanent and truly existent—qualities that have already been refuted.

Care must be taken not to be enchanted by mystical-sounding words that no one actually understands or can define. Try to correctly identify the root of duḥkha—self-grasping ignorance—and its conceived object—true existence—by relying on definitive sūtras such as the Perfection of Wisdom sūtras and commentaries by Nāgārjuna, Candrakīrti, and others. Then cultivate the wisdom realizing the emptiness of true existence and employ it to counteract self-grasping ignorance. By proving to ourselves that true existence cannot possibly exist, our ignorance, and consequently our saṃsāra, will cease.

Some people develop the above misunderstanding about buddha nature further, saying a buddha who is already inside us is replete with the signs and marks of a buddha. They claim a buddha's nonmistaken mind that knows reality is already within each of us. It is independent and wasn't created by causes and conditions; it has existed from beginningless time and is naturally awakened. It is the ultimate truth and an independent, positive phenomenon that truly exists. They conclude that to cut the root of duḥkha it is not necessary to eliminate the elaborations of true existence by realizing emptiness. Realizing and perceiving this truly existent ultimate truth is the way to end saṃsāra. This, too, is an absolutist view in which true-grasping is left comfortably alone.

Prāsaṅgikas counter that meditating on a positive, truly existent phenomenon does not eliminate the ignorance grasping true existence. Thinking that such meditation is the key to cutting the root of duḥkha is like a person who is afraid of a poisonous snake in the east saying to himself, "There is a tree in the west." This does nothing to eliminate his false idea or his fear. Knowing what the snake would look like if it existed, he must search in the east and discover that no snake is there. Only then will his fear be extinguished.

Prāsaṅgikas explain that the ultimate truth, emptiness, is a nonaffirming negative; it is the absence of true existence. Nothing else is affirmed. Emptiness is realized by negating true existence on its bases—conventionally existing objects. Emptiness, too, does not exist from its own side. It is a dependent phenomenon and relies on its bases, phenomena that are empty. It too exists by being merely designated.

## *Causes and Effects, Permanent and Impermanent*

Buddhist philosophy firmly supports Asaṅga's three principles of causality. However, some ancient Indian schools disagree. The Vaiśeṣikas assert smallest particles that are the building blocks of the universe. These particles are not produced, but themselves join together to produce other objects. This idea is similar to that of some scientists who search for the smallest subatomic particle that is permanent (which means it must be unproduced) and forms the basis for all other atoms. Vaiśeṣikas say these smallest particles are permanent even though they are causes but not effects. Buddhists respond that these particles must undergo change to produce larger objects. Anything that changes must be impermanent, and whatever is impermanent is the result of causes and conditions.

Vaiśeṣikas also claim that the smallest particles are directionally partless, to which Buddhists reply: How can they coalesce to form larger objects? If they have no sides, then when two particles meet, they would merge into each other and could not produce something larger. If they joined one next to the other, then they would have parts—one side connected to the particle on its left, the other side connected to the particle on its right. If a particle didn't have a left side, right side, and middle, it would be invisible and couldn't join to any other particles.

Vaidāntikas say time is a cause but not an effect. It is a cause because depending on the season (time), a seed will either grow or not grow into a sprout. Time is the key factor allowing the seed, water, and fertilizer to produce a sprout. Buddhists respond that time must also be an effect because without there being an effect, we cannot establish something as a cause. Something being a cause depends on it having the possibility of producing an effect. If not, tomato seeds would not be the cause of tomato plants.

Questioning your deeply held beliefs or intuitions may not be an activity that you are accustomed to doing, and it may initially be uncomfortable. Nevertheless, clearing away confusion and establishing the truth brings confidence and mental peace. Challenging the incorrect acquired views you have learned is a first necessary step that prepares you to challenge the innate erroneous views that are the real source of saṃsāra. Although many of the arguments above do not focus on refuting inherent existence, they lay the foundation for doing so. Without these foundational understandings, the refutations of inherent existence will be difficult to comprehend.

In short, repeatedly contemplate Asaṅga's three principles for causality and observe how they apply to your life and what you see around you. Also contemplate these points: a permanent phenomenon cannot produce anything; causes must cease for their results to arise; permanent functioning things cannot exist; and any impermanent thing is both an effect of its cause and the cause for a future effect in that it has the potential to give rise to an effect. Āryadeva reminds us that anything that functions—be it a person, a tree, a cause, or an effect—cannot be permanent, unitary, and independent (CŚ 202):

> There is not anywhere any [functioning] thing
> that ever exists without depending.
> Thus never is there anywhere
> anything that is permanent.

Philosophical texts often use the example of seeds and sprouts to explain causality and the lack of inherent existence, because they are easy to understand. As your comprehension increases, apply these principles of causality to other topics such as your body, mind, feelings, emotions, situations you encounter, and so on. Doing this will encourage the habit of questioning assumptions. Use them to deepen your understanding of the twelve links of dependent origination. When meditating on emptiness, do not leave your usual beliefs and sensibilities to one side and meditate on some external, exotic nothingness that is unrelated to how you perceive and conceive of yourself and the people and things around you. Rather, become aware of your subtle, long-held beliefs and with rigor and honesty examine if they are correct or not.

## *Buddhism and Other Religions*

At the initial level of spiritual practice, the teachings of all religions are similar. They stress reducing anger and increasing love, compassion, and forgiveness, abandoning actions that harm others, and cultivating self-discipline, ethical conduct, and contentment. Although each faith has a slightly different approach to cultivate these qualities, the goal of developing them is the same. For this reason, I think that beginning practitioners can be half Christian and half Buddhist, or half Jewish, Muslim, or Hindu and half Buddhist. But just as all students learn to read and write at the beginning of their education and later specialize in a particular field, so too spiritual practitioners may initially do a general practice but later must clarify their beliefs so they can go deeper in one path. Although someone may initially practice another religion together with some aspects of Buddhism, when the view of the ultimate nature of reality becomes more important in their practice, they must investigate and decide which view seems more reasonable to them.

Each religion must retain its distinctive qualities. Because human beings have a variety of dispositions, the existence of many religions serves an important purpose in that it enables individuals to find a path that is suitable for them. The question is not "Which religion is best?" but "Which religion is most suitable for me?" The value of a particular medicine is determined by its effectiveness in curing one's own particular illness. An antibiotic is best for someone suffering from a bacterial infection, but it doesn't help a person with a broken foot. Therefore, instead of proclaiming one or another religion as best for everyone, we should identify the one that is most fitting for our disposition and interests.

Religious harmony does not and should not depend on saying that the theory and goal of all religions are the same. When we haven't even accomplished the final aim of our own faith, how can we say the goals of other faiths are the same? We should explore the richness of diverse philosophies, notice their similarities and differences, and respect the practitioners of all of them.

Several decades ago, I visited Montserrat, the home of the Black Madonna, near Barcelona. There I met a Catholic monk who so far had spent five years as a hermit in the mountains behind the monastery. He consumed only bread and water, and when I asked him what he had been practicing, he responded, "Meditation on love." As he said this, his eyes sparkled with joy, and when I looked into his eyes, there was some special feeling there. I admire and respect him greatly.

A few years after that, I (Chodron) visited Montserrat and with two or three friends found our way to this hermit's abode. We arrived completely unexpectedly, and he welcomed us in. On an altar in the center of the room was a kata (a Tibetan ceremonial scarf) and an image of One-Thousand Armed Chenrezig. We meditated in silence with him for a while before departing. It was clear that his meditation practice was profound and that he and His Holiness had a strong spiritual connection.

Many years ago, I (Dalai Lama) was with Father John Main, a Catholic priest who was my friend. We were sitting together in a room in Canada—Father John, a musician, another person, my translator, and me. Father John prayed and chanted as the musician played spiritual hymns, and tears began to roll down his cheeks. He was having a very powerful experience that arose from his extremely strong faith.

Someone with strong single-pointed faith and belief can have a vision of the divine being of their faith. From a Buddhist perspective, this divine being could be an emanation of a highly realized bodhisattva or buddha. To benefit particular people, a buddha or bodhisattva may teach about another divine being because that doctrine is suitable for the dispositions of those particular people. A buddha or bodhisattva may even emanate as a religious figure of another faith, and a follower of that faith could have a vision of that figure.

Buddhist scriptures contain accounts of the Buddha manifesting in different forms to benefit particular sentient beings. To tame an arrogant musician, he manifested as a violinist who played sublimely. To give a practitioner the opportunity to overcome prejudice arising from attachment to appearances, he manifested as a leper who needed help crossing a river. Because the Buddha's purpose is to benefit sentient beings and gradually lead all of them to full awakening, he may emanate as the teacher of a non-Buddhist path to instruct a person who is a proper vessel for that teaching. Through such skillful means, the Buddha leads others by teaching them a doctrine that suits them most at that moment, even if it is not the Buddha's ultimate thought or his ultimate teaching.

## *Awakening and Other Spiritual Traditions*

Is it possible to attain awakening by following other religions? This depends on the tenets of that faith and how it sets forth the basis, path, and result. How does it define duḥkha, its cause, the final goal, and the path to that goal? According to the Buddhadharma, attaining liberation and awakening depend on eliminating the cause of duḥkha, the ignorance grasping inherent existence, by cultivating the correct view of emptiness and the nonconceptual wisdom that realizes it. If other spiritual paths identify the cause of duḥkha as ignorance grasping inherent existence and have the correct view of emptiness that is taught as the antidote to it, then that path will lead to liberation and awakening. But if a spiritual tradition does not correctly point out the conceived object of the self-grasping ignorance and cannot explain the correct view of emptiness that disproves it, it would be extremely difficult to attain liberation and awakening by practicing that path.

Proponents of many religions and philosophies, as well as proponents of many Buddhist tenet systems, accept inherent existence. Meditation according to those systems does not overcome subtle ignorance and therefore cannot lead to liberation or awakening because the view of selflessness is incomplete. Similarly, people who accept an independent soul and a permanent creator will resist the idea of the emptiness of inherent existence. As long as they hold their present views, they will be unable to gain a correct inference of emptiness let alone a direct realization of it.

Take the case of a Yogācārin who holds the strong philosophical view that other-powered phenomena and thoroughly established phenomena exist inherently. He may meditate on selflessness according to that view, but he could not realize emptiness as described by the Prāsaṅgikas. Although understanding the Yogācāra view of emptiness can be a helpful step in the right direction, that person will first need to relinquish the Yogācāra view in order to gain the correct view of emptiness as explained by the Prāsaṅgikas. If this is the case for Buddhists who hold the tenets of lower systems, needless to say it would be so for those holding the views of non-Buddhist paths that accept a permanent, external creator or an inherently existent substance from which everything arises.

Can heaven as described in Christian teachings be attained through Buddhist practice? I don't think so. When the goal of practice is different, the method to attain it will also differ. Nevertheless, both religions encourage ethical behavior and encourage followers to engage in virtuous actions that lead to happy results.

Our conceptual framework and worldview greatly influence what we experience in meditation. If we believe in a creator, realizing emptiness will be difficult, because the qualities of a creator—permanence, omnipotence, independence of causes and conditions—are antithetical to the doctrine of emptiness. Similarly, doing a meditation technique that originated in Buddhism while holding the beliefs of another religion will not bring insights that accord with the Buddha's teachings. I (Chodron) heard of a rabbi who practiced Zazen in a retreat. The principal conclusion he reached from his meditation was that God existed. Although that benefited him in practicing his own religion, it was not the same conclusion someone doing Zazen within a Buddhist framework would come to.

Nowadays many people are interested in Buddhist meditation. Catholic roshis teach Zazen, and scientists and therapists teach mindfulness meditation. Although this benefits people, it is highly unlikely that these people will gain realizations of the Buddhist path by doing these practices, since their worldview includes notions of a permanent creator or lacks any notion of selflessness. In addition, the meditation techniques themselves have been changed to accommodate a secular perspective. It's wonderful that non-Buddhists benefit from those meditation practices, but the results will differ from meditation techniques taught by the Buddha and Buddhist masters.

When the Buddha was alive, he talked about spiritual practice and philosophy with a wide diversity of people who had an equally broad diversity of views. As many sūtras in the Pāli Nikāyas show, the Buddha went to great lengths to point out distorted views and describe right views. In the eightfold path of the āryas, right view comes first, followed by right intention. This order emphasizes the importance of finding the right view of both the law of karma and its effects and of selflessness, and cultivating the right intention to attain the results of the path taught by the Buddha.

Can someone who is unfamiliar with the doctrine of emptiness nevertheless realize it quickly and easily? There are accounts of a few exceptional practitioners realizing the ultimate nature during a teaching on emptiness by a high lama and a few stories of practitioners attaining liberation shortly after realizing emptiness, but this is extremely rare. King Indrabhūti (Indrabodhi) from Oḍḍiyāna is one such example; he realized emptiness and was liberated simultaneously. However, he was not an ordinary person. He had cultivated the path and experienced the wisdoms arising from hearing, contemplation, and meditation in many previous lifetimes.

REFLECTION

1. All religions are designed to benefit sentient beings by teaching ethical conduct, love, compassion, forgiveness, and so forth; thus it is important to respect all faiths.
2. One religion will not fulfill the needs of all sentient beings. People must choose a faith that helps them the most. Thus it is important to respect all religious practitioners as well as all non-believers.
3. Although we respect other religions and their practitioners, we can still discuss and debate our beliefs with a friendly attitude.

## *Free Will and Predetermination*

The issue of free will and predetermination has plagued Western philosophers for centuries. Do we have choice or are the events in our lives predetermined? Interestingly, this topic was not among the topics of interest that Indian and Tibetan Buddhist sages debated. There is no mention of this issue in scriptures that I know of. Perhaps that is because the theme of dependent arising permeates the Buddha's teachings, deflecting such questions early on.

The potential to make choices is always present. Our taking a fortunate or unfortunate rebirth is in our hands. Although ignorance prevents us ordinary beings from choosing the specific body we will take in our next rebirth, we make conscious choices during our lives to engage in constructive or destructive actions, which are the principal causes of the type of rebirth we will have.

Actions done in our previous lives influence the type of body we are reborn into: that of a human being, animal, and so forth. The rebirth we take gives us some options, but circumscribes other choices: as human beings we have the potential to engage in complex intellectual pursuits that are not available to someone born as an animal. On the other hand, birds can flap their wings and fly, whereas humans cannot. Our previous karma may cause us to be reborn with a healthy body or one prone to illness, and these physical circumstances will limit our choices to some extent. Our previously created karma causes us to be reborn in one country rather than another; then the ongoing conditioning of this life takes over as the culture of the country where we grow up influences the way we think, our opportunities as a man or woman, and the religion we encounter and follow.

The habitual emotional and thought patterns cultivated in previous lives influence the ones we have today. They also condition our inclinations, interests, likes, and dislikes. None of these things are predetermined in the sense of being fixed and inflexible. On the other hand, past actions and thoughts influence present ones. Some children are naturally compassionate toward their playmates and animals from a young age, whereas other children are chronically unhappy and disgruntled. Of course, their upbringing, education, and societal conditioning in this life can alter these tendencies, either increasing or decreasing their strength.

We lack total freedom to do anything we want at any particular moment. Although it would be helpful to speak Chinese, I cannot choose to speak it fluently five minutes from now because I haven't created the causes to be able to do that.

While the conditions we are born into may circumscribe our choices, the key lies in how we respond to those conditions. This is where our choice lies. While a difficult situation may be the result of the ripening of previous destructive karma, we still have the choice to respond to it with fear, indignation, and anger, or with acceptance, compassion, and wisdom. As we practice the mind-training teachings and the meditations on the stages of the path, our worldview will broaden, and we will see that our emotional states and physical and verbal responses to situations are not fixed. We don't have to react to every criticism by becoming defensive. It is not compulsory that we become jealous whenever someone has something we want. Take, for example, a situation described in *The Thirty-Seven Practices of Bodhisattvas* (VV 14):

> Even if someone broadcasts all kinds of unpleasant remarks
> about you throughout the three thousand worlds,
> in return, with a loving mind,
> speak of his good qualities—
> this is the practice of bodhisattvas.

We may have a habitual response to criticism, one coming from previous lives and nourished in this life, to retaliate when someone broadcasts unpleasant remarks about us to many people. But a choice exists. Do we criticize, humiliate, or ruin the reputation of the other person? Or do we contemplate that being criticized is not the end of the world and could have some benefits that we don't see now? Do we understand that the other person is suffering and behave in a kind manner with him? Depending on the choice we make, we will experience either happiness or suffering now and in future lives.

The critical point is whether we realize that we have choice and choose to exercise it. Mindfulness and introspective awareness help us to slow down and become more observant of our thoughts and feelings and to cultivate new habits of choosing our emotional, verbal, and physical responses to situations.

The Buddha knows that the outcome of harsh speech will be unpleasant. He also knows that the karmic seed from insulting or ridiculing others can be purified and instructs us in the four opponent powers for purification. The choice of whether to engage in these four and purify the karmic seed lies with us.

It is said that the Buddha sees the future. Must the future be predetermined for him to do so? No, it does not. The future is what has the potential to arise but has not yet arisen. Present circumstances influence future possibilities. But if present causes and conditions change, what happens in the future will change as well. It may seem to our limited knowledge that all the conditions point to a specific future outcome, but conditions may arise that we don't know about now. In short, we don't know the future until it happens.

That the Buddha has the clarity of mind to see the complex interaction of causes and conditions in the future does not mean future events are predetermined or independent of other factors. We know the sun will bring daylight to the Earth tomorrow, but that does not mean it is predetermined. It depends on the rotation of the Earth, the cloud cover, weather patterns, and so forth.

# 11 Pāli Tradition: Abandoning the Two Extremes

## *Wisdom*

The higher training in wisdom is the third of the three higher trainings, the first two being ethical conduct (*śīla*) and concentration (*samādhi*). Although there are many types of wisdom (*prajñā, paññā*), here our concern is with the wisdom that directly leads to nirvāṇa.[91] The Pāli commentarial tradition distinguishes two types of wisdom involved in the attainment of nirvāṇa: insight wisdom (P. *vipassanā-paññā*) and path wisdom (P. *magga-pañña*). Insight wisdom understands the three characteristics. It is cultivated gradually and leads to path wisdom. Path wisdom realizes nirvāṇa and comes with a clear realization seeing the deathless, nirvāṇa.[92] Insight wisdom is considered mundane because it has to do with analyzing the three characteristics of conditioned phenomena that are polluted, whereas path wisdom is supramundane because it is focused on the unconditioned, nirvāṇa.

In the context of the eightfold path, wisdom is right view. Because there are two types of right view—right view that is based purely on intellectual understanding and right view based on direct experience of the four noble truths—there are also two corresponding forms of wisdom. Intellectual wisdom is cultivated by listening to teachings and thinking deeply about them in order to arrive at the correct understanding of them. Although this wisdom is conceptual, it is very powerful. Experiential wisdom is direct penetration of the truth—nirvāṇa and the four truths—in our own experience.

Both forms of wisdom are important because experiential wisdom arises on the basis of a correct conceptual understanding. We must cultivate and employ correct discrimination, investigation, and analysis on the conceptual level to shatter false conceptions before experiential wisdom knowing the truth can arise. Some of these false conceptions are so much a part of our ordinary outlook that we do not recognize them as false and simply accept them unquestioningly. By studying and reflecting on the Buddha's teachings, we must learn to identify these false conceptions and develop correct conceptions.

This point is important, because some people mistakenly believe that all conceptual processes are useless and that wisdom is an intuitive experience that arises suddenly, seemingly without cause. This, however, is not the case. Cultivation and practice are necessary. Many intuitions and experiences in meditation may occur, but we lack any reliable means to check if they are trustworthy. This underlines the importance of practicing under the guidance of a wise and experienced teacher and of having a conceptual understanding of the path derived through study of the sūtras and other scriptures.

An experience in meditation is one thing; what we think it was after we arise from meditation is another. After the meditation session, our conceptual mind is functioning; it interprets and imputes meaning to the experience. If this is done incorrectly, harmful consequences may ensue. We may become arrogant, thinking we have attained something we have not. Or we may be disappointed, wondering why the wonderful experience cannot be replicated in future meditations. Or we may be frustrated because we thought this experience should have eliminated certain afflictions and problems in our lives only to discover that they remain. These difficulties arise not because of the meditation experience but because of our mistaken interpretation of it afterward. For these reasons, having correct conceptions and proper guidance from experienced teachers is important to prevent going astray.

## *Penetrating the Four Truths*

Penetrating and seeing the four truths comes about through the development of wisdom, which is based on concentration. First the mind must be focused and brought to a state of unification with single-pointed concentration. Such concentration makes the mind a powerful tool for investigating the nature of our experiences and existence.

Theravādin masters have diverse ideas on the degree of concentration needed to do insight meditation. Some say the attainment of full samādhi is not necessary, that even a relatively new practitioner can begin doing insight meditation.[93] Others say that one of the dhyānas is necessary for insight meditation. Still others say that some concentration must be cultivated, even if it is not full dhyāna. They direct their students to begin by practicing mindfulness to make the mind more focused until eventually it can remain without distraction on the constantly changing series of ever-changing moments of body and mind. Although they do not develop mindfulness that leads to the appearance of the sign (P. *nimitta*)—a mental image that arises in stabilizing meditation and is then used as the meditation object to attain single-pointed concentration—their concentration is sufficient to begin insight meditation.[94]

Insight wisdom practiced with a mind of samādhi examines the five aggregates that compose the person—the body, feelings, discriminations, miscellaneous factors, and consciousness.[95] This wisdom comes to see and to experience that this seemingly solid, monolithic body is actually a stream of material events that are arising and ceasing in each moment. Insight wisdom is directed to feelings, discriminations, and miscellaneous factors and experiences them as continuously arising and passing away. As insight deepens, experiencing everything in the first four aggregates as arising and passing away is superseded by perception of everything in the body and mind as disintegrating and dissolving moment by moment.

Insight then proceeds to investigate consciousness, where ignorance hides in its most subtle forms. When wisdom investigates consciousness, it too is revealed as nothing more than impersonal moments of mind that continuously arise and vanish. As the mind becomes more fine-tuned to impermanence, all five aggregates are seen as disintegrating, dissolving, and vanishing in each moment. Nothing substantial remains in the collection of aggregates.

Since the five aggregates are continuously ceasing, they are known as unable to bring lasting happiness and are therefore unsatisfactory. Being impermanent and unsatisfactory, they are unsuitable to be an everlasting blissful self. There is nothing in them to grasp as being I, mine, or my self.

In the *Mindfulness of Breathing Sutta* (*Ānāpānasati Sūtra*, MN 118), the last four aspects illustrate the path preceding and leading up to the breakthrough to the unconditioned. These four are contemplating impermanence, contemplating fading away, contemplating cessation, and contemplating relinquishment. When contemplating impermanence, meditators observe changes in the rhythm, frequency, and texture of the breath. Going deeper, they see that each phase of the breath—the beginning, middle, and end of the in-breath and the out-breath—changes continuously. Wisdom then examines the rest of the body, seeing that it, too, is in constant, unstoppable flux. Similarly, feelings, discriminations, primary consciousnesses, and mental factors arise and pass away in each moment. As wisdom and concentration become more refined, the process of arising and passing away is seen directly, more subtly, and more rapidly.

As meditation continues, the phase of arising recedes into the background, and the phase of disintegrating becomes more prominent. In evermore tiny microseconds the five aggregates are seen as disintegrating. This progresses to simply being aware of their cessation, the continuous stream of cessations of the body-mind complex in all of its aspects. The last stage, relinquishment, is giving up attachment to and identification with the five aggregates as a self. What we cling to as I and mine is just a collection of impermanent, impersonal factors that are continuously ceasing. There is nothing within or among them to be grasped as I or mine.

The meditator continues contemplating the five aggregates as impermanent, unsatisfactory, and not-self, making the mind more and more familiar with these truths. As insight deepens, it comes to a point where wisdom presses up against the boundaries of the conditioned and then breaks through the façade of conditioned phenomena. At this time, the meditator attains realization of the unconditioned, nirvāṇa. Penetration into the four truths in the path moments occurs in a sudden flash, a single breakthrough into all four truths simultaneously. However, this does not mean that all four truths are perceived simultaneously. According to the commentaries, the supramundane path and fruit take nirvāṇa (true cessation) as their object, not the other three truths. However, the path-consciousness is said to penetrate all four truths simultaneously. While it directly perceives only its object, the third truth, it penetrates the other three truths in terms of its function.

After arising from the experience of the path and fruition, meditators experience the five aggregates in a totally different way. Not clinging to the aggregates as I and mine, they fully understand the first noble truth—that the five aggregates are unsatisfactory in nature. They have lessened ignorance and craving to some extent, thus abandoning a portion of the true origin of duḥkha. Because the āryan eight path factors were present when realizing the third truth, they know the true path, the fourth truth.

Just for a moment the clouds of ignorance disperse, supramundane wisdom shines forth, and the third truth—true cessation of duḥkha and its origins—is seen clearly. Simultaneous with seeing true cessation, the other three noble truths are also seen and understood as being just empty, insubstantial, impermanent phenomena. Wisdom understands that ignorance and craving keep us bound in saṃsāra and that the path of wisdom leads to the cessation of duḥkha and its origin—this is the unconditioned, nirvāṇa. This breakthrough, which lasts only a short while, in which all four truths are known directly and simultaneously as they really are, establishes one as a stream-enterer. Meditators then continue to practice, gradually eradicating defilements, and experience nirvāṇa more deeply, passing through the stages of once-returner and nonreturner until arhatship is attained.

## *Subduing Defilements*

Afflictions have plagued us and caused us misery since beginningless time. Although it would be wonderful if they would disappear by themselves, this is not possible. Just like a shrewd enemy, they hide where we do not expect them to and appear at times when we thought they would not. To overcome them, we must be more clever than they are. To do this, we must study them well, know their habits, detect their weak points, and then, with wisdom, destroy them.

Defilements—afflictions, hindrances, fetters, and so on—have different degrees of strength and intensity at different times. For this reason, certain antidotes are more appropriate according to the strength of the defilement, and different degrees of abandonment are brought about by these antidotes. By being aware of this, we will understand why the three higher trainings and the insight wisdom and path wisdom they develop are essential for liberation.

The three general degrees or stages of defilements, going from coarse to subtle, are:

(1) *Expressed defilements* are motivating forces for our physical and verbal

behavior and are expressed through the actions of our body and speech. The coarsest level of defilements, expressed defilements, are usually strong and contribute to the creation of nonvirtuous karma. Living with ethical conduct—specifically taking and keeping precepts—restraining the senses, and practicing the seven virtuous actions of body and speech are effective ways to counter these defilements. For example, to impress others, Sam lies about his abilities. Attachment to reputation is the defiled motivation expressed through his verbal destructive action. Recognizing the disadvantages of uncontrolled speech and wanting to prevent it in the future, Sam takes the precept to avoid lying. Should a similar situation arise in the future, keeping this precept will deter him from lying. Observing precepts is *specific factor abandonment.*

Alternatively, Sam could remember that lying is nonvirtuous and stop himself from doing it because he aspires for a good rebirth. He could also practice sense restraint by not paying so much attention to gossip in the office. This level of abandonment is useful but is not stable because afflictions easily arise and overwhelm the mind, motivating us to express the defilements in our mind through speech and action.

(2) *Manifest and active defilements* are those present in the mind that haven't yet erupted into nonvirtuous physical or verbal actions. These are the defilements that were present when Sam was worrying about his reputation and seeking to impress others. Reflecting on one of the antidotes to attachment, such as mindfulness of death, will temporarily relax the attachment. This is a rudimentary form of abandonment called "factor substitution." Actual abandonment by factor substitution is substituting the defilement with insight knowledge that directly opposes the defilement. This is likened to abandoning darkness by turning on a light. Grasping permanence is abandoned by understanding impermanence; wrong views about karma and its effects are abandoned by meditation on conditionality.

Another way to prevent attachment from manifesting and being active in the mind is through cultivating deep states of concentration, such as access concentration or one of the dhyānas. Such deep concentration temporarily suppresses, but does not eradicate, the hindrances. The underlying tendencies still remain and, once the person comes out of meditation, manifest afflictions may arise. They don't necessarily arise again in the same life; skilled yogis can suppress the defilements so they don't arise, but they remain operative at the level of underlying tendencies (*anuśaya*, *anusaya*). Nevertheless, *suppression abandonment* gives the mind some repose and prevents coarse afflictive emotions from disturbing the mind.

(3) *Latent defilements* are underlying tendencies (P. *anusaya*) that are ingrained and innate. Only wisdom has the ability to cut the continuity of the underlying tendencies of afflictions. This wisdom is of two types. The first is insight wisdom, which is cultivated while meditating on the three characteristics. It weakens, but does not eliminate, the underlying tendencies. However, when all the conditions come together and a practitioner's faculties are mature,[96] the wisdom of clear realization arises and eradicates the defilements in such a way that even traces of them no longer exist in the mind. *Eradication abandonment* is the abandoning of defilements that are the true origin of duḥkha by destroying them completely so that they can never occur again. This is accomplished by the four supramundane paths and occurs in the mental continuums of the four types of āryas.[97]

DEFILEMENTS, ANTIDOTES, AND TYPES OF ABANDONMENT

| LEVEL OR DEGREE OF DEFILEMENT | MINIMAL ANTIDOTE | ABANDONMENT |
|---|---|---|
| **Expressed defilements** are expressed by bodily or verbal action. | Ethical conduct: precepts, sense restraint, practicing virtue, etc. | Specific factor: observing a precept stops the expression of a defilement in our actions. |
| **Active or manifest defilements** are active as thoughts and emotions in the mind. | 1. Factor substitution<br>2. Concentration: access-concentration or full dhyāna concentration | 1. Specific factor: using a particular antidote to deal with a particular hindrance<br>2. Suppression abandonment: using dhyāna concentration to suppress all hindrances |
| **Latent defilements or underlying tendencies** are defilements lying dormant deep within the mind, ready to become manifest when stimulated. | Wisdom:<br>1. insight wisdom weakens the latent tendencies<br>2. wisdom of clear realization (path wisdom) eradicates them | 1. Specific factor abandonment occurs through insight wisdom<br>2. Eradication abandonment occurs through the wisdom of clear realization. |

Just as a child does not begin her schooling in university, we do not begin the path by generating insight wisdom or path wisdom. Starting at the beginning by adhering to precepts and ethical values is a practical and effective method to stop the physical and verbal expression of defilements. From there we progress to generating concentration as the way to suppress manifest defilements. Continuing to practice, we generate path wisdom that is capable of uprooting them completely. To whatever degree we are capable of abandoning defilements, to that degree our mind will be more peaceful.

REFLECTION

1. Make examples of expressed defilements in your life. What is the minimal antidote to apply to them? Imagine applying those antidotes to calm your mind.
2. Do this for active (manifest) defilements and latent defilements (underlying tendencies).
3. What are the three abandonments? How can you develop them?

## *The Importance of Realizing Selflessness*

The importance of realizing selflessness to attain nirvāṇa becomes evident as we examine the four truths. When asked what constitutes the truth of duḥkha, we point to the five aggregates that are called *sakkāya* (S. *satkāya*), the collection of aggregates subject to clinging. Our psychophysical aggregates are not free from clinging and are under the control of clinging.[98] *Sakkāya* is often translated as personality or personal identity. In the Tibetan term *'jig tshogs*, *'jig* means to perish or decay, and *tshogs* means collection and refers to the collection of perishing aggregates.

Our life is an interplay of the five aggregates. Through the sense faculties in the body meeting sense objects, consciousness of the world arises together with contact, discrimination, feeling, intention, and other mental factors, all of which are true duḥkha. How do these five aggregates that constitute the person come into being? What is their origin? Craving is the chief source. Normally we think that first we exist, then we crave. Although from one perspective that is true, from another perspective because craving exists, the five aggregates come into being and we exist. In the *Discourse on the Six Sets of Six*, the Buddha says that the origin of the five aggregates is regarding any of the aggregates as "this is mine; this I am; this is my self"—three sentences that appear frequently in the sūtras. The conception or grasping that any part of this body-mind complex is mine, I, or my self is a decisive cause that perpetuates saṃsāra. We usually don't think that thoughts have such power, but they do. The thoughts grasping the ideas of "mine," "I," and "my self" have the ability to propel this cycle of rebirth.

Three graspings (*grāha, gāha*) lie behind these three afflictive thoughts: craving, conceit, and wrong views. In particular, craving supports the thought "this is mine," because craving wants to possess the aggregates or whatever else it sees as desirable. Conceit lies behind the thought "this I am," because conceit holds the I to be a solid and independent entity.[99] Wrong views underlie the idea "this is my self," because views formulate philosophical stances of what I truly am and what my real nature is, thus constructing a view of the self. The three graspings drive this round of existence from life to life. The perishing aggregates are true duḥkha, and these three graspings are true origins.

Because we do not understand the five aggregates as they are—as impermanent, unsatisfactory, and selfless—ignorance and craving continue and much misery is experienced. When we do not understand the six sense objects (the external sources), the six sense faculties (the internal sources), consciousness, contact, and feeling, we become enmeshed in craving for all these factors that play a role in cognition and experience. For example, we meet a person and experience pleasure being with him. Immediately the mind becomes attached to the sights, sounds, fragrances, tastes, tactile sensations, and mental images of that person. Attachment also arises for our sense faculties—the eye, ear, nose, tongue, tactile, and mental faculties—that enable consciousness to perceive him after contact has occurred. Attachment arises not only for those consciousnesses and contacts but also for the pleasant feelings. Not seeing feeling as it actually is becomes particularly disturbing to our well-being because craving and other afflictions arise in direct response to feelings. Experiencing pleasure, we want more and better. This craving propels us to do this and that, go here and there, continually looking for happiness from external people and objects. In the *Great Sixfold Base Sūtra*, the Buddha warns (MN 149.4):

> When one abides inflamed by sensual desire, fettered, infatuated, contemplating gratification [that we hope to receive from external people and things], then the five aggregates subject to clinging are built up for oneself in the future; and one's craving—which brings renewal of being (rebirth in saṃsāra), is accompanied by delight and sensual desire, and delights in this and that—increases. One's physical and mental troubles increase, one's physical and mental torments increase, one's physical and mental fevers (longing) increase, and one experiences physical and mental suffering.

Craving fixates on all the factors involved in producing feeling, and we find ourselves in the grip of attachment, bound by attachment, confused in our infatuation, and continually thinking of the gratifying pleasure we hope to receive from objects of the senses. When we do not receive the pleasure we crave, unhappiness and anger set in. A restless mental state, disturbed by either longing or animosity, can affect our physical health. This is suffering we experience here and now as a result of craving. In addition, craving perpetuates saṃsāra by propelling a new set of aggregates to arise in the future birth. That future birth, in turn, is the basis for the arising of further craving for the objects of the senses, sense faculties, consciousnesses, contacts, and feelings that manifest in that lifetime.

Meditation on the above explanation is effective for energizing our Dharma practice. Do this by considering many examples of this process as it occurs in your own life. The clearer you see the reality of your situation in saṃsāra, the greater will be your determination to be free from it. In addition, understanding the dependent arising of objects, sense faculties, consciousness, contact, and feeling in your daily experiences sets the stage for insight meditation.

To disband these five aggregates and attain liberation, we must challenge the three afflictive thoughts "This is mine. This I am. This is my self." This is done by seeing all factors of the body-mind complex as they really are—that is, by regarding them as "this is not mine; I am not this; this is not my self." The eightfold path converges on this meditation in which right view is applied to all factors of our saṃsāric existence, which are subsumed in the five aggregates and the twelve sources.[100] When we know with right insight that they are not mine, not I, and not my self, it becomes possible to stop certain defilements from arising in active form. Seeing the impermanence, unsatisfactory nature, dependent existence, and selflessness of these factors prevents craving for pleasure, craving to be free from pain, and craving for neutral feelings not to subside.[101]

Meditation on all the various parts of the aggregates as "this is not mine; this I am not; this is not my self" is another way of formulating the true path. To see the three characteristics entails the cultivation of insight wisdom. As insight wisdom gradually becomes stronger and more penetrative, the path wisdom of an ārya arises, and one catches a glimpse of nirvāṇa. Through path wisdom and direct knowledge, the fetters and pollutants are eliminated step by step on the ārya path, until ignorance is completely eradicated and the four truths are fully seen as they are. The eradication of these three distorted conceptions, the three graspings that lie behind them, and the five aggregates that result from them is true cessation. The meditation bringing about this cessation is the true path.

## REFLECTION

Observe the three graspings in your own experience.

1. Craving supports the thought "this is mine." Notice how craving wants to possess the aggregates, possessions, people, reputation, and so on. It divides the world into what is desirable and what isn't. How does craving influence your life?

2. Conceit lies behind the thought "this I am." Notice how there is conceit even when thinking "I"—there is pride just in existing.

3. Wrong views underlie the thought "this is my self." Do you get tangled up in a proliferation of thoughts about what you are and what your real nature is?

## *Cultivating Wisdom and Gaining Realization*

Wisdom is cultivated in stages, first by restraining the natural tendencies to react to pleasant feelings with attachment, to respond to painful ones with aversion, and to remain ignorant about the nature of neutral feelings. With this background, practitioners observe the nature of feelings, and after doing that over time, they will be able to penetrate their nature more deeply and clearly. Through this process, the underlying tendencies—latent dispositions that enable manifest afflictions to arise when the causes and conditions are present—are gradually weakened, until the point is reached when insight is strong and profound enough to cut off those tendencies altogether.

What does it mean to penetrate or understand the nature of feelings? Here feelings are used as an example of the many things to penetrate and understand, such as the five aggregates, six sources, the constituents, and so forth.

First we cultivate mindfulness and train in identifying the feelings in our own experience. Through training in mindfulness, we become able to identify even subtle happy and unhappy feelings when they arise. The following schema of gratification, danger, and escape is often applied to mindfulness of the five aggregates, six sources, and the elements as well. We first become aware of the gratification or pleasure we receive from contact with sense objects. Then we contemplate the danger of being attached to these feelings and how that perpetuates our saṃsāra. Upon realizing how this traps us in saṃsāra, we generate the wish to escape from attachment to feelings.

The *origin* (P. *samudaya*) of feelings is their causes and conditions. This is understood by tracing the causal process of contact occurring through the meeting of consciousness and the object by means of the sense faculty, and contact then leading to the generation of feelings. The *disappearance* (P. *atthangama*) of feelings is their cessation when their conditioning factors cease. When contact does not occur, feelings do not arise.

*Gratification* (P. *assāda*) refers to the pleasure and joy we derive from feelings, even when this involves the creation of misery. For example, we sometimes indulge in unhappy feelings because that gives us the "pleasure" of feeling sorry for ourselves. We delight in pleasant feelings because they anesthetize our deep-rooted dissatisfaction, in the same way that an alcoholic delights in the next drink that masks—and perpetuates—his unhappiness.

The *danger* or *drawbacks* (P. *ādīnava*) of feelings is that they are impermanent, unsatisfactory, and subject to change. Feelings are dangerous when we ignorantly react to them, perpetuating bondage in saṃsāra. Pleasant feelings bring attachment, unpleasant feelings breed anger, and neutral feelings lead to apathy and confusion. These disturbing emotions continue to run our lives, create destructive karma, and ensure rebirth in saṃsāra.

*Escape* (P. *nissaraṇa*) entails relinquishing attachment and desire for these feelings, which is accomplished through mindfulness and wisdom. Escape is the antidote that remedies the danger, and at its fullest is nirvāṇa.

When the sense faculties, objects, consciousnesses, contacts, and feelings are known as they really are, we are not inflamed with sensual desire. That allows for space to contemplate their danger and disadvantages—in particular their being impermanent, unsatisfactory, and subject to change. Such contemplation leads to the vanishing of physical and mental troubles and the arising of physical and mental bliss. Knowing and seeing things as they really are is the practice of wisdom and brings about the ending of craving, the cessation of the five aggregates subject to clinging, and liberation from saṃsāra.

This practice embodies the entire eightfold path. A practitioner who has contemplated the three characteristics and knows and sees things as they are has right view. Her intention—her motivation and purpose—is right intention. The effort she makes in that contemplation is right effort. Her mindfulness of the sense object, sense faculty, consciousness, contact, and feeling arising from contact as they really are—as impermanent, unsatisfactory, and selfless—is right mindfulness. The absorption of mind in that contemplation is right concentration. At the highest level of insight wisdom, just before she attains the ārya path, these five factors of the eightfold path are active. The other three factors—right speech, right action, and right livelihood—have been purified before entering into insight meditation and do not need further development at this moment. When the practitioner breaks through to the supramundane path and becomes an ārya, all eight path factors are present simultaneously, each playing its own role in eradicating the defilements. As the practitioner continues to develop the eightfold path of the āryas, all the other factors of the thirty-seven harmonies with awakening simultaneously come to fulfillment.

## *Calming Reactivity to Feelings*

Reactivity to physical and mental feelings of pleasure, pain, and neutrality creates disturbance in our lives here and now and interferes with the cultivation of serenity and insight. We cannot endure discomfort, let alone pain, and constantly seek pleasure and comfort. Such attachment and aversion dominate our lives. Learning to calm these reactions and maintain equanimity toward whatever feeling arises in our mind is a necessary step to cultivate both serenity and insight.

To do this, followers of many religions are encouraged to adopt some form of ascetic practice. But how useful are such practices for purifying the mind and progressing on the path? The Buddha noted that when someone who is undeveloped in body experiences a pleasant feeling, she enjoys the pleasure with attachment and craves more. When someone who is undeveloped in mind experiences a painful feeling, it invades the mind and persists, the mind becoming overwhelmed with aversion toward that feeling. However, when someone who is developed in body experiences a pleasant feeling, the mind does not become obsessed with it and does not crave more, and when someone who is developed in mind experiences a painful feeling, the mind does not become overwhelmed with aversion toward that feeling.

*Development of body* means that the person has developed insight. With insight, she understands that any pleasant feeling is impermanent, unsatisfactory, and not-self. With this wisdom she loses interest in these feelings. *Development of mind* indicates samādhi: when deep concentration is present, painful feelings cannot invade and overwhelm the mind because the practitioner is able to withdraw the mind from those feelings.

The Buddha's life story tells us that after his renunciation he engaged in ascetic practices for six years. The *Greater Discourse to Saccaka* (MN 36) relates that during that time three similes occurred to him. First, fire cannot arise from a wet, sappy stick in water. Similarly, practitioners who do not live physically withdrawn from sense pleasures cannot internally suppress their attachment to them. When they experience pain, they also are not able to gain realizations because the pain and their aversion to it overwhelm the mind, rendering them unable to concentrate or reflect on the Dharma. Even when they do not experience pain, they are still incapable of knowledge and vision because they are overwhelmed by distraction.

The stick lying in water symbolizes enjoying sense pleasures while seeking awakening. The stick being wet and sappy inside is analogous to the sensual desire that has not been internally subdued by samādhi. These practitioners cannot attain awakening, no matter whether they engage in ascetic practices or not. They suffer from two obstructions: physically they are immersed in sense pleasures and internally their desire has not been stilled. Thus for them, ascetic practices are futile.

In the second simile, the wet, sappy wood is on dry land; however, it still cannot produce fire. This is analogous to practitioners who live physically withdrawn from sense pleasures but whose desire for these pleasures has been neither abandoned nor suppressed internally. When they experience painful feelings by engaging in ascetic practices, they are incapable of knowledge and vision and supreme awakening. Even when they do not experience painful feelings, they are incapable of awakening. These people have met one condition by living physically withdrawn from sense pleasure, but their sensual desire is not stilled because they do not know how to train the mind, or if they do know, they do not practice it. In this case, too, whether or not they do ascetic practices, they cannot attain awakening.

The third simile is a dry sapless stick on dry land; this stick is capable of producing fire. Similarly, practitioners who are physically withdrawn from sense pleasures and have internally suppressed sensual desire are capable of attaining awakening whether or not they experience painful feelings. They have met both conditions: they are physically withdrawn from sense objects and their minds are stilled. So whether or not they engage in ascetic practices, they will be able to attain awakening.

From this we may conclude that engaging in ascetic practices is not the key to attaining awakening. Physically distancing ourselves from sense pleasures by living a modest lifestyle and mentally removing our mind from sensual desire by cultivating samādhi will benefit us. Samādhi is the basis for insight to arise, and insight uproots the deep tendencies in our mind for sensual craving. Samādhi enables a practitioner to temporarily abandon or to suppress afflictions by means of entering deep states of concentration. Insight gives the ability to abandon afflictions so they will never return.

Those non-Buddhists who engage in painful ascetic practices seek to tame their attachment and aversion. However, the method they employ does not work. Other non-Buddhists are instructed by their teachers not to see forms with their eyes, nor hear sounds with their ears, and so forth (MN 152). If not seeing, not hearing, and so forth were the way to avoid responding to sense objects with attachment, aversion, and apathy, the Buddha commented that then the blind and deaf would have excelled in developing their mental faculties.

At this point in the sūtra, Ānanda requests the Buddha to explain the supreme development of the faculties—the development of the mind—in the āryas' discipline. In his reply, the Buddha assumes that practitioners are already practicing restraint of the sense faculties (P. *indriyasaṃvara*) by restricting contact with sense objects so that the mind doesn't get carried away by its reactions to them. The next step in developing the faculties is to establish insight while perceiving the object. This is done by understanding (MN 152.4):

> There has arisen in me what is agreeable, there has arisen what is disagreeable, there has arisen what is both agreeable and disagreeable. But that is conditioned, gross, dependently arisen; this is peaceful, this is sublime, namely equanimity.

Here practitioners notice that liking, disliking, or apathy has arisen toward the perceived object and counteract that by focusing on other attributes of the object—the fact that it is conditioned, gross, and dependently arisen. Through this, the equanimity of insight is established and, by dwelling in that, they release attraction, aversion, and apathy. This is the supreme development of the faculties in āryas' discipline.

When seeing a form, hearing a sound, and so forth (up to cognizing a mental object), how does a disciple in higher training (someone who has entered the path) practice? If liking, disliking, or apathy arise in her mind, she recognizes it as a hindrance and, turning her mind away from these reactions, she reestablishes the equanimity of insight.

The Buddha proceeds by explaining how arhats practice when agreeable, disagreeable, or neutral feelings arise when contacting sense objects. Note that here he speaks of arhats who have perfected these methods. In other instances, the Buddha teaches them to ordinary practitioners as methods to abandon attachment, anger, and ignorance in training. These are:

(1) Perceiving the unrepulsive in the repulsive is to meditate on love

toward a person we find disagreeable or to contemplate a person or object as simply a collection of impersonal parts or elements. Doing this brings the mind to a neutral state that is open, receptive, and has arisen through implementing a virtuous Dharma method.

(2) Perceiving the repulsive in the unrepulsive is to contemplate the body of an attractive person as foul or to understand an attractive object as impermanent.

(3) Perceiving the unrepulsive in both the repulsive and the unrepulsive is to apply the first two methods to both repulsive and unrepulsive objects.

(4) Perceiving the repulsive in both the unrepulsive and the repulsive is to apply the first two methods to both repulsive and unrepulsive objects.

(5) By avoiding both the repulsive and unrepulsive, abide in equanimity, mindful and fully aware. This abandons joy and sorrow in reaction to objects of the six senses and allows us to abide in equanimity.

The Buddha closes this sūtra with heartfelt encouragement (MN 152.18):

> What should be done for his disciples out of compassion by a Teacher who seeks their welfare and has compassion for them, that I have done for you, Ānanda. There are these roots of trees, these empty huts. Meditate, Ānanda, do not delay, or else you will regret it later. This is my instruction to you.

By teaching us with compassion, the Buddha has done what he could to lead us out of saṃsāra and to nirvāṇa. Now we must practice. Since we do not know when death will come, we should not delay, because dallying on the path will only bring regret and pain later on.

## *Unique Qualities of the Buddha's Teaching*

The teachings on conditionality (causal dependence) and selflessness are unique aspects of the Buddha's doctrine. In the *Shorter Sutta on the Lion's Roar* (MN 11), the Buddha emphasizes the necessity of uprooting all views of self, especially the views of existence (absolutism, P. *bhavadiṭṭhi*) and of nonexistence (nihilism, P. *vibhavadiṭṭhi*). Only by the thorough cultivation of true knowledge (*vijjā*) are ignorance (*avijjā*) and all forms of clinging eliminated, resulting in the attainment of nirvāṇa.

The *Held by Views Sūtra* discusses the views of existence and nonexistence (Iti 2.22).

> Held by two kinds of views, some devas and human beings hold back and some overreach; only those with vision see.
>
> And how, monastics, do some hold back? Devas and humans enjoy existence, delight in existence, are satisfied with existence. When Dhamma is taught to them for liberation from existence, their minds do not enter into it or acquire confidence in it or settle upon it or become resolved upon it. It is in this way, monastics, that some hold back.
>
> How, monastics, do some overreach? Now some are troubled, ashamed, and disgusted by this very same existence and they rejoice in [the idea of] nonexistence, asserting: "In as much as this self, good sirs, when the body perishes at death, is annihilated and destroyed and does not exist after death—this is peaceful, this is excellent, this is the real!" It is in this way, monastics, that some overreach.
>
> How, monastics, do those with vision see? Herein a monastic sees what has come to be as having come to be. Having seen it thus, he practices the way for disenchantment, for dispassion, for the cessation of what has come to be. It is in this way, monastics, that those with vision see.

Here the Buddha speaks of three types of people. The first, those who hold back, are confined and limited by their wrong views. Not knowing any other type of existence, they enjoy saṃsāra and delight in its pleasures. Some people who crave for saṃsāric existence develop a view of it that gives intellectual support to their craving. Other people just assume there is a permanent soul or a substantial self that continues after death; they want to go on existing forever. Some seek rebirth specifically as a deva or human being with great wealth, reputation, family, and power.

The second are people overreach. Some are disgusted with life, are in great pain, or despair about the state of the world. At the time of death, they crave for nonexistence in order to terminate their misery. Others enjoy life but think that the mind is just a property of the brain and that the self ceases at the time of death. Both of these ideas assume that when the body dies the consciousness and the person become nonexistent. They see the cessation of all existence at the time of death as peaceful and do not consider or prepare for future lives.

The third alternative is the one the Buddha presents; these people see with correct vision of wisdom and insight. They see "what has come to be as having come to be"—they see that five aggregates have arisen through conditions. Because the five aggregates are controlled by ignorance and karma, they become disenchanted with them, cease to crave them, and attain freedom from them by overcoming their causes. This cessation is not the absolutism of those who hold back or the nihilism of those who overreach, but is the Middle Way of the Buddha that upholds dependent origination in saṃsāra and its cessation.

### REFLECTION

1. Some people hold back from the Dharma because they are completely wrapped up and infatuated with this life and the external world with its desirable people and attractive experiences. They find Dharma uninteresting.

2. Some people overreach because they cannot find harmony with people and the world. They are depressed and discouraged and see death or nonexistence as the peace they seek. They are unable to make effort in the Dharma or dislike doing so.

3. Those who see with vision see the world and beings in it with wisdom, as they are, and seek liberation.

## *Relinquishing Wrong Views*

Wrong views must be relinquished to generate correct views. Many wrong views are based on philosophical machinations, and clinging to them brings misery here and now and impedes the ability to think clearly. In the *Net of Brahmā Sūtra* (DN 1), the Buddha outlines sixty-two wrong views to renounce. In the *Shorter Series of Questions and Answers* (MN 44), Bhikkhunī Dhammadinnā outlines twenty wrong views of self to be given up. In the *Discourse on the Simile of the Snake*, the Buddha talks about various views of permanence, pointing out their disadvantages; for example (MN 22.18):

> . . . someone thinks thus: "Alas, I had it! Alas, I have it no longer! Alas, may I have it! Alas, I do not get it!" Then he sorrows, grieves, and laments; he weeps, beating his breast, and becomes distraught.

Holding this view, we think our possessions are permanent, everlasting, and not subject to change. When we later lose a cherished possession or relationship, we exclaim in distress, "Alas, I had it! Alas, I have it no longer!" and are distraught with grief and often with anger or depression as well. The mind vacillates, being attached to those things when we have them and lamenting when we lose them. Or, as indicated by thinking "Alas, may I have it! Alas, I do not get it!" we crave desirable things we don't have, and when our wishes or longing are stifled, we mourn in distress. On the other hand, someone who does not hold a view of permanent possessions, status, or relationships is not subjected to these emotional vacillations that are rooted in craving.

Someone may hold an extreme absolutist view thinking that at death our individual self will continue on unchanged and exist eternally, or thinking our soul will merge with the universe and in that way be permanent and everlasting. When people who cling to such views encounter the Buddha's teachings, they easily misinterpret them, thinking the Buddha is saying that at death they will be annihilated and cease to exist altogether. They then become terrified and agitated and reject the Dharma. Clinging to this wrong view has obscured their wisdom.

Is it possible to hold any doctrine of self without experiencing unfortunate repercussions? The Buddha challenges the monastics (MN 22.23):

> Monastics, you may well cling to that doctrine of self that would not arouse sorrow, lamentation, pain, grief, and despair in one who clings to it. But do you see any such doctrine of self?

After the monastics reply that they do not, the Buddha agrees. Although not said directly, the implication is that holding any wrong view leads to clinging to that view, and when a wrong view is clung to and cherished, misfortune will eventually come. That misfortune may not arise immediately or in an obvious way. In fact, some people may derive satisfaction and security from their wrong views, and other people may restrain from destructive behavior due to them. However, in the long term these views will lead to disappointment, justification for harmful actions, rejection of correct views, and continued existence in saṃsāra.

Several sūtras in the *Suttanipāta* contain passages about giving up even the subtlest clinging to views.

> Those who hold rules (precepts) to be the highest thing,
> thinking purity comes from [practice of] self-restraint,
> take up rites and observe them [dutifully],
> [thinking] "if we learn this, then we'll learn purity"—
> [these] self-proclaimed experts are bound for rebirth.
>
> When someone is deficient in rules and rituals,
> having failed to perform some act, he trembles,
> he yearns and longs for purity here,
> like one who has left home [but] lost the caravan.
>
> So renounce rules and rituals,
> all actions that bring praise and blame;
> without yearning [for] "purity, impurity!"
> [a person] should live free, not grasping at peace.
>
> When a person in the world, abiding in views,
> esteems something especially "the highest,"
> then he says that all others are inferior;
> in this way he is not beyond disputes.
>
> The person who holds opinions, defining [things] for himself,
> comes to further quarrels in the world;
> [only] when a person renounces all opinions
> does he make no quarrel with the world.[102]

Clinging to views—be they views concerning precepts, rituals, or philosophical topics—takes us far from the purpose of the Dharma into egotistic thinking. Arrogance flares up and we are lost in comparing ourselves with others, thinking we are best because we hold the correct views and others are inferior because they hold foolish views. We find ourselves in disputes with others, desperately endeavoring to be victorious in debates in a frantic attempt to prop up our self-esteem. This is not the path to nirvāṇa.

Relinquishing clinging to views doesn't mean we don't believe in anything, are afraid to join a discussion, or ignorantly vacillate between views. We need to learn to think clearly without attachment or confusion. Right views in the eightfold path can be supported by reason.

The *Sutta to Pasūra* speaks of the disadvantages of clinging to views and discourages doing so. It also advises how to reply to someone who is intent on arguing about views for the sake of praise and recognition (Sn 4.8):

> "Only here is there purity"—that's what they say. "No other doctrines are pure"—so they say. Insisting that what they depend on is good, they are deeply entrenched in their personal truths.
>
> Seeking controversy, they plunge into an assembly, regarding one another as fools. Relying on others' authority, they speak in debate. Desiring praise, they claim to be skilled. . . .
>
> Those who, grasping at views, argue and say "Only this is truth," to them you should say when talk begins, "There are none here to reply to you in strife."
>
> Among those who live above confrontation, not pitting view against view, whom would you gain as opponent, Pasūra, among those here who are grasping no more?

The *Aṭṭhakavagga* and the *Pārāyanavagga*, small collections of some of the earliest sūtras, are found in the *Suttanipāta*. These sūtras seem to anticipate Nāgārjuna's emphasis on not clinging to precepts and practices and even to the most cherished philosophical views that we are certain will lead us to awakening. Nāgārjuna's instruction isn't simply to abandon clinging to views in the sense of not demanding "my view is right, yours is wrong," but to release clinging to the view of grasping inherent existence. He warns us against holding the reified extreme of absolutism that grasps inherent existence as well as the annihilating view of nihilism that negates what in fact exists.

Unwilling to assent to any view of inherent existence, Nāgārjuna says that the emptiness of inherent existence itself is also empty. In place of the wrong views of absolutism and nihilism, he asserts that although all phenomena—even emptiness itself and his own views—lack inherent existence, they still exist and function, and therefore adopting the correct view is important. In the culminating verse of *Treatise on the Middle Way*, he says (MMK 27.30):

> I prostrate to Gautama,
> who, through great compassion,
> taught the exalted Dharma
> that leads to the relinquishing of all views.

Some people have misinterpreted Nāgārjuna's words, thinking that Mādhyamikas only refute others' views but do not have any of their own. This is not correct; Mādhyamikas have positions and make assertions. Nāgārjuna explains that Mādhyamikas' assertions as well as refutations of wrong views are empty of inherent existence, yet exist dependently.

Although there are some similarities between Madhyamaka and some passages in the *Suttanipāta*, they are not the same. Nāgārjuna explains in detail how to realize emptiness, which is the antidote to all views, whereas the *Suttanipāta* does not. However, as a collection of short sūtras it gives us points to contemplate, and some of its sūtras speak of emptiness or of non-grasping. In the *Sutta on Violence*, the Buddha instructs (Sn 4.15.949–51):

> Dry out that which is past,
> let there be nothing for you in the future.
> If you do not grasp at anything in the present,
> you will go about at peace.
>
> One who, in regard to this entire mind-body complex,
> has no cherishing of it as "mine,"
> who does not grieve for what is nonexistent,
> truly suffers no loss in the world.

> For him there is no thought of anything as
> "This is mine" or "This is another's."
> Not finding any state of ownership,
> and realizing "nothing is mine," he does not grieve.

In short, not clinging to anything in saṃsāra, be it sense objects, people, or views, is the key to liberation. Whether someone asserts grasping a self-sufficient substantially existent person or grasping inherently existent phenomena as the final grasping to be relinquished, everyone agrees that embellishing reality with our wrong conceptions leads to duḥkha.

# 12 Pāli Tradition: Cultivating Insight Knowledge

THE PĀLI AND SANSKRIT TRADITIONS share many of the same analytical methods to realize selflessness. Some differences in approach exist too. According to the Pāli tradition, the realization of the three characteristics of conditioned phenomena—impermanence, duḥkha, and selflessness or not-self—is worldly insight knowledge because these three are characteristics of true duḥkha, the phenomena of saṃsāra. Realization of the three characteristics is prerequisite to penetrating nirvāṇa—the unconditioned, the ultimate. The supramundane wisdom that knows nirvāṇa is employed over the ārya stages of stream-enterer, once-returner, and nonreturner, and culminates in arhatship.

In the Sanskrit tradition, understanding impermanence and duḥkha is accomplished by conventional reliable cognizers. The various tenet systems have different views of what selflessness is, according to how they describe the object of negation. In the Prāsaṅgika system, selflessness is equivalent to emptiness; it applies to all persons and phenomena, and direct, nonconceptual realization of selflessness is an ārya path that, when fully developed, leads to liberation or full awakening.

In both traditions, wisdom is praised for unlocking the door to nirvāṇa, the state of actual peace. Therefore, the Buddha and Buddhist sages encourage us to treasure wisdom and do our best to cultivate it. The Buddha counsels (AN 1.77–81):

> Insignificant, monastics, is the loss of relatives, wealth, and fame;
> the loss of wisdom is the greatest loss.

> Insignificant, monastics, is the increase of relatives, wealth, and fame; the increase of wisdom is the greatest.
>
> Therefore, monastics, you should train yourselves thus, "We will increase in wisdom."

Cultivating insight wisdom entails understanding our experiences and ourselves, the person experiencing them. To understand ourselves, it is necessary to understand the five aggregates that compose the person, and this is done by comprehending their common characteristics—impermanence (*anitya, anicca*), unsatisfactoriness (*duḥkhatā, dukkhatā*), and selflessness, or not-self (*anātman, anattā*)—and comprehending how the aggregates relate to the self who is experiencing and clinging to them. Mindful observation of the aggregates sets the stage for insight analyzing their nature and the nature of the person.

## *Schemas to Use and Phenomena to Examine*

In the sūtras the Buddha repeatedly uses certain schemas of phenomena as the objects on which to develop insight wisdom and path wisdom. These include, but are not limited to, the three characteristics; the four truths; dependent origination; gratification, danger, and escape; and disenchantment (*nibbidā*), dispassion (*virāga*), and liberation (*vimutti*).

The principal schema to cultivate insight wisdom is the three characteristics of conditioned phenomena in saṃsāra: impermanence, duḥkha, and selflessness. The Buddha often uses these three to help disciples come to three conclusions about conditioned phenomena: they are not mine, they are not I, and they are not my self.

The schema of the four truths is employed to examine each phenomenon in terms of its specific nature, its arising, its cessation, and the path to its cessation. This is also the pattern used to contemplate dependent origination. In one sūtra, Śāriputra describes each of the twelve links of dependent origination, the conditions for its arising, and the conditions for its cessation, and prescribes the eightfold path as the means to cease saṃsāra. This schema highlights the conditioned nature of things—that nothing is an isolated event, separate from other things. Rather our life is part of a complex interconnected web in which one thing conditions another, which, in turn, conditions another. Understanding this opposes the misconception of independent existence and impacts the way we view ourselves and our relationship to people and things.[103]

While analyzing the arising and ceasing of each link, it comes to light that the process of rebirth continues without a substantial self that is reborn. Conditionality *itself* is what makes the continuity from one life to the next occur: no soul, independent self, or controlling self is required. For example, New York City exists, and whether we think about it or experience it directly, it appears to us to be one city. Yet upon examination, we find many neighborhoods, buildings, people, and activities there. From one day to the next, each of these different elements continues on, becoming something new in each passing day. Do any of these constantly changing elements that constitute the city need a real, findable New York City to make them continue? No. Is there a findable thing that is New York in any of these elements individually or in their collection? No. If the name "New York" were removed, would everything fall apart? No. Similarly, the flow of the aggregates continues without there being a findable self that makes all these parts cohere.

Another schema the Buddha employs is that of gratification, danger, and escape. Gratification refers to the attraction sentient beings have for polluted objects and the enjoyment they derive from them, danger refers to the unpleasant consequences stemming from afflicted involvement with them, and escape refers to the peace of nirvāṇa that is free from them.

In addition, the Buddha employs the schema of disenchantment, dispassion, and liberation with respect to each conditioned thing in saṃsāra. Disenchantment is the sense of revulsion toward saṃsāra, dispassion is the fading away of desire for polluted objects, and liberation is attaining the path and experiencing nirvāṇa. Alternatively, disenchantment is the last stage of insight, dispassion is the attainment of the supramundane path, and liberation is the fruit of the path.

Other schemas can be used to examine the phenomena that compose the five aggregates. These include the twelve sources and eighteen constituents,[104] as well as the six types of consciousness, six contacts, six feelings, and six cravings taken together. The six elements—earth, water, fire, wind (air), space, and consciousness—are another formulation of phenomena included in the five aggregates.

Why are there so many ways to classify phenomena and so many schemas through which to examine them? Our ignorance is deep and approaching the same thing from different angles brings a more robust understanding. In addition, because people have different dispositions, an individual may find one or another schema or one or another way of grouping phenomena to be more useful for their meditation. In the next volume of the *Library of Wisdom and Compassion* you will see different schemas applied to various topics and objects. Here we'll begin with the three characteristics.

## *The Three Characteristics*

Cultivating insight into the three characteristics enables us to look at the components of our being in a realistic way and thus is a central element of the path to liberation. It is recommended to meditate on these three on the basis of a general understanding of some of the prominent themes in the Buddha's teachings: conditionality, dependence, and how they pertain to the twelve links of dependent origination. This background prepares us to investigate each conditioned and dependent factor of our saṃsāric existence and to understand that all of them share three characteristics: they are impermanent, unsatisfactory, and selfless. Although they have these characteristics, ignorance clouds our mind and we see conditioned things as permanent, satisfactory, and having a self.

Ignorance functions in two ways. First, as mental darkness, it conceals and obscures the true nature of phenomena. Second, it creates false appearances or distortions in the mind so that we see things in a way that is opposite to what they actually are. The distortions operate on three levels: in our perceptions, thoughts, and understanding or views.

First, we *perceive* things incorrectly. Based on these incorrect perceptions, we *think* about them in a wrong way. Drawing our thoughts together, we create a narrative that interprets and *understands* our experience incorrectly. This results in constructing a philosophy that we then cling to, identify with, and defend. Needless to say, this has brought incredible misery to sentient beings throughout history. For example, Alfred perceives himself as a substantial being. When a colleague gives him some feedback about his work, he thinks the colleague is criticizing him. Ruminating on this, he understands that his job may be in danger if his boss hears about this criticism.

He also notes that the colleague is from a particular country. Remembering incorrect information about that country that he heard as a child, he creates an "us versus them" philosophy whereby his country seems endangered by immigrants from the other country. Alfred then pledges to stop immigrants from entering his country by joining a vigilante group that polices the border. Meanwhile, others who heard the feedback the colleague gave Alfred saw it as a helpful tip, not as criticism.

The Buddha spoke of four distortions, each of which occurs at the three levels above. These four are: (1) regarding what is foul as attractive, (2) regarding what is impermanent as permanent, (3) regarding what is unsatisfactory as the source of true happiness, and (4) regarding what is not self as self.

In a mind obscured by ignorance and confused by these four distortions, clinging, attachment, and other afflictions continuously operate. Ignorance gives rise to craving, which seeks to expand the territory of this supposed self so that it can control everything. We want this imagined self to continue in the future and be immortal. The four distortions sustain saṃsāra, distracting us by the lure of happiness in the world. The mind is caught up in illusions, which give rise to craving, conceit, and wrong views. In the meantime we frantically seek confirmation of our selfhood and remain perpetually frustrated as this eludes us. Only by turning the mind inward to investigate our experience with mindfulness and wisdom can these corroding activities and the duḥkha they bring be ceased.

The way to liberation lies in seeing that the three characteristics are the nature of all phenomena that constitute our body and mind. This leads us to stop identifying the aggregates as a substantial self—to see that they are not mine, not I, and not my self. By knowing the selflessness of these phenomena with correct wisdom and releasing the identification of the five aggregates as a self, craving and clinging cease as the mind becomes disenchanted, dispassionate, and liberated.

The first distortion—seeing what is foul as attractive and pure—applies particularly to the body. Although the body is a collection of elements and organs that are foul, we project attractiveness onto it. The antidote to this is meditation on the thirty-two parts of the body.

The antidote to the next three distortions is understanding the three characteristics of impermanence, duḥkha, and selflessness. The Buddha encourages us to understand the three characteristics by explaining six advantages of comprehending each of the three (AN 6:102–4):

> When a monastic sees six advantages, it is enough for him to establish unlimited perception of impermanence in all conditioned things. What six? All conditioned things will appear to me as transient. My mind will not delight in anything worldly. My mind will emerge from the entire world. My mind will incline to nibbāna. My fetters will be abandoned. And I come to possess supreme asceticism. . . .
>
> When a monastic sees six advantages, it is enough for him to establish unlimited perception of dukkha in all conditioned things. What six? A perception of disenchantment will be established in me toward all conditioned things, as toward a murderer with uplifted dagger. My mind will emerge from the entire world, I will see nibbāna as peaceful. The underlying tendencies will be uprooted. I shall be one who has completed his task. And I shall have served the Teacher with loving-kindness.
>
> When a monastic sees six advantages, it should be enough for him to establish unlimited perception of not-self in all conditioned things. What six? I shall be without identification (craving and views) in the entire world. Notions of "I" will cease in me. Notions of "mine" will cease in me. I shall possess knowledge not shared [with worldlings]. I shall clearly understand causes and the phenomena that arise from them. And I shall have clearly seen causally arisen phenomena.

When those who sincerely aspire to be free from saṃsāra contemplate these advantages, it will inspire and energize them to contemplate the three characteristics. But for those who are not yet convinced that lasting happiness is not to be found in saṃsāra, these advantages will appear uninteresting. To develop their minds, they should reflect again on the disadvantages of saṃsāra in terms of their own experience. In that way, a wish to be free from saṃsāra will arise and increase.

The three characteristics are intricately related to one another, and realizing them leads to the clear realization of a stream-enterer who directly knows nirvāṇa. The Buddha questioned his disciples regarding the three characteristics in *The Simile of the Snake Sūtra* (MN 22.26):

> "Monastics, what do you think? Is material form permanent or impermanent?" "Impermanent, Venerable Sir." "Is what is impermanent unsatisfactory or happiness?" "Unsatisfactory, Venerable Sir." "Is what is impermanent, unsatisfactory, and subject to change fit to be regarded thus: 'This is mine, this I am, this is my self'?"—"No, Venerable Sir."

The Buddha then continued to ask the same series of questions concerning feeling, discrimination, miscellaneous factors, and consciousness, to which the monastics gave the same reply. He then said that any kind of material form, feeling, discrimination, miscellaneous factor, or consciousness whatsoever—"past, present, or future, gross or subtle, inferior or superior, far or near—should be seen as it actually is with proper wisdom thus: 'This is not mine, this I am not, this is not my self.'"

The same argument appears many times in the sūtras, especially in the *Book of Aggregates* in the *Connected Discourses* (SN 22–24). While the body is often used as an example because it comes first in the list of five aggregates, the same arguments should be applied to feelings, discriminations, miscellaneous factors such as emotions and attitudes, and consciousnesses.

## REFLECTION

1. Contemplate the six advantages of understanding impermanence: All conditioned things will appear as transient. Your mind will not delight in anything worldly. Your mind will emerge from worldly worries. Your mind will incline toward nirvāṇa. You will abandon all fetters and you will come to possess supreme asceticism.

2. Contemplate the six advantages of understanding duḥkha: You will not be hooked or swept away by conditioned things. Your mind will emerge from the world and will see nirvāṇa as peaceful. The underlying tendencies will be uprooted. You will complete the task of attaining liberation and will have served the Teacher with loving-kindness.

3. Contemplate the six advantages of understanding not-self: You will be without craving and views. Notions of "I" will cease; notions of "mine" will cease. You will possess knowledge not shared with worldly people; you will clearly understand causes and the phenomena that arise from them. And you will clearly see causally arisen phenomena.

---

*Impermanence*

The Buddha describes subtle impermanence as "arising and passing away" or as "origination and disintegration." Understanding arising or origination dispels the misconception of nihilism, which believes that either things do not exist at all or the person completely discontinues after death, so that there is no continuity of karma and its effects. Understanding passing away or disintegration dispels the misconception of absolutism, according to which people and things have a substantial, permanent, eternal reality.

Occasionally, the sūtras speak about knowing feelings, discriminations, and thoughts "as they arise, as they are present, as they disappear" (MN 123.23), outlining three characteristics of the conditioned: arising, changing while abiding, and passing away. The Abhidharma formalizes this into the theory that at the micro level any conditioned phenomenon has three phases: the phases of arising, presence, and dissolution. These three points are without temporal duration. Change occurs not from the actual change of a persisting thing, but from the successive arisings of discrete phenomena in an unbroken sequence with imperceptible rapidity.

In meditation, it is more helpful to focus on the sūtra presentation of arising and passing away, and within those two, especially on dissolution or passing away, as that highlights impermanence in a very forceful way.

By beginning with the analysis of form's impermanence, the Buddha appeals to the direct experience of our body. We know our body is constantly changing; we know it is aging and will eventually cease to exist. This is a comparatively gross form of impermanence, whereas the understanding of subtle impermanence frees us from the illusion of the body being permanent.

Subtle impermanence is more difficult to understand. Scientists tell us of the constant changes in subatomic particles, but since these are not visible to our ordinary perceptions and the physical objects around us seem to be stable, we assume that our five aggregates and the world around us are immutable and fixed. In fact, our body, feelings, and so on are dynamic processes in which every aspect of them is arising and passing away in each moment. Nothing is static, even though it may appear to be firm and unchanging because our perception is not sharp enough to detect the subtle changes occurring in each moment. The obscured mind puts together these unique moments of ever-changing existence and sees them as solid objects so that the ignorant mind can deal with the world. A stable, solid body is a mental image superimposed onto a stream of events in the same way that a spinning propeller is seen as a circle. The constant succession of discrete acts of cognition or feeling appears as a monolithic event, just as the rapid change of frames in a film appears as a smooth continuum.

By practicing mindfulness and paying careful attention to the body and mental processes, we will gradually see that what appear as unified objects or events are momentary phenomena that are arising and passing away in a fraction of a nanosecond. This constant change occurs due to causes and conditions, which themselves are in constant flux. Similarly the elements that compose the body are actually dynamic processes that arise and cease in each moment. As mindfulness deepens, subtle impermanence is seen clearly, not in an intellectual or conceptual manner, but as direct experience.

To approach subtle impermanence, begin by examining your body. Is it the same from one year to the next? Is it the same from one month, week, day, hour, minute, and second to the next? Is it the same from one split-second to the next? Questioning in this way makes it clear that our body changes from split-second to split-second. Similarly, each part of our body and each atom of our body changes from one split-second to the next. Feelings, discriminations, miscellaneous factors, and consciousnesses also do not remain the same from one nanosecond to the next. Everything comes into existence, persists for the tiniest fraction of a moment, and then ceases; in fact, even in that split-second while it persists, it is changing. This is followed by something new that arises, persists for a changing fraction of a moment, and disintegrates. There is no way to stop this process: change is in the very nature of conditioned things.

The experience of a pleasant feeling is dependent on an object, the sense faculty, consciousness, and contact, but once the feeling arises, could it be permanent during the time it endures? Bhikkhu Nandaka, when instructing a group of five hundred bhikṣuṇīs, asked (MN 146.9):

> Monastics, suppose an oil lamp is burning: its oil is impermanent and subject to change, its wick is impermanent and subject to change, its flame is impermanent and subject to change, and its radiance is impermanent and subject to change. Now would anyone be speaking rightly who spoke thus: "While this oil lamp is burning, its oil, wick, and flame are impermanent and subject to change, but its radiance is permanent, everlasting, eternal, not subject to change?"

To this the bhikṣuṇīs responded that such permanence is not possible. Anything that arises dependent on causes and conditions—even if it endures for a period of time—cannot itself be permanent and unchanging. It too perishes, and something new arises in each split-second of its continuity.

Our ordinary consciousness sees feelings as solid and substantial, but by directing our attention inward to our moment-to-moment experience, it is possible to realize the arising and ceasing of contact—the cause of feeling—in each split-second. As contact is seen—and it too is momentary and transient—so is the ceasing of each moment of feeling that has arisen based on that contact. By not understanding pleasant feelings as impermanent, sensual desire is ignited; by not understanding unpleasant feelings as impermanent, anger flares; and by not understanding neutral feelings as impermanent, confusion is activated. For this reason, the Buddha emphasizes understanding feelings with correct wisdom, because doing so prevents the arising of these afflictions and will eventually lead to their total eradication.

By increasing our mindfulness of each of the five aggregates, insight knowledge will arise that directly knows subtle impermanence. When this happens, it almost seems as if nothing is there, because whatever arises is gone in the next moment. The present cannot be stopped.

*Unsatisfactoriness*

The *Path of Purification* says that duḥkha has the meaning of "oppression by rising and passing away." In the passage from the *Simile of the Snake Sūtra* above, the Buddha points to the connection between impermanence and duḥkha by asking, "Is what is impermanent suffering or happiness?" Given that the five aggregates are transient and do not endure a second moment, they are unsatisfactory in nature; they are not secure, predictable, or dependable. The body may experience some temporary pleasure, but it is incapable of providing lasting, stable happiness that is invulnerable to changes in circumstances. Since our health and physical energy decline as we age, the body cannot be a source of true happiness.

Similarly, feelings are unsatisfactory by nature. Feelings are unstable—they are pleasant, then unpleasant; happy, then unhappy. The same unsatisfactoriness is found with discriminations, miscellaneous factors, and consciousnesses. In short, because the aggregates are under the control of afflictions and karma, they are not beyond duḥkha. By releasing false assumptions about each of the five aggregates, we see that they have the nature of duḥkha and our false expectations and clinging to them cease.

### *Selflessness*

Selflessness (not-self) is the most difficult to glean of the three characteristics. To understand it, follow up on the first two characteristics and ask: Is what is impermanent and unsatisfactory fit to be regarded as "this is mine; this I am, this is my self"?

Underlying the answer is the ancient Indian idea of what is fitting to be regarded as I, mine, and my self, as well as our basic human notion of what we assume our true self to be. The ancient Indian conception of the self is a permanent, eternal, and intrinsically blissful self. The self is the master of the aggregates, able to accomplish what it wishes without depending on anything else. Clearly a self that is transient and under the influence of afflictions and polluted karma does not meet this description.

As for what we take to be our true self, impermanent things such as our five polluted aggregates that are bound up with duḥkha will not meet the mark because the self does not have ultimate mastery over these. Certainly we do not want to identify the polluted aggregates as being truly ours, truly what we are, or our true selves. Not finding something we can point to as our true selves puts in question the entire notion of whether such a true self exists.

The Buddha does not deny the conventional existence of the self. He used the word "I" when communicating with people. Conventionally and appropriately, the words "I," "you," "they," and so forth are used to distinguish different people. The doctrine of not-self does not negate the existence of persons or of the designations used to refer to them. What is being refuted is a substantial ego entity, a permanent subject existing at the core of the psychophysical aggregates. The doctrine of not-self does not deny the existence of a person designated in dependence on the body-mind complex. It denies that the person exists as a self, as an enduring, substantial, independent entity. Saying the person exists is to say the five aggregates are present. Saying the person is selfless or that there is no self means the aggregates cannot be identified as self and do not contain a self. No inner nucleus of selfhood can be found within or behind the conventional person composed of the five aggregates.

This is contrary to our ordinary way of thinking of ourselves. We think and feel that we are a self. We identify the body or mind as self or think a self stands behind the aggregates. According to our ingrained notion of "self," the self has certain qualities. First, it appears to be an entity that endures through time. It might endure temporarily, coming into existence at birth and ceasing to exist at death. Or it might endure eternally, without ever ceasing after death. Second, the self is conceived to be one unified, indivisible whole that does not have parts. Third, the self seems to be self-sufficient and not dependent on causes and conditions. Fourth, it controls the aggregates. The self that is seen as our essence has mastery over itself. There should be no conflict between what we want ourselves to be and what we are.

Let's examine the five aggregates and see if any of them fits this description of self. If such a self exists, we should be able to apply analysis to pin it down and find what it is. Conceiving a self can only be done in relationship to what is experienced, the five aggregates. While a number of different relationships between the self and the aggregates are possible, they can be subsumed in two. A real self should be either (1) the same as the aggregates—the self should be identifiable with some aspect of the body-mind complex—or (2) different from the aggregates—the self is separate from the aggregates and can be found as a distinct entity either inside the collection of the aggregates, behind them, or as their invisible owner.

In the *first option*, the aggregates would be the self. But do any of the aggregates have the four attributes that befits a real self?

- We think the self should be permanent, but the aggregates are impermanent. The body is a mass of physical processes, arising and passing away. The mind is a series of momentary events of awareness.
- We believe the self to be an indivisible whole, but there are five aggregates. Each of these aggregates in turn consists of a multiplicity of elements and events. Which one of the parts of the body would be the self? Which one of the moments of any of the four mental aggregates could be a single, unified self?
- We think the self is self-sufficient and independent of causes and conditions, yet the aggregates are conditioned and dependent on causes and conditions. The body arises from the sperm and egg of our parents, and it continues by depending on the nourishment provided by food. The mental processes arise from their own previous moments; they are influenced by the state of the body and arise reliant on the various sense faculties.
- We expect the self to be in control, but the aggregates are simply processes with no supervisor overseeing them. There is no one behind the mental processes controlling them or making them be a certain way. If there were a true essence, it should be able to bring the aggregates under its domination. But the five aggregates are not under the control of a findable self. If they were, then since the self doesn't want to suffer, it would be able to stop the body from aging and dying and stop the mind from experiencing painful feelings or having nonvirtuous intentions.

Although a true self should have these four attributes, the aggregates have none of them and in fact have four opposite attributes. The aggregates are insubstantial. The body is like a ball of foam, lacking any substance. Feelings are like bubbles, arising and breaking up very quickly. Discriminations are like a mirage, appearing but not being found when searched for. Miscellaneous factors are hollow like the trunk of a plantain tree. Consciousness is like a magical illusion, appearing but lacking any substance. There is no core in any of the aggregates. They are empty of any independent, substantial, or findable essence.

Similarly, the collection of the aggregates cannot be a self. If a self cannot be found in each aggregate individually, how could it be found in the collection of aggregates? For example, if a house has five rooms and there isn't a table in any of the rooms, a table certainly couldn't be found in the collection of the five rooms.

Nothing can be identified as self. Everything we take to be our self—any of the aggregates that we grasp to be I or mine—is not self. This fact contradicts our ingrained thought that centers around notions of "I," "mine," and "my self." These notions are the source of duḥkha; cultivating insight wisdom enables us to break out of clinging to ideas of self.

According to the *second option*, the self would be findable distinct from the aggregates but would be contained within them or lying behind them. But when we try to identify anything that the self does, such as walking or thinking, we can only see the aggregates doing those actions. There is no separate, substantial self to be found.

In short, when we analyze each aggregate, we find that it is impermanent, changing in every moment; it is in the nature of duḥkha, unable to bring stable happiness or security; it is not a substantial self, independent of causes and conditions; it is neither a controller self nor something controlled by such a self. Therefore, none of the aggregates are suitable to be considered "this is mine, this I am, this is my self." The seeming presence of a self is an illusion.

That each aggregate is not mine, not I, and not my self counteracts three obsessions or graspings—craving, conceit, and wrong views—respectively. Understanding that the aggregates are not mine eliminates the obsession of craving, because craving thinks "this is mine" or "I want to make this mine." The body, feelings, discriminations, miscellaneous factors, and consciousnesses are not the property of a substantial self. They are impersonal factors, each performing its own function without the help of a supervisory self. Since such a self does not exist, thinking that anything belongs to it is foolishness. Thus craving is relaxed.

Seeing that the aggregates are not I counteracts the fundamental conceit, the conceit "I am." Based on the thought "I am," other types of conceit and comparison manifest: I am superior to this person; I am equal to that one; I am inferior to this one. I am someone with such-and-such a position, therefore others should treat me with respect. My race, gender, nationality, socioeconomic class, or so on is higher than the others. Since the aggregates cannot be identified as I, how can we justify holding the conceit "I am"? Thus conceit is deflated.

So many views are based on the five aggregates—thinking the aggregates are the self, as in "my body is me, my feelings are me," or thinking "I am the aggregates," as in "I am my emotions, I am my thoughts, I am the thinker, the perceiver, the cognizer." The Buddha described twenty types of view of a personal identity that lay out different relationships of the self and the aggregates that the confused mind interpolates. But seeing that the five aggregates are not our self neutralizes the multitude of wrong views. By understanding selflessness, we see that the aggregates are neither an independent self nor the possessions of such a self. In fact, the aggregates themselves are not independent things.

Knowing the aggregates in this way, as they actually are—as not I, mine, or my self—is seeing them with proper wisdom. The Buddha says (MN 22.28–29):

> Seeing thus, monastics, a well-taught ariya disciple becomes disenchanted with material form, disenchanted with feelings, disenchanted with discriminations, disenchanted with miscellaneous factors, disenchanted with consciousness.
>
> Being disenchanted, he becomes dispassionate. Through dispassion [his mind] is liberated. When it is liberated there comes the knowledge: "It is liberated." He understands, "Birth is destroyed, the holy life (*brahmacarya*, *brahmacariya*) has been lived, what had to be done has been done, there is no more coming to any state of being."

The knowledge and vision of things as they really are includes knowing the five aggregates in terms of all three characteristics. One who has done that has reached the final stages of insight meditation and becomes *disenchanted* with the aggregates. She sees through their appearance of being stable, bringing happiness, and being a self and thus loses fascination with them. She then attains the supramundane path and becomes *dispassionate* with respect to the aggregates, releasing the deep attachment to them. Through releasing clinging to the aggregates, the yogi attains the fruit of *liberation* and is now forever free from the pollutants—the primordial defilements of sensual desire, attachment to saṃsāric existence, and ignorance that have kept her trapped in saṃsāra since beginningless time. Emerging from meditation, the reviewing knowledge (*paccavekkhaṇañāṇa*) confirms that she has completed her mission and is now free from the cycle of rebirth. This is the knowledge and vision of liberation, the assurance that what had to be done has been done.

### REFLECTION

1. Contemplate each of the five aggregates one by one as being impermanent, duḥkha, and not-self, as described above. Become disenchanted with them. Relinquish fascination with them and turn your mind to the Dharma.
2. Imagine attaining the supramundane path and becoming dispassionate toward the aggregates. Put your energy and attention toward perception of nirvāṇa.
3. Imagine escaping from saṃsāra and attaining liberation, freedom from rebirth under the control of afflictions and karma.

## *Abandon What Is Not Yours*

After instructing his disciples to analyze the three characteristics and refute a true I and mine, the Buddha teaches a swift method for releasing grasping. In the *Discourse on the Simile of the Snake*, he advises (MN 22.40–41):

> Therefore, monastics, whatever is not yours, abandon it; when you have abandoned it, that will lead to your welfare and happiness for a long time. What is it that is not yours? Material form is not yours. Abandon it . . . long time. Feeling is not yours. Abandon it . . . long time. Discrimination is not yours. Abandon it . . . long time. Miscellaneous factors are not yours. Abandon it . . . long time. Consciousness is not yours. Abandon it. When you

> have abandoned it, that will lead to your welfare and happiness for a long time.
>
> Monastics, what do you think? If people carried off the grass, sticks, branches, and leaves in this Jeta Grove, or burned them, or did what they liked with them, would you think: "People are carrying us off or burning us or doing what they like with us?"
>
> (Monastics): No, venerable sir. Why not? Because that is neither our self nor what belongs to our self.
>
> (Buddha): So, too, monastics whatever is not yours, abandon it. When you have abandoned it, that will lead to your welfare and happiness for a long time.

Craving and clinging want to make almost everything into I or mine; we want to control and possess whatever is possible. Here the Buddha recommends abandoning grasping for what is not ours. Since there is no findable self, how could there be an established mine that possesses things? There is no [substantial] I that is the aggregates or that owns the aggregates. When craving and clinging for what is not ours—our body, feelings, discriminations, opinions, ideas, emotions, attitudes, plans, consciousnesses, and innermost sources of awareness—have been relinquished, the mind abides in peace. This is a powerful teaching to remember at times when grasping I and mine afflicts us. Applying it brings instant relief.

## REFLECTION

1. Think of a time when attachment to your body arose strongly—for example, you were sick and afraid of death, lying in the warm sunshine on the beach, injured and fearful of pain, or blissfully having a massage at a spa.
2. Ask yourself, "Is this body I'm so attached to mine? Is it I? Is it my self?" Who possesses this body?
3. When you can't identify an I that owns the body, an I that is the body, and a self that is the body, relinquish the attachment to the body and feel freedom from craving.

4. If your mind resists doing this or gets stuck while investigating, examine that defensiveness in the mind.

5. Do this reflection for your feelings, discriminations, various emotions, and types of consciousness to see if you can locate mine, I, or myself.

---

## *Insight Knowledge*

Insight knowledge (P. *vipassanā-ñāṇa*), which is equivalent to insight wisdom (P. *vipassanā-paññā*), is an essential step to liberation, one that must be cultivated carefully and correctly. The general procedure for meditation on the three characteristics that leads to insight was described earlier in this chapter. Direct seeing of the three characteristics is the knowledge and vision of things as they really are (*yathā-bhūta-ñāna-dassana*), a concentrated mind knowing the reality of things that leads to disenchantment, dispassion, and liberation.[105]

Many different objects can be investigated in a variety of ways with insight, but they can be synthesized into examining phenomena as dependently arisen and conditioned and thus seeing them as impermanent, duḥkha, and no-self. Because the nature of the aggregates and other phenomena is impermanent, unsatisfactory, and insubstantial, they cannot be a substantial self. Here a meditator is not only negating a self-existing self but also changing the way she views the aggregates and phenomena in general. It is not the case that she leaves her ordinary perception of phenomena alone, accepting it as true. Rather, she comes to see that it is erroneous—what appears to be permanent, or to be one unified whole, or to exist independent of causes and conditions does not exist in those ways. Through seeing that the aggregates do not exist in the way she thought, she then negates their being a person who is truly there.

Now we will look at some of the methods the Buddha outlined in the sūtras that incorporate analysis of the three characteristics and cultivate insight. First is the method described in the *Discourse on the Six Sets of Six*, in which the six internal sources, six external sources, six classes of consciousness, six types of contact, six classes of feelings, and six kinds of craving are analyzed with insight. Because these arise and cease, the self that depends on them must also arise and cease. Since this is discordant with our conception of a substantial self, the existence of such a self is refuted.

Cultivating insight through analysis of the four great elements and the forms derived from them as taught in the *Greater Discourse on the Simile of the Elephant's Footprint* (MN 28) is another method, one that powerfully severs our identification with the body. The analysis of the derivative forms is especially interesting because Śāriputra ties all five aggregates together in the process of cognition, dissecting an instance of cognition into the five aggregates to show their dependent nature, conditionality, and selflessness.

In the *Greater Discourse to Mālunkyāputta* (MN 64), the Buddha analyzes the meditative absorptions in terms of the five aggregates, demonstrating how they too are impermanent, unsatisfactory, and selfless. In the *Discourse to the Man from Aṭṭhakanāgara* (MN 52), Ānanda investigates the meditative absorptions of the form and formless realms, showing them to be mentally conditioned and intentionally produced, and thereby not the self.

## *The Six Sets of Six*

In the *Discourse on the Six Sets of Six* (MN 148), the Buddha examines the components of the person to determine if they are a self and to develop the insight wisdom that leads to full realization.[106] He begins by setting out the phenomena to be analyzed—the six sets of six phenomena or thirty-six factors: the six internal sources (six sense faculties), six external sources (six objects), six classes of consciousness, six types of contact, six classes of feeling, and six kinds of craving.

*The six internal sources* are the sense faculties—the eye, ear, nose, tongue, body, and mind—that are the source or base for the arising of consciousness. The Buddha was not concerned with looking at the sense faculties anatomically or physiologically; his interest was in the conscious experience of sentient beings and how the faculties relate to the object and function to produce consciousness.

According to the Abhidharma, the five physical sense faculties are subtle material housed in the gross organs of the eye, ear, nose, tongue, and body. This subtle material is sensitive and responsive to its respective object—the eye to visible form, the ear to sounds, and so forth. The mental source is the mind as a sense faculty; the *bhavaṅga* or subliminal consciousness is at work here.[107] The mental faculty is not a physical organ such as the brain. At the time of the Buddha, there was no thought of there being a physical basis for the mind; only in modern times is brain activity seen as related to mental activity. These six sources are said to be internal because they belong to the continuum of the person. As part of the psychophysical organism, they are the doors through which objects and consciousness come together.[108]

*The six external sources* are external objects such as visible forms, sounds, smells, tastes, tactile sensations, and mental phenomena that are known by the six consciousnesses via the six internal sources.

*The six classes of consciousness* are the visual consciousness, auditory consciousness, olfactory consciousness, gustatory consciousness, tactile consciousness, and mental consciousness. Each consciousness arises dependent on its respective external and internal sources. The first five types of consciousness cognize raw sensory data, without necessarily understanding their meaning. For example, the eye sense source enables the visual consciousness to perceive red and white, but it does not know that the object is a stop sign. The mental faculty transmits the sensory data to the mental consciousness, which synthesizes the various moments of seeing red and white shapes and, drawing on past experiences, forms the idea and meaning of a stop sign. The activities of identifying objects, labeling them, and knowing their meaning are done by the mental consciousness.

Our experience seems to be one seamless whole, but with refined mindfulness, we will gradually see that it is made of individual moments of consciousness. Sometimes one of the six consciousnesses is more prominent, and a moment later another is. Sometimes a consciousness perceives one object, and a moment later it perceives another. Even when a consciousness appears to be seeing the same object for a period of time, there are actually fleeting mind-moments arising and passing away. The sense faculty and its object are likewise arising and passing away in each moment, although they too appear to be one thing.

As mindfulness becomes more refined, it is possible to distinguish the successive moments of hearing a sound followed by the mental cognition of it. Refined mindfulness brings the ability to distinguish between the moment of tasting at the bare sensory level and the mental consciousness that recognizes the taste as sweet. The precise moments of enjoying the taste and of wanting more of it also appear clearly to a mindful and concentrated mind. In this way, the flow of experience is known to be a series of moments arising and passing away.

Such awareness helps us distinguish the information that is actually entering through our senses from our mental elaborations of that raw data. This mindfulness notices the liking and disliking, the favoring and opposing, the grasping at I, mine, and my self—multiple elaborations of the conceptual mind that is distorted by underlying tendencies such as attachment, hostility, and ignorance.

*The six types of contact* are the meeting of the six consciousnesses with their respective objects by means of their respective sense faculties. Contact is simply the coming together of the nose faculty, a smell, and the olfactory consciousness, for example. Their coming together does not mean that they mix together, but that the object is known by the consciousness due to the functioning of the sense faculty. Contact is very brief and it instantly gives way to feeling, discrimination, and so forth. Then thoughts about the object pop into the mind, as do various emotions that trigger karmic actions.

Each of the six contacts can be of three types—contact bringing a pleasant, unpleasant, or neutral feeling. Although contact itself does not experience the object as pleasant, unpleasant, or neutral—that is the function of feeling—it is differentiated in terms of the feeling it will produce.

*The six classes of feeling* arise from the six types of contact that occur when the six consciousnesses meet the six objects by means of the six sources. Occurring with each moment of consciousness, feeling is the experience of the object as pleasurable, painful, or neutral. The transition from contact to feeling occurs so quickly that we ordinary beings do not perceive it.

*The six kinds of craving* are the thirst for the sense object that has arisen from the six feelings that came from the six types of contact of the six consciousnesses with the six objects by means of the six internal sources. The Buddha laid out the sequence (MN 148.9):

> Dependent on the eye and forms, visual consciousness arises; the meeting of the three is contact. With contact as condition, there is feeling, with feeling as condition, there is craving.

He then spelled out the other five kinds of craving in a similar way, showing that the six sets of six all culminate in craving.

To break this chain, we must first understand how craving originates. In this context, the Buddha explains it slightly differently than in the presentation of the twelve links of dependent origination, although factors in the two presentations overlap. Dependent origination is not a fixed formula that always progresses in a predetermined order. It is a complex process with streams of causation working in different directions, intersecting one another. The twelve links show the progressive chain of links through which rebirth in saṃsāra occurs over a series of lifetimes. The presentation of the six sets of six shows the dependent origination of craving as it occurs in daily life, once a lifetime is already in process. Through this, we begin to see that the daily experiences we take for granted are the fuel for craving. By repeatedly welcoming craving into our minds and yielding to its seductive power, we suffer here and now and perpetuate our existence in saṃsāra as well.

Bill wakes up in the morning and smells freshly baked muffins in the kitchen. The nose faculty connects the aroma of the muffins with the olfactory consciousness and with contact, he smells the sweet fragrance. A pleasant feeling arises, and the mental consciousness discerns: "Yum, there are freshly baked muffins." Craving rears its head, and the thought "I haven't eaten freshly baked muffins in ages and want to eat these!" instantly arises. With a mental image of how delicious the muffins will taste, he goes to the kitchen and starts eating, but his spouse tells him the muffins are for guests coming that evening. Disappointed because his desire has been frustrated, Bill gives in to a grouchy mood that sets him up to quarrel with his spouse.

In the process leading to the arising of craving, some links occur without choice: Dependent on the nose faculty and aromas, the olfactory consciousness arises. The meeting of these three is contact. All this happens in a continuous flow. When the sense source, object, and consciousness come together, we cannot stop contact. With contact as a condition, feeling automatically arises. Choice is present now—we decide how to respond to the feeling. When mindfulness is lacking, craving easily flows on from feeling. But when mindfulness, introspective awareness, concentration, and wisdom function even to a small degree, it is possible to interrupt this process and stop the arising of craving and its companions—anger, arrogance, jealousy, and so on.

In this life, craving leaves us dissatisfied, frustrated, and longing for something to fill the psychological void inside. Craving also motivates actions, which in turn lead to rebirth. Following rebirth comes the inevitability of aging and death, as well as sorrow, lamentation, pain, grief, despair, and the whole mass of duḥkha.

Propelled by craving, the mind continually looks for excitement by contacting objects with the six senses. Craving operates in the mind to hold the sense faculties to the external objects, producing more contact. In discussing whether the sense faculties are the fetters for their respective objects or the objects are the fetters for their respective sense faculties, Śāriputra asks Koṭṭhita (SN 35.232):

> Suppose, friend, a black ox and a white ox were yoked together by a single harness or yoke. Would one be speaking rightly if one were to say: "The black ox is the fetter of the white ox, the white ox is the fetter of the black ox?"
>
> (Koṭṭhita): No, friend. The black ox is not the fetter of the white ox, nor is the white ox the fetter of the black ox. Rather the single harness or yoke by which the two are yoked together; that is the fetter there.
>
> (Śāriputra): So too friend, the eye is not the fetter of forms nor are forms the fetter of the eye. Rather the desire and sensual attachment that arise there in dependence on both; that is the fetter there.

Śāriputra then says the same regarding each sense source and its object. In other words, the fetter, yoke, and rope that tie sense faculty and object together is craving. Ārya wisdom, which is a product of the seven awakening factors, is the main tool to cut this craving. When it does, the sense faculties and their objects are still there; cognition and feeling occur but craving is no longer. Arhats still have eyes, ears, and so forth, and objects still exist. Arhats cognize these objects, but the delight and sensual desire that bind the mind to them through the sense faculties do not arise.

However, when unopposed, craving induces clinging and grasping. Grasping holds the five aggregates as "this is mine; this I am; this is my self." What sustains craving, enabling it to wreak havoc in our lives? Ignorance. Wisdom is the antidote to ignorance, and the selfless nature of all phenomena that we ordinarily identify as mine, I, or my self is the object to be realized by wisdom. By seeing the aggregates as "this is not mine; this I am not; this is not my self," wisdom stops craving.

In the sūtra, the Buddha proceeds to demonstrate how none of the thirty-six factors are mine, I, or my self. In doing so, he is not asserting that there is no self whatsoever, as the translation "no-self" may imply. Nor, by saying that these thirty-six factors are not the self, is he implying that something else is the self or that a subtle self exists behind or within the aggregates. Rather his aim is to break the identification of any of the aggregates or any part of one aggregate as the self.

The Buddha uses the word "self" as a valid conventional notion when referring to the person as the one who creates karma and experiences its result. He encourages people to purify themselves and to be responsible for their own actions. Speaking of the self in this way is not problematic; only when the self becomes an object of grasping or of metaphysical speculation must we question: What is this self?

## *Analysis of the Thirty-Six Factors as Not-Self*

Throughout history elaborate theories and philosophies about the self have been concocted. Some people assert "the self is ineffable and blissful," "the self is love," or "an eternal unitary self is reborn and attains liberation." Other people who don't examine or develop theories about the self simply have a natural grasping, "this is mine; this I am; this is my self," based on the aggregates. Whenever anyone approached the Buddha with a theory about the true self and said that he had a self, the Buddha would ask the person what they identified as that self. The Buddha then inquired if that thing they are taking to be the self is permanent or impermanent. Once the person saw that it is impermanent, the Buddha led them to realize that what is impermanent is duḥkha by nature and cannot be a self.

Beginning with the first of the thirty-six factors and then using the same argument for each of the others, the Buddha says (MN 148.10):

> If anyone says "The eye is self," that is not tenable. The rise and fall of the eye are discerned, and since its rise and fall are discerned, it would follow: "My self rises and falls." That is why it

> is not tenable for anyone to say "The eye is self." Thus the eye is not self.

Very few people would actually think the eye source was the self. However, it is likely that we take the collection of the aggregates or the mental consciousness as the self. In any case, the structure of the argument presented for the eye is the same for all the other factors.

To review, before understanding why the eye and so forth are not the self, we have to know what is meant by "self." What kind of self are we looking for? According to Indian thought at the time of the Buddha, the self was something everlasting, with stable and continual existence; it was what went from one life to the next, bringing karmic seeds along with it. Indian metaphysics aside, ordinary people have the sense of an I that is continual and enduring—a self that retains the same identity over time; a secure, reliable, continuous self, something that is truly me.

We don't think of our self as coming into existence and going out of existence in every split-second, but that is exactly what a substantial self would have to do if the eye or any other factor in the five aggregates were the self. Why? If the eye were the self, the eye and the self would have the same characteristics. One characteristic of the eye is that it is composed of individual moments of the eye that are constantly coming into and going out of existence. In each split-second, brief moments of the eye arise and pass away many times, producing new moments of the eye that similarly arise and pass away. If the eye were arising and passing away billions of times in each split-second, the self would have to be changing that quickly as well. However, such a transient self does not fit our feeling of a stable, enduring, everlasting self. Therefore the eye cannot be the self. Do this investigation with the mental consciousness or the collection of aggregates as the self, as these notions more typically arise in our mind.

If we insist that the mental consciousness is the self, which moment of mental consciousness is the self? The mental consciousness that exists at 6:00 is not the same as the mental consciousness that exists at 6:01, which in turn is different from the mental consciousness at 6:02 and 6:03. Which one of these mental consciousnesses would be the self? If one moment of the mental consciousness were the self, then when it ceases in the next split-second, the self would similarly cease. And just as a new mental consciousness arises in the next moment, a new self would also come into existence in each moment. A different self would exist in each fleeting moment. None of these options is possible if the self were permanent, everlasting, and maintained the same identity throughout time.

In short, to identify something as the self, it would have to be permanent and unchanging. Insight directly perceives that each of the thirty-six factors is impermanent. Therefore, none of them is the self. In other words, the thirty-six factors are not the self because they are characterized by subtle impermanence, whereas a self must be permanent.

In meditation, a practitioner takes each of the thirty-six factors and examines it, seeing if it could be a continuous self that retains its identity from one moment to the next. It is important to examine each factor individually. Simply understanding the argument for one factor and then jumping to the conclusion that none of the factors can be a self will not bring true insight. We need to analyze and investigate with careful and precise attention, deeply examining if anything can be identified as the self that we so deeply believe exists.

Directly seeing the subtle impermanence of any of the thirty-six factors requires mindfulness, concentration, and insight. Of course, we can get a sense of the impermanence of the eye or the mental consciousness by reflecting on their gross impermanence. We may also use reasoning to become familiar with their transient nature, or reflect on the constantly changing nature of subatomic particles based on scientific evidence. According to some physicists, many subatomic particles are flashes of energy that appear and disappear. However, to arrive at a deeper level of understanding, deep mindfulness and concentration are needed to observe the arising and passing away of the aggregates and all their parts in progressively shorter periods of time. Meditators with strong mindfulness and deep samādhi perceive this as clearly as we see a pearl in the palm of our hand.

If a person identifies their body as the self, they must dissect the body mentally and investigate: Is the color of the body my self? Is the sound, smell, taste, tactile sensation, or mental image of the body who I am? Examining external objects is a way to investigate the concept of "mine." We may think that this object is *mine* and want to retain continuous, permanent possession of it. But these external items also arise and disintegrate in each moment, and eventually even their continuum will cease. In that case, how could anything ultimately be mine? Everything that we cling to and take to be mine not only perishes in each split-second but eventually will be struck by gross impermanence. A treasured photograph changes in each moment and one day will crumble into bits or be destroyed by fire, water, or other means. What can truly be mine about such a passing phenomenon?

Similarly, if someone says that the eye consciousness is the self, that too is not tenable because that consciousness arises and passes away in each moment. Eye contact too occurs so quickly that it is unlikely that anyone would think that is their abiding self. Is the feeling generated through eye contact the self? This is not possible, because like all previous factors, a feeling does not endure as exactly the same thing in the second moment. Any and all feelings of pleasure, pain, or neutrality arise dependent on their conditions. Because the sense source, object, consciousness, and contact that were the causes for a particular feeling are also momentarily changing, so too is the feeling that is dependent on them.

Could craving be the self? To the extent that we enjoy craving and take it as the source of enjoyment, we might think craving is our true self. Some philosophers think that the will to live is our true identity; it is the self. But that will to live is just another name for craving, because we crave saṃsāric embodiment. But craving arises and passes away in each brief moment, making it unsuitable to be a secure, constant self.

While observing in meditation the arising and ceasing of the internal and external sources, consciousness, contact, feeling, and craving, turn your attention to the meditating consciousness—the consciousness that is observing these momentary phenomena. Is that your self? It arises and passes away in the briefest of moments; there is nothing there that can be a true self or identity. When you analyze what you usually identify as self—the five aggregates or some part of them—you discover that it arises and ceases in each split-second. Because it is transient, it is not a basis for secure and true happiness; it is unsatisfactory by nature. Something that is impermanent and unsatisfactory is not suitable to hold as a self—a true, substantial, enduring basis of individual identity. The only possible conclusion from this analysis is that none of the aggregates is the self and that such a permanent, partless, substantial self that is a controller does not exist.

The Buddha repeatedly asked if any of these phenomena are the self to encourage us to investigate phenomena and to examine our notion of self.

He didn't just say, "There is no self." Such a statement presents a foregone conclusion and stifles the inquirer from researching the issue themselves and reaching their own conclusion. The Buddha did not present selflessness as a metaphysical position that cannot be tested. Instead he explained the field of grasping—the five aggregates—and said these are what ignorance clings to as the self. He then encouraged us to search for and try to find anything that could plausibly be a substantial, everlasting self.

Through the above investigation, we see that impermanence is the foundation for understanding selflessness. With refined meditation, sharp-faculty meditators can see subtle impermanence and move directly to understanding selflessness. For other people, the Buddha used the fact of duḥkha to help them release their grasping at mine, I, and my self and to realize selflessness. Seeing that the aggregates have the characteristic of subtle impermanence and that whatever is impermanent is unsatisfactory, unpredictable, and bound up with duḥkha, they then reflect: Is it worthwhile to continue holding what is duḥkha in nature and bound up with suffering as I, mine, or my self? Or is this grasping to be relinquished in order to attain lasting happiness?

## *Understanding Selflessness by Means of the Elements*

In the *Greater Discourse of the Simile of the Elephant's Footprint* (MN 28), Śāriputra, the Buddha's disciple who was foremost in wisdom, explains not-self with respect to material form. In doing so, he bases his analysis on the accepted outlook of his time in which material form was composed of the four primary or great elements (earth, water, fire, and wind) and forms derived from them (the six sense faculties and their objects). Understanding how form is related to the arising of consciousness, feeling, clinging, bondage, and liberation is conducive for realizing nirvāṇa.

In general, "form" refers to any material form, but in many contexts it refers to the body. The body is one of the five aggregates subject to clinging. It is the object of clinging, and it came into existence as a result of clinging. The form aggregate, as are the other four aggregates, is included in the first truth, true duḥkha. The form aggregate is of two types: the four primary elements and material form derived from them. Although the sūtras speak about the four primary elements, they mention derived forms but do not explain them in depth. That is done in the Abhidharma, where derived forms include the five sense faculties and the four objects—color, sound, smell, and taste. Tangibles are the four primary elements themselves.

The four coarse elements should not be thought of as things such as the ground, the ocean, a campfire, and the breeze on a windy day—but as four properties or aspects of material form. The earth element is the aspect of hardness, resistance, and mass. The water element is the aspect of fluidity and cohesion because things that are damp stick together easily. The fire element is the property of heat and maturation because warmth makes plants grow and fruit mature, and the wind element is the aspect of expansion, contraction, pressure, and movement. The four elements are conditions for one another and are inseparably bound together. They exist in dependence on one another.

Although all material things are a combination of all four elements, one among the four is usually predominant in a specific object. In the space around us, the wind element is predominant, but there are also particles of dust in the air. The earth element is stronger in the dust; however, there is a certain amount of water in it too. The water causes smaller particles to coalesce to form a dust mote. Blood is mostly the water element, but the cells in it contain the earth and fire elements; blood moves, indicating the presence of the wind element.

Understanding selflessness by means of the four elements involves reflecting on each element in detail by analyzing the internal and external elements to determine if they are mine, I, or my self, and seeing their subtle impermanence.

To use the earth element as an example: The earth element may be internal or external. The internal earth element includes parts of the body in which hardness and resistance are dominant qualities. In the list of thirty-two parts of the body found in the establishment of mindfulness of the body, the hair, nails, teeth, skin, muscles, bones, spleen, lungs, intestines, liver, and feces are among the parts of the body in which the earth element is predominant. The external earth element is found in things in others' bodies and in the environment that are characterized by hardness and resistance—vegetables, fruit, trees, buildings, an insect's body, and so on.

Both the internal and external earth elements are just earth element. When we think about it, there is not much difference between the two. We usually think "this body is mine," or when we're in pain or need surgery, we think "this body is me." In our mind there is a clear delineation between what is outside and therefore is not me, and what is inside and therefore me or mine. But the quality of hardness and resistance is the same in both places.

The distinction between the internal and external earth elements is not so clear. Our hair consists predominantly of the internal earth element, and we consider it part of us. But after cutting it, we throw it away and it becomes the external earth element. We no longer think of it as mine. Vegetables are the external earth element; they are not us or part of us. But after we eat them, they become part of the internal earth element of our body, and they are seen as mine or as part of me. When portions of the vegetables are eliminated as feces, we again consider that as the external earth element that is other than us.

In this way an interplay between the internal and external earth elements continuously occurs. Everything in our body that is hard and resistant began as the external earth element and later became the internal earth element of our body that we cherish and cling to. Then when the body dies, it is buried or cremated and the internal earth element is recycled in nature, becoming the external earth element. What we eat is made up of the earth element that used to be part of the bodies of sentient beings who lived on the planet millions of years before us.

Because of strong habit, mental fabrications, and grasping, the sense of I, me, mine, and my self become focused on the body. We judge people based on their body—their skin color, the shape of their eyes, their gender—and because of this some people are oppressed and others are privileged; some receive an education and others do not. Human beings fight, torture, rape, and kill others due to grasping at the body as mine, me, and my self and holding others' bodies as other, different, and therefore suspect. In fact, all bodies are made of the same earth element, as are so many things in our environment. Which earth element is me and mine? Which is other? Which is impersonal in nature? Through deep analysis, we conclude that there is nothing in the body to cling to as being a person; there is nothing in the body that is I, mine, my self, or you, yours, your self. Proper wisdom understands this clearly. Śāriputra makes the point (MN 28.6):

> Now both the internal earth element and the external earth element are simply earth element. And that should be seen as it actually is with proper wisdom thus: "This is not mine, this I am not, this is not my self." When one sees it thus as it actually is with proper wisdom, one becomes disenchanted with the earth element and makes the mind dispassionate toward the earth element.

There is a useful distinction between what is conventionally considered oneself and what is external to oneself. Your arm is not the same as a stone. However, this does not imply the existence of a substantial self. The body is not the property of a substantial self.

Once we see both the internal and external earth elements for what they are and understand that the earth element is not mine, not I, not my self, disenchantment with the earth element and the body arises. There isn't anything spectacular about the earth element, is there? There isn't anything to be attached to in the qualities of hardness and resistance. Nothing about the earth element is me, mine, or my self. Being disenchanted, we become dispassionate and relinquish clinging to the earth element and the body; we cease to identify the body with the self.

## REFLECTION

1. Be aware of and experience the inner earth element—the bones, muscles, inner organs, and so on in your body.
2. Be aware of the outer earth element—the ground, buildings, animals, and vegetation around you.
3. Consider that the same earth element composes both your body, others' bodies, and things in your environment.
4. Observe that when you eat, what was the outer earth element becomes the inner earth element as it assimilates into and forms your body. Watch the mind begin to consider what was the outer earth element and is now the inner earth element to be mine, I, or my self. Is it reasonable to consider it in this way?

5. Observe that when you have a bowel movement, some inner earth element becomes outer earth element that you consider unrelated to you and even disgusting. But isn't it the same earth element? Is it now I, mine, or my self?

6. What is I, mine, and my self?

---

A second way to break down identification with the body and grasping the body as I and mine is to reflect on the impermanent nature of the earth element. According to ancient Indian cosmology, a universe evolves, exists, dissolves, and becomes nothing. This happens due to imbalance in the four elements. For example, there will be a time at the end of an eon when water swallows up the external earth element, which then vanishes under it. Since the great earth element, which seems so reliable, stable, and permanent, will end one day, what can be said about this body, which exists only for a comparatively short time? This body is always disintegrating and most unreliable. What in it could possibly be I, mine, or my self? Remember: in asking these questions, we are checking to see if the body can be a substantial I that is permanent, pleasurable, independent of causes and conditions, and the controller of the aggregates.

The two meditations above—seeing the internal and external earth element as they actually are with proper wisdom and seeing their subtle impermanence—should be applied to the other three elements—water, fire, and wind. In the body, the water element is prominent in bile, phlegm, pus, blood, sweat, tears, spit, mucus, urine, and other bodily fluids. The water element is found in liquids in the environment as well—in ponds, rivers, rain, aquifers, and oceans. When these liquids are drunk they become part of our body, and when they are expelled, the internal water element in our body is recycled and becomes part of the external water element.

According to Indian cosmology, at the end of an eon the external water element evaporates completely. Since this is the case, how much more so is the internal water element in our body short-lived and unreliable? Whether external or internal, the water element is impersonal, with nothing in it suitable to be considered mine, I, or my self.

The fire element is the heat in the body. Active in digestion and metabolism, the fire element promotes aging of the body. The external fire element heats our homes and burns them down. The internal wind element is apparent in the breath as well as in the subtle winds or qi that course through the limbs, causing them to move. According to Indian physiology, thought and intention activate the wind element, which is transmitted to the limbs, stimulating them to move. (The contemporary equivalent may be nerve currents.) The external wind element enables all movement—of clouds, ocean waves, and earthquakes. The internal and external elements of fire and wind are simply the impersonal fire element and the impersonal wind element. They are not suitable to be considered as I, mine, or my self.

Śāriputra clinches the argument concerning the selfless nature of the body by saying (MN 28.26):

> Friends, just as when a space is enclosed by timber and creepers, grass and clay, it comes to be termed "house," so too, when a space is enclosed by bones and sinews, flesh and skin, it comes to be termed "body."

What we see as our body is nothing more than a space with bones as its structure; muscles, internal organs, and tissue filling it in; and skin holding it together. There is nothing in this collection of elements or in any part of it that is a real body. This being the case, there is nothing in it that could be a self or person.[109]

When meditating on the establishment of mindfulness on the body, in addition to scrutinizing all parts and aspects of the body with wisdom, bear in mind that it is composed simply of impersonal elements. Including the above explanation in your meditation will strengthen your understanding of the body and of not-self.

## *Understanding Selflessness by Means of Derived Forms*

In addition to the meditation on the four primary elements to realize selflessness, Śāriputra taught a meditation on the conditioned and dependent nature of forms derived from these elements. This meditation too is for the purpose of realizing the four truths and nirvāṇa. The eye faculty is used as an example, the argument being applicable to the other senses as well.

For a full visual cognition to arise, several factors must be intact—there must be the eye faculty, a visible form in range of the eye, and the mind placing attention on and engaging with that object. If any of these are lacking, a fully conscious visual cognition will not arise. The various aspects of a full visual cognition can be subsumed in the five aggregates. The visible form (the red color of a blossom), the eye faculty, and the person's body that houses that sense faculty are included in the form aggregate. The feeling aspect arising from that cognition (probably a pleasant feeling) is included in the feeling aggregate. Identifying the flower is the aspect of discrimination in that cognition; it is part of the aggregate of discrimination. Mental factors such as intention, attention, contact, mindfulness, and concentration that arise with that full visual cognition are included in the aggregate of miscellaneous factors. The visual consciousness (the basic entity that sees the flower) is included in the aggregate of consciousness. In this way, all five aggregates are present, functioning, and intertwined in this one act of cognition of the red color of a blossom.[110] Having explained this, Śāriputra then makes one of the most famous statements in the early sūtras (MN 28.38):[111]

> Now this has been said by the Blessed One (the Buddha): "One who sees dependent arising sees the Dhamma; one who sees the Dhamma sees dependent arising."

This statement underscores that understanding dependent arising is the key to understanding the entire Buddhist doctrine; it is the cardinal point to realize reality and the four truths; it is the most important factor to attain nirvāṇa. These five aggregates subject to clinging are dependently arisen: they repeatedly arise in dependence on the sense faculties being intact, a form being in range of the faculties, and the mind placing attention on that form. Depending on those conditions, a cognition arises and together with it arise factors of all five aggregates.[112]

These five aggregates subject to clinging are the first truth, true duḥkha. The deeper significance of duḥkha is the fact that the five aggregates come into being through polluted conditions stemming from ignorance. Our internal world of experience and the external world that we apprehend and engage with all originate due to such polluted conditions. They are not reliable and stable; moreover, they are not mine, I, or my self.

Craving is one of the principal factors that bring the five aggregates into existence. Ordinary beings crave experiences through the five aggregates. Craving and clinging—elements that themselves are part of the five aggregates—perpetuate the arising of the five aggregates in one birth after another. In one life after the next, a new set of aggregates arises that, in turn, has all the elements necessary to create more sets of aggregates in future lives.

How do we bring this process to an end? Since the aggregates are dependent on conditions, when those conditions cease, compulsive rebirth also ceases. Because the origin of duḥkha is impermanent and conditioned, when these conditions are destroyed, the duḥkha that results from them cannot arise. The āryas' eightfold path that damages and eventually eradicates the origins of duḥkha is also conditioned, so it can be practiced and cultivated. Cultivating the path will eradicate the origin of duḥkha, leading us to the unconditioned, nirvāṇa, at which time true peace is found.

In this volume of the *Library of Wisdom and Compassion*, we have plunged into the topics of selflessness and emptiness that were mentioned in earlier volumes. We have learned some of the fundamental concepts regarding the ultimate nature and how it can be approached through the understanding of dependent arising. We have also begun to learn some of the reasonings and meditation methods employed to realize the ultimate nature. The next volume will delve into some of these numerous reasonings and meditation methods that lead to this realization.

By investigating both the Pāli tradition's and Sanskrit tradition's approach to the ultimate nature, we discover a basic unity in that both emphasize the analytical method and dependent arising as an important topic to analyze. We have also seen divergent views, specifically the Sanskrit tradition's explanation of the selflessness of phenomena in addition to the selflessness of persons explained in the Pāli tradition, and the different levels of the object of negation in the meditation of the selflessness of persons.

Both the commonalities and differences point to the Buddha's skill as a teacher who makes his teachings suitable for a wide variety of disciples. We are incredibly fortunate to have encountered these teachings, to have the opportunity to learn and practice them, and to have the receptivity to trust and have faith in them. May all merit from our efforts be dedicated to the full awakening of all sentient beings.

# Coda: The Pāli Abhidharma

One purpose of the *Library of Wisdom and Compassion* is to familiarize Buddhists with the doctrine of other Buddhist traditions. Along this line, this coda will explain a few aspects of the Abhidharma as taught in the Pāli tradition. The Pāli explications of the dharmas that compose material objects are briefly presented so that people who are interested in tenet systems and who have studied Buddhist tenets can expand their knowledge.[113] Many Tibetans believe the Pāli tradition to be equivalent to the Vaibhāṣika or Sautrāntika tenet systems. Although it does share some similarities with these, there are some important differences.

Due to geographical distances and doctrinal issues, eighteen schools developed after the Buddha's parinirvāṇa. It seems that most of these had their own systems of Abhidharma. The Pāli Abhidharma developed in south India, Sri Lanka, and other Theravāda countries. The Sarvāstivāda Abhidharma developed in Kashmir and northern India. There were other Abhidharma systems as well among the eighteen early schools, but only texts from the Theravāda, Sarvāstivāda, and Dharmaguptaka schools are extant today.[114] Later masters in countries following the Pāli or Sanskrit tradition wrote subsequent Abhidharma texts.[115]

Although both the Pāli and Sarvāstivāda Abhidharma Piṭakas have seven canonical Abhidharma treatises, these seven are not the same. The themes in these two sets of seven treatises overlap to some extent, but in some instances their interpretations differ. Present-day Theravāda follows the Pāli Abhidharma, whereas the Abhidharma texts known in Tibetan Buddhism descend from the Sarvāstivāda and Mūlasarvāstivāda Abhidharmas.

The early Abhidharmikas who lived just after the Buddha probably shared similar ideas. In the third century BCE, Buddhism spread to Sri Lanka, where the Pāli Abhidharma developed. Sri Lanka is far from northern India where the Sarvāstivāda Abhidharma evolved. As time went on, some terms that were common to both Abhidharmas came to have slightly different meanings. For example, the word "ultimate" (*paramārtha*, *paramattha*) was used by the early commentators in one way but it came to have a different meaning in the early Abhidharma, and even other diverse meanings in the Yogācāra and Madhyamaka tenet systems. Furthermore, the Sarvāstivāda and Pāli Abhidharmas differed in what they considered ultimate.

Unless otherwise mentioned, the views below are those of the Pāli Abhidharmikas. As we reflect on them, we will see that the Vaibhāṣika doctrine that arose from the Sarvāstivāda school differs from the Pāli system. In general, the Sarvāstivāda system tends more toward substantialist assertions than does the Pāli system. Please note that, as will be seen below, the notion that modern-day Theravādins hold Vaibhāṣika or Sautrāntika tenets is incorrect, although they do share some similar views.

## *Formulating a Philosophy Rooted in the Buddha's Teachings*

When the Buddha taught the sūtras that were later systematized to form the Pāli canon, his teachings were practice oriented. He instructed people of diverse backgrounds, spiritual dispositions, and interests to live a good life in the present, to create the causes for good rebirths by observing the law of karma and its effects, and to attain liberation by practicing the three higher trainings. At that time, his teachings were not an organized theory about diverse phenomena or their mode of existence. Formulating such a philosophy from the Buddha's teachings was the work of future generations, beginning with the Abhidharmikas.

The Abhidharma is one of the three baskets of the Buddha's teachings. "Abhidharma" indicates a discipline or study of the Dharma. The word "dharma" has multiple meanings, including phenomena, the Buddha's teachings, and the physical and mental elements into which all phenomena can be resolved. Of the three higher trainings, the Abhidharma is associated with the higher training in wisdom.

Theravāda scholars and practitioners have varying views regarding the origins of the Abhidharma: Some say it was first spoken by the Buddha and later related by Śāriputra. Others say it was composed by arhats and sages. However, all agree that the Abhidharma developed and was systematized after the Buddha's parinirvāṇa. The aim of the early Abhidharmikas was to discuss the underlying structure of the Buddha's teachings in a systematic way that would apply in all circumstances and help practitioners in their meditative practice, so they would attain awakening.

One way they did this was by forming lists of phenomena and matrixes to point out the unique characteristics of each phenomenon as well as its relationships with other phenomena. By doing this, they emphasized the Buddha's aim of helping us to understand that the world and the beings in it are not how we commonly think of them. Things are not permanent, pleasant, arising from an underlying metaphysical substance, or governed by a findable, real self. They are processes, not isolated objects. The people and objects we encounter in our daily life arise dependently and are interconnected and interlocking physical and mental phenomena, arising and ceasing in every instant due to their causes and conditions. By dissecting things into their components, the Abhidharmikas highlighted that a real self cannot be found.

While teachings on selflessness and emptiness in present-day Buddhist traditions began with the Buddha's sūtras, they were further elaborated by the Abhidharmikas. The theories and structures they developed, in turn, were later influenced by the philosophies of non-Buddhist schools as well as by Abhidharmikas from the other Buddhist schools. This led to new Abhidharma writings as well as to other treatises on wisdom and the nature of reality by later Indian sages such as Nāgārjuna and Dharmakīrti. There has been a great deal of interchange, debate, revision, and amplification of various theories articulated by the early Abhidharmikas. This history is not easy to untangle since not all the relevant texts are extant today. However, a cursory look will help us understand the evolution of the philosophies of today's Buddhist traditions.

For people who have studied in the Tibetan tradition, some of what you read below may not accord with the tenets texts that you have studied. Furthermore, within the Tibetan tradition, various subschools describe the assertions of ancient Indian philosophical schools differently. The willingness to hear other approaches is crucial.

## *The Early Abhidharmikas*

While deconstructive analysis has consistently been valued in Buddhism, in the early years it did not focus on the ontological status of objects, but on distinguishing the constituents of phenomena and their relationships with one another. As one of the seven awakening factors, the discrimination of states (*dharmapravicaya, dhammavicaya*) was highly valued in meditation and was used to develop right view, insight, and wisdom for the purpose of attaining awakening. It was employed to evaluate various mental states and practices and differentiate the virtuous ones to cultivate from the nonvirtuous ones to abandon. In this way, practitioners would live ethically and develop deep concentration.

Discrimination was also used to identify the actual constituents and structures of commonplace objects in order to eliminate attachment and animosity toward them. Furthermore, discrimination helped practitioners to see the interdependence among phenomena, which aided in realizing selflessness. In this way, they emphasized that the teachings on dependent arising are essential to attain liberation.

To fulfill these purposes, the Abhidharmikas drew on lists found in the sūtras. They examined questions such as "What are the afflictions, the pollutants, the auxiliary afflictions? In which of the three realms of existence—desire, form, and formless—are they found? Which ones are virtuous, nonvirtuous, or neutral?" This led to comprehensive analysis of mental states—the principal topic of the first chapter of the *Enumeration of Factors* (*Dhammasaṅgaṇi*), the first book of the Pāli Abhidharma. The analysis of virtue and nonvirtue led to in-depth discussions on karma. The thirty-seven harmonies with awakening were analyzed to reveal the way to practice the path. As time went on, Abhidharma commentators spelled out the paths and stages of awakening and related them to various defilements that were reduced or eradicated on each path and at each stage.

The theories of the early Abhidharmikas who appeared just after the Buddha's parinirvāṇa were rooted in three principal doctrines that the Buddha expounded:

1. Momentary impermanence. All conditioned phenomena arise and pass away each moment due to their causes and conditions.

2. Selflessness. There is no substantiality to either the person or the five aggregates that compose the person.
3. Dependent origination. Phenomena arise in dependence on other phenomena—their causes and conditions—and they exist in relation to other phenomena. There is no underlying substance out of which phenomena appear or are formed. Nor is there an absolute, external creator that created mind and matter.

By describing and analyzing phenomena, the Abhidharmikas engaged in two important activities: first, they analyzed phenomena in depth, clearly describing the unique character of each phenomenon; second, by analyzing phenomena into their component parts, they created more detailed lists of classifications of phenomena, and the relationships among these phenomena developed into what is called the "dharma theory."

Beginning with categories of phenomena in the sūtras—the five aggregates, the twelve sources, the eighteen constituents—they analyzed each one and described its relationships to the others. They investigated how the five aggregates correspond to the twelve sources and eighteen constituents and which sources and constituents are included in each aggregate.

By analyzing phenomena into their smallest constituents, practitioners see that there is no underlying substance from which everything was created. This contradicts the assertions of non-Buddhist schools such as the Sāṃkhyas who say that all manifest objects are transformations of the fundamental nature (primal substance, *prakṛti*, *pakati*). It also invalidates the beliefs that everything is created from one unifying cosmic substance, that one universal mind underlies all that exists, and that everything is created by and will dissolve back into a permanent and absolute creator. By stating that everything in the world appears, changes, and ceases due to causes and conditions, Buddhism disproves theories of fatalistic predetermination or causeless, random arising.

By showing that the constituent parts of phenomena do not exist in isolation unrelated to anything else, Abhidharmikas emphasized causal relationships. Things have direct causes and cooperative conditions: wood is the direct cause of a table and the carpenter is its cooperative condition. Some phenomena are "co-nascent conditions" in that they arise together and mutually condition each other. In other words, if one is present, so is the other.

In the process of selecting the topics to discuss, the early Abhidharmikas also pointed out the major topics and teachings for Buddhists to explore and understand. In this way, attention was drawn to our states of mind, the material world, realms of existence, karma and its results, the paths to and fruits of awakening, time, motion, and so on.

## *The Dharma Theory*

The dharma theory arose as a way to understand what is known and experienced in meditation and to point out to practitioners what to observe when they do practices such as the four establishments of mindfulness.[116] Since practitioners seek nirvāṇa and the path to nirvāṇa entails insight into the nature of the self, analysis of the components of the self is important. To see the world—our internal experience and external objects—correctly involves seeing the bare phenomena of which we and our world are composed.

The dharma theory centers around identifying the building blocks of our experience, the bare phenomena that compose our being and the world. These are conditioned phenomena that arise and cease in each moment. Describing how they interrelate to form other phenomena and later recombine to form yet other phenomena, the dharma theory shows that our belief that our mental states and the world around us consist of unified, "solid" phenomena is erroneous.

In particular the Abhidharma analysis demonstrates that what appears to be a continuous flow of consciousness is actually composed of different moments of mind, each of which consists of a primary mind and its concomitant mental factors. This marks the beginning of the systematization of Buddhist psychology, a psychology directed toward awakening and thus concerned with discerning defiled and undefiled mental states. The Abhidharma matrixes also illustrate that one mental factor can appear in different forms and with different names in various lists. We begin to investigate, for example, how malice, as one of the three nonvirtues, relates to anger, which is one of the three roots, and how anger relates to resentment, wrath, and so forth. Similarly, we understand mindfulness in an expansive way as the establishment of mindfulness, faculty of mindfulness, power of mindfulness, awakening factor of mindfulness, and right mindfulness.

The dharma theory evolved over time as new questions arose, as implications of the existing theory were examined, and as contradictions were discovered or resolved. In the Pāli tradition, this resulted in a series of Abhidharma texts, lengthy commentaries, and subcommentaries that were later summarized into shorter texts. After that, more commentaries were written on these shorter texts.

The dharma theory is presupposed, although not clearly set forth, in the canonical Abhidharma texts. It is more fully developed in the commentaries that explore its implications. As more questions arose, other theories, such as the two truths and the division into substantial and imputed existence, were developed in response.

In the sūtras the Buddha proposed five groups into which phenomena, particularly those related to the self, could be analyzed: (1) body and mind (P. *nāma-rūpa*); (2) five aggregates (*skandha, khandha*); (3) six elements (*dhātu, dhātu*) of earth, water, fire, wind, space, and consciousness; (4) twelve sense sources (*āyatana, āyatana*); and (5) eighteen constituents (*dhātu, dhātu*).

The Buddha had a reason for speaking of each of these sets. Categorizing things into the five aggregates clearly differentiates between material (body) and mind. Meditation on the five aggregates enables practitioners to discover that there is no independent self to be found either within the aggregates or separate from them. The Buddha repeatedly says, "This is not mine; this I am not; this is not my self." That is, none of the aggregates belongs to me, they do not correspond to I, and they are not my self. There are only impersonal physical and mental parts.

Classifying those same phenomena into twelve sense sources and eighteen constituents emphasizes the conditions necessary for perception and cognition to occur. Discriminating them in this way brings home the point that the mind is not a soul or an independent phenomenon, but is produced by causes and conditions.

These five sets are not distinct from one another; they overlap. Body and mind can be expanded to become the five aggregates—the body is the form aggregate and the mind consists of the four remaining aggregates. Body and mind and the five aggregates can be expanded into the six elements, with the body/physical aggregate including the elements of earth, water, fire, wind, and space, and mind (four mental aggregates) being condensed into the sixth element, consciousness. The five aggregates can be expanded to form the twelve sources, which can be further expanded into the eighteen constituents. None of these sets forms the final mode of analysis because each can be broken down into smaller parts.[117]

The dharma theory facilitates even more refined analysis when each dharma is seen as the smallest factor that can be identified. However, identifying the smallest particles of matter does not imply that these particles or dharmas are partless. There is no discussion of phenomena being composed of partless particles in the Pāli Abhidharma.[118] Rather, these dharmas are simply the smallest material units that can be identified. In this case, the form aggregate is broken down into twenty-eight form dharmas.

The Abhidharma focuses primarily on the mental factors that compose various types of consciousnesses. The primary consciousnesses and mental factors are important factors to examine to realize selflessness. In addition, knowing the various states of mind aids meditators when they cultivate concentration to gain meditative absorptions of the form and formless realms. These mental dharmas are more numerous than the material ones: the aggregates of feeling, discrimination, and miscellaneous factors together are composed of fifty-two mental factors (*caitta, cetasika*). The last aggregate, consciousness, is comprised of eighty-nine types.

In summary, the canonical Abhidharma defines, classifies, and shows the relationships among the dharmas. Consisting of many lists and matrixes, it aids practitioners to identify and understand the dharmas in their meditation. Abhidharma entails not only analysis to identify each dharma but also synthesis to show their interconnections. For example, the first book of the Pāli Abhidharma, the *Enumeration of Factors* (*Dhammasaṅgaṇi*), defines and classifies the mental factors among other things, whereas the last book, the *Foundational Conditions or Relations* (*Paṭṭhāna*), lists the various types of conditional relationships among the dharmas. Analysis deconstructs phenomena to show there is no self and no underlying, primal, or fundamental substance (*prakṛti*) from which everything originates. Synthesis complements this, illustrating that the dharmas are not separate, isolated entities, but are dependent—the classifications and precise definitions are artificial categories delineated only for the sake of identifying and describing the dharmas. Our experience is in fact a complex web of interconnected relationships of dharmas.

According to the Pāli tradition, the material dharmas are elements of experience. They are spoken of as characteristics and functions, but not as particles. For example, the earth element is the property of solidity. It is the characteristic of hardness, and its function is to serve as a support or basis for the other elements. The water element is the property of cohesion. It has the characteristic of flowing or fluidity, and it functions to bind other dharmas together.

The dharma theory of the Pāli Abhidharma is not based on a dichotomy between substance and qualities, for such a dichotomy could easily lead to the assumption of a substantial self (P. *attavāda*), which the Buddha emphatically denies. That is, a dharma is not an inherent quality of another dharma, and a dharma is not the substrata or substance out of which another dharma is produced. The dharmas themselves are conditions for other dharmas, as described by the set of twenty-four conditions that show the dependent arising of all dharmas both in terms of their temporal and spatial relationships.

The Sarvāstivāda Abhidharma speaks of the dharmas in a different way. They are isolated, partless particles, with their own-nature (*svabhāva, sabhāva*). This results in the Sarvāstivādin's assertion that the dharmas exist as ultimate and discrete entities in all three times—the past, present, and future—a position refuted by Nāgārjuna and later Mādhyamikas.

## *The Development of the Dharma Theory*

Doctrinal questions and controversies influenced the development of the dharma theory over time. According to the canonical Abhidharma, there was no enduring essence that was the person either inside the aggregates—and by extension inside the dharmas that compose the aggregates—or totally separate from the aggregates and the dharmas. However, some Buddhists—specifically the Puggalavādins—questioned how rebirth could occur and karma continue into future lives if there is no self. To resolve this conundrum, the Puggalavādins asserted that the person is real and ultimate. This was refuted in *Points of Controversy* (*Kathāvatthu*), one of the seven canonical Abhidharma texts that was said to have been written by Moggaliputta Tissa in the third century BCE.

When refuting that the person is real and ultimate, these later Abhidharmikas said that the dharmas and aggregates that compose the person are real and ultimate. But "real and ultimate" does not mean that they were distinct and absolute entities existing in their own right. Rather *ultimate* means that the dharmas are the final limit of our experience in that they cannot be further reduced. However, there is no absolute substance that underlies them, no metaphysical entity from which they manifest and into which they later dissolve. Their being called "ultimate" does not contradict the early Abhidharma's insistence that all things are impermanent and arise dependently due to causes and conditions. The dharmas are said to be *real*—meaning that they occur when their causes and conditions are present.

This makes evident that there are two levels of existents: Some, like the person, can be analyzed into their constituent parts. Others, like the dharmas, cannot be further analyzed because they are the elementary constituents of phenomena.

To understand the evolution of some of the ideas in the Abhidharma, it is helpful to look at a later Abhidharma text, the *Abhidhammattha Sangaha* by Anuruddhācariya, which has been widely used from the twelfth century onward, and see the way it categorizes phenomena and the reasons behind it. This text states that there are two kinds of realities: conventional (P. *sammuti*) and ultimate (P. *paramattha*).[119] They are differentiated based on whether they are referents of conceptual thought (P. *paññatti*) and conventional terms or have their own-nature (P. *sabhāva*). Conventional realities are referents of concepts and terms. Some examples of conventional realities are persons, human beings, animals, cups, tables, and trees. As designated objects and products of mental construction, they exist due to conception, are without own-nature, and are not irreducible components of existence.

Ultimate realities, on the other hand, have their own-nature and are the final, ultimate constituents of existence. When conventional realities are analyzed into their components, we discover the ultimate realities—the dharmas—that cannot be further reduced. For example, a person appears to be an ultimate reality, but when analyzed we find only the person's components—the five aggregates. As a collection of impermanent mental and physical processes, a person is a conventional thing that exists only due to terms and concepts. While "person" is a conceptual construct that cannot be found when searched for, the dharmas, which are a person's most elementary impermanent components, cannot be further reduced. Thus ontologically the dharmas are ultimate realities because they have their own-nature, and epistemologically they are the final objects of correct knowledge.

The meaning of the five aggregates being ultimate realities requires clarification. The coarse body, for example, is not an ultimate reality, for it can be reduced to the four primary elements. The primary elements, however, cannot be further reduced. They are subtle, and it is difficult for us ordinary people to actually perceive them. We have to investigate with mindfulness and appropriate attention to perceive the ultimate realities such as the four great elements. Because they are directly known with a subtler meditative consciousness, which is considered an ultimate or supreme knower, they are called "ultimate" or "supreme objects."

Ultimate existents (ultimate realities) are of four types:

1. Mind (*citta, citta*) corresponds to the aggregate of consciousness. Included in mind are the minds of the desire, form, and formless realms. Mind is defined in three ways: an agent that cognizes an object, the instrument by means of which the mental factors cognize an object, and the activity of cognition. The first two definitions imply that mind is one thing and the action of cognizing is another. These definitions are given to overcome the distorted view that there is a permanent self or soul that is the agent or instrument of cognition. The third definition is the most accurate: mind is the process of cognizing and cannot be known apart from the action of cognizing; it is nothing other than the act of cognizing.
2. The mental factors include the aggregates of feeling, discrimination, and miscellaneous factors. The Abhidhamma lists fifty-two mental factors, which occur together with mind and perform diverse functions. The aggregates of feeling and discrimination are two of the mental factors. The other fifty are found in the aggregate of miscellaneous factors, which includes emotions, views, attitudes, moods, and other mental functions. The mental factors that accompany any mind arise and cease together with that mind, have the same object, and arise due to the same sense source.
3. Matter or form (*rūpa*) refers to the material dharmas and is the same in both the Abhidharma scheme and the scheme of the five aggregates.

4. Nirvāṇa, the cessation of duḥkha and its causes, is the only unconditioned dharma. Neither created nor destroyed, nirvāṇa is deathless and completely beyond the conditioned world and the bonds of time and space. Nirvāṇa is said to have its own-nature (Vism 16:72) because it is a dharma—it is not a designation and does not depend on conceptual constructs.

Of these four ultimate realities, the first three comprise all impermanent, conditioned things. The five aggregates can be subsumed in these first three—the form aggregate being matter, the aggregates of feeling, discrimination, and miscellaneous factors being mental factors, and the consciousness aggregate being mind. The fourth ultimate reality, nirvāṇa, is the unconditioned.

Here the aggregate of form does not mean the coarse body, which is a conventional reality, but the components of the body into which it is ultimately analyzed—the dharmas. Similarly, the aggregate of consciousness does not refer to the mind in general, which is a conventional reality, but to the fleeting moments of consciousness of which the mind is composed. Discerning the difference between the person, which is a conventional reality, and the five aggregates, which are ultimate realities, is an essential part of cultivating the wisdom of selflessness in the Pāli tradition. Understanding this is the goal of insight meditation and is an important step toward the realization of nirvāṇa.

## *Substance and Own-Nature*

The *Śāriputrābhidharma Śāstra*[120] appears to be the first Abhidharma text to use the expressions own-nature (self-nature) and other-nature. It says, "Self-nature contains self-nature; other-nature does not contain self-nature. Self-nature associates with self-nature; self-nature does not associate with other-nature." This indicates that things with the same attributes belong to a self-nature group and those with different attributes belong to an other-nature group. Here this term delineates between different groups and has nothing to do with phenomena's mode of existence.

In later Abhidharma śāstras self-nature gradually came to mean inherent nature. This connotation first appears in the *Abhidharma-vibhāṣā-śāstra* of the Sarvāstivāda school. It divides things into seventy-five basic constituents and regards these as the real essence of all things. They are indivisible, endowed with their own unique nature, and real, while composites made from them are unreal. For example, the person is unreal, but its basic constituents are real—that is, they are substantially existent. The person, meanwhile, is imputedly existent and less real than the basic constituents. While the Sarvāstivādins believed they correctly understood the Buddha's teachings on selflessness, in fact they established a Buddhist realism that contradicts the Buddha's core teachings on no-self and emptiness. It seems their notion of substantial existence was the main target of Nāgārjuna's Madhyamaka approach.

This doctrinal controversy, which also influenced the Theravāda dharma theory, centered around the Sarvāstivādin assertion that phenomena exist in the three times. It arose from the questions: Since things only exist in the present, how could a cause that is not existent (because it has already ceased in order to give rise to a result) produce a result? How could a result that is not existent (because it has not yet arisen) be produced by a cause that exists? To resolve this quandary, the Sarvāstivādins posited that phenomena substantially exist in the past, present, and future. This suddenly gave an ontological twist to the dharma theory, which until then had simply been a descriptive account of empirical experience. From the Theravāda viewpoint, this Sarvāstivāda assertion accorded an unnecessary, inherent nature to the dharmas.

Although the Pāli tradition rejected this assertion of own-nature and its implications, it still impacted the dharma theory as explained in Sri Lankan commentaries. Whereas the canonical Abhidharma did not give a formal definition of "dharma," Sri Lankan Abhidharma commentators defined a dharma as that which holds or bears its own-nature. This does not, however, imply a duality between a dharma and its nature; a dharma is not a separate agent that holds its own-nature as an underlying substance. Rather, "own-nature" is used to mean "that which is not held in common by others": each dharma is a fact of empirical existence that is not the same as other empirically discerned facts. "Own-nature" simply indicates the mere fact of being a dharma. It does not mean that there is an enduring substance supporting a dharma. If anything, equating dharma and own-nature means that there is only the constantly changing arising and ceasing of mental and material phenomena, each of which has its own unique characteristics.

An earlier Pāli canonical text, the *Path of Discrimination* (*Paṭisambhidāmagga*), found in the Khuddaka Nikāya and ascribed to Śāriputra, says that the five aggregates are empty of own-nature (P. *sabhāvena-suñña*). If the aggregates lack own-nature, then surely the parts into which they can be analyzed must also lack own-nature. To reconcile this statement and the new definition of dharma as "that which bears its own-nature" without suggesting that dharmas exist in their own right, Pāli commentators supplemented the above definition with a new one: a dharma is that which is borne by its own conditions. That is, a dharma is not an autonomous agent but is something that depends on its conditions and is supported by its conditions. This definition emphasizes that dharmas do *not* exist in their own right and that "own-nature" does not mean inherent substance.[121] Dharmas occur due to appropriate conditions. Here we see that although the word "sabhāva" was incorporated into Theravāda Abhidharma thought, it was not interpreted to mean a substantial mode of being. Rather, it was the conditionally dependent nature of things.

## *Own-Characteristic*

Similarly, saying that a dharma is that which bears its own-characteristic (*svalakṣaṇa, salakkhaṇa*) does not mean that there is duality between a dharma and its characteristics. Definitions (characteristics) and definiendums (what is being characterized) are used for convenience in expression; they do not have ultimate meaning. Each dharma has its own distinguishing characteristics. For example, visibility is the specific characteristic of color. Saying the earth element is that which has the characteristic of solidity is provisional, not ultimate. In fact, solidity is the earth element.

Commenting on the title of the *Discourse on the Root of All Things*, the subcommentary explains the meaning of "things" (*dharma*):[122]

> "They bear their own characteristics": Although there are no dhammas devoid of their own characteristics, this is still said for the purpose of showing that these are mere dhammas endowed with their specific natures devoid of such attributions as that of

> a "being," etc. Whereas such entities as self, beauty, pleasurableness, and permanence, etc., or [fundamental] nature, substance, soul, body, etc., which are mere misconstructions due to craving and views, or such entities as sky-flower, etc., which are mere expressions of conventional discourse, cannot be discovered as ultimately real actualities (P. *saccikaṭṭhaparamatthato*), these dhammas (those endowed with a specific nature) can. These dhammas are discovered as ultimately real actualities. Although there is no real distinction (between these dhammas and their characteristics), still, in order to facilitate understanding, the exposition makes a distinction as a mere metaphorical device. Or else they are borne, they are discerned, known, according to their specific nature, thus they are dhammas.

Saying dharmas have their own characteristics is done to show they have a specific nature and to distinguish them from distorted conceptions such as seeing that which lacks self as having self, seeing the foul as beautiful, seeing what is unsatisfactory in nature as pleasurable, and seeing what is impermanent as permanent. Having their own characteristics also indicates they are not created out of a primal substance or other metaphysical entities that are fabricated due to craving and views. Because they have their own characteristics, dharmas are different from sky-flowers and other such nonexistents that we imagine. This, then, is the meaning of saying that they are ultimately real actualities. It does not mean they exist by their own characteristics.

The basic characteristic of a dharma is not altered over time and cannot be transferred to another dharma. Even when it is in association with other dharmas, each dharma retains its own characteristic. Solidity or earth element remains solidity, even when associated with water or other elements.

Own-characteristics or specific characteristics are those unique to each dharma; they are the dharmas. The dharmas are the final limits of subtle analysis. They cannot be known individually with our senses. A group of them or a continuum of moments in the case of feelings and so forth is needed for cognition to occur. Likewise, specific characteristics are not directly cognized, although a group of them can be directly perceived as a conceptual object.

General characteristics (*sāmānya-lakṣaṇa, sāmañña-lakkhaṇa*) are characteristics, such as impermanence, unsatisfactoriness, and not-self, that are common to all mundane dharmas. General characteristics are mental constructs imputed by mind to dharmas. Superimposed on the ultimate data of empirical existence, general characteristics are known by inference. When yogis perceive a general characteristic such as impermanence, their yogic direct perceiver cognizes the dharmas that arise and cease. They know their impermanence indirectly. The sūtras speak of three general characteristics of conditioned things. These three general characteristics are not dharmas or discrete entities. They are mental constructs imputed on groups of phenomena: (1) arising: production (*utpāda*, *uppāda*), (2) passing away: ceasing (*vyaya*, *vyaya*), and (3) aging: alteration of that which exists (*sthityanyathatva*, *ṭhitassa aññathatta*).

A cup, for example, is an imputed object, a mental construct, that is nothing more than the collection of dharmas—solidity, cohesion, temperature, and so forth—of which it is composed. Our senses directly perceive white, solidity, smoothness, and by these means we know "here is a cup." The dharmas are ultimate in that they can actually be experienced and perceived directly; they are sense data. Our mind puts the sense data together, creates a mental construct, and designates "cup."

In general, "ultimate" means that which has reached the highest or the last. In this case, dharmas are ultimate in the sense that they cannot be further reduced through analysis, unlike the person, which is not real and ultimate. Dharmas came to be called not only "own-nature" but also "ultimate nature" (P. *paramattha-sabhāva*). For the Pāli tradition, these terms do not have substantialist implications. Rather, they emphasize that mental and material dharmas are elements of present experience; they are not seen as having a real nature that persists through the past, present, and future, as asserted by the Sarvāstivādins.

Similarly, saying that the dharmas have ultimate or objective existence (P. *paramatthato vijjamānatā*) means that they are the irreducible components of empirical experience. Saying that the dharmas are ultimately cognizable indicates that the contents of our cognition can be analyzed into these irreducible elements.

Both dharmas and designated objects (*prajñapti*, *paññatti*) are objects of knowledge. Even though imputed objects are artificially created by the mind and lack objective counterparts that are directly known by the senses, they are still knowable and thus are knowable objects. Here we come upon another meaning of the term "dharma" that is also found in the Abhidharma: phenomena, existents. In this sense, all phenomena—both those that are ultimate realities and those that are mental constructs—are considered dharmas.

Two other traits also apply to dharmas: inseparability and conditioned origination. *Inseparability* means that in any given instance of material or mind, the dharmas of which it is composed are not separable from one another. In association like this, the dharmas form a unity. The primary mind and mental factors that are concomitant with it are inseparable in that neither can occur without the other. Together they form one cognizer. Similarly, the color, taste, smell, and hardness of an apple cannot be physically separated but occur together.

Although the dharmas are inseparable, they are distinguishable and can be cognized as if they were separate. Although the color, taste, smell, and texture of an apple are inseparable, these qualities are distinguished separately by the different sense cognizers. Mental dharmas, however, are much more difficult to distinguish separately. It is hard to differentiate feeling, intention, attention, and so forth in our experience.

Like inseparability, *conditioned origination* describes dharmas in terms of their associations with one another. There are five axioms of conditioned origination that are stated either explicitly or implicitly:

1. There is no absolute original cause or beginning of anything. There is simply the continuity of ever-changing, conditioned things.
2. Things only arise from their concordant causes; they cannot arise from causes and conditions that lack the ability to produce them.
3. Things do not arise from a single cause such as an absolute creator or a primal substance.
4. Things do not arise as isolated phenomena. Whenever change occurs due to causes, the effects are multiple.
5. Several causes and conditions produce several results. Many dharmas produce many other dharmas.

Dharmas arise in association with and at the same time as other dharmas. For example, a primary mind and its seven omnipresent mental factors[123]—

contact, feeling, discrimination, intention, attention, one-pointedness, and psychic life—arise together. None of these—either the primary mind or any of the concomitant mental factors—can arise alone without the others. Even one moment of mind is a complex phenomenon with many components.

Similarly, the smallest unit of matter is a cluster (P. *kalāpa*), a combination of eight material dharmas—the four primary elements of solidity (earth), cohesion (water), temperature (fire), and motility (air) and the four secondary elements of color, odor, taste, and nutritive essence (the ability to sustain life). Sound is not considered an inseparable secondary element because things do not continuously produce sound.

None of these eight can arise separate from the others. They are not located in different physical areas or at different times. The fact that the dharmas are inseparable and arise in combination with one another and yet are distinguishable as having their own unique characteristics illustrates the analytical and synthesizing approaches of the Abhidharma. Through analysis they are individually discerned, through synthesis they are seen as co-arising.

## *Designations and Concepts*

The dharma theory also enables us to distinguish distinct empirical entities from cognizing minds and imputed phenomena that are created by the conceptual mind. It helps us to understand the relationship between the dharmas and the objects we perceive in our daily lives. It also brings into question the extent to which objects correspond to the terms that refer to them.

Designations or imputations were first mentioned in the *Dhammasaṅgaṇi*, where the designation itself is the *paññatti* (S. *prajñapti*), and all dharmas (in the broad sense of all things) are the "pathway of designations"—that is, they are what is designated. Paññatti are the names, terms, and designations that express both ultimate existents—the dharmas—and the larger objects that are combinations of dharmas. Later commentators included in paññatti not only the names of things—be they objects real or nominal—but also the objects and meanings that correspond to them. This does not imply, however, that dharmas exist in dependence on designation and conceptualization by mind. The theory of paññatti was implied by the sūtras but was developed by the Abhidharmikas. "Person" became known as the conventional designation given to the collection of the dependently arisen, impermanent psychophysical aggregates. Similarly, "cart" was the conventional name given to the collection of parts that formed a vehicle. However, the early Buddhist idea of conventional designation was not explained in contrast to ultimate or real existents such as the dharmas. This was done later by the Abhidharmikas in the Abhidharma Piṭaka.

There are two types of designations: (1) *Term-designations* (P. *nāma-paññatti*) are the names, words, or symbols that designate real or unreal things. These are established by worldly usage. An example is the word "cup." (2) *Designated objects* (P. *attha-paññatti*) are the designated or conceptualized objects and meanings that correspond to the names, words, and symbols. These objects are mental constructs that come into being by the mind's interpreting the appearances of the real elements in certain arrangements. An example is the cup.

Term-designations and object-designations are interdependent and refer to the same thing seen from two different angles: the verbalization that makes things known and what is made known (what is constructed by thought). It is important to note the difference between object-designations and dharmas. While dharmas can be conceptualized and made known by names and symbols, their existence is not dependent on them. Object-designations, on the other hand, do not exist unless conceptualization is involved.

The later commentaries explain designations in more depth. Designations lack corresponding reality and are things without their own-nature; this differentiates them from dharmas, which are the objective elements of existence. Designations are not ultimate existents and lack the attributes of arising, abiding, and disintegrating. They are not produced by causes and conditions; they do not have own-nature that is displayed while they are present. Whereas temporal distinctions such as past, present, and future apply to dharmas, they do not apply to designations. Designations are not included in the five aggregates, and they are neither conditioned (P. *saṅkhata*) nor unconditioned (P. *asaṅkhata*). Although they exist, designations are unreal and abstract. They lack objective existence and are "mind-dependent," whereas dharmas exist by their own-nature (*svabhāvasiddhi*, *sabhāvasiddha*) and have their own distinct characteristics. Designations are conceptualized and exist only due to thought (P. *parikappasiddha*). As mental constructs superimposed on reality, designations give the illusion of being one object to things that are in fact complex assemblies of dharmas.

When wheels, axles, and planks are arranged in a certain fashion, "cart" is designated to them and they are conventionally known as a cart. But when analyzed into dharmas—their ultimate and irreducible components—there is no cart. When roots, trunk, branches, and leaves are arranged in a particular manner, they are commonly called "tree," but when each part is examined there is no tree there. Similarly, together the five aggregates are called "person," "I," or "being," but when analyzed into their ultimate components, there is no person there at all.

## *The Two Truths*

The ancient non-Buddhist Indian traditions that adhered to the notions of a "soul" or "Self" (*ātman*, *attan*) had a substantialist view of existence and saw time and space as absolutes. The Buddha and the Abhidharmikas refuted these views. To form a cohesive philosophy that could explain all existents free from the erroneous philosophical assumptions of non-Buddhists, the Abhidharmikas formulated the doctrine of the two truths. This doctrine was also influenced by the discussion of designations and concepts that developed as a result of the dharma theory.

While the doctrine of the two truths—conventional and ultimate truths—is first discussed by Abhidharmikas, not in the sūtras themselves, the distinction made in the sūtras between definitive (*nītārtha*, *nītattha*) and interpretable (*neyārtha*, *neyyattha*) sūtras appears to be a relevant antecedent. A sūtra in the Aṅguttara Nikāya says (AN 2.24):

> Monastics, these two misrepresent the Tathāgata. Which two? One who explains a discourse whose meaning requires interpretation as a discourse whose meaning is definitive, and one who explains a discourse whose meaning is definitive as a discourse whose meaning requires interpretation.

The meaning of definitive statements has been drawn out and made clear. They express their meaning explicitly and can be taken as they are. Interpretable statements are indirect and their true meanings must be drawn out and revealed.[124] Buddhaghoṣa establishes a connection between definitive and interpretable meanings and the two truths.[125] Here, it seems that the initial notion of the "two truths," as well as the notion of "definitive and interpretable discourses," served to help early Buddhists reconcile scriptural passages that appeared to be contradictory. As time went on, the doctrine of the two truths became a way of categorizing phenomena. The commentary to the *Kathāvatthu* states:[126]

> The Awakened One, the best of all teachers, propounded two truths, conventional and ultimate; we do not see a third. A statement governed [purely] by agreement is true because of the world's conventions. An ultimate statement is true in that it characterizes things as they are.

The two truths are conventional (P. *sammuti-sacca*) and ultimate (P. *paramattha-sacca*). *Sammuti* refers to convention and general agreement, so conventional truths are truths based on general agreement and societal conventions. Ultimate truths are explanations that use terms indicative of the real elements of existence—the dharmas—which do not depend on mental construction. Statements about ultimates are ultimate truths. Although the dharmas are said to be ultimate realities, they are not ultimate truths. Only dharmas are real, and what is not a dharma is not real. Both conventional and ultimate truths are paññattis, designations, because they must be conveyed through the symbolic medium of language.

In early Buddhism, there was no formulated doctrine of real existence. What was analyzed (the person, for example) was called "conventional," but what it was analyzed into—the dharmas—were not called "ultimate." Ultimate was used only to refer to the "supreme goal, supreme good," nirvāṇa. Later paramattha acquired the meaning of "supreme meaning," and then "ultimately existent."

Later, in the Abhidharma, ultimate came to have the ontological meaning of that which really exists. In this way, the meaning of "ultimate" was expanded to include the dharmas. That is, "ultimate" came to denote real existence, the dharmas that have their own-nature. However, there is no mention of the dharmas being ultimate truths.

Thus it seems that the meaning of "ultimate" and "ultimate truth" changed over time with the addition of the Abhidharma and its commentaries. In the sūtras, nirvāṇa is the supreme or ultimate truth because its nature is undeceptive. The Buddha says in the *Sūtra on the Exposition of the Elements* (MN 140.26):

> For that is false, monastics, which has a deceptive nature, and that is true which has an undeceptive nature—nibbāna. For this, monastics, is the supreme [ultimate] truth of the ariyas, namely, nibbāna, which has an undeceptive nature.

The Abhidharma distinguishes between what is mentally constructed and what has its own-nature. Conventionally based things (P. *sanketa*) are things that come into being due to designations; they depend on mental interpretations that are superimposed on collections of dharmas. But dharmas are ultimate because they are real existents that can be directly known. A table, for example, is conventional because "table" is designated on the multitude of dharmas that are its components. "Table" does not refer to an objective phenomenon that corresponds to the term but is designated when the mind interprets a collection of dharmas in a certain way. The mind superimposes "table" on this collection; thus the table is a convention, a designation. Although the table is not an entity separate from its component dharmas, it is said to exist because according to our social conventions and agreements, it is regarded as a separate entity. The dharmas that compose it, however, have their own-nature that does not depend on convention; the dharmas are empirical reality. They exist dependent on causes and conditions but are not dependent on mental designation.

Some people mistakenly believe the Pāli tradition values ultimate truths more highly than conventional truths. To the contrary, Pāli scriptures explain that to sentient beings who could be guided to nirvāṇa by means of speech regarding the conventional, the Buddha spoke of the conventional. To sentient beings who could be led to nirvāṇa by means of speaking of the ultimate, he spoke of the ultimate. And to those who required a combination of the two, he spoke of both. Just as a person who is multilingual speaks to another person in the other's native tongue to facilitate that person understanding his meaning, so too does the Buddha speak of conventions, ultimates, and both according to the most expedient method for guiding a particular being to arhatship. Neither method is superior to the other.

Furthermore, the commentary to the Aṅguttara Nikāya explains that whatever the Buddha says is true. For example, saying "The person exists" is true speech regarding the conventional. Only if someone thinks there is a substantially existent person in the aggregates does this statement become false. If we try too hard to speak in terms of the ultimate, such as saying "The dharmas composing the five aggregates are walking down the street," we fail to communicate well because we have disregarded the conventional usages of words. Both conventional and ultimate truths exist and are useful, and speech regarding the conventional and the ultimate likewise are useful. It is not necessary to rank one higher than the other. In fact, we could say that the two truths are two ways of presenting the truth, two ways of talking about our experience.

## *The Theory of Form*

While the principles outlined above apply equally to the mental and material dharmas, here we'll look more closely at form (*rūpa, rūpa*), which is also referred to as material or matter.

The Pāli Abhidharma defines form as that which has the characteristic of being subject to physical change and disintegration. According to the Abhidharma theory of momentariness, one moment of material gives way to another. One moment of form disappears and another appears. The succeeding material is not the same as the immediately preceding material, principally due to the influence of infinitesimal changes in temperature.

The Sarvāstivāda Abhidharma, in contrast, defines form as having the characteristic of resistance or impenetrability. This emphasizes that form is located within space and can exist only where another form does not exist.

In the Pāli Abhidharma, four primary elements of form are delineated. Although these are called "earth, water, fire, and air," they actually indicate qualities of material. To review, the earth element is solidity and resistance. The water element is fluidity and cohesion that binds the other elements together. Cohesion forms solidity into recognizable objects such as tables and trees. The fire element is heat. Cold is merely the absence of heat; it is not a distinct quality by itself. The air element is mobility, expansion and contraction, and fluctuation. These four are the natural forces of which material is composed. Being spatially and temporally inseparable, these four exist at the same time and in the same place, whether they are the smallest units of matter or components of huge mountains. Thus every instance of form has some solidity, cohesion, heat, and mobility. Although these four are inseparable, they can be distinguished. But the fact that they can be spoken of differently does not mean they exist independently, unrelated to anything else. The interplay of the elements becomes the material objects we recognize.

The four elements have different characteristics, functions, and manifestations. Each one is influenced by the others but does not lose its individual characteristic. They can neither be condensed into one substance nor transformed into another element. The four primary elements arise and exist together; they are mutually co-arising and co-conditioning. *The Path of Purification* explains (Vism 11.109):

> The earth element, which is held together by water, maintained by fire, and distended by air, is a condition for the other three primary elements by acting as their foundation. The water element, which is founded on earth, maintained by fire, and distended by air is a condition for the other three primary elements by acting as their cohesion. The fire element, which is founded on earth, held together by water, and distended by air is a condition for the other three primary elements by acting as their maintaining. The air element, which is founded on earth, held together by water, and maintained by fire is a condition for the other three primary elements by acting as their distension.

Each element is present in every instance of material. What differentiates various material objects is not the quantity of each element that composes it but its intensity. For example, although all four primary material elements are present in both metal and milk, the element of solidity is more intense in the metal and the element of fluidity more intense in milk.

Our tactile sense does not necessarily know all the elements simultaneously. This often has to do with what we pay attention to. If we put our hand in hot water, the experience of heat is foremost, although fluidity is certainly present. What our tactile sense perceives may depend on which element is prominent; if we step on a nail, solidity is prominent and becomes the object of mind, although the other three elements are also present.

Interestingly, the Pāli Abhidharma does not consider the water element to be a tactile object but an object of mind (P. *dhammāyatana*). When we touch water, its softness is due to the earth element and its temperature is due to the fire element. We cannot touch cohesion or fluidity directly. While Theravādins do not consider cold as a characteristic of the water element, the Sarvāstivādins do. Thus Sarvāstivādins consider the water element to be a tactile object because when touching it, we can experience its coolness.

The primary elements depend on one another to arise, whereas the secondary elements depend on and are supported by the primary ones, although they arise simultaneously with them. It is for this reason that they are considered secondary.

In the canonical Abhidharma, many types of form are mentioned. These are coalesced into fourteen secondary types of form in the commentaries:

(1–5) The five physical sense organs or faculties—the organs of sight, sound, smell, taste, and touch. These are not the coarse organs, such as the eyeball or the ear, but a type of subtle, translucent matter located in these physical organs. Each faculty has its own field of perception: the eye faculty perceives colors, not sounds, and so forth.

(6–9) The four types of sense data: color, sound, smell, and taste. Tactile objects are omitted because they consist of three of the four primary elements (solidity, temperature, and mobility). Only earth, temperature, and mobility are tactile objects. The water-element represents fluidity and viscidity and is not directly cognized by the sense of touch; it is known through a process of inference. This idea is limited to the Theravāda Abhidharma. Other Buddhist schools say that all the four great elements are objects of touch.[127]

In the canonical Pāli Abhidharma as well as in the Sarvāstivāda Abhidharma, both color and shape are considered objects of sight. However, in the Pāli Abhidharma formulated in Sri Lanka, only color is an object of sight. Shape cannot be directly perceived; we see a shape in dependence upon seeing the location of color. Therefore, shape is considered a mental construct that lacks an objective counterpart. There are two views regarding sound, one of which says that it travels like waves in a series.

(10–11) The two faculties of sex, which are subtle matter that differentiate male and female.

(12) The material faculty of life, which maintains and stabilizes the sense faculties, the sexual faculties, and the physical basis of mind.

(13) The nutritive quality of matter, the ability to nourish the biological form and to sustain life.

(14) The physical basis of mind. This is not mentioned in the sūtras but is found in the *Paṭṭhāna*, the last book in the Pāli Abhidharma Piṭaka. It is a form that is the physical basis for the mind-source and the mental consciousness constituent. However, what it is precisely is not specified, although later commentators identified it with the heart (*hṛdaya*, *hadaya*). This refers not to the physical heart, but to a subtle matter located in or near it. Interestingly, while the other five physical sense faculties are also considered controlling faculties (*indriya*, *indriya*), the mental consciousness is not.

These fourteen plus the four primary elements are the eighteen concrete material elements that constitute actually existent material dhammas in the Pāli Abhidharma. An additional ten material elements are modes or stages of those eighteen. Some of these exist both internally and externally, as parts of living beings as well as in the inanimate environment. Others—the five physical sense faculties, the two faculties of sex, the material faculty of life, and the physical basis of mental activity—are only found in conjunction with living beings. Here we see that the Abhidharma examines both the physical components of living beings as well as their external environment, seeing all of them as dependently arisen, impermanent phenomena that lack a self or primal substance as their controller.

## *The Theory of Smallest Particles*

There is a lot of discussion about smallest particles of matter by both contemporary scientists and ancient Abhidharma scholars. However, this discussion is absent in the Pāli canon; it was developed later in Sri Lanka and seems to have been influenced by the Buddhist schools in India, in particular the Sarvāstivāda and Vaibhāṣika schools.[128]

According to the Sarvāstivādas and Vaibhāṣikas, the *paramāṇu* (S. *paramāṇu*) is the smallest unit of material. It is without parts and has no spatial dimensions. The Vaibhāṣika master Saṅghabhadra says:[129]

> Among the material elements susceptible to resistance, the smallest unit, which is not further amenable to division either by another material thing or by mind, is called the *paramāṇu*. Because it has no parts, it is called the smallest, just as the *kṣaṇa* (moment, instant) is considered the smallest unit of time, as it is not further divisible into semi-kṣaṇas.

A paramāṇu always arises and exists together with other paramāṇus, forming a unity or an aggregate called a *saṃghāta*. The saṃghāta is made of the four primary elements and four of the secondary elements. A paramāṇu is partless and lacks resistance because particles without spatial dimensions cannot have resistance.

According to Theravāda scholarship, the Sautrāntikas took issue with this, saying that the smallest particle cannot be without parts and resistance.[130] The Vaibhāṣikas replied that while a smallest particle lacks parts and resistance, since they don't occur in isolation but in combination with other smallest particles, when they form an aggregation they have resistance. The Sautrāntikas pointed out the fallacy in this, saying that if the smallest particle is partless and lacks resistance, then an aggregation must also be partless and lack resistance, for how could many things that individually lack resistance come to have resistance when they come together?

The Sautrāntikas also questioned how these partless particles can join together to form an aggregate. Do they touch one another or not? If they touch one another, then since they lack parts and spatial dimensions (for example, directional parts such as east, south, and so on) and resistance, then they should merge into one, in which case there would never be any coarse forms. If they touch one another partially, then they must have parts and directions, which contradicts the Vaibhāṣikas' own assertion. Furthermore, if partless particles touched, they should exist for two moments, one in which they arise and the second during which they touch. This contradicts the commonly accepted assertion that all dharmas are momentary.

In response to this, the Vaibhāṣikas say that partless particles do not come into contact with one another but there is infinitesimal intervening space between them. The particles stay joined together due to the influence of the air element. But the Sautrāntikas questioned this as well: How could partless particles join together with space between them? They would have to have parts and resistance to do so.

The Theravādins say a paramāṇu is an infinitesimally small unit of material. Unlike the Vaibhāṣikas, they do not say this is the smallest unit of each of the primary elements. Instead, a paramāṇu refers to the smallest cluster that consists of the four primary and four secondary elements. To emphasize the smallness of this particle, one Pāli commentary said it is like "a particle of space." The paramāṇu is called a "material cluster" (P. *rūpa-kalāpa*) to show that although it is infinitesimally tiny, it is an aggregation of material elements.

Theravādins speak of *kalāpaṅga*—a "limb of the group"—that is, a constituent material element of a *kalāpa* (smallest particle).[131] While the Vaibhāṣikas say the smallest particle is an instance of a primary element, according to the Theravādins the smallest particle is a conglomerate (*kalāpa*) of the four primary and four secondary elements. While logically one could say that the kalāpaṅgas were smaller than the kalāpa, since no kalāpaṅga exists in isolation, it is not said to be the smallest instance of a material. The kalāpaṅgas and kalāpas both have spatial dimensions—there is no talk of partless particles in the Pāli Abhidharma. The *Visuddhimargasannaya* of King Parakaramabahu II says:[132]

> The intervening space between two smallest particles (*kalāpa*) has the function of delimiting the atom as "this is the lower side of the smallest particle and that is the upper side of the smallest particle."

Theravādins assert that each smallest particle of material (*rūpa-kalāpa*) is separated from other smallest particles by an infinitesimally small space. Thus the smallest particles do not touch one another. The reason they cannot touch is that if they did, then they would have to be spatially inseparable like the kalāpaṅgas. In that case two smallest particles would merge to form a bigger particle. If this continued, with more and more particles merging, the world would be one huge rūpa-kalāpa. So while the Vaibhāṣikas say the smallest particles cannot touch because they would merge and become one infinitesimally small particle, the Theravādins say they cannot touch because they would become one infinitesimally huge particle!

## *The Theory of Momentariness (Instantaneous Being)*

Parallel to a theory of the smallest unit of material is the theory of the smallest unit of time (*kṣaṇa, khaṇa*), a moment. While the rudiments of this theory can be traced to the canonical Abhidharma, it was fully developed in the Sri Lankan Abhidharma literature. As mentioned above, the sūtras spoke of three characteristics of the conditioned (AN 3.47): arising, passing away, and aging (arising, vanishing, and alteration while persisting), which are general characteristics. Later these three submoments of experience were called "arising," "abiding," and "disintegrating."

Sarvāstivādins also had a theory of momentariness, which reflects this school's substantialist tendencies. It was the first school to mention four characteristic marks of every mental and material dharma: arising, abiding, modification (*jarata, jaratā*), and passing away. They define a moment as the time in which all four of these accomplish their activities. A moment is the length of time it takes to cut a silk thread with a sharp knife, and sixty-four moments constitute the length of time of a finger snap.

Again, from the Theravāda perspective, Sautrāntikas refute this, saying that if these four occur serially, then a moment has four distinct phases, and therefore it is divisible and cannot be the smallest unit of time. But if these four occur simultaneously in one moment, then they would cancel each other out. The four characteristics cannot apply to a single momentary dharma, only to a series of momentary dharmas, which is an empirically observable thing. The Sautrāntikas assert that the four characteristics are a series, which itself is called "subsistence." Something that is momentary cannot subsist or be modified because whatever arises perishes; there is no time for it to subsist or be modified.

Within Theravāda, there are diverse ideas about this. The sūtras often present two phases: arising and ceasing. Once a dharma arises, it is perishing;

there is no time for it to abide.[133] Arising dispels nihilism, which says either that the person does not exist or that it ceases at death with no continuity. Ceasing dispels absolutism, which holds that things have a substantial permanent reality. This view harmonizes with meditative experience, especially when the phase of dissolution is emphasized to bring home the impermanence of conditioned phenomena.

Some Theravādins said that although something that arises will cease, there is an intermediate moment when that thing turns toward its own cessation. This moment, when it is faced with its own perishing, is called "abiding." This moment of existence is necessary, for something cannot do two opposite activities—arise and cease—in the same moment.

However, some sūtras, such as the *Sutta of the Wonderful and Marvelous* (MN 123.23), speak of knowing things such as feelings, discriminations, and thoughts "as they arise, as they are present, as they disappear." The Abhidharmikas formalized this to become the theory that conditioned dharmas arise, abide, and disintegrate. That is, each mental and physical dharma goes through three moments: a moment of origination, a moment of existence, and a moment of cessation. These are not three dharmas but one dharma that goes through three phases, arising in the first moment, abiding in the second, and ceasing in the third.

In ancient times there was much discussion about the theory of change. There are only two ways in which change can occur: partially or totally. Partial change means that while the entity remains the same, some qualities or parts of it change. This is counter to Buddhist ideas, for something cannot be both permanent and impermanent. There is no duality between substance and quality such that the former can remain static while the qualities arise and cease.

On the other hand, if there is total change, then the new thing is completely different. If something arises and then changes totally before it ceases, we cannot say that the same thing that arises also ceases, for a totally different thing would cease.[134]

This quandary led to the redefinition of change. Instead of change being the transformation of the same element from one stage to another, change was now seen as the replacement of one momentary dharma by another. Change is the cessation of one element and the arising of another in its place. This is in contrast to the non-Buddhist substantialist view of there being a permanent underlying substance that remains the same in its subsequent moments but superficially changes.

The theory of momentariness caused the redefinition of change, and it also brought about the definition of motion. Just as a momentary dharma has no time to change but ceases immediately, similarly it has no time to move to another place. Movement is not one thing going from one place to another but a new momentary thing appearing in an adjacent place. Although we say a green pepper was moved from the cutting board to the frying pan, in fact it did not move. Rather a new instance of green pepper appeared at each moment in each infinitesimally small location along the route from the cutting board to the frying pan.[135]

## *The Theory of Time*

Just as Buddhism refutes the notion of an underlying primal substance, it also denies the existence of absolute time—that is, time as a real, all-pervading substance or container in which things exist and events occur. The Buddhist perspective is that time is a designation imputed by the conceptual mind in dependence on changes in arising and perishing dharmas. Past, present, and future are posited in relation to dharmas—in reference to a specific dharma, the past is what has arisen and ceased, the present is what has arisen but not yet ceased, and the future is the not yet arisen. Buddhaghoṣa says:[136]

> Chronological time denoted by reference to this or that event is merely a conventional expression.

There is no permanent or absolute moment of time. Specifically, a particular primary consciousness—which has no content per se—arises simultaneously with its attendant mental factors—which fill it out and supply its content. A moment of time is designated to the duration of the combination of mental factors that are concomitant with a primary mind. Seventeen moments of a mental dharma is the length of time a form exists, the mind moments changing at a much faster rate than material particles.

## *The Theory of Space*

Just as absolute time is rejected, so too is absolute space. Only one Buddhist school[137] adheres to the idea of real space: it says that space is omnipresent, infinite, eternal, and non-obstructive in that it does not obstruct the matter that exists in it and it is not obstructed or pushed away by matter. This space isn't just the lack of obstruction but something positive—a real element or substance that is the container in which everything exists and moves.

According to the Pāli tradition, which refutes the above theory, although space is sometimes listed in conjunction with and just after the four primary elements of earth, water, fire, and air, that does not mean it too is a primary element of material. When space and consciousness appear after the four primary elements (*mahābhūta, mahābhūta*), the group of six is called "elements" (*dhātu, dhātu*). Thus space and consciousness are not considered additional primary elements of matter.

The first book of the Pāli Abhidharma Piṭaka lists space as a secondary material element. In doing so, it shows that space exists only in reference to form, and in that sense it is a derivative of form. Nevertheless, space lacks independent existence and exists only as a concept. The *Kathāvatthu* describes a debate about the reality of space. Someone says that space is real and visible, citing the space that can be seen between two trees or the space in a keyhole. The *Kathāvatthu* refutes this, saying that what we are actually seeing is the color of the two trees. In dependence on this, we impute that there is space between them. Similarly, we see the color of the surrounding material of the keyhole and give the designation "the space of a keyhole." This space is known via a conceptual process, not by direct perception. Thus it is dependent on the conceptual processes of the mind.

The Sautrāntikas also reject space as something real and define it as "the mere nonexistence of form, which has the characteristic of impenetrability or lack of resistance." Saying that it is the "mere nonexistence of matter . . ." emphasizes that it is a mere negation. Space is not a substance that is the opposite of form, but a mere absence of the obstructibility of form. They agree with the Pāli tradition that space exists imputedly (P. *kappana-siddha*) and does not exist by its own-nature (P. *sabhāvasiddha*). This explains the Buddha's refusal to answer a question non-Buddhists often posed to him about whether space was infinite or finite. Because it is created by conception, it cannot be said to be either.

## *The Evolution of Abhidharma*

The early Abhidharmikas in the first two centuries after the Buddha's parinirvāṇa probably lived in areas not so distant from one another, so their theories were fairly similar. But once Buddhism began to spread far and wide in South Asia, there was little communication among the various Abhidharma commentators, and thus there was more diversity in their assertions. As time went on, new issues that occupied the later commentators arose because of contact with non-Buddhist influences. At that time many philosophers and renunciants in India were involved in studying and developing theories about epistemology, ontology, and language, among other topics. Philosophical schools such as the Sāṃkhya, Jain, and Vaiśeṣika promoted ideas that challenged the Buddhists and stimulated them to formulate responses that concorded with general Buddhist doctrine. It was within this milieu that the Sarvāstivāda Abhidharma developed.

In early Abhidharma, the dharmas were seen as dynamic processes and conditioned events. Later, non-Buddhist schools in India began to discuss existence (*bhāva*, *bhāva*), own-nature (*svabhāva*, *sabhāva*), substance (*dravya*, *dabba*), imputation and designation, own-characteristics or specific characteristics, and general characteristics. These terms came to have a variety of meanings, and new concepts arose, leading to much debate, not only between Buddhists and non-Buddhists but also among Buddhist traditions and even within different sects of one tradition. In addition, the meanings of these words were constantly changing even within one sect!

For example, the term *dravya*, which after the rise of the Madhyamaka was equated with inherent existence, was previously used by the non-Buddhist philosopher Patañjali to indicate an individual object or an aggregation of qualities. Then it was juxtaposed with *guṇa* (qualities), and the Sāṃkhya said dravya had both an unchanging substrate as well as properties that changed. The Vaiśeṣika had yet another meaning for dravya, and the Jains defined it as existence (S. *sat*), which possessed arising, abiding, and passing away.

In addition to the sets of phenomena noted above, Abhidharmikas also began new modes of classification, such as the twenty-two faculties (*indriya, indriya*).[138] Later the Sarvāstivādins delineated a fivefold taxonomy of phenomena: form, primary minds, mental factors, abstract composites (S. *cittaviprayuktasaṃskāra*), and unconditioned or permanent phenomena (S. *asaṃskṛta*). Like the sūtras, this classification differentiates form and mind. However, now mental factors—which the Sarvāstivāda list as forty-six in number—are distinguished from primary minds and given their own category. In addition, there are new categories of phenomena—abstract composites and unconditioned phenomena—that were not initially listed in the five aggregates, twelve sense sources, and eighteen constituents. Abstract composites are impermanent phenomena that are neither form nor mind. Unconditioned phenomena include not only nirvāṇa and unconditioned space but also other unchanging phenomena.

It is hard to know to what extent people previously had conceptualized such groups, and to what extent these new categories were the result of questions and debates that arose after the Buddha's life. Viewed from a historical perspective, these new developments in understanding the Buddha's teachings led to the creation of new classes of phenomena. Although the previous classifications into the five aggregates and so forth were useful to realize that there is no self among the components of the person, later there was more concern with ontology. Also, because more people had engaged in analysis over the years, more dharmas, each with its own distinctive name and function, were identified.

Previously dharmas were seen as impermanent processes and events that mutually condition one another. Adding the category of unconditioned phenomena changed that because permanent phenomena were said to have a function, which distinguished them as existents and as dharmas. But unlike conditioned phenomena, their function was not to produce an effect. For example, the function of unconditioned space was to give material objects a place to occur. According to the Sarvāstivāda Abhidharma text the *Great Detailed Explanation* (*Mahāvibhāṣā Śāstra*), space was a real entity, a dharma, not a designation (*prajñaptita*). Furthermore, the Sarvāstivādins said that all phenomena, be they conditioned or unconditioned, had a fixed inherent nature (*svabhāva*) and existed substantially as real entities (S. *dravyatā*) in all three times—past, present, and future.

Meanwhile, the word *svabhāva* continued to change. In the canonical texts, own-nature was juxtaposed to other-nature and said to be the criterion by which dharmas are included in one category or another. In other words, dharmas and categories are defined by their svabhāva; they do not possess a separate nature but are constituted of and determined by their svabhāva. The Sarvāstivādas began the transition of the meaning of svabhāva from phenomena having their own-nature to their having an inherent nature.

## *Some Reflections*

I (Chodron) would like to offer some reflections, rudimentary as they are, so that we see the Buddha's teachings in the context of the circumstances in which they blossomed and how the change in those circumstances influenced the explanations of the teachings by future generations. Too often some of us see the Buddhadharma we are taught as immune to external influences such as culture, politics, the economy, science, and so forth. While this topic is very broad, I will just mention a few points.

At the time of the early Abhidharmikas and the early Indian Buddhist pandits of the Nālandā tradition, India had many sects of renunciants, each with its own doctrine. Their panditas and teachers engaged in a lively culture of debate, whereby the disciples of those who could not maintain their assertions in the face of reasoning converted and became followers of those who could. At the same time as each party defended their own system, they were being challenged to explain various points in more depth, leading to the evolution of beliefs and the expansion of topics to debate. The Buddhism that has come to us now is a product of that. Although the true Dharma does not change, its outward expression and some of the topics it deems important change with time.

Topics that were of great importance in Tibet in the seventh century, the fifteenth century, and at present are not necessarily the same ones discussed by the early Abhidharmikas or the ones of interest in contemporary Theravāda studies. One reason for this is that questions and debates appeared gradually over time. Another is that certain topics were of more or less interest to people in different places and cultures. Let's look at some instances of this.

The Pāli Abhidharma does not speak of partless particles, a topic that is still widely refuted in contemporary Tibetan studies. In the Pāli

Abhidharma, the four great elements are not spoken of as particles, but as qualities, and the combination of the four great elements and the four secondary qualities are considered the smallest units of form. From this viewpoint, these smallest units of form are interdependent and arise and cease due to causes and conditions; they have parts. The Sarvāstivādins, on the other hand, assert partless particles. The Yogācāra and Madhyamaka refutations of partless particles, therefore, are in response to the Sarvāstivādins, not the Pāli Abhidharmikas.

In the canonical Pāli Abhidharma texts and the Indian and Sri Lankan commentaries, there is no mention of phenomena being truly existent or non-truly existent. It seems that the term "true existence" came into use later.[139] Early on svabhāva—own-nature or intrinsic nature—meant that dharmas have their own conventional entity. Different sects, both Buddhist and non-Buddhist, had their own meanings for that term, many of which were ambiguous. The expressions "inherently existent" and "existent by their own characteristics" were not used.

The same is true for the early Sarvāstivāda Abhidharma, but because of their substantialist assertion that dharmas substantially exist in all three times, it seems they were more inclined to accept reified ways of existence. Thus, the Madhyamaka negation of inherent existence and existing by its own characteristics is especially in response to the views of the Sarvāstivādins and Vaibhāṣikas.

In the early Pāli Abhidharma as well as the early Sarvāstivāda Abhidharma, the terms "selflessness of persons" and "selflessness of phenomena" are not found. The Pāli commentators explicitly stated that the aggregates are not the self and are not objects of use of a self, and they assumed that everything—persons and phenomena—existed dependently. They refuted assertions of non-Buddhist schools that people and phenomena are created by an external creator or that they are produced from an absolute substance that is their substrata—ideas that future generations said were acquired and not innate afflictive views. Instead, Pāli Abhidharmikas said a person is a designation on a collection of impersonal material and mental dharmas.[140]

Looking from a historical perspective, I find the evolving meanings and usages of words fascinating. There was no mention of ultimate and conventional in the early Abhidharmas. When the term "ultimate" was introduced in the Pāli Abhidharma, it was ascribed to the dharmas, meaning that they are the basic things out of which minds and matter are composed. Similarly, the meaning of "own-nature," "own-characteristics," and "specific and general characteristics" evolved over the centuries within each tradition. Nor is the term "object of negation" found in either the sūtras or Pāli commentaries.

It would be very interesting to research the evolving meanings of some of the prominent terms now used when investigating the deeper mode of existence of phenomena and to explore the new philosophical terms that have arisen over the centuries. This would be a great topic for a doctoral dissertation.

The Abhidharma began in order to formulate the Buddha's teachings into a philosophy and a system for the purpose of furthering the Buddhist practitioners' aspiration for liberation. It was used as an aid to meditation on not-self in that it analyzed complex mental and material phenomena so that practitioners could see there is no findable person in the aggregates and no primal substance in material. Because the Abhidharmikas also emphasized synthesis of the dharmas, their explanations also aided practitioners in understanding dependent arising.

As time went on, ontological issues arose and became prominent, especially with the introduction of the term and concept of *svabhāva/sabhāva*. While this term was not used by the Buddha in the sūtras and is rarely found in the Pāli canon in general, it became an important concept in post-canonical times. Furthermore, later scholar-adepts drew out the epistemological implications of the early Abhidharma, expounding on the various types of cognizers and how objects are known by them. Add to this the ideas found in the Perfection of Wisdom sūtras, and there is an abundance of theories to debate and to employ in meditation.

Many texts and topics studied in contemporary Tibetan Buddhism, such as paths and grounds (T. *sa lam*), have their roots in the early Abhidharma works that described the stages of realization of disciples (śrāvakas and solitary realizers). To these were added descriptions of the bodhisattva grounds from Mahāyāna sūtras, such as the *Sūtra of the Ten Grounds*. Indian sages such as Maitreya and Asaṅga elaborated on the paths and grounds of the three vehicles, and from all this material Tibetan scholars later developed the genre of texts known as Paths and Grounds describing the paths and grounds of the three vehicles from the Svātantrika as well as the Prāsaṅgika viewpoints. These are included in the current monastic curriculum.

The Collected Topics texts (*Dudra*) and Mind and Awareness (*Blo rig*) texts studied in contemporary Tibetan monasteries also have their origins in these early Abhidharma texts. The scheme in which all phenomena are categorized into permanent (*nitya*, *nicca*) and thing (S. *bhāva*), the subcategories of these two, the classifications of the various types of causes and effects, and the systematization of the types of minds and mental factors all originate in the Abhidharma. The interrelationships among the minds and mental factors and the causes of cognition likewise follow from the early Abhidharma texts.

Having a historical perspective on the development of ideas within Buddhism helps us to understand the various theories and the great Indian sages who were their proponents. It also illustrates why certain issues were and continue to be so important. As Buddhist doctrines encounter Western philosophy, new questions and topics of discussion will emerge. How will these be dealt with using the richness of the scriptural tradition as a resource? The question of free will and predetermination—so prominent in Western philosophy—was not examined by the great minds of India, Sri Lanka, China, and Tibet. Why was this topic so uninteresting that it didn't even occur to them? How can Buddhist tenets be applied to discuss it now? Similarly, the question of the interdependence of brain and mind—a non-issue in ancient cultures—is another area where Buddhist philosophy will develop in modern times.

## *The Abhidharmikas and Later Indian Philosophers*

Because the Middle Way is studied in depth before the Abhidharma in the Tibetan monastic curriculum, and because the historical development of ideas in Buddhism is not emphasized in their education, practitioners in the Tibetan tradition may not see the connection between the development of the Abhidharma and the Middle Way as taught by Nāgārjuna.

In the Pāli sūtras, the Buddha does not assert inherent existence, nor does he deny it. Sometimes when the Buddha talks of not-self in the Pāli sūtras, he negates the aggregates being a person. At other times it seems that he is negating the aggregates having their own inherent nature, although he does not use that terminology. In Pāli sūtras, the Buddha explains how phenomena are subject to constant arising and passing away. Can someone who has clear meditative and experiential insight with deep mindfulness of the continuous/constant passing away of the aggregates still assert that they have an inherent essence that exists from one moment to the next?

Antecedents to Nāgārjuna's thoughts and writings exist in the Pāli tradition, as they surely did in all early schools. The format as well as the content of Nāgārjuna's famous tetralemma that rejects arising from self, other, both, and causelessly is found in the Pāli sūtras, when in the *Book of Causation* (SN 12.17) the naked ascetic Kassapa asks the Buddha if suffering is created by oneself, another, both oneself and another, or fortuitously. The Buddha responded, "It is not so" to each option.

The idea that some phenomena are mental constructs imputed by the mind was initially spelled out in the early Abhidharma literature. The implications of this idea were drawn out by Indian masters and their Tibetan descendants. For many Indian masters, mental constructs are juxtaposed with "real" phenomena (which each school defines slightly differently), so that various phenomena are said to have different degrees or types of existence. In his *Treatise on the Middle Way,* Nāgārjuna examines many of the same topics as the Abhidharmikas—causality; motion; the sense sources; aggregates; elements; arising, abiding, and ceasing; essence; time; and becoming and destruction—and concludes that there are not different degrees of existence but that all phenomena equally exist by mere imputation.

Many of the topics explored by early Sarvāstivāda Abhidharmikas and unpacked by later commentators became the basis of the Madhyamaka critique. Of the various early Buddhist schools, the Sarvāstivāda were very substantialist. The meanings of many terms—for example, "own-nature" and "own-characteristics"—took on different meanings for different people and schools. In addition, these meanings changed over time, and new philosophical terms became popular. The writings of Indian Mahāyāna panditas responded to these old and new words and their diverse meanings. For example, later scholar-adepts questioned: What is the difference between an object having its own-nature and existing by its own-nature? Can an object have its own characteristics but not exist by its own characteristics? The various philosophical schools that developed in India have their own definitions of these terms and their own positions on these questions.

Because Nāgārjuna lived for some time in North India, where the Sarvāstivādins and the Vaibhāṣikas were strong, he likely had more contact with these schools. Thus his refutation of inherent existence and existence by its own characteristics was directed at their assertions when he clarified the meaning of the Middle Way free from the two extremes.

Many of the topics that are presently issues of debate or issues of great importance in the Tibetan Gelug understanding of emptiness were not considered by the Pāli tradition or other early schools. For example, the Pāli tradition assumed that people had a common conventional understanding of the word "mine" and did not go into lengthy discussions about the meaning of "mine" in view of a personal identity grasping I and mine. In the same vein, in the Pāli canon the Buddha does not state that phenomena exist inherently, nor does he say that there is only the selflessness of persons and no selflessness of phenomena. None of these terms were in common usage until later, and even then, their meaning evolved over time as the great Buddhist thinkers explored different areas.

Although my knowledge is just in its infancy, if we approach the Pāli sūtras with a fresh mind, we will see tantalizing hints of Nāgārjuna's philosophy in them. Similarly, when we approach the Abhidharma texts of the various early schools, we will see the development of ideas that led to Nāgārjuna's refutation of the inherent existence of all phenomena. Some of the ideas found in the canonical Abhidharma and its later commentaries are ones that Nāgārjuna refuted, whereas others supported his refutation of inherent existence.

# Notes

1. You'll find discussion of the Vinaya, samādhi, insight, and the thirty-seven harmonies with awakening in *Following in the Buddha's Footsteps.*
2. It seems that both these Sanskrit terms are not found in Buddhist Sanskrit literature.
3. This is according to the Prāsaṅgikas. For followers of the Tathāgatagarbha philosophy in China, "suchness" has a different meaning.
4. For more on the three turnings of the Dharma wheel, see chapter 9 of *Approaching the Buddhist Path.*
5. The three kinds of faith are admiring faith, aspiring faith, and believing faith. See chapter 9 of *Approaching the Buddhist Path.*
6. These are the three Perfection of Wisdom sūtras: the extensive sūtra in one hundred thousand lines (or verses), the middle-length sūtra in twenty-five thousand lines, and the condensed sūtra in eight thousand lines.
7. This refers to the three higher trainings in ethical conduct, concentration, and wisdom.
8. This refers to the initial, middle, and advanced levels of practitioners. See chapter 8 in *Approaching the Buddhist Path.*
9. Translated by the Venerable Geshe Lhakdor in Dharamsala, February 26, 2002; revised by Tenzin Wangdue, Nicholas Vreeland, and Jeremy Russell, December 2020.
10. Saying that someone is a student of Nāgārjuna doesn't mean that they met him directly during their lifetime, but that they followed his views.
11. For a full explanation of these, see chapter 3 of *In Praise of Great Compassion.*
12. Private correspondence, Geshe Dadul Namgyal, May 1, 2010.
13. In Gelug, the main tenet texts are *Great Exposition of Tenets* (*Grub mtha' chen mo*) by Jamyang Shepa; *Precious Garland of Tenets* (*Grub pa'i mtha'i rnam par bzhag pa rin po che'i phreng ba*) by Könchok Jigme Wongpo, Jamyang Shepa's incarnation; and *Ornament of the Mountain of Tenets* (*Grub mtha' lhun po'i mdzes rgyan*) by Changkya Rolpai Dorje. The main Nyingma tenet text, *Treasury of Tenets: Illuminating the Meaning of All Vehicles* (*Theg pa mtha' dag gi don gsal bar byed pa grub pa'i mtha' rin po che'i mdzod*), was written by Longchen Rabjam. Sakya Pandita's *Thorough Explanation of the Systems* (*Gzhung lugs legs par bshad pa*), also

known as *Differentiation of Tenets* (*Grub mtha' rnam 'byed*), is the main Sakya tenet text, and Taktsang Sherab Rinchen, a Sakya scholar, wrote *Explanation of "Freedom from Extremes through Knowing All Tenets"* (*Grub mtha' kun shes nas mtha' bral grub pa zhes bya ba'i bstan bcos*). A popular Kagyu and Rime tenet text was written by Jamgon Kongtrul Lodro Taye and is included in his masterpiece, *Treasury of Knowledge* (*Shes bya kun la khyab pe mdzod*), *Book Six, Part Three: Frameworks of Buddhist Philosophy.*

14. For an excellent discussion of the purpose of the tenet schools in the Gelug tradition see Blumenthal, *Ornament of the Middle Way*, 227–32.
15. Please see chapter 4, "The Spread of the Buddhadharma and Buddhist Canons," in *Approaching the Buddhist Path* for comments on the early meaning of the name Theravāda.
16. The other five treatises on emptiness that Nāgārjuna is said to have written are *Precious Garland of Advice for the King* (*Ratnāvalī*), *Refutations of Objections* (*Vigrahavyāvartanī*), *Seventy Stanzas on Emptiness* (*Śūnyatāsaptati*), *Sixty Stanzas of Reasoning* (*Yuktiṣaṣṭikākārikā*), and *Treatise Called the "Finely Woven"* (*Vaidalyasūtranāma*).
17. Nowadays the debate continues whether, according to the Prāsaṅgika system, a syllogism is necessary to generate the correct view.
18. Also called the "self-cognizing mind" (T. *rang rig*).
19. The two *Knowledges* are the *Treasury of Knowledge* by Vasubandhu and the *Compendium of Knowledge* by Asaṅga.
20. See Cozort and Preston, *Buddhist Philosophy*; Tenzin Yangzom, *Presentation of Buddhist Tenets by Jetsun Chokyi Gyaltsen: Tibetan, English, Mandarin*; Geshé Namgyal Wangchen, *Brief Presentation of the Fundamentals of Buddhist Tenets and Modern Science.*
21. Some translators have translated *'dzin* as "conception" and thus say "the conception of true existence." This translation can be misleading because we usually consider conception a rather gross mind, whereas grasping true existence is an innate mind that is subtler.
22. Tibetan scholars say that all eighteen of the early Buddhist schools can be included under the heading of "Vaibhāṣika." However, modern scholars and most Buddhists in other Asian countries do not agree. Many modern scholars believe that the Vaibhāṣikas were a branch of the Sarvāstivāda because the Vaibhāṣikas' main text, the *Mahāvibhāṣā Śāstra* (*Great Detailed Explanation*), is a commentary on the final book of the Sarvāstivāda Abhidharma, the *Foundation of Knowledge* (*Jñānaprasthāna*).
23. The same is true of form in general. A car is an example of form. A car is a conventional truth and imputedly exists, but form in general is not because when form is physically or mentally broken into smaller pieces, form is still present.
24. "Imputedly existent" and "substantially existent" have different meanings according to the tenet system. They are being used here as follows:
    - Vaibhāṣikas: Something is imputedly existent because when it is broken into smaller pieces or moments of time, it can no longer be ascertained. Some-

thing is substantially existent when it can be identified even when broken into smaller pieces or moments of time.

- Sautrāntikas up to Svātantrika Mādhyamikas: Something is imputedly existent when another object must be identified in order to identify it. It is substantially existent when it can be known directly, without another object being identified.
- Prāsaṅgikas: All phenomena are imputedly existent because they exist by being merely imputed by term and concept. Substantial existence is equivalent to inherent existence and nothing exists in that way.

For a different description of substantial existent and imputed existent according to the Drepung Gomang *Collected Topics* text, see Perdue, *Debate in Tibetan Buddhism*, 758–71.

25. That the Vaibhāṣikas and Sautrāntikas don't assert a selflessness of phenomena affects their tenets on other topics. For example, they accept that the five aggregates and the external environment truly exist and that the way they appear to direct perceivers is not erroneous—these things are truly existent as they appear to be. Since that is the case, the five aggregates and so forth are inherently polluted and can never be purified. Thus when arhats pass away and attain nirvāṇa without remainder, their polluted aggregates cease, as does the continuity of the person. For that reason, there are three final vehicles, and śrāvakas and solitary realizers will never enter the Mahāyāna and become buddhas. Since not everyone will become a buddha, their generating bodhicitta is not necessary. Because the aggregates and environment are inherently polluted, the Buddha as well as highly realized yogis do not see them as pure. Because the continuity of the person and aggregates ends with the attainment of nirvāṇa without remainder, they do not accept the four buddha kāyas, which include the truth body, which is a buddha's omniscient mind, and the two form bodies through which buddhas benefit sentient beings and lead them on the path.
26. In describing this, Tsongkhapa quoted the ninth chapter of the *Autocommentary on the Treasury of Knowledge*.
27. According to Prāsaṅgikas, substantial existence comes to the same point as objective or inherent existence. Although Prāsaṅgikas accept that some things are imputed existents as described by Asaṅga, they assert many levels of imputation. The one described above is coarse, while the subtlest meaning of imputed existent is that all phenomena exist by being *merely* imputed by mind and term. "Merely" excludes it being inherently existent.
28. It is called "Yogācāra" because its followers practice four yogic grounds: the yogic grounds of realizing the selflessness of persons, observing mind only, observing suchness, and dwelling in nonappearance.
29. *Grounds of Yogic Practice* (*Yogācārabhūmi*), *Compendium of Ascertainments* (*Nirṇayasaṃgraha*), *Compendium of Bases* (*Vastusaṃgraha*), *Compendium of Enumerations* (*Paryāyasaṃgraha*), *Compendium of Explanations* (*Vyākhyānasaṃgrahaṇī*). *Grounds of Yogic Practice* includes *Bodhisattva Grounds* (*Bodhisattvabhūmi*), *Śrāvaka Grounds* (*Śrāvakabhūmi*), and *Solitary Realizer Grounds* (*Pratyekabuddhabhūmi*).

30. *Inquiry into Relations* (*Sambandhaparīkṣā*), *Ascertainment of Reliable Cognition* (*Pramāṇaviniścaya*), *Commentary on Reliable Cognition* (*Pramāṇavārttika*), *Drops of Reasoning* (*Nyāyabindu*), *Drops of Logic* (*Hetubindu*), *Proof of Other Minds* (*Saṃtānāntarasiddhi*), and *Reasoning of Debate* (*Vādanyāya*).
31. "Posit" can either have the meaning to designate, which is done by a conceptual consciousness, or to establish, which can be done by a conceptual or nonconceptual consciousness.
32. Apperception (*svasaṃvedana*, T. *rang rig*) is rejected by the Vaibhāṣikas, Sautrāntika-Svātantrikas, and Prāsaṅgikas because if it existed, the subject and object of a cognition would be confused. Furthermore, there would be an infinite regress of apperception. Some scholars say the Sautrāntika Scripture Proponents also reject apperception.
33. Jamyang Shepa (1648–1721/22) has a unique perspective on the self-sufficient substantially existent person, saying that there are both coarse and subtle versions. Unlike grasping the coarse self-sufficient substantially existent person, grasping a subtle self-sufficient substantially existent person views the person and the mind-body as related, but still sees the person as the boss and the mind and body as the employees that the person leads and directs. The I is in control and dominates the aggregates, bossing them around. Here the boss is a worker just like the employees, but is more important and powerful than them. We experience this object of negation when we feel that there is an I that is one of the aggregates; for example, when the mental consciousness appears to be the I that controls the other aggregates. Jamyang Shepa says that this is the object of negation in the meditation on the selflessness of persons for all non-Prāsaṅgika schools. Its nonexistence is the subtle selflessness of a self-sufficient substantially existent person.
34. The five Saṃmitiya subschools of the Vaibhāṣikas assert a self-sufficient substantially existent person.
35. Not all imaginaries are findable when we seek the object that their term refers to, because some imaginaries are nonexistent. However, as a class, imaginaries exist and are findable when the object to which the term "imaginary" is attributed is sought.
36. This applies to modest-faculty disciples. For sharp-faculty disciples, the Buddha may teach Prāsaṅgika tenets directly.
37. The sequence described in detail is: first the aggregates appear to inherently exist, and ignorance grasps them as inherently existent. This is self-grasping of phenomena. The I is designated on the basis of the aggregates, and it too appears inherently existent. Grasping the I as inherently existent follows. This is the self-grasping of persons. The aggregates and other items are seen as "mine," which leads to attachment to *my* things. More afflictions ensue, polluted karma is created, and saṃsāra continues on.
38. Subtle afflictions that grasp inherent existence are a unique assertion of Prāsaṅgikas. Most of our daily life afflictions are coarse; they do not grasp inherent existence themselves but are supported by grasping a self-sufficient substantially existent person as well as grasping inherent existence.

39. In some cases the term "interpretable" is used, implying that we must interpret the meaning of a passage; at other times the word "provisional" is used, implying that the passage does not convey the final meaning. The Sanskrit term is the same in both cases.
40. MP 235.
41. See MP 268–69.
42. These Yogācārins say that when sharp-faculty disciples study the *Prajñāpāramitā Sūtras* of the second turning, they understand the Yogācāra explanation of the three natures and three non-natures without having to study sūtras of the third turning. However, modest-faculty Yogācāra disciples must study sūtras such as the *Sūtra Unraveling the Thought* to correctly understand the Yogācāra view of these topics.
43. See MP 315.
44. This argument is spelled out more elaborately in the first chapter in the section "Emptiness, Its Nature, Its Purpose, and Its Meaning."
45. It seems this text is not available in Sanskrit or Tibetan, but exists in Chinese as a set of gāthās attributed to Nāgārjuna.
46. A rough example of the meaning here is saying "one" presupposes more than one. If we say there is one cup, someone knows there are not two cups.
47. See chapters 6 and 9 in *Following in the Buddha's Footsteps* for more about objects of concentration in the Pāli and Sanskrit traditions.
48. For a more in-depth description of this process, see *Courageous Compassion*, chapters 8 onward.
49. The Sanskrit tradition would call this a direct perceiver of emptiness.
50. See *Courageous Compassion*, chapters 6 and 7, for more on the paths of the śrāvakas and solitary realizers.
51. See *The Foundation of Buddhist Practice*, 69–76.
52. Tsongkhapa, *The Great Exposition of Secret Mantra, Volume One: Tantra in Tibet*; commentary by the Dalai Lama; translation, editing, and explanatory material by Jeffrey Hopkins (Boulder, CO: Snow Lion, 2016), 214.
53. The observed or focal object can be understood in two ways: (1) It is the object that is the basis of observation of a particular characteristic. For example, for a mind perceiving the impermanence of a table, the table is the observed object and its impermanence is the aspected object (T. *rnam pa'i yul*). (2) It is the main object that the mind focuses on, such as the table.
54. The Yogācārins, however, consider consciousnesses that apprehend external objects or objects that are not the same nature as the consciousnesses perceiving them to be mistaken.
55. There are different opinions regarding this. Some people say that a single moon is the appearing object because it is what triggered the perception of a double moon, but other people say a single moon is not the appearing object because it is falsely perceived.
56. The observed object of this wisdom is the object whose mode of existence is analyzed and whose emptiness is realized. However, the observed object does not

appear to that wisdom directly realizing emptiness; only emptiness itself appears and is apprehended by that wisdom. The wisdom directly realizing the emptiness of I and mine directly realizes the emptiness of all phenomena.

57. "Superimposition" (*samāropa*, T. *sgro btags, sgro 'dogs*) refers to imputing something that does not exist—for example, the self of persons or the self of phenomena. These superimpositions are objects of negation.
58. Candrakīrti says (MMA 1.3cd):

> First, with the thought "I," the beings cling to a self;
> then, with the thought "mine," they become attached to things [such as the aggregates].

From Nāgārjuna's verse in *Precious Garland*, it seems that grasping the aggregates as truly existent arises prior to grasping the I as truly existent, but Candrakīrti seems to be saying the opposite, that first grasping I arises, then grasping the aggregates and becoming attached to them as mine. How do we resolve this seeming contradiction?

Nāgārjuna is describing the process by which self-grasping I arises—it is underpinned by having grasped the aggregates as inherently existent. For example, based on grasping a sad feeling as truly existent, we say "I am sad" and grasp the I as truly existent. Candrakīrti is speaking of the view of a personal identity in which the observed object is I or mine, not the aggregates. He is not saying that the self-grasping of persons precedes the self-grasping of the aggregates, but that grasping the I as inherently existent precedes grasping mine as inherently existent. "Mine" is another way of looking at the person. Although the notion of "mine" is based on things such as the aggregates—we say "this body is mine"—it does not grasp them as inherently existent; it grasps the I that makes things mine as inherently existent.

59. This differs from flashbacks and panic attacks caused by previous trauma.
60. The word *rtog pa* is the Tibetan translation for two Sanskrit words. The first is *kalpanā*, which has the meaning of conceptuality as described here. The second is investigation (*vitarka, vitakka*), which is a mental factor that engages with its object in a coarse way. It is also helpful to distinguish *rtog pa* from *rtogs pa*, which means realization (*adhigama*).
61. The meaning of conceptual consciousness and conceptual appearance is discussed in *The Foundation of Buddhist Practice*, 69–76.
62. See *Saṃsāra, Nirvāṇa, and Buddha Nature*, 20–21 and 107–8, for more on distorted conceptions.
63. In the homage in *Commentary on (Dignāga's) "Compendium of Reliable Cognition,"* Dharmakīrti pays homage to Buddha Śākyamuni by referring to him as "the one who has eliminated the net of conceptualizations." Here conceptualizations can be interpreted in two ways—as distorted conceptualizations such as self-grasping, or as conceptualizations in general. In terms of the inferential realization of emptiness, a conceptual consciousness that is an asset on the path, as a meditator advances on the path, the veil of conceptuality gradually falls away

and they see emptiness directly as it is. Such a nonconceptual realization has the power to eradicate afflictions completely. In the case of bodhicitta, it is said that a buddha's bodhicitta is also nonconceptual.

64. In the Sakya tradition, the meaning of "mind-basis-of-all" is different than in the Yogācāra system.
65. In this context, the term "mind" is used in a general sense that covers all types of cognitive events, without distinguishing between *sems* (mind) and *rig pa* (pristine awareness).
66. Of the three, understanding emptiness by hearing, thinking, and meditating, His Holiness is referring to the latter. By repeatedly meditating with a correct understanding of emptiness, an experience of emptiness will naturally arise.
67. Some scholars say that when meditating on the ultimate nature of the I, the I and emptiness appear to the inferential realization, but only emptiness is apprehended, whereas others say the I does not appear to this mind.
68. The Tibetan word *snang ba* can be translated as both appear (appearance) and perceive (perception). Cognitive obscurations are qualities of the subject, the mind that is obscured. They are not the object that the mind perceives. The "appearance" of inherent existence is the object or content of the mind that continues to perceive phenomena as inherently existent.
69. Please see *Saṃsāra, Nirvāṇa, and Buddha Nature*, 259–61, for more explanation on the two obscurations, and chapter 5 for more about afflictions, their seeds, and their latencies.
70. From "Recognizing My Mother" by Changkya Rolpai Dorje in *Songs of Spiritual Experience*, trans. Thupten Jinpa and Jas Elsner (Boston: Shambhala Publications, 2000), 109.
71. For more on these three types of phenomena, see *The Foundation of Buddhist Practice*, 18.
72. For more about the valid sense of I, see Khensur Jampa Tegchok, *Insight into Emptiness*, ed. Thubten Chodron (Somerville, MA: Wisdom Publications, 2012), 86–92.
73. Jamyang Shepa says grasping a self-sufficient substantially existent person has two forms: (1) The coarse form grasps the person and the aggregates as having discordant characteristics. He says this is what the Svātantrika and below assert as the conceived object of innate self-grasping of persons. (2) The subtle form grasps the I and the aggregates as having concordant characteristics. He says grasping this self is the grasping that Candrakīrti says is extinguished on the fourth ground. For more about Jamyang Shepa's presentation of the levels of the object of negation for the selflessness of persons and the type of self-sufficient substantially existent person refuted by the lower systems, see MP 651–54.
74. In the Gelug tradition, there is a debate about what "mine" refers to in the view of a personal identity. In both canonical and commentarial texts in the Pāli tradition, there does not seem to be a philosophical debate regarding the meaning of "mine."
75. The meaning of "emptiness dawns as the meaning of dependent arising" will be explored in more depth in volume 8 of the *Library of Wisdom and Compassion*.

76. There is a subtler level of disparity in that the reflection itself mistakenly appears to exist from its own side. This is explained further in volume 9 of the *Library of Wisdom and Compassion*. However, now we are using the reflection of a face as an analogy.
77. Stream-enterers have the initial realization of selflessness and will become arhats within seven lives at the most. Once-returners will be reborn in the desire realm one more time before attaining arhatship, while nonreturners will not. Arhats (foe destroyers) have attained liberation. See chapter 1 in *Following in the Buddha's Footsteps* and chapters 6 and 7 in *Courageous Compassion* for more on these four pairs of Saṅgha in the Fundamental Vehicle.
78. Of the 108 phenomena, fifty-three are from the afflictive class and fifty-five from the pure class. The fifty-three afflictive phenomena are: 1–5 five aggregates; 6–11 six sense faculties (eye, ear, nose, tongue, body, mental); 12–17 six consciousnesses that depend on the six sense faculties; 18–23 six objects of those six consciousnesses; 24–29 six contacts that arise due to the coming together of a sense faculty, consciousness, and object; 30–35 six feelings that arise dependent on the six contacts; 36–41 six elements (earth, water, fire, wind, space, consciousness); 42–53 twelve links of dependent origination.

    The fifty-five phenomena of the pure class are: 1–6 six perfections; 7–24 eighteen emptinesses; 25 four establishments of mindfulness; 26 four supreme strivings; 27 four bases of spiritual power; 28 five faculties; 29 five powers; 30 seven awakening factors; 31 eightfold path of the āryas (note that 25–31 are the thirty-seven harmonies with awakening); 32 four truths of the āryas; 33 four dhyānas; 34 four immeasurables; 35 four formless absorptions; 36 eight liberations; 37 nine serial absorptions; 38 paths of insight (concentrations on the three doors of liberation); 39 five superknowledges; 40 four concentrations (going as a hero, sky treasury, stainless, and loftily looking lion); 41 four doors of retention (of patience, secret speech, words, meaning); 42 ten powers of a buddha; 43 four kinds of self-confidence (four fearlessnesses); 44 four sciences; 45 great love; 46 great compassion; 47 eighteen unshared qualities of a buddha; 48–52 five beings who actualize the paths (stream-enterers, once-returners, nonreturners, arhats, solitary realizers); 53–55 three knowers (knower of the base, knower of paths, exalted knower of all aspects).
79. See chapter 2 of *The Foundation of Buddhist Practice* for more about the importance of syllogisms and the three criteria.
80. See chapter 2 of *Approaching the Buddhist Path* and chapter 7 of *The Foundation of Buddhist Practice* for more about rebirth.
81. Truly existent assertions are assertions that the opponent claims exist truly.
82. India's classical period was approximately 320–543, during the Gupta Empire.
83. For more on the coarse and subtle four truths, see chapter 1 of *Saṃsāra, Nirvāṇa, and Buddha Nature.*
84. Chokyi Gyaltsen says impermanence, the first of the sixteen characteristics of the four truths, is momentariness. Because this is the same for all tenet systems, it

cannot be divided into coarse and subtle, like the other fifteen attributes. Jamyang Shepa says there are both coarse and subtle impermanence.

85. http://emahofoundation.org/images/documents/DiamondSutraText.pdf, 4.
86. See chapter 9 of *Courageous Compassion*.
87. See Shenghai Li, "Candrakīrti's Āgama: A Study of the Concept and Uses of Scripture in Classical Indian Buddhism," PhD diss., University of Wisconsin–Madison, 2012, 207–10.
88. Similarly, some Mahāyāna practitioners may hold Fundamental Vehicle tenets and not realize the emptiness of inherent existence, while others may hold Prāsaṅgika tenets and realize subtle emptiness.
89. Unlike other Buddhists, Vaibhāṣikas claim that functioning thing, existent, and knowable object are equivalent. They divide functioning things into those that are permanent and those that are impermanent. For them a functioning thing does not necessarily arise from a cause and produce a result. Unconditioned space is a permanent functioning thing because it performs the function of allowing movement to occur.
90. See chapters 12–14 of *Saṃsāra, Nirvāṇa, and Buddha Nature* for a more extensive explanation of buddha nature.
91. See chapter 11 in *Saṃsāra, Nirvāṇa, and Buddha Nature* for an explanation of nirvāṇa and its relationship to emptiness.
92. Nirvāṇa is called "the deathless" in the sense that once nirvāṇa has been attained, there is no more birth in saṃsāra, and without birth, there is no death.
93. For instructions on the development of concentration, serenity, and dhyāna, see chapters 4–10 in *Following in the Buddha's Footsteps*.
94. Because the level of concentration with which one embarks on insight meditation may differ, the level of concentration at the time of breakthrough to the unconditioned does as well. According to the *Visuddhimagga* and Abhidhamma, a meditator practices insight in a state of concentration that is not dhyāna. Other commentaries call this state *vipassanā-samādhi*. Then, when the meditator makes the breakthrough to the supramundane path, the mind naturally goes into a dhyānic state. For a meditator who proceeds by the path of "dry insight" (insight without prior attainment of dhyāna), the path and fruit will occur at the level of the first dhyāna, but if the meditator has previously attained dhyāna, the path and fruit will occur at the level of dhyāna attained (see Vism 21.112ff.).
95. This is predicated on meditation on the four establishments of mindfulness. For instruction on this practice, see chapters 12–14 in *Following in the Buddha's Footsteps*.
96. The expression "mature or ripe faculties" appears in both the Sanskrit and Pāli traditions, as does the differentiation of practitioners according to their faculties being either sharp or modest. In the Pāli tradition, faculties usually refer to the five faculties of faith, effort, mindfulness, concentration, and wisdom. In the living meditative tradition of the Theravāda, "mature faculties" often has the broader meaning of being ready to gain insight or realization or having enough pāramīs to attain realization. Here "pāramīs" refer to the merit created through the practice

of the ten pāramīs of the Theravāda path, which everyone, not just those on the bodhisattva path, must fulfill to attain the clear realization of nirvāṇa.

97. In addition to the above three types of abandonment, there are two more. One is *subsiding abandonment*, which is the subsiding of the defilements at the four moments of fruition that follow the four supramundane paths; this abandonment occurs at the moment of becoming a stream-enterer, once-returner, nonreturner, and arhat. The second is *abandonment by escape*, which is nirvāṇa in which all conditioned phenomena have been abandoned.
98. In Tibetan these are referred to as the appropriated aggregates. I (Chodron) find the Pāli term more compelling.
99. The difference between the conceit "I am" and the view of the self is subtle. The view of self takes one or another of the five aggregates or the collection of the aggregates and grasps it to be the self. The subtle view of self arises in all beings, whether they know philosophy or not. Some people speculate on what the self really is and develop a variety of complex explanations that they grasp to be true. Developing philosophical stances is a coarser form of the view of self.

    The coarser form of conceit is pride, which can be based on the five aggregates, although it does not grasp them as our self. For example the pride thinking "I'm attractive" is based on the body, but it doesn't grasp the body to be the self, and the pride thinking "I scored well on this test because I'm intelligent" is based on the mind, but doesn't grasp the mind to be the self.

    The conceit "I am" is much subtler; it is the spontaneous idea that I exist. This idea "I exist" does not grasp one or another aggregate to be the self; it is simply the thought that a true, findable I exists. This idea arises even in stream-enterers, once-returners, and nonreturners who have eliminated the view of a personal identity. These āryas know the thought "I am" is false, whereas when an ordinary person thinks "I am," they hold it as true and let it influence how they think and act.
100. The twelve sources consist of six external sense sources (forms, sounds, odors, tastes, tangible objects, and other phenomena) and six internal sense sources (eye, ear, nose, tongue, body, and mental sense faculties).
101. Sentient beings especially crave the neutral feeling in the meditative absorption of the fourth dhyāna and the four formless absorptions. This neutral feeling is so peaceful and satisfying that subtle attachment can arise for it, binding sentient beings in saṃsāra.
102. Steven Collins, *Selfless Persons* (Cambridge: Cambridge University Press, 1982), 129–30.
103. See chapters 7 and 8 in *Saṃsāra, Nirvāṇa, and Buddha Nature* for an explanation of the twelve links of dependent origination.
104. The eighteen constituents encompass all existents, both permanent and impermanent. The eighteen are the six objects, six sense faculties, and six consciousnesses.
105. Knowledge and vision of things as they really are is one of eighteen types of insight knowledge.
106. Based on the early sūtras in the Pāli canon and their commentaries, Buddhaghoṣa

in the *Path of Purification* set out the stages of insight knowledge (*vipassanā-ñāṇa*) in detail. Beginning with the early Abhidhamma schools and continuing through the arising of Mahāyāna, each Buddhist tradition worked out the process of developing insight in its own way.

107. Spoken of in the commentaries and the Abhidhamma, but not the sūtras, the bhavaṅga is a passive, underlying stream of consciousness from which active consciousness arises. It occurs in the absence of any cognitive process and serves to connect all active states of consciousness; it is not a permanent consciousness or self. It is included in the mental source because due to it, active mental consciousness arises. At the microscopic level of individual mind moments in the waking state, the mind could be going in and out of the bhavaṅga so quickly that we do not notice it. During sleep, the mind is in bhavaṅga for a longer time, emerging to dream and then returning to dreamless sleep in the bhavaṅga. The bhavaṅga is also present when fainting.
108. Sometimes it is said that the consciousness "goes out to the object." This is speaking metaphorically and indicates that the consciousness is receptive and cognizes the object. It does not mean the consciousness leaves the body and goes to the place where the sight or sound is. At other times it is said that the object comes into the consciousness through the sense doors. This, too, is metaphoric and indicates that cognition of object by the consciousness occurs.
109. Applying Madhyamaka philosophy, the quotation above emphasizes the dependent nature of the body and its being designated in dependence on the basis of designation, the collection of elements. This paragraph speaks of both the selflessness of phenomena (the body) and selflessness of persons.
110. This is one of the few places that shows how the five aggregates arise through the six sense sources. Usually these two sets—the aggregates and the sense sources—are discussed separately. In this case, Śāriputra brings them together in a way that demonstrates their interdependent and related natures.
111. Interestingly, this statement does not seem to be said by the Buddha in any of the Pāli sūtras. But not everything the Buddha said was necessarily recorded and transmitted in a complete form throughout the centuries due to human error.
112. This is one way of describing the dependent arising of the five aggregates. The forward sequence of the twelve links of dependent origination is another way to explain the dependent arising of the five aggregates. There are other ways as well.
113. The Pāli Abhidharma, extant in the Theravāda tradition, explains many more topics than mentioned here, including consciousness, mental factors, cognitive processes, realms of rebirth, karma, the process of death and rebirth, matter, defilements, dhyānas and formless absorptions, meditation objects, conditionality, paths and results, and purification. The material covered in this coda is only a very thin slice of the Pāli Abhidharma.
114. The title of an Abhidharma work from the Dharmaguptaka school preserved in Chinese translation is equivalent to the Śāriputra-Abhidharma-Śāstra in Sanskrit.
115. See chapter 4 of *Approaching the Buddhist Path* for more about the Buddhist canons and the three baskets of teachings, of which Abhidharma is the third.

116. See chapters 12 and 13 in *Following in the Buddha's Footsteps* for an explanation of the four establishments of mindfulness.
117. In Vasubandhu's *Treasury of Knowledge*, the twelve sources and eighteen constituents include permanent phenomena such as unconditioned space and nirvāṇa. In the Pāli Abhidharma, the twelve sources and eighteen constituents include nirvāṇa, but there are no other permanent dharmas.
118. Vaibhāṣikas and Sautrāntikas assert partless particles (T. *rdul phran cha med*), whereas Yogācārins and Mādhyamikas refute their existence.
119. See Bhikkhu Bodhi, *Comprehensive Manual of Abhidharma*, 25–26, for more discussion of ultimate reality.
120. Yinshun, a great Chinese scholar-adept in the twentieth century, says this text is a very early Abhidharma text of the Sthaviravāda school. Most Western scholars say it is a Dharmaguptaka text. The Dharmaguptakas were a branch of the Vibhajyavādins, which came under the division of the Sthavira branch of the early Saṅgha (as contrasted with the Mahāsāṃghika), so there is no contradiction between what Yinshun says and the view of Western scholars.
121. It seems that for the ancient Pāli commentators, *sabhāva* ("own-nature") has multiple meanings, some acceptable, others not. The same point was made by Mādhyamikas as well, as will be explained in a future volume.
122. *The Discourse on the Root of Existence* (*Mūlapariyāya Sutta and Its Commentaries*), trans. Bhikkhu Bodhi (Kandy: Buddhist Publication Society, 2006), 38.
123. Tibetan texts on Mind and Awareness (*Blo rig*) list five omnipresent mental factors.
124. The topic of definitive and interpretable (provisional) teachings is emphasized in Tibetan Buddhism as well. See Robert A. F. Thurman, *The Central Philosophy of Tibet: A Study and Translation of Jey Tsonkhapa's Essence of True Eloquence* (Princeton, NJ: Princeton University Press, 1991).
125. There is a parallel distinction in the explanation of the Prāsaṅgika-Mādhyamika. Emptiness of inherent existence, which is ultimate truth, is definitive, as are the scriptures that explain it. Conventional truths and the scriptures that explain them are interpretable or provisional.
126. The Cowherds, *Moonshadows: Conventional Truth in Buddhist Philosophy* (Oxford: Oxford University Press, 2001), 6.
127. The non-Theravāda schools consider cold as an attribute of water-element, but according to the Theravāda, cold is the relative absence of heat, which is represented by the temperature-element.
128. In general, scholars of history say the Vaibhāṣika was a later branch that developed out of the Sarvāstivāda school.
129. Y. Karunadasa, *The Buddhist Theory of Matter as Presented in the Theravāda Buddhism with Special Reference to the Abhidharmma*, PhD diss., University of London, 1963, 344–45.
130. According to the tenet systems presented in the Gelug branch of Tibetan Buddhism, Vaibhāṣikas and Sautrāntikas accepted partless particles, whereas Yogācārins and Mādhyamikas refuted their existence. However, some Gelug scholars say that one branch of the Sautrāntika do not accept partless particles.

131. Paramāṇu and kalāpa are the same thing. It is called *paramāṇu*, or atom, because it is the smallest. It is called *kalāpa*, or cluster, because although it is the smallest, it is a cluster or group of material elements.
132. Karunadasa, *Buddhist Theory of Matter*, 368–69.
133. This view is shared by the Yogācārins and Mādhyamikas. Whatever arises is perishing; there is no need for an external force to operate on it to cause its cessation. Arising due to causes and conditions alone is enough to ensure its immediate cessation. According to the Gelug tradition, the Sautrāntikas, Yogācārins, and Mādhyamikas say that the characteristics of a thing include three activities: the activities of arising, of abiding or persisting, and of ceasing. Vaibhāṣikas say they are separate agents that act on forms and so forth, causing them to arise, abide, and cease. Prāsaṅgikas assert that the arising, abiding, and ceasing of impermanent things occur simultaneously. A thing's arising is its being the new creation of what didn't exist; its abiding is its similarity to what preceded it; its aging is its being a different entity from the previous moment, and its ceasing (disintegrating) is its not lasting another moment.
134. These are the kind of conundrums that arise when we see phenomena as inherently existent. Prāsaṅgikas use them to refute inherent existence. See chapters 11 and 15 of Āryadeva's *The Four Hundred* for examples of this.
135. See MMK chapter 2 on "Coming and Going" for another perspective on movement. Tsongkhapa's commentary, *Ocean of Reasoning*, helps to explicate this.
136. In Y. Karunadasa, *The Theravāda Abhidhamma: Inquiry into the Nature of Conditioned Existence* (Boston: Wisdom Publications, 2019), 274.
137. Some Theravādins identify this school as the Kashmiri Vaibhāṣikas.
138. The term *indriya* is also used to refer to the five sense faculties as well as the group of five faculties in the thirty-seven harmonies with awakening.
139. I asked Bhikkhu Bodhi about this and in private correspondence, May 5, 2010, he wrote, "Interestingly, I just did a search for *saccasiddhi* (the Pāli equivalent of the Sanskrit term *satyasiddhi*, or true existence) in the Sixth Council Tripiṭaka CD. It shows three results. They all refer to the same passage in three different subcommentaries. But the meaning is quite different from *satyasiddhi* as 'true existence.' Here the meaning is 'success through truthfulness.' The text is explaining the order of the ten pāramīs in the Theravāda tradition and says that 'determination comes immediately after truthfulness because there is the success of truthfulness through determination. . . .When one is bound to truthfulness, one remains unshakable in accord with one's precepts regarding generosity, and so forth.'"
140. This differs from Prāsaṅgikas, who say that a person is *imputed in dependence on* the collection of aggregates. Did the ancient scholars think of the difference between "dependent on" and "in dependence on"? It seems such issues arose much later, as debaters asked more and more questions.

# Glossary

*absolutism* (eternalism or permanence, *śāśvatānta, sassata*). The belief that phenomena inherently exist.

*abstract composites* (*viprayukta-saṃskāra*). Impermanent phenomena that are neither forms nor consciousnesses.

*access concentration* (P. *upacāra samādhi*). The preparatory stage of the first dhyāna. Here the five hindrances have been suppressed but the five absorption factors are not yet firm.

*acquired afflictions* (*parikalpita*, T. *kun btags*). Afflictions learned in this life through contact with false philosophies and psychologies.

*acquisition* (*prāpti*, T. *'thob pa*). Asserted by Vaibhāṣikas, it is like a rope that ensures karma will go from one life to the next.

*affirming negation* (*paryudāsapratiṣedha*, T. *ma yin dgag*). A negation that is realized upon explicitly eliminating an object of negation and that projects another phenomenon in the wake of that negation.

*afflictions* (*kleśa*). Mental factors that disturb the tranquility of the mind. These include disturbing emotions and wrong views.

*afflictive obscurations* (*kleśāvaraṇa*, T. *nyon mongs kyi sgrib pa*). Obscurations that mainly prevent liberation; afflictions and their seeds.

*aging* (*sthityanyathatva*, *thitassa annathatta*). Alteration of that which exists.

*aggregates* (*skandha*, *khandha*). The four or five components that make up a living being: form (except for beings born in the formless realm), feelings, discriminations, miscellaneous factors, and consciousnesses.

*analysis* (*vicāra*, T. *dpyod pa*). A mental factor that examines an object in detail.

*analytical meditation* (*vicārabhāvanā*, T. *dpyad sgom*). Meditation done to understand an object.

*appearing object* (*pratibhāsa-viṣaya*, T. *snang yul*). The object that actually appears to a consciousness. The appearing object of a conceptual consciousness is a conceptual appearance of something.

*apperception* (*svasaṃvedana*, T. *rang rig*): a "secondary" consciousness that knows the main consciousness itself directly and nondualistically. Asserted by some tenet systems, it is negated by Prāsaṅgikas and others.

*apprehended object* (engaged object, *muṣṭibandhaviṣaya*, T. *'dzin stangs kyi yul*). The main object with which the mind is concerned—that is, the object that the mind is getting at or understands.

*arhat* (P. *arahant*, T. *dgra bcom pa*). Someone who has eliminated all afflictive obscurations and attained liberation.

*arising/production* (*utpāda*, *uppāada*, T. *skye ba*). The coming into being of an impermanent phenomenon that wasn't present before.

*ārya* (P. *ariya*). Someone who has directly and nonconceptually realized the emptiness of inherent existence.

*autonomous syllogism* (*svatantra-prayoga*, T. *rang rgyud kyi sbyor ba*). A syllogism in which the parties involved agree that all parts of the syllogism inherently exist; Svātantrikas' preferred form of reasoning.

*basis of designation* (basis of imputation, T. *gdags gzhi*). The collection of parts or factors in dependence on which an object is designated or imputed.

*bhavaṅga*. A passive stream of subliminal consciousness that exists during all occasions when a clearly cognizing consciousness is not present. It is described in the Pāli commentaries and Abhidharma but not in the sūtras.

*bodhicitta*. A main mental consciousness induced by an aspiration to bring about the welfare of others and accompanied by an aspiration to attain full awakening oneself.

*bodhisattva*. Someone who has spontaneous bodhicitta and is training to become a buddha.

*bodhisattva ground*. A consciousness in the continuum of an ārya bodhisattva characterized by wisdom and compassion. It is the basis for the development of good qualities and the basis for the eradication of ignorance and mistaken appearances.

*brahmacarya*. Pure conduct, especially sexual abstinence.

*character natureless* (*laksaṇa-niḥsvabhāvatā*, T. *mtshan nyid ngo bo nyid med pa*). A quality of imaginaries that do not exist by their own characteristics.

*characteristics* (*lakṣaṇa*, T. *mtshan nyid*). Attributes or features of an object.

*coarse afflictions*. Afflictions stemming from grasping a self-sufficient substantially existent person, as contrasted with subtle afflictions.

*cognitive faculty/sensory faculty* (*indriya*). The subtle material in the gross sense organ that enables perception of sense objects; for the mental consciousness, it is the previous moment of any of the six consciousnesses.

*cognitive obscurations* (*jñeyāvaraṇa*, T. *shes bya'i sgrib pa*). Obscurations that mainly prevent full awakening; the latencies of ignorance and the subtle dualistic view that they give rise to.

*collection of merit* (*puṇyasaṃbhāra*). A virtuous action motivated by bodhicitta that is a main cause of attaining the form body of a buddha.

*collection of wisdom* (*jñānasaṃbhāra*). A virtuous mental action motivated by bodhicitta that is a main cause of attaining the truth body of a buddha.

*common four truths*. The four truths accepted in common by the four Buddhist tenet systems. These center around coarse afflictions.

*comprehended object* (*prameya*, T. *gzhal bya*). That which is the object known or cognized by a reliable cognizer.

*conceived object* (*adhyavasāya-viṣaya*, T. *zhen yul*). The object conceived by a conceptual consciousness; it is the apprehended or engaged object of a conceptual consciousness.

*concentration* (*samādhi*). A mental factor that has the potential to dwell single-pointedly for a sustained period of time on one object; a state of deep meditative absorption; single-pointed concentration that is free from discursive thought.

*conceptual appearance* (*artha-sāmānya*, T. *don spyi*). A mental image of an object that appears to a conceptual consciousness.

*conceptual consciousness* (*kalpanā*, T. *rtog pa'i shes pa*). A consciousness that knows its object by means of a conceptual appearance.

*conceptual fabrications*. False modes of existence and false ideas imputed by a conceptual consciousness.

*conceptuality* (*kalpanā*, T. *rtog pa*). Thought.

*conceptualizations* (*vikalpa viparyāsa*, T. *rnam rtog*). Distorted thoughts that range from exaggerating the desirability or beauty of an object to grasping impermanent things as permanent, and so forth.

*concomitant* (T. *mtshungs ldan*). Accompanying or occurring together in the same mental state.

*conditionality* (causal dependence). Dependence on causes and conditions.

*confusion* (*moha*, T. *gti mug*). Ignorance.

*consciousness* (*vijñāna*, *viññāṇa*, T. *rnam shes*). That which is clear and cognizant.

*consequence* (*prasaṅga*, T. *thal 'gyur*). A form of reasoning that shows the other party the inconsistencies in their assertions; the form of reasoning widely used by the Prāsaṅgikas.

*conventional existence* (*saṃvṛtisat*). Existence.

*conventional truths* (veiled truth, *saṃvṛtisatya*, *sammuti-sacca*, T. *kun rdzob bden pa*). That which is true only from the perspective of ignorance. This includes all phenomena except ultimate truths.

*death* (*maraṇabhava*). The last moment of a lifetime when the subtlest clear light mind manifests.

*defilement* (*mala*, T. *dri ma*). Either an afflictive obscuration or a cognitive obscuration.

*definitive* (*nītārtha*, *nītattha*, T. *nges don*). Prāsaṅgikas: A sūtra or statement that mainly and explicitly teaches ultimate truths.

*dependent arising* (*pratītyasamutpāda*). This is of three types: (1) causal dependence—things arising due to causes and conditions, (2) mutual dependence—phenomena existing in relation to other phenomena, and (3) dependent designation—phenomena existing by being merely designated by terms and concepts.

*designation* (*prajñapti*, *paññatti*, T. *btags pa*). The object designated by term and concept in dependence on its basis of designation.

*desire realm* (*kāmadhātu*). One of the three realms of cyclic existence, where sentient beings are overwhelmed by attraction to and desire for sense objects.

*dhyāna* (P. *jhāna*). A meditative stabilization of the form realm.

*different* (*nānātva*, T. *tha dad*). Phenomena that are diverse; phenomena that are not identical.

*different nature*. Two things can exist at different times and different places.

*direct perceiver* (*pratyakṣa*, T. *mngon sum*). A nonmistaken awareness that is free from conceptuality. According to Prāsaṅgika: an awareness that is free from conceptuality.

*direct reliable cognizer* (*pratyakṣa-pramāṇa*). A new nondeceptive nonmistaken awareness that is free from conceptuality. According to Prāsaṅgikas, it is a nondeceptive awareness that knows its object without depending on a reason.

*discordant characteristics*. The characteristics of two objects that are not the same. For example, one object is permanent while the other is impermanent.

*distorted conception* (inappropriate attention, *ayoniśo-manaskāra*, T. *tshul bzhin ma yin pa'i yid la byed pa*). Distorted thoughts that project exaggerations and erroneous qualities on objects, leading to the arising of afflictions.

*dualistic appearance* (T. *gnyis snang*). The appearance of subject and object as separate or the appearance of inherent existence.

*duḥkha* (P. *dukkha*). The unsatisfactory experiences of cyclic existence.

*Dzogchen*. A tantric practice emphasizing meditation on the nature of mind, practiced primarily in the Nyingma tradition.

*eight worldly concerns* (*aṣṭalokadharma*). Attachment to material gain, fame, praise, and pleasure and aversion to loss, disrepute, blame, and pain.

*eighteen constituents* (*dhātu*, T. *khams*). These are the six objects, six sense faculties, and six consciousnesses.

*elaborations* (proliferations, *prapañca*, *papañca*, T. *spros pa*). Ignorance and other mental fabrications that obscure the ultimate nature of phenomena, their emptiness.

*emptiness* (*śūnyatā*, T. *stong pa nyid*). The lack of inherent existence and true existence.

*engaged object* (apprehended object, *pravṛtti-viṣaya*, T. *'jug yul*). The main object with which the mind is concerned.

*erroneous* (*viparyāsa*, T. *phyin ci log pa*). Wrong, incorrect, perverted.

*essentialists* (proponents of true existence, T. *dngos por smra ba*). Buddhist and non-Buddhist philosophers following a non-Madhyamaka tenet system who assert that the person and aggregates truly exist.

*exalted knower* (*jñāna*, T. *mkhyen pa*). A realization in the continuum of someone who has entered a path. It exists from the path of accumulation to the buddha ground. Exalted knower, path, ground, pristine wisdom, and clear realization are mutually inclusive.

*existence by its own characteristics* (*svalakṣaṇa*, T. *rang gi mtshan nyid kyis grub pa*). Existence from its own side.

*existent* (*sat*). That which is perceivable by mind.

*fetters* (*saṃyojana*). Factors that keep us bound to cyclic existence and impede the attainment of liberation. The five lower fetters—view of a personal identity, deluded doubt, view of rules and practices, sensual desire, and malice—bind us to rebirth in the desire realm. The five higher fetters—desire for existence in the form realm, desire for existence in the formless realm, arrogance, restlessness, and ignorance—prevent nonreturners from becoming arhats.

*focal object* (*viṣaya*, T. *dmigs pa*). The main object the mind refers to or focuses on.

*form body* (*rūpakāya*). The buddha body in which a buddha appears to sentient beings; it includes the emanation and enjoyment bodies.

*form realm* (*rūpadhātu*). The saṃsāric realm in which beings have bodies made of subtle material; they are born there due to having attained various states of concentration.

*formless realm* (*ārūpyadhātu*). The saṃsāric realm in which sentient beings do not have a material body; they are born there due to having attained various states of meditative absorption.

*foundation consciousness* (*ālayavijñāna*, T. *kun gzhi rnam shes*). A storehouse consciousness where all latencies and karmic seeds are placed. It carries this from one life to the next and is the self according to Yogācāra Scripture Proponents.

*four truths of the āryas* (four noble truths, *catvāry āryasatyāni*). The truth of duḥkha, its origin, its cessation, and the path to that cessation.

*free from conceptuality* (*kalpanā-apoḍha*, T. *rtog bral*). Without any conceptual appearances.

*full awakening* (*samyaksaṃbodhi*). Buddhahood; the state in which all obscurations have been abandoned and all good qualities have been developed limitlessly.

*Fundamental Vehicle*. The vehicle of śrāvakas and solitary realizers, the path that leads to liberation.

*general characteristics* (*sāmānya-lakṣaṇa*, *sāmañña-lakkhaṇa*, T. *spyi'i mtshan nyid*). Characteristics, such as impermanence, unsatisfactoriness, and not-self that are common to all functioning things.

*grasping inherent existence* (*svabhāvagraha*). Grasping persons and phenomena to exist truly or inherently. Synonymous with grasping true existence (Prāsaṅgika).

*grasping true existence* (true grasping, *satyagrāha*). Grasping persons and phenomena to exist with an intrinsic essence.

*hell being* (*nāraka*). A being born in one of the unfortunate classes of beings who suffer intense physical pain as a result of their strong destructive karma.

*hungry ghost* (*preta*). A being born in one of the unfortunate classes of beings who suffer from intense hunger and thirst.

*ignorance* (*avidyā*). A mental factor that is obscured and grasps the opposite of what exists. There are two main types: ignorance regarding ultimate truth and ignorance regarding karma and its effects.

*illustration-isolate self* (T. *gang zag gzhi ldog*). What is found when the person is searched for.

*impermanence* (*anitya, anicca*). Momentariness; not remaining in the next moment. Coarse impermanence is the ending of a continuum; subtle impermanence is something not remaining the same in the very next moment.

*imputedly existent* (*prajñaptisat*, T. *btags yod*). (1) Vaibhāṣikas: Something that when it is broken into smaller pieces or moments of time can no longer be ascertained. (2) Sautrāntikas up to Svātantrikas: Something that can be identified only by identifying something else. (3) Prāsaṅgikas: Something that exists by being merely designated by term and concept.

*inappropriate attention*. *See* distorted conception.

*inference* (*anumāna*, T. *rjes su dpag pa*). (1) A cognizer that knows its object through reasoning, (2) a conclusion reached through a syllogism on the basis of evidence and reasoning.

*inferential reliable cognizer* (*anumāna-pramāṇa*). An awareness that knows its object—a slightly obscure phenomenon—nondeceptively, purely in dependence on a reason.

*inherent existence* (*svabhāvasiddhi, sabhāvasiddha*, T. *rang bzhin gyis grub pa*). Existence without depending on any other factors; independent existence. For Prāsaṅgikas, to be negated both ultimately and conventionally.

*innate* (*sahaja*, T. *lhan skyes*). Existing with the mind from beginningless time, something not acquired anew in this life.

*inner heat* (*candālī*, T. *gtum mo*). A practice of highest yoga tantra to draw the winds inside.

*insight* (*vipaśyanā*, *vipassanā*, T. *lhag mthong*). A wisdom of thorough discrimination of phenomena conjoined with special pliancy induced by the power of analysis.

*insight knowledge* (P. *vipassanā-ñāṇa*). Mundane (*lokiya*) knowledge of the three characteristics gained through insight. It leads to supramundane (*lokuttara*) path knowledge that realizes the four truths and nirvāṇa.

*insight wisdom* (P. *vipassanā-paññā*). Knowledge of the three characteristics gained through insight and leading to stream-entry.

*interpretable* (*neyārtha*, *neyyattha*, T. *drang don*). A scripture or statement that speaks about the variety of phenomena and/or cannot be taken literally.

*investigation* (*vitarka*, *vitarka*, T. *rtog pa*). A mental factor that seeks a rough idea about an object.

*karma*. Intentional action of body, speech, or mind.

*karmic seeds*. The potency from previously created actions that will bring their results.

*knowable object* (*jñeya*, T. *shes bya*). That which is suitable to serve as an object of an awareness.

*latencies* (*vāsanā*). Predispositions, imprints, or tendencies.

*liberated path* (*vimuktimārga*, *T. rnam grol lam*). A wisdom directly realizing emptiness that has completely eradicated its corresponding portion of defilements.

*liberation* (*mokṣa*, T. *thar pa*). A true cessation that is the complete abandonment of all afflictive obscurations; nirvāṇa, the state of freedom from cyclic existence.

*liberation* (*vimukti*, *vimutti*, T. *rnam grol*). Sanskrit tradition: Complete freedom from saṃsāra; Pāli tradition: a conditioned event that brings nirvāṇa.

*Madhyamaka*: A Mahāyāna tenet system that refutes true existence.

*Mahāmudrā*. A type of meditation that focuses on the conventional and ultimate natures of the mind.

*manifest afflictions*. Afflictions active in the mind at the present moment (contrasted with seeds of afflictions).

*meditative equipoise on emptiness*. An ārya's mind focused single-pointedly on the emptiness of inherent existence.

*mental consciousness* (*mano-vijñāna*). A primary consciousness that knows mental phenomena in contradistinction to sense primary consciousnesses that know physical objects.

*mental factor* (*caitta*). An aspect of mind that accompanies a primary consciousness and fills out the cognition, apprehending particular attributes of the object or performing a specific function.

*mind* (*citta*). The part of living beings that cognizes, experiences, thinks, feels, and so on. In some contexts it is equivalent to primary consciousness.

*mindfulness* (*smṛti, sati*). A mental factor that brings to mind a phenomenon of previous acquaintance without forgetting it and prevents distraction to other objects.

*mindstream* (*cittasaṃtāna*). The continuity of mind.

*mistaken awareness*. An awareness that is mistaken in terms of its appearing object.

*momentary* (*kṣaṇika*). Not enduring in the next moment without changing.

*monastic*. Someone who has received monastic ordination; a monk or nun.

*nature truth body* (*svabhāvika dharmakāya*). The buddha body that is either the emptiness of a buddha's mind or the true cessations in that buddha's continuum.

*naturelessness* (*niḥsvabhāva*, T. *ngo bo nyid med pa*). The lack of a certain nature.

*negative* (*pratiṣedha*, T. *dgag pa*). An object (1) whose name eliminates an object of negation, or (2) that explicitly appears in a way that an object of negation has been negated. Equivalent with exclusion (*apoha*, T. *sel ba*), other exclusion (*anyāpoha*, T. *gzhan sel*), and isolate (*vyatireka, ldog pa*).

*nihilism* (*ucchedānta*, *vibhavadiṭṭhi*). The belief that our actions have no ethical dimension; the belief that nothing exists.

*Nirgranthas*. Jains; followers of Mahāvira, a contemporary of the Buddha.

*nirvāṇa*. The state of liberation of an arhat; the emptiness of a mind that has been totally cleansed of afflictive obscurations.

*nominal truths* (*vyavahārasatya*, T. *tha snyad bden pa*). *See* conventional truths.

*nominally different*. Two phenomena are nominally different when they are not the same thing and can be distinguished by conception.

*nonabiding nirvāṇa* (*apratiṣṭha-nirvāṇa*). A buddha's nirvāṇa that does not abide in either the extreme of cyclic existence or in the extreme of personal liberation.

*nonaffirming negative* (*prasajyapratiṣedha*, T. *med dgag*). A negative phenomenon in which, upon the explicit elimination of the object of negation by an awareness, another phenomenon is not suggested or established. A phenomenon that is the mere absence of an object of negation.

*nonconceptual consciousness* (*nirvikalpaka*, T. *rtog med shes pa*). A consciousness that knows its object directly, not by means of a conceptual appearance.

*nondeceptive* (*avisaṃvādi*, T. *mi slu ba*). Incontrovertible, correct; the way it appears to a reliable cognizer directly realizing it is in accord with the way it exists.

*nonduality*. The nonappearance of subject and object, of inherent existence, of conventional truths, and/or of conceptual appearances in an ārya's meditative equipoise on emptiness.

*nonerroneous* (*aviparīta*, T. *phyin ci ma log pa*). Correct, right.

*nonexistent* (*asat*). That which is not perceivable by mind.

*nonmistaken* (*abhrānta*, T. *ma 'khrul ba*). (1) Sautrāntikas: not mistaken with respect to a consciousness's appearing object. (2) Prāsaṅgikas: a consciousness without the appearance of inherent existence.

*non-thing* (*abhāva*, T. *dngos med*). (1) Permanent phenomena; (2) phenomena that cannot perform a function.

*non-wastage* (*avipraṇāśa*, T. *chud mi za ba*). Asserted by Vaibhāṣikas, it is likened to an IOU, voucher, or seal that ensures karma will go from one life to the next.

*object* (*viṣaya*, T. *yul*). That which is known by an awareness.

*object of negation* (*pratiṣedhya* or *niṣedhya*, *T. dgag bya*). What is negated or refuted.

*observed object* (*ālambana*, *ārammaṇa*, T. *dmigs yul*). The basic object that the mind refers to or focuses on while apprehending certain aspects of that object.

*one* (*ekatva*, T. *gcig*). A singular phenomenon; a phenomenon that is not diverse; identical.

*one nature*. Two phenomena that exist at the same time and do not appear separate to direct perception are one nature.

*ordinary being* (*pṛthagjana*, *puthujjana*, T. *so so skye bo*). Someone who is not an ārya.

*own-characteristics/specific characteristics* (*svalakṣaṇa*, *salakkhaṇa*, T. *rang mtshan*, *rang gi mtshan nyid*). The specific characteristics unique to each phenomenon. Things have their own characteristics, but they do not exist by their own characteristics.

*passing away* (*vyaya*, *vaya*, T. *'jig pa*). Ceasing, disintegrating.

*path* (*mārga*, *magga*, T. *lam*). An exalted knower that is conjoined with uncontrived renunciation.

*path knowledge* (P. *magga-ñāṇa*). A supramundane path that knows the four truths and nirvāṇa.

*path of accumulation* (*sambhāramārga*, T. *tshogs lam*). First of the five paths. In the Śrāvaka or Solitary Realizer Vehicle, it begins when one aspires for liberation day and night; in the Mahāyāna, it begins when one has spontaneous bodhicitta.

*path of meditation* (*bhāvanāmārga*, T. *sgom lam*). The fourth of the five paths. This begins when a meditator begins to eradicate innate afflictions from the root.

*path of no-more-learning* (*aśaikṣamārga*, T. *mi slob lam*). The last of the five paths; arhatship or buddhahood.

*path of preparation* (*prayogamārga*, T. *sbyor lam*) The second of the five paths. It begins when a meditator attains the union of serenity and insight on emptiness.

*path of seeing* (*darśanamārga*, T. *mthong lam*). Third of the five paths. It begins when a meditator first has direct, nonconceptual realization of the emptiness of inherent existence.

*permanent* (*nitya*, *nicca*, T. *rtag pa*). Unchanging, static, not momentarily changing. It does not mean eternal.

*permanent, unitary, independent self.* A soul or self (ātman) asserted by non-Buddhists.

*person* (*pudgala*, T. *skya bo*). A living being designated in dependence on its four or five aggregates.

*pollutant* (*āsrava*, *āsava*). A set of three or four deeply rooted defilements: sensual desire, existence (craving to exist in a saṃsāric form), and ignorance. Some lists add view.

*polluted* (P. *āsava*). Under the influence of ignorance or its latencies.

*posit* (*vyavasthāna*, T. *bzhag pa*). To establish, determine, or postulate an object; to designate.

*positive* (affirmative, *vidhi*, T. *sgrub pa*). A phenomenon that is not realized by the conceptual consciousness apprehending it by explicitly eliminating an object of negation.

*Prāsaṅgika Madhyamaka.* A Mahāyāna tenet system that asserts that all phenomena lack inherent existence both conventionally and ultimately.

*prātimokṣa.* The different sets of ethical precepts for monastics and lay followers that assist in attaining liberation.

*primal substance* (fundamental nature, *prakṛti*, *pakati*, *T. rang bzhin*). A truly existent substance out of which everything is created, asserted by the non-Buddhist Sāṃkhya school.

*primary consciousness* (*vijñāna*). A consciousness that apprehends the presence or basic entity of an object; there are six types of primary consciousnesses: visual, auditory, olfactory, gustatory, tactile, and mental.

*pristine wisdom* (*jñāna*, T. *ye shes*). A realization in the continuum of someone who has entered a path.

*probing awareness* (reasoning consciousness, *yuktijñāna*, T. *rigs shes*). A consciousness using or having used reasoning to analyze the ultimate nature of an object. It can be either conceptual or nonconceptual.

*production natureless* (*utpatti-niḥsvabhāvatā*, T. *skye ba ngo bo nyid med pa*). A quality of dependent natures: they arise from causes that are a different nature than themselves and do not arise from causes that are the same nature as themselves.

*pure lands*. Places created by the unshakable resolve and merit of buddhas where all external conditions are conducive for Dharma practice.

*realization* (*adhigama*, T. *rtogs pa*). An awareness that eliminates superimpositions on an object and is able to induce ascertainment of a phenomenon. It may be either inferential or direct.

*reliable cognizer* (*pramāṇa*). A nondeceptive awareness that is incontrovertible with respect to its apprehended object and that enables us to accomplish our purpose.

*reviewing knowledge* (P. *paccavekkhaṇañāṇa*). In stream-enterers, once-returners, and nonreturners, it is a knowledge in post-meditation time that reviews the path, its fruition, the defilements abandoned, the defilements that remain, and nirvāṇa. Arhats have no reviewing knowledge of defilements that remain.

*samādhi*. *See* concentration.

*Sāṃkhya*. A school of Hindu philosophy that asserts a primal substance and that says effects exist in a nonmanifest state in their causes.

*saṃsāra*. The cycle of rebirth that occurs under the control of afflictions and karma.

*Sautrāntika*. A Fundamental Vehicle tenet system that asserts that functional things are ultimate truths and that phenomena that exist by being imputed by thought are conventional truths.

*Sautrāntika-Svātantrika Madhyamaka*. A Mahāyāna tenet system that accepts external objects and refutes inherent existence ultimately but not conventionally.

*self* (*ātman*, *attan*, T. *bdag*). (1) A person, (2) inherent existence, or (3) a permanent, unitary independent soul or self.

*self-grasping* (*ātmagrāha*). Grasping inherent existence.

*self-isolate person* (T. *gang zag rang ldog*). The general person, the imputedly existent person.

*selflessness of persons* (*pudgalanairātmya*, T. *gang zag gi bdag med*). Prāsaṅgikas: the nonexistence of a self-sufficient substantially existent person is the coarse selflessness of persons, and the nonexistence of an inherently existent person is the subtle selflessness of persons.

*selflessness of phenomena* (*dharmanairātmya*, T. *chos kyi bdag med pa*). Prāsaṅgikas: the nonexistence of inherently existent phenomena other than persons.

*self-sufficient substantially existent person* (T. *gang zag rang rkya thub pa'i rdzas yod*). A person that can be identified without identifying its aggregates; a self that is the controller of the body and mind. Such a self does not exist.

*self-sufficient* (T. *rang rkya ba*). Being a different entity from its parts.

*sense direct reliable cognizers*. Incontrovertible awarenesses that know their objects—sights, sounds, smells, tastes, and tangible objects—directly by depending on a physical cognitive faculty.

*sentient being* (*sattva*). Any being with a mind, except for a buddha.

*serenity* (*śamatha*, *samatha*). Sanskrit tradition: concentration arisen from meditation that is accompanied by the bliss of mental and physical pliancy in which the mind abides effortlessly without fluctuation for as long as one wishes on whatever virtuous object the mind has been placed. Pāli tradition: one-pointedness of mind; the eight attainments (meditative absorptions) that are the basis for insight.

*sign* (*nimitta*). A mental image that arises in stabilizing meditation and is used to attain single-pointed concentration.

*signlessness* (*ānimitta*, T. *mtshan ma med pa*). The emptiness that is the absence of inherent existence of the cause of any phenomenon.

*six perfections* (*ṣaḍpāramitā*). The practices of generosity, ethical conduct, fortitude, joyous effort, meditative stability, and wisdom that are motivated by bodhicitta.

*slightly obscure phenomena* (*parokṣa*). Phenomena that ordinary beings can initially know only through factual inference.

*solitary realizer* (*pratyekabuddha*). A person following the Fundamental Vehicle who seeks liberation and emphasizes understanding the twelve links of dependent arising.

*śrāvaka* (hearer, P. *sāvaka*). Someone who practices the Fundamental Vehicle path leading to arhatship and who emphasizes meditation on the four truths.

*stabilizing meditation* (*sthāpyabhāvanā*, T. *'jog sgom*). Meditation to focus and concentrate the mind on an object.

*substantial cause* (*upādāna-kāraṇa*). The cause that becomes the result, as opposed to cooperative causes that aid the substantial cause in becoming the result.

*substantially existent* (*dravyasat*, *dabbasat*, T. *rdzas yod*). (1) Vaibhāṣikas: An object that can be identified even when broken into smaller pieces or moments of time. (2) Sautrāntikas up to Svātantrikas: An object that can be known directly, without another object being identified. (3) Prāsaṅgikas: inherently existent.

*suchness* (*tattva*, T. *de kho na nyid*). Emptiness, the way things really are.

*superimposition* (*samāropa*, T. *sgro btags, sgro 'dogs*). The imputing or projecting of something that does not exist—for example, a self of persons.

*supramundane* (transcendental, *lokottara*, *lokuttara*). Pertaining to the elimination of fetters and afflictions; pertaining to āryas.

*subtle afflictions*. Afflictions stemming from grasping inherent existence (contrasted with coarse afflictions).

*Svātantrika Madhyamaka*. A Mahāyāna tenet system that asserts that phenomena do not exist inherently on the ultimate level but do exist inherently on the conventional level.

*syllogism* (*prayoga*). A statement consisting of a subject, predicate, and reason, and in many cases, an example.

*tathāgata*. A buddha.

*tenet* (*siddhānta*, T. *grub mtha'*). A philosophical assertion or belief.

*tenet system/school*. A set of philosophical assertions regarding the basis, path, and result that is shared by a group of people.

*thesis* (*pratijñā*). What is to be proven—the combination of the subject and the predicate—in a syllogism.

*thing* (*bhāva*, T. *dngos po*). (1) Something that can perform a function, synonymous with product; (2) inherent existence.

*thought* (*kalpanā*). Conceptual consciousness.

*three characteristics*. Three qualities of conditioned phenomena: impermanence, duḥkha, and selfless (not-self).

*three criteria for existent phenomena*. It is known to a conventional consciousness; its existence is not invalidated by another conventional reliable cognizer; it is not invalidated by a mind analyzing emptiness.

*three criteria of a correct inference or syllogism*. Presence of the reason in the subject, pervasion or entailment, and counterpervasion.

*three realms* (*tridhātuka*, *tedhātuka*). Desire, form, and formless realms.

*true cessation* (*nirodhasatya*). The cessation of a portion of afflictions or all afflictions; the cessation of a portion of cognitive obscurations or all cognitive obscurations.

*true existence* (*satyasat*). Existence having its own mode of being; existence having its own reality.

*true grasping*. *See* grasping true existence.

*truth body* (*dharmakāya*). The buddha body that includes the nature truth body and the wisdom truth body.

*twelve links of dependent origination* (*dvādaśāṅga-pratītyasamutpāda*). A system of twelve factors that explains how we take rebirth in saṃsāra and how we can be liberated from it.

*twelve sources* (*āyatana*, T. *skye mched*). That which opens or increases the arising of consciousness. They consist of six external sense sources (forms, sounds, odors, tastes, tangible object, and other phenomena) and six internal sense sources (eye, ear, nose, tongue, body, and mental sense faculties).

*two truths* (*satyadvaya*). Ultimate truths and veiled (conventional) truths.

*ultimate analysis* (T. *don dam pa'i dpyod pa*). Analysis that examines what an object really is and its deeper mode of existence.

*ultimate natureless* (*paramārtha-niḥsvabhāvatā*). A quality of consummate natures; the ultimate nature of phenomena that is perceived by the ultimate purifying consciousnesses.

*ultimate truth* (*paramārthasatya*, *paramatthasacca*, T. *don dam bden pa*). The ultimate mode of existence of all persons and phenomena; emptiness; objects that are true and appear true to their main cognizer, a wisdom nonconceptually and directly realizing emptiness.

*uncommon four truths.* The four truths accepted only by Prāsaṅgika-Mādhyamikas. These center around subtle afflictions.

*underlying tendencies* (*anuśaya*, *anusaya*). Latent dispositions on the mind that enable manifest afflictions to arise when the appropriate causes and conditions are present. These are attachment to sensuality, anger, views, deluded doubt, arrogance, existence (in the three realms), and ignorance.

*unfortunate states* (*apāya*). Unfortunate states of rebirth as a hell being, hungry ghost, or animal.

*uninterrupted path* (*ānantaryamārga*, T. *bar ched med lam*). A wisdom directly realizing emptiness that is in the process of eliminating its corresponding portion of defilements.

*union of serenity and insight.* A path that consists of both serenity and insight and in which the bliss of mental and physical pliancy has been induced by analysis.

*unpolluted* (*anāsrava*). Not under the influence of ignorance.

*Vaibhāṣika*. A Fundamental Vehicle tenet system that accepts directionally partless particles and temporally partless moments of consciousness as ultimate truths and asserts truly established external objects.

*veiled truths* (conventional truths, *saṃvṛtisatya*). Objects that are true only to ignorance; objects that appear to exist inherently to their main cognizer, ignorance.

*view of a personal identity* (view of the transitory collection, *satkāyadṛṣṭi*, *sakkāyadiṭṭhi*). Grasping an inherently existent I or mine (according to the Prāsaṅgika system).

*view of a personal identity grasping I* (*ahaṃkāra*, T. *ngar 'dzin gyi 'jig lta*). An afflictive view that holds the I to be inherently existent.

*view of a personal identity grasping mine* (*mamakāra*, T. *nga yi bar 'dzin pa'i 'jig lta*). An afflictive view holding what makes things mine as inherently existent.

*Vinaya*. Monastic discipline.

*wind* (*prāṇa*, T. *rlung*). One of the four elements; energy in the body that influences bodily functions; subtle energy on which levels of consciousness ride.

*wisdom truth body* (*jñāna dharmakāya*). The buddha body that is a buddha's omniscient mind.

*wishlessness* (*apraṇihita*, T. *smon pa med pa*). The ultimate nature of the effects of things.

*wrong or erroneous awareness* (*viparyaya jñāna*). A mind that is erroneous with respect to its apprehended object.

*Yogācāra* (*Cittamātra*). A Mahāyāna tenet system that accepts eight consciousnesses, including a foundation consciousness and an afflictive consciousness, and asserts the true existence of other-powered (dependent) phenomena but does not assert external objects.

*Yogācāra-Svātantrika Madhyamaka.* A Mahāyāna tenet system that does not assert external objects, asserts six consciousnesses, and refutes inherent existence ultimately but not conventionally.

*yogi/yoginī.* A meditator on suchness.

*yogic direct reliable cognizers.* Nondeceptive mental consciousnesses that know their objects by depending on a union of serenity and insight.

# Recommended Reading

Bhikkhu Bodhi, ed. *A Comprehensive Manual of Abhidhamma: The Abhidhamma Sangaha of Ācariya Anuruddha*. Pāli text originally edited and translated by Mahāthera Nārada. Translation revised by Bhikkhu Bodhi. Kandi: Buddhist Publication Society, 1993.

Blumenthal, James. *The Ornament of the Middle Way: A Study of the Madhyamaka Thought of Śāntarakṣita*. Ithaca, NY: Snow Lion Publications, 2004.

Cozort, Daniel, and Craig Preston. *Buddhist Philosophy: Losang Gonchok's Short Commentary to Jamyang Shayba's Root Text on Tenets*. Ithaca, NY: Snow Lion Publications, 2003.

*Diamond Cutter Sūtra*. http://emahofoundation.org/images/documents/DiamondSutraText.pdf.

H. H. the Dalai Lama. *Science and Philospophy in the Indian Buddhist Classics, Volume 2: The Mind*. Boston: Wisdom Publications, 2020.

Hopkins, Jeffrey. *Meditation on Emptiness*. Boston: Wisdom Publications, 1996.

———. *Tsong-kha-pa's Final Exposition of Wisdom*. Ithaca, NY: Snow Lion Publications, 2008.

Jinpa, Thupten. *Mind Training: The Great Collection*. Boston: Wisdom Publications, 2006.

———. *Self, Reality, and Reason in Tibetan Philosophy*. New York: RoutledgeCurzon, 2002.

Karunadasa, Yakupitiyage. *Early Buddhist Teachings*. Somerville, MA: Wisdom Publications, 2018.

———. *The Buddhist Analysis of Matter*. Somerville, MA: Wisdom Publications, 2020.

———. *The Theravāda Abhidhamma: Inquiry into the Nature of Conditioned Existence*. Somerville, MA: Wisdom Publications, 2019.

Klein, Anne Caroline. *Path to the Middle: Oral Mādhyamika Philosophy in Tibet*. Albany, NY: State University of New York Press, 1994.

Lindtner, Christian. *Master of Wisdom: Writings of the Buddhist Master Nāgārjuna*. Berkeley, CA: Dharma Publishing, 1997.

Nāgārjuna. *A Commentary on the Awakening Mind* (*Bodhicittavivaraṇa*). Translated by Geshe Thupten Jinpa. http://www.kurukulla.org/resources/Nagarjuna_Teaching_Booklet_English.pdf (Kurukulla.org).

Newland, Guy. *The Two Truths*. Ithaca, NY: Snow Lion Publications, 1992.

———. *Appearance and Reality*. Ithaca, NY: Snow Lion Publications, 1999.

Perdue, Daniel. *Debate in Tibetan Buddhism*. Ithaca, NY: Snow Lion Publications, 1992.

Rje Tsong khapa. *Ocean of Reasoning: A Great Commentary on Nāgārjuna's Mūlamadhyamakakārikā*. Translated by Geshe Ngawang Samten and Jay Garfield. New York: Oxford University Press, 2006.

Sopa, Geshe Lhundup, and Jeffrey Hopkins. *Cutting Through Appearances: Practice and Theory of Tibetan Buddhism*. Ithaca, NY: Snow Lion Publications, 1989.

Tegchok, Geshe Jampa, and Thubten Chodron. *Practical Ethics and Profound Emptiness: A Commentary on Nagarjuna's Precious Garland*. Somerville, MA: Wisdom Publications, 2017.

———. *Insight into Emptiness*. Boston: Wisdom Publications, 2012.

Thabkhe, Geshé Yeshe. *The Rice Seedling Sutra*. Somerville, MA: Wisdom Publications, 2020.

Tsongkhapa. *Illuminating the Intent: An Exposition of Candrakīrti's* Entering the Middle Way. Translated by Thupten Jinpa. Somerville, MA: Wisdom Publications, 2021.

Vasubandhu. *Abhidharmakośabhāṣyam of Vasubandhu*. 4 vols. Translated into French by Louis de La Vallée Poussin. English translation by Leo M. Pruden. Fremont, CA: Asian Humanities Press, 1991.

Wangchen, Geshé Namgyal. *Brief Presentation of the Fundamentals of Buddhist Tenets and Modern Science*. Translated by Gavin Kilty. Dharamsala: Library of Tibetan Works and Archives, 2019.

Yangzom, Tenzin. *Presentation of Buddhist Tenets by Jetsun Chokyi Gyaltsen: Tibetan, English, Mandarin*. Independently published, 2019.

# Index

# About the Authors

THE DALAI LAMA is the spiritual leader of the Tibetan people, a Nobel Peace Prize recipient, and an advocate for compassion and peace throughout the world. He promotes harmony among the world's religions and engages in dialogue with leading scientists. Ordained as a Buddhist monk when he was a child, he completed the traditional monastic studies and earned his geshe degree (equivalent to a PhD). Renowned for his erudite and open-minded scholarship, his meditative attainments, and his humility, Bhikṣu Tenzin Gyatso says, "I am a simple Buddhist monk."

Peter Aronson

BHIKṢUṆĪ THUBTEN CHODRON has been a Buddhist nun since 1977. Growing up in Los Angeles, she graduated with honors in history from the University of California at Los Angeles and did graduate work in education at the University of Southern California. After years studying and teaching Buddhism in Asia, Europe, and the United States, she became the founder and abbess of Sravasti Abbey in Washington State. A popular speaker for her practical explanations of how to apply Buddhist teachings in daily life, she is the author of several books on Buddhism, including *Buddhism for Beginners*. She is the editor of Khensur Jampa Tegchok's *Insight into Emptiness*. For more information, visit sravastiabbey.org and thubtenchodron.org.

## Also Available from the Dalai Lama and Wisdom Publications

**Buddhism**
*One Teacher, Many Traditions*

**The Compassionate Life**

**Ecology, Ethics, and Interdependence**
*The Dalai Lama in Conversation with Leading Thinkers on Climate Change*

**Essence of the Heart Sutra**
*The Dalai Lama's Heart of Wisdom Teachings*

**The Essence of Tsongkhapa's Teachings**
*The Dalai Lama on the Three Principal Aspects of the Path*

**The Good Heart**
*A Buddhist Perspective on the Teachings of Jesus*

**Imagine All the People**
*A Conversation with the Dalai Lama on Money, Politics, and Life as It Could Be*

**Kalachakra Tantra**
*Rite of Initiation*

**The Life of My Teacher**
*A Biography of Kyabjé Ling Rinpoche*

**Meditation on the Nature of Mind**

**The Middle Way**
*Faith Grounded in Reason*

**Mind in Comfort and Ease**
*The Vision of Enlightenment in the Great Perfection*

**MindScience**
*An East-West Dialogue*

**Opening the Eye of New Awareness**

**Practicing Wisdom**
*The Perfection of Shantideva's Bodhisattva Way*

**Science and Philosophy in the Indian Buddhist Classics, vol. 1**
*The Physical World*

**Science and Philosophy in the Indian Buddhist Classics, vol. 2**
*The Mind*

**Sleeping, Dreaming, and Dying**
*An Exploration of Consciousness*

**The Wheel of Life**
*Buddhist Perspectives on Cause and Effect*

**The World of Tibetan Buddhism**
*An Overview of Its Philosophy and Practice*

# Also Available from Thubten Chodron

**Insight into Emptiness**
Khensur Jampa Tegchok
Edited and introduced by Thubten Chodron

"One of the best introductions to the philosophy of emptiness I have ever read."—José Ignacio Cabezón

**Practical Ethics and Profound Emptiness**
*A Commentary on Nagarjuna's Precious Garland*
Khensur Jampa Tegchok
Edited by Thubten Chodron

"A beautifully clear translation and systematic explanation of Nagarjuna's most accessible and wide-ranging work. Dharma students everywhere will benefit from careful attention to its pages."
—Guy Newland, author of *Introduction to Emptiness*

**Awakening Every Day**
*365 Buddhist Reflections to Invite Mindfulness and Joy*

**Buddhism for Beginners**

**The Compassionate Kitchen**

**Cultivating a Compassionate Heart**
*The Yoga Method of Chenrezig*

**Don't Believe Everything You Think**
*Living with Wisdom and Compassion*

**Guided Meditations on the Stages of the Path**

**How to Free Your Mind**
*Tara the Liberator*

**Living with an Open Heart**
*How to Cultivate Compassion in Daily Life*

**Open Heart, Clear Mind**

**Taming the Mind**

**Working with Anger**

# About Wisdom Publications

Wisdom Publications is the leading publisher of classic and contemporary Buddhist books and practical works on mindfulness. To learn more about us or to explore our other books, please visit our website at wisdomexperience.org or contact us at the address below.

Wisdom Publications
199 Elm Street
Somerville, MA 02144 USA

We are a 501(c)(3) organization, and donations in support of our mission are tax deductible.

Wisdom Publications is affiliated with the Foundation for the Preservation of the Mahayana Tradition (FPMT).